The King and his kingdom

The King and his kingdom

The Gospel of Matthew simply explained

John Legg

EVANGELICAL PRESS

EVANGELICAL PRESS
Faverdale North Industrial Estate, Darlington, DL3 0PH, England

Evangelical Press USA
P. O. Box 825, Webster, New York 14580, USA

email: sales@evangelicalpress.org

web: http://www.evangelicalpress.org

First published 2004

British Library Cataloguing in Publication Data available

ISBN 0 85234 561 5

Printed and bound in Great Britain by Creative Print & Design Wales, Ebbw Vale

For the members and friends of
Shrewsbury Evangelical Church

Contents

Part 7: The sufferings and triumph of the King
(26:1 – 28:20)

Introduction

According to the Lord Jesus Christ, our first priority must be to seek the kingdom of God (Matt. 6:33). The aim of Matthew's Gospel is to help the Christian to fulfil that duty. To do this, we must above all honour, trust and serve the King himself, Jesus Christ. This commentary must, therefore, be both Christ-centred and practical. Its focus will be the King and his kingdom.

Four Gospels

Matthew is a long book by New Testament standards, so we must not waste valuable space by dealing at length with technical, introductory questions, which do not concern most readers. However, it is important to face the issue of why we have four Gospels.

Some avoid this subject by including material from the other Gospels in what is often referred to as a harmony. This can be useful in showing that there is no contradiction between the four treatments, but in a commentary, even in the hands of the master commentator, John Calvin, it is a disadvantage. In fact, the effect of combining the four Gospels is the reverse of harmony! In musical harmony the individual lines are retained, while producing a rich and complex sound. The Gospel 'harmony' does the reverse, eliminating the variety and producing an artificial unity, a unison lacking the richness of God's design. Thus T. V. Moore writes, 'The gospel is a harp with four strings, and the attempts to twist them all into one string really destroy the harmony, instead of creating it.'[1]

Since the Lord has given us four Gospels, not just one, we must assume there was a purpose and ask why each one was written, what specific point is being made, what angle is being covered that is not dealt with by the others. We may also find help in interpreting a particular passage by asking why the author chose to include this item which another Gospel-writer passed over. This is not to suggest that the author has changed or invented material in order to make his point — as some modernist critics maintain![2] On the contrary, in asking this question we are recognizing that the Holy Spirit has led different authors to bring out different aspects of the truth — truth which is already there in the events and words of history.

This agrees with the fact that these Gospels are not biographies in our modern sense of the word. They do, in general, follow the chronological sequence of Christ's life, but there is much missing that a modern biographer would consider essential, while other matters receive undue prominence, if judged by the same criterion. They are, in fact, Gospels — presentations of the same good news of Christ, but each from a different perspective, and this must govern our approach.

Author and themes

This Gospel, like the others, has no name attached in the text. Tradition affirms that the author is Matthew, the apostle, otherwise known as Levi, the tax collector. We shall assume that this is true, as there is no good reason to reject it and it gains some support from 9:9 and 10:3, which refer to Matthew in a slightly self-deprecating way. It seems likely that he has based his Gospel on Mark, abridging it somewhat, but adding other material which makes his work longer overall. Some will disagree with this theory, for such it remains, but the issue is not vital.[3] In any case, we must take note of some words of Dr Leon Morris on the subject of Matthew's use of his sources: 'It is more important to understand what the words mean in their new situation than to engage in scholarly niceties about how they came to be there.'[4]

Various attempts have been made to define the central theme of the Gospel. I believe they are all in measure correct. In fact, Matthew keeps at least five different themes going at the same time, rather like a juggler keeping five balls in the air! Under God's direction, this is the work of a literary genius. The five themes are:

    1. the biography — only in outline, but progressing to the cross;

    2. the revelation of Christ's person, with the climax at Peter's confession;

    3. the training and development of the disciples, especially after 16:21;

    4. the place of the Gentiles in the expanding kingdom; and, overall,

    5. the nature of the kingdom of heaven, the kingship of Christ.

The structure of the Gospel is based on the five lengthy discourses (chapters 5-7; 10; 13; 18; 24-25), each of which leads into a similar transitional verse or two, e.g., 'When Jesus had finished saying these things…' (7:28-29; 11:1; 13:53; 19:1; 26:1-2). Each section deals with one aspect of Christ's kingdom (though not exclusively), which is then expounded in the concluding discourse. The last three chapters, describing the final days of Christ's ministry, his death and resurrection, do not follow this pattern, but they do not constitute a mere conclusion. They form a significant section in its own right — a culmination, not an anti-climax.

The basic theme of the kingdom is looked at from an essentially Jewish position, as we can see from some of the author's assumptions, e.g. his stress on the law, and also his use of the term 'kingdom of heaven', which possibly allows for Jewish susceptibilities by avoiding the use of the name of God. This, of course, makes it all the more remarkable that he stresses the extension of the Messiah's reign to the Gentiles.

Part 1:
Prologue — The birth of the King (1:1 – 2:23)

1.
Jesus the Christ

Please read Matthew 1

Jewish sixties' pop-star Helen Shapiro was searching for something. Stirred by the story of how Stan Telchin's daughter became a Christian,[1] she found herself a Bible. In her own words, 'I took a deep breath, decided, "In for a penny, in for a pound" and opened up at the New Testament. I didn't know what to expect, other than an anti-Semitic diatribe. The thing that shook me to the core on that first reading was ... the genealogy of Jesus, which went through Zerubbabel via King David, to the tribe of Judah and back to the patriarch Abraham... I could relate the events to me and my culture.'[2]

This should warn the reader, Jew or Gentile, not to skip the first seventeen verses of the Gospel, saying, 'Who these days is interested in genealogies?' Matthew begins his Gospel with a prologue in which he introduces the main themes of his book or, more precisely, the Lord himself, who is the subject of the book. The genealogy is an essential part of this. Since the theme of the Gospel as a whole is the kingship of Christ, the prologue deals specifically with his descent from King David. This is not done in a merely technical way. Jesus came to the throne of his father David in order to bring in the kingdom of God and achieve a great salvation, and in these two chapters Matthew is already challenging his readers to submit to and benefit from this kingship, as Helen Shapiro did.

The genealogy of Jesus

Matthew begins his Gospel by demonstrating beyond any doubt at all that the Jesus about whom he is going to write is the long-expected Messiah, or **'Christ the son of David, the son of Abraham'** (1:1). To do this he sets down his genealogy. Genealogies, or family trees, are not the most exciting parts of the Bible. They are, however, very necessary and most effective in showing that the biblical record is factual, not a mere fairy tale, as is so often claimed. The Bible deals with real people and real events, so Matthew begins with our Lord's line of descent.

Luke's version of this is very different: it goes in the reverse direction, traces Christ's descent right back to Adam, 'the son of God', and has many variants in the more recent part. It has often been claimed that this is because one is the line through Joseph and the other through Mary, but this does not really fit the text. It is more likely that Luke traces the physical descent of Joseph and Matthew his legal, and royal, descent, thus establishing Jesus' claim to David's throne as his heir, the Messiah.

According to verse 17, the genealogy is arranged artificially in three fourteens of generations (possibly to help memory as 'was customary among Jewish authors'[3]), which clearly necessitated some omissions. It may be that Jeconiah has to be counted twice to make the names fit. It seems likely that the significance of the number fourteen comes from the numerical value of the consonants in the Hebrew form of David; $d = 4$, $v = 6$, so $4 + 6 + 4 = 14$.[4] The important thing to notice is that the turning-points after the initial call of Abraham are the reign of David (explicitly called **'King'**, 1:6) and the exile: the high and low points of the history of the monarchy and of the people of Israel.[5] Genealogies can be dull, but this one is full of surprising details.

From Abraham to David (1:1-6a)

Beginning the genealogy with Abraham rather than David takes us back even beyond the founding of the nation. Matthew's concern is not merely with Israel, but with the world. His vision of the kingdom is as universal as was God's covenant with Abraham and his descendants. This does not, of course, exclude the Jews, but it does prepare for the inclusion of the Gentiles. In Genesis 12 Abraham was promised not only that he would become a great nation and receive a blessing; he was also told, 'All peoples on earth will be blessed through you.' In Genesis 22:18 this was enlarged as he was told, 'Through your offspring all nations on earth will be blessed.' Right from the beginning the hope of the coming Messiah, the offspring of Abraham, was associated with the blessing of all nations, not just the descendants of **'Jacob the father of Judah and his brothers'** (1:2). Later references to the kingdom being given to another people should come as no shock.

It is not, therefore, surprising, though it is remarkable, that in the first section of the genealogy we have not just certain women mentioned, but Gentile women! True, these are the exceptions, but that is enough to foreshadow the later extension of the kingdom. **'Tamar'**, mentioned in verse 3 as the mother of the twins, **'Perez and Zerah'**, was in fact the wife of Judah's son Er and, probably, a Canaanite girl. The twins were born as the result of her seduction of Judah in revenge for his wrong treatment of her (Gen. 38). **'Rahab'**, whose story is recounted in Joshua 2:1-21 and 6:25, became a believer, according to Hebrews 11:31 and James 2:25, but was a Canaanite by birth all the same, an exception to the general slaughter of the inhabitants of Jericho. **'Ruth'**, of course, was a very different character, but nevertheless a Moabite, one of the nation which had been banned from the congregation of Israel for ten generations! (Deut. 23:3). And these women, not Sarah or Rebekah or Leah, are the ones included in Messiah's genealogy!

Even without mentioning Bathsheba, the wife of a Hittite, from
the next section, it is clear that Matthew is making a point. It was
always God's intention to include the Gentiles. Even David could
say:

All the nations you have made
  will come and worship before you, O Lord; .
  they will bring glory to your name

                                                (Ps. 86:9).

Now, with the coming of the King in whose line they are to be
found, the time has come for them to be called more generally.
Throughout the Gospel we find the suggestions that, although Jesus
himself is sent only to the Jews, the gospel will soon be sent to all
nations. It is not only that Jewish outsiders, like Matthew himself,
are to be welcomed, but also those who hitherto had been excluded, the unclean heathen. This should stimulate us even more
to proclaim the gospel worldwide. How sad that some today use
the concept of the kingdom to exclude the Gentiles from the blessings promised to Messiah's people and look for a return to the old
days of exclusion in a future millennium! That is a direct contradiction of Matthew's teaching here and elsewhere. ✗

From David to the exile to Babylon (1:6b-11)

This section of the genealogy demonstrates the triumph of God's
grace. The Messiah has come and God has kept his promises, not
because of Israel's righteousness, but in spite of Israel's sin. It is
not just a matter of amazement at the people God can use, but a
more general principle that salvation at every stage is all of grace.
This point had been made in devastating fashion centuries before:
'The Lord did not set his affection on you and choose you because you were more numerous than other peoples, for you were

the fewest of all peoples. But it was because the LORD loved you...'
(Deut. 7:7-8). The chosen people had no right to be proud of
themselves; their election was all of grace.

Of course, all the individuals, both men and women, mentioned
in the list were sinners, even Abraham and Isaac and Boaz, however godly they became. Some, however, were outstanding or
notorious sinners. In the first section 'Tamar' stands out for this
reason and is specifically mentioned, not glossed over as one might
have expected. (In fact, Judah was the more sinful one in that
case, as we have seen already.) In this second period between
King David and **'the exile to Babylon'** we find some righteous
kings, like **'Asa'** and **'Jehoshaphat'**, but there are others who
are clearly wicked. Even David's sin with Bathsheba, **'Uriah's
wife'**, is referred to (1:6), and **'Ahaz'**, **'Manasseh'** and **'Amon'**
are included in the list of Christ's ancestors. It is not just their
individual wickedness that is significant. Their collective and cu-
mulative sin led inevitably to the exile. Is this, perhaps, the meaning of the reference to **'Jeconiah and his brothers'** (1:11), i.e.
not his physical brothers, but his fellow-Israelites, the whole nation
going into exile?

With that event all seemed to be lost. The line of David, although it did not die out altogether, ceased to occupy the throne
of Israel. Indeed, for many years there was not even a throne to
occupy! Thus we see that Christ came to deliver Israel from the
consequences of their sin. Matthew is teaching by implication that
Christ is the Saviour of sinners, just as he will say explicitly later in
the chapter.

From the exile to the Christ (1:12-17)

Matthew now traces the royal line through the period when Israel
had no king, but during which God was keeping his purpose in
operation and hope alive in the hearts of believing Israelites.

'Jeconiah' appears to have been chosen to mark the new beginning, rather than Jehoiakim or Zedekiah, because it was he whom the Babylonian king, Evil-Merodach, treated well, thus giving an assurance that Israel would survive and return (2 Kings 25:27-30). The chastisement was over; God's promise had not been lost. The names from **'Abiud'** to **'Jacob the father of Joseph'** are not known from other sources. God's purpose continues its course, irrespective of human fame or influence, until the time comes for the Christ to be born. Salvation, it is made clear, is the result of God's secret, hidden purpose, not man's working. Did any of these men know that he was in the Messiah's line?

The last link in the chain is not a physical one: **'Joseph, the husband of Mary, of whom was born Jesus, who is called Christ'** (1:16). Christ is not, of course, a modern-type surname, but a title, as verse 17 makes clear: **'from the exile to the Christ'**. The Hebrew 'Messiah' and the Greek 'Christ' both mean 'anointed', and although in the Old Testament we have references to priests and prophets being anointed with oil, it is chiefly the king who is in mind when this term is used. David was the Lord's Anointed, pointing forward to the one who would come and who would be anointed, not with oil, but with the Holy Spirit (Isa. 61:1; Acts 10:38). In fact Jesus, as the Christ, fulfilled the offices of all three Old Testament mediators — prophet, priest and king — but in Matthew's Gospel it is mainly the kingship that is in view.

Just as the first table showed God's universal purpose and the second his sovereign grace, so this third one demonstrates his power. In spite of Israel's folly and sin, in spite of the strength of their enemies and the hopelessness of the exile, God has brought his purpose to pass. The fact that this happened by means of a miraculous birth only stresses what is already clear. This foreshadows the rest of the Gospel. All three themes constantly recur: for example, God's power ('With God all things are possible', 19:26); his grace ('Don't I have the right to do what I want with my own money? Or are you envious because I am generous?',

20:15); and his universal purpose ('Therefore go and make disciples of all nations', 28:19).

This genealogy, then, far from being a mere list of names, is, implicitly at least, a challenge to examine our doctrine of salvation. Do we too believe in salvation by God's power alone, by grace alone, but for all nations?

The birth of Jesus Christ (1:18-20)

From the genealogy's preparatory details, Matthew passes to a narrative of the event itself. Immediately he makes clear that this is a supernatural, virginal conception (the birth itself was normal). Mary was, indeed, **'pledged to be married to Joseph, but before they came together, she was found to be with child through the Holy Spirit'** (1:18). There is no possibility in the biblical record that Joseph was the father of Christ in the physical sense. It is only after Joseph has discovered the fact of Mary's pregnancy that he is informed by an angel that what is conceived in her is from the Holy Spirit.

Betrothal was a much more serious matter than a modern engagement is, so Joseph is described as considering divorce. It is clear from this that the strict application of the law concerning adultery has passed away. In fact, the Old Testament itself makes this clear, as the Lord speaks of divorcing Israel because of her sin, thus tacitly endorsing the commuting of the death penalty for adultery to divorce (Jer. 3:8; Isa. 50:1). Thus Joseph can be described as **'a righteous man'**, as well as being shown to be compassionate in not wanting **'to expose her to public disgrace'**. The assurance by **'an angel of the Lord'** that Mary's pregnancy was **'from the Holy Spirit'** gives Joseph the necessary confidence to proceed with the marriage, although verse 25 tells us that there was no sexual intercourse until after the birth of our Lord. He also tells him the name by which the baby is to be known.

Jesus (1:21)

Jesus is the Greek form of Joshua, which means 'Jehovah [or, better, Yahweh] saves' or 'is salvation'. The reason for this is also given: **'because he will save his people from their sins'**. This probably refers back to Psalm 130:8: 'He himself [the LORD] will redeem Israel from all their sins.' It seems likely, therefore, that the name **'Jesus'** is intended to show that Jesus is himself Yahweh who saves, not just the one through whom Yahweh saves.

With this name the angel makes clear that the primary purpose of Christ's coming is to bring salvation. His kingdom is one of redemption, salvation from sin, not some kind of nationalistic deliverance from Rome, or a moralistic crusade against evil. Doubtless this will have an effect on the 'sinful structures' with which so many are obsessed in these days, but it is with sin — its guilt, power and corruption in the individual — that he is primarily concerned, not with revolution or social liberation. The deliverance of creation as a whole must, in the main, await his glorious return.

And this work he will perform. The words do not suggest an attempt, dependent on the willingness of man, a mere making possible so that man can do the rest himself. God's purpose in his coming is actual salvation. Jesus himself made this clear: 'For I have come ... not to do my will but to do the will of him who sent me. And this is the will of him who sent me, that I shall lose none of all that he has given me, but raise them up at the last day' (John 6:38-39).

This reference to 'all that he has given me' links with the next element of the meaning of Christ's name. He has been given a **'people'**, a known and specific people for whose salvation he has come. Just what Joseph understood by this we cannot know, but the rest of Matthew shows that this people is both narrower and wider than national Israel. It refers first to the believing remnant of the Jews, but includes also those Gentiles who have been chosen by God and who will in due course believe. The apostle

Paul is told about these people in the words of the Lord at Corinth: 'Do not be afraid; keep on speaking, do not be silent. For I am with you, and no one is going to attack and harm you, because I have many people in this city' (Acts 18:9-10). As in Matthew 1:21, the people are known in advance, before they actually come to believe.

Messiah's people are God's elect, chosen before the foundation of the world, given to the Son to redeem and in time called by God's grace to repent and believe. This truth is expressed in various ways in the New Testament. As well as the idea of Christ saving his people, those given to him by the Father, we have the Good Shepherd laying down his life for his sheep (John 10:11,15) and the great Bridegroom loving the church and giving himself up for her (Eph. 5:25). It is thus apparent that he will save his people by dying for them, but for Matthew's readers this will only become clear later on.

Immanuel (1:22-25)

It makes little difference whether verses 22 and 23 were spoken by the angel or are Matthew's comment. The form of the statement suggests the former, in which case the perfect tense may be rendered in the normal fashion: 'All this has taken place.' Either way the stress is on the fact that this fulfils the prophecy in Isaiah 7:14. The biblical doctrine of the inspiration of the Scriptures is seen in the finely-balanced statement: **'what the Lord had said through the prophet'** (1:22). This reference poses some difficulties, but a brief consideration of them should show why the quotation is given and what spiritual profit is intended.

The wording of the quotation raises the issue of whether **'virgin'** or 'young woman' (1:23) is the correct translation. There is no doubt about the Greek word; it is 'virgin'. The meaning of the Hebrew word is more debatable; it is often argued that it means only 'a young woman'. Evangelical scholars stoutly defend the traditional rendering of 'virgin'. The argument is not simply one of linguistics; there is also the issue of belief in the supernatural.

Linked with this is the question of whether Isaiah's words were a directly Messianic prophecy or not. Some argue for a double fulfilment, i.e. first in an ordinary child born to a young woman, possibly still a virgin at the time of the prophecy, as a sign to King Ahaz, and then later in the birth of Christ of a virgin. This comes up against the double difficulty that the initial event was hardly surprising enough to constitute a sign and, on the other hand, that the second fulfilment necessitates a change in the meaning of the word.

Others see the virgin as 'the virgin daughter of Zion' (Isa. 37:22), whose son is the faithful remnant which came to surround the prophet and is identified as Immanuel, whose land it is (Isa. 8:8,18).[6] This would fit with Matthew's identification of the godly remnant ('my son') with Jesus in chapter 2:15. If, on the other hand, we take Isaiah 7:14 as a direct prophecy of the birth of the Messiah, eight hundred years later, it is difficult to see how this could be a sign to Ahaz. However, J. A. Motyer most helpfully explains the prophecy as a future sign, which will confirm God's judgement on Ahaz for his present unwillingness to trust the Lord.[7] He finds a similar future sign given to Moses in Exodus 3:12, where the future worshipping of God on Sinai will be a sign confirming that Moses was right to trust God to rescue them from Egypt. In the same way, Jesus himself refuses to give the Pharisees a sign, except that of the prophet Jonah — that is, his resurrection (Matt. 12:38-41). That will confirm that the Pharisees were wrong not to repent, in contrast with the men of Nineveh. ✻

This reference to Ahaz helps with the last problem: does **'Immanuel'** refer to Jesus himself as **'God with us'**, or merely to God being with us through Jesus? It also gives a clue to the spiritual point that is being made. In recent years it has become generally accepted that in New Testament quotations from the Old

Testament the whole context, not just the quoted words, must be taken into account. In Isaiah the sign prophecy occurs in a lengthy section which culminates in the description of the Messiah's birth in chapter 9:6. There he is called 'Mighty God'. Jesus is God with us. In addition, just as the sign condemned Ahaz for refusing to trust God when he was confronted by great enemies, so its fulfilment now comes as an encouragement to God's people that the Christ has come to defend them against their enemies; they should trust him whatever their need.

Zechariah, the father of John the Baptist, states the same thing in his prophecy:

> Praise be to the Lord, the God of Israel,
> because he has come and has redeemed his people.
> He has raised up a horn of salvation for us
> in the house of his servant David
> (as he said through his holy prophets of long ago)
> salvation from our enemies
> and from the hand of all who hate us
>
> (Luke 1:68-71).

Taken together with verse 21, this prophecy defines our enemies in terms of sin. God will deliver his people from spiritual enemies of every kind. Jesus, the Christ, is truly another David. The rest of the Gospel will show Jesus defeating all these enemies: Satan, demons and sin itself. Finally, of course, Satan's grip on the world will be broken as the disciples go forth to make disciples of all nations. And the promise which they will take with them? 'Surely I am with you always, to the very end of the age' (28:20) — God with us.

Matthew has begun his Gospel with a clear declaration that the Jesus of whom he is writing is the Messiah/Christ, the son of David. Moreover, he is the Saviour of sinners. He has already fulfilled Old Testament prophecies and will continue to do so until sin and

Satan are finally destroyed. This is the kind of reign that Christ has come to inaugurate. And those who gain the benefits of his kingdom are those who trust him as their Saviour from sin. Right from the beginning, Matthew is clear that belonging to the kingdom is not a matter of trying to earn acceptance by obeying God's laws, but trusting and serving the Saviour-King.

2.
King Herod and King Jesus

Please read Matthew 2

Reaction to this chapter varies from sentimental speculation to critical despair. Too many concentrate on the identity and number of the wise men (with imaginative fables about three kings, Melchior, Balthasar and Caspar), the nature of the star (natural or supernatural), the bloodstained history of King Herod (who murdered his wife, Mariamne, and at least two of his sons) or the chronology of Luke's Gospel (see below). While these things do have some significance, Matthew's interest, as always, is in **'the one who has been born king of the Jews'** (2:2).

The visit of the Magi (2:1-11)

The ecclesiastical Feast of Epiphany may not be of great concern to many readers, but at least it focuses on this aspect. 'Epiphany' means 'manifestation'; later in the New Testament it is used of Christ's Second Coming, but here it refers to the revelation of Christ to the Gentile world. Already in chapter 1 there has been more than a suggestion that his kingdom is universal. Now this hint becomes more explicit as Magi from the east come to Bethlehem, representatives of the Gentile world coming to worship the Saviour.

At least six weeks have passed since the birth of Jesus **'in Bethlehem in Judea'** (2:1). According to Luke's account, Jesus has been taken to Jerusalem by his parents to be presented to the Lord and for them to fulfil the requirements of the law for Mary's cleansing. Now the family has moved into a **'house'** (2:11) — contrary to the many nativity plays which show the 'kings' visiting the stable alongside the shepherds. To this house God directs the Magi by a **'star in the east'** (2:2,9-10), which they follow to Jerusalem. Many have tried to establish the precise nature of this star. Was it a conjunction of two stars, or an especially bright one, or something completely original and supernatural? None of these attempts has been very successful, but the extraordinary nature of God's leading these men to Bethlehem from a distant and heathen country should alert us to the great significance of the event.

The word 'magi' (or *magoi*) has various meanings. These men come from **'the east'**, which probably means Babylon, where there had been men who acted as priests with especial ability, so it was thought, to interpret dreams. The word is used of Daniel and others (Dan. 1:20), and also of Elymas, the sorcerer (Acts 13:6,8). There were still many Jews in Babylon and although these magi were probably astrologers, they seem to have had access to Jewish books, from which they learned of the promised King, whom they linked to the star which had appeared.

Far from justifying astrological beliefs, the Magi's visit illustrates the great variety in God's providential direction of all whom he wills to bring to his Son. The means God uses are his prerogative, not our duty, whether dreams and visions, or the amazing 'coincidence' in which, for instance, a man came across one of Spurgeon's sermons in a newspaper lying on the counter in a public house in the Australian outback and as a result was converted.[1] Those whom God has chosen by grace to be saved, he will bring by his providence to hear the message of salvation and so find Christ.

Herod is disturbed at the suggestion of a rival king, **'and all Jerusalem with him'** (2:3), although the people's reason probably has more to do with Herod's likely response than love of his

rule. The **'chief priests and teachers of the law'** are consulted
and tell Herod that the Messiah is due to be born in Bethlehem. In
addition to Micah 5:2[2] they quote 2 Samuel 5:2 (but see also Micah
5:4), from which Matthew may be implying the caring, shepherding character of the Christ, in contrast with Herod's cruelty. In
addition to this we are then shown the king's amazing hypocrisy in
asking for a report of the child's whereabouts so that he **'too may
go and worship him'**!

The Magi were clearly deceived by Herod's apparent honesty
and went on to Bethlehem. We should not press verse 9 to mean
that the star indicated the exact house where Jesus was, but any
theories about its nature must reckon with this more specific guidance which **'stopped'**, or stood, over Bethlehem. The Magi entered the house, **'bowed down and worshipped'** the infant Jesus
(2:11). The word 'worship' may mean no more than paying hom-
age — i.e. to the King of the Jews — but given the first chapter's
revelations the reader is surely expected to infer much more: 'The
Magi "worshipped" better than they knew.'[3] The tradition that the
Magi were kings probably derives from Old Testament verses
such as Psalm 72:10-11, Isaiah 49:7 and 60:3, which say that
kings will come and worship the Messiah. These do, at least,
emphasize that the Gentile nations will be brought into the kingdom. The number 'three' is a reasonable, but not necessary, deduction from the three kinds of gift in verse 11. Traditionally **'gold'**
has been taken to indicate royalty, **'incense'** (frankincense, a valuable, spicy perfume) Christ's deity, and **'myrrh'** his sufferings and
death. The Magi are more likely to have thought of their value
(**'they opened their treasures'**) and appropriateness for a king.

We do not know just how much the Magi understood, but
their willingness to travel a great distance to worship him shows
that they were more than merely curious. Like the Queen of Sheba,
who travelled 'from the ends of the earth' to visit King Solomon,
they put to shame many who make no effort at all to seek out
Jesus (see Luke 11:31). What a contrast with King Herod, who

was 'on the spot' but, far from looking for the Messiah, tried to destroy him, and with his advisers, who could quote the relevant scriptures but made no attempt to find and worship the Lord! They may be a rebuke to many of us, too.

Providential care (2:12-23)

Now the reader will fear for the child's safety and, indeed, for the wise men's. However, God's providence has not yet finished with them. Guidance is followed by protection, not just for them, but also, and especially, for the baby Jesus. It is implied that the warning dream, like that of Joseph in verse 13, is from the Lord. So the Magi took note and **'returned to their country by another route'** (2:12). God is not, of course, taken by surprise by Herod's enmity and his command **'to kill all the boys in Bethlehem and its vicinity who were two years old and under'** (2:16). He intervenes beforehand to protect his Servant and fulfil his purpose. These verses introduce another, and vital, instalment in the age-long conflict between the seed of the woman and the seed of the serpent (Gen. 3:15).

As, earlier, Satan had inspired Pharaoh and then Haman (Exod. 1:15-16; Esth. 3:6) to annihilate the Jews, so now Herod attempted to remove the threat to his throne and, unwittingly perhaps, do even more: wipe out the threat to Satan's kingdom. Revelation 12:1-5 describes the same conflict in symbolic language. The woman, representing God's covenant people in every age, gives birth to a man-child, 'who will rule all the nations with an iron sceptre' (v. 5). The dragon, representing persecuting authority in every age, attempts to destroy the woman's son, the Messiah, but 'Her child was snatched up to God and to his throne.' Revelation looks far beyond Bethlehem to the resurrection, ascension and beyond, but this incident is a part of the whole battle. Matthew's Gospel is not only about the coming of God's reign; it is also about the defeat of Satan's kingdom, represented here by Herod.

So Joseph took Mary and Jesus into the safety of **'Egypt, where he stayed until the death of Herod'** (2:14-15). God's care continues as a further dream tells Joseph that it is safe to return **'to the land of Israel'** and yet another warns him to go back to Nazareth, out of reach of **'Archelaus'**, Herod's son and successor, **'in Judea'** (2:19-20,22). All these movements fulfil **'what was said through the prophets'** (2:23), but the modern mind finds this difficult. Some, of course, refuse to accept the reality of predictive prophecy, but the problem here is rather more complicated than that. The actual quotations in this chapter seem to have little genuine reference to the events described. This is similar to the problem of Matthew's reference to Isaiah 7:14 considered above. However, if we try to gain the same perspective as Matthew, we can not only see the justification for using the word **'fulfilled'**, but also gain spiritual profit and encouragement.

Hosea 11:1, quoted in verse 15, has no direct reference to the coming of Jesus; it is actually looking back to the Exodus, not forward to the incarnation. In addition, Jesus is going into **'Egypt'**, not coming **'out'** as Hosea says. 'Fulfil' in Matthew does not refer only to direct predictions by the prophets, but has a broader significance, including the types and shadows of the law and historical books (see further in the commentary on 5:17). It is clear from Isaiah's prophecy that Jesus is regarded as the true Servant of the Lord, unlike Israel, the blind and deaf one (contrast Isa. 41:8-9; 42:19 with 42:1; 49:5 etc.). He is the true Son of God, doing what Israel failed to do (Exod. 4:22-23, Deut. 32:5-6; Matt. 4:1-11). In the light of this, Matthew is assuring us that just as God protected his son, Israel, in the history referred to by Hosea, so he would protect his true Son, Jesus. In context, Hosea was telling Israel that God would not leave them under judgement, but would call them back to himself (Hosea 11:10-11). The implication is that just as God brought Israel safely out of Egypt and back from exile, so he will bring back his Son, Jesus, as he did in verse 21, and fulfil his purposes of grace through him. So we, as members of the true Israel in Christ, may be assured of God's continuing care and protection. The kingdom of God may be subject to enmity and persecution, but God's love will protect and redeem.

The reference to Jeremiah 31:15 is more than a mere association of words — boys in Bethlehem = children in Ramah, with the added connection that Rachel died near Ephrath, i.e. near Bethlehem (Gen. 35:16-19). The real point is that the context in Jeremiah is one of hope: 'Your children will return to their own land' (Jer. 31:17). So Matthew is telling us that, in spite of Herod's cruelty and the sorrows of Bethlehem, God's purpose of grace will be fulfilled. Jesus, the Messiah, has come, and salvation and comfort will follow. God's kingdom involves suffering and sorrow, especially for the suffering Messiah, but his purpose for that kingdom is to bring blessing out of the sorrow. Once again the suffering of the Messiah, as in Genesis 3:15, will bring salvation and hope. God will be victorious.

The reference in verse 23, describing how Jesus was to be brought up in Nazareth, is also difficult. There is no obvious Old Testament text that is being quoted. Only here does Matthew refer to the plural, **'prophets'**, and instead of 'saying' he uses a form which most likely indicates an indirect quotation. What we have, therefore, is a summary of Old Testament teaching, not a specific prediction. The word is clearly **'Nazarene'** (not 'Nazirite'), referring to an inhabitant of Nazareth. Such people in general were despised, as Nathanael shows by his scornful remark in John 1:46: 'Nazareth! Can anything good come from there?' In the light of this it is better to see Matthew's reference as giving 'the substance of several passages',[4] that the Messiah would be both hidden and despised, for example Isaiah 53:2-3. Matthew takes up this theme in later passages. Jesus came, not in the open, public way that men expected, but in a hidden way, only gradually revealed, but nevertheless he is the true Messiah. Contrary to much current church practice, we should not be led astray by the desire to be famous or popular. Very often God's way is hidden, despised by the world, approved only by the Lord.

So we should be encouraged by this account. In spite of the opposition of Satan, persecution by ungodly authorities and the scorn of the world, God's kingdom will come. The offspring of Eve, the true Son of God, will defeat the devil and his kingdom will be established. We must not fear, or despair, or slip into worldliness, but be confident and encouraged. The Gentiles will be called; the kingdom will spread to all nations; and Satan is unable to prevent it (Rev. 20:3).

At the end of the prologue to his Gospel, Matthew has announced many of its major themes: the Lord's unfailing purpose to bring salvation for his people, both Jews and Gentiles, grace which overcomes sin, suffering, protection and victory, his overruling providence and the responsibility of man to seek the Lord. Right from the beginning of his Gospel, Matthew calls us to decide where we stand. Are we like the Magi — ready to make every effort to come to find the Saviour and worship and serve him? Or are we like Herod and his advisers — in possession of the facts, knowing the Scriptures, but unwilling to make any effort to enter the kingdom? Take notice of Christ's exhortation: 'Make every effort to enter through the narrow door' (Luke 13:24). Or are we actually in opposition to it? Be assured that God's kingdom will prosper; it will overcome all opposition, turn despair to hope and one day be manifest in all its glory, when the victorious Messiah comes again.

Part 2:
The nature of the kingdom (3:1 – 7:29)

3.
Jesus and John the Baptist

Please read Matthew 3

In the prologue Matthew has introduced us to the subject of his Gospel: Jesus, the promised King. Now he describes how the King's coming was announced (by John the Baptist and Jesus himself). He explains the response that was required, repentance (3:2; 4:17), and then expounds the nature of the kingdom that has come near: righteousness (6:33). So, right at the beginning of the Gospel, we are told that this cannot be just another intellectual enquiry. King Jesus demands a response. You and I must be prepared to treat this as a matter of the utmost seriousness.

It would be difficult to overstate the importance of John the Baptist. All four Gospels record his ministry. He was, says Jesus, a prophet, but 'more than a prophet' (11:9). He was the appointed herald and forerunner of the King. Indeed, of him Jesus asserted: 'I tell you the truth: Among those born of women there has not risen anyone greater than John the Baptist; yet', he adds significantly, 'he who is least in the kingdom of heaven is greater than he' (11:11).

John announced the presence of the King (3:1-6)

As far as this Gospel is concerned, John appears suddenly, without background or biographical introduction. His importance lies entirely in his function as the herald of the King. He simply 'comes';

he appears **'in the Desert of Judea'** with a demand for repentance on the basis of the good news that **'The kingdom of heaven
is near'** (3:1,2). From being far away, known only in prophecy,
the kingdom has now come near; the King has come, and with
him the kingdom. The word only rarely refers to territory, as in the
expression, 'United Kingdom'. The main idea is of reign or rule.
The King has come to reign over his people.[1]

Matthew identifies John as the herald, the **'voice of one calling in the desert'**, spoken of in Isaiah 40:3.[2] The bleakness of
the wilderness setting and the harsh clothing and diet all point to a
severity of ministry like that of Elijah, which prepares us to hear
the demand for repentance. The **'way for the Lord'** is not a road
for the exiles to leave Babylon and return to Israel, but for the
Lord (Yahweh/Jehovah, here referring to Jesus) to come to them
to save them. The smoothing, or making straight, of the way is to
be understood as the repentance that must precede the reception
of God's salvation (3:2), and the confession (3:6) that leads to
forgiveness. (Thus Isaiah 40:5 speaks of 'the glory of the LORD'
being revealed, which is equivalent to salvation, see Luke 3:6.)
This is to be achieved through John's ministry (cf. Mal. 3:1; 4:5-6).

Too often John's ministry is seen as legalistic and moralistic,
which is a complete misunderstanding. Nor is it just a matter of
ritual — baptism as a formal requirement for membership of the
kingdom. The preaching of the good news, that the King has come,
precedes both repentance and the mention of baptism (3:6). We
must never allow the concept of the kingdom to degenerate into a
mere giving of commandments, as with much modern liberal teaching. The King rescues and saves his people before ruling and defending them in righteousness, as foreshadowed by King David.

John called for repentance (3:7-10)

Repentance is a frequently ignored idea today. Sadly, even when
it is not ignored, it is very often totally misunderstood. As John

speaks to **'the Pharisees and Sadducees'** who come to check up on him, he sets repentance in its context and shows the implications which are too often neglected.

The origins of the word translated **'repentance'** have to do with a change of mind, but we can go wrong if we merely understand it in this way. Throughout the Old Testament the equivalent word is used for something more than just a change of mind, however thoroughgoing. It is not merely feeling sorry for your sins. This is, no doubt, included, and confession of sin is necessary (3:6), but the word was used by the prophets for something more radical. It expressed God's 'frequent summons to Israel to "return" to God, to abandon their rebellion and come back to covenant-obedience'.[3] In other words, it is equivalent to conversion, a radical change of heart as well as mind, leading to a changed life.

Repentance is necessary because of the declared displeasure and wrath of God. Somewhat ironically, John asks **'who'** has **'warned'** the Jewish leaders **'to flee from the coming wrath'** (3:7). He declares that judgement is imminent (3:10). **'The axe'** of God's judgement **'is already at the root of the trees'**, beginning with Israel. (As the rest of the Gospel will make clear, this will come to fruition only at the return of Christ, see 3:12.) The only way of escape is through repentance, bringing forgiveness through the King who has come. In particular the leaders must not rely on their status as God's people, the children of Abraham (3:9). John anticipates Paul's assertion: 'Not all who are descended from Israel are Israel' (Rom. 9:6). Not all who are descended from Abraham are the seed of Abraham. The point of John's saying about the **'stones'** is that God can, and will, produce true believers, true covenant children of Abraham and of God, from the Gentiles. Isaiah had foreseen this when he announced, in the same prophecy that spoke of John, not only that God's glory would be revealed, but that 'All mankind together will see it' (Isa. 40:5).

Such repentance must be genuine; it must produce the appropriate fruit — good, matching fruit **'in keeping with repentance'**

(3:8), fruit that would pass the test of the judgement of God (3:10). Later, Paul would demand the same. In Acts 26:20 he summed up his ministry as he 'declared first to those in Damascus and in Jerusalem, and throughout all the region of Judea, and then to the Gentiles, that they should repent, turn to God, and do works befitting repentance' (NKJV). Many are so afraid of teaching justification by works that they omit this aspect of the gospel requirement. Sins must be confessed; new life must begin; good works must be performed; but this does not earn acceptance with God. That is by faith in Christ alone. Nevertheless, if the faith is real and the repentance is true, they will produce such fitting, worthy (matching), appropriate works. The biblical pattern must not be abandoned because of fears, or accusations, of teaching a works religion.

John pointed to Jesus, the true Baptizer (3:11-12)

Baptism was mentioned in verse 6, but only in verse 11 does John explain its significance. It was intended to point to the real baptism with the Holy Spirit. This does not mean that John's disciples were not saved, but that it was not his baptism with water that saved them. Nor was it his preaching, apart from the **'more powerful'** Christ whom he proclaimed, that delivered them from sin. Since repentance had to precede baptism (3:6), **'for repentance'** may mean 'with reference to baptism' or be a general description of John's ministry (cf. 21:25), which was aimed at bringing men to repentance (Mark 1:4; Luke 3:3).[4]

What is this baptism **'with the Holy Spirit'**? First, it is not, as it is often mistakenly called, a baptism *by* the Holy Spirit? Christ is the great Baptizer. He baptizes *with* the Spirit and fire.[5] Secondly, some find two baptisms here — one of purification, by the Spirit, and another of judgement, by fire (cf. 3:12). However, the word 'with' comes only once, so there is only one baptism, not two. The fire, as well as the Holy Spirit, speaks of cleansing and purification (see Isa. 4:4). John is saying that the Messiah will give his Holy Spirit to his true people and so change their hearts and lives. This is later identified with what happened at Pentecost (Acts 1:4-5), but is also now a personal gift and indwelling for all who believe (Acts 2:38-39).

Verse 12 tells us that the Messiah's coming includes judgement, as well as salvation. The picture is of wheat thrown into the air by the **'winnowing fork'**. The heavier grain falls to the ground and is collected, while the lighter chaff is blown away, swept up and burnt. The **'unquenchable fire'** is that of eternal punishment (Mark 9:45,46,48). John is looking ahead to the final judgement, although at this stage he sees the Messiah's coming from the Old Testament perspective as one event, which later causes him difficulties (see comments on 11:1-6). John's hearers are faced with the alternatives; a decision for repentance is demanded.

John baptized Jesus to fulfil all righteousness (3:13-17)

We are told that Jesus came all the way **'from Galilee to the Jordan'** in Judea to be baptized, showing how important this was to him — necessary, as well as **'proper'** (3:15). Why, then, did John try to refuse his request? It was not because he knew Jesus was the Messiah, for John 1:33 shows that John only realized this afterwards. However, John was no doubt aware of a great difference between himself and his cousin, sufficient to persuade him that the roles should be reversed. Jesus persuaded him to go ahead with the baptism **'now'** and so **'fulfil all righteousness'** (3:15). What does this mean?

It is no accident that the keyword 'righteousness' is used. Jesus was not a sinner needing to repent and be cleansed. Nor was righteousness just a good thing to do and be seen doing. Receiving baptism was the righteous act of a true Israelite. The 'now' reminds us that the day of the Messiah had arrived and that, therefore, John must set aside his otherwise valid objection. It was as Messiah that Jesus would undergo baptism. The use in Matthew 2:15 of the quotation from Hosea 11:1 showed that he was to be regarded as the true Son of God, the true Israel. So here he identified himself with his people and their sin, making clear that, as God's obedient and righteous Servant, he would do whatever was necessary to provide a righteousness for them and for their salvation.

The descent of the **'Spirit of God ... like a dove'** and the **'voice from heaven'** are clearly the consequence of his submitting to baptism. In fact, we have here all three persons of the Trinity involved in a significant stage in the work of salvation. Anointing with oil in the Old Testament had the double significance of setting apart and also equipping for the service of God. The Holy Spirit came upon Jesus, anointing him as God's Servant in fulfilment of Isaiah 42:1 and 61:1 and endowing him with all the necessary gifts for his work (Isa. 11:2-5; John 3:34). **'He saw'** in verse 16 refers to Jesus, who was thus given assurance of all this before entering on his ministry, and especially before the temptations, but John also was assured that this was truly the one whom he had come to herald, the one who would baptize with the Spirit and fire (3:11; cf. John 1:33).

The symbolism of the dove has mystified commentators, producing many imaginative solutions. There is little Old Testament background to the idea, but Hosea 7:11 does refer to Israel as a dove, and it may be that once again Jesus is being pointed to as the true Israel. Further, the words of Matthew 10:16 ('as innocent as doves') may be relevant here: Jesus is identified with sinful Israel, but is not himself sinful at all.

Perhaps even more important are the words of God's voice from heaven: **'This is my Son, whom I love; with him I am well pleased'** (3:17). These words are a combination of Psalm 2:7 ('You are my Son') and Isaiah 42:1, which Matthew later quotes as 'Here is my servant whom I have chosen, the one I love, in whom I delight' (12:18). In the light of this, 'love' must include the idea of 'chosen'. The Father chose the Son before the foundation of the world to be his Servant, 'a covenant for the people and a light for the Gentiles' (Isa. 42:6). While the basic idea of sonship in Psalm 2 is that of the Messianic kingship, we can never exclude the eternal sonship from our thoughts. Christ does not become the Son because he is the Servant, but is eminently suited to be the Servant because he is God's beloved Son.

The baptism of Jesus is too often ignored, apart from debates about Christian baptism. It was clearly of great importance for him, giving assurance at the outset of his ministry. This assurance is also applicable to us. We need have no fear. Our Saviour is fully able to save; he has every gift and ability that is necessary for our salvation. He gives the Spirit to his people to cleanse and purify and set apart for his service. If we ignore this we miss out on much strength and assurance of his help for our times of trial.

Equally, however, we must not presume upon his mercy. The kingdom and the King still require our heartfelt and thorough repentance. If you claim to belong to the kingdom of heaven, do you display the appropriate fruit, the works that match repentance? Does your life demonstrate the power of the Spirit of God and reflect the purity and innocence of the Saviour?

4.
A declaration of war

Please read Matthew 4

Martin Luther said, 'Temptation and adversity are the two best books in my library.'[1] Here we see the Son of God, preparing to enter on his ministry, undergoing these same elements, especially temptation. It was God who took the initiative, not Satan. **'Jesus was led by the Spirit into the desert to be tempted by the devil.'** As he looked forward to beginning the preaching of the gospel of the kingdom, he met the enemy, the prince of this world, the occupying power, as it were.

This confrontation is looked for, not just as a preparation for ministry, but as a part of that ministry: an entry on the battle, a declaration of war. It is vital to see this remarkable incident, sadly grown so familiar as to seem unremarkable, in a positive way. It is surely not wrong to use this passage to learn from our Lord's method of dealing with temptation, for instance by the correct use of Scripture, but that is not the real point. That is purely defensive; the real point is that our Lord is on the attack. God's King has come from heaven to invade the enemy's territory, to begin the war of liberation, to free sinners in bondage to Satan.

The last Adam (4:1-2)

In the light of this it is significant that for his answers to the Evil One, Jesus went to the book of Deuteronomy, using quotations that applied originally to the Israelites. This is not a misuse of Scripture, but an insight into its true meaning and relevance. It shows that he stood alongside his people, that he was the true Israel, as we have seen already in chapter 2:15. He is the representative man, the Servant of the Lord.

He came as another Adam to represent all his people, both Jews and Gentiles, as Adam represented all men, and on their behalf to win the victory. Where Adam disobeyed and sinned and so brought sin and death to all mankind, Jesus obeyed and earned a righteousness for those whom he represented. The apostle Paul spells it out in his letter to the church in Rome: 'Consequently, just as the result of one trespass was condemnation for all men, so also the result of one act of righteousness was justification that brings life for all men. For just as through the disobedience of the one man the many were made sinners, so also through the obedience of the one man the many will be made righteous' (Rom. 5:18-19).

We must remember here that Jesus was (and is) a real man, not a spirit or God in a human form. However difficult we find it to accept, he was really tempted, genuinely under pressure, in fact even more so than we can be or imagine, because he resisted throughout and so provoked increasingly hard temptation. We do not get this far; we give in before we can encounter temptations as hard as those he faced and defeated. Jesus, the representative man, suffered when he was tempted (Heb. 2:18). This was a new and crucial stage in the age-long struggle between the seed of the woman and the seed of the serpent (Gen. 3:15). Like Adam, he was a real man. Unlike Adam, he faced temptation in the worst possible circumstances. Adam was in paradise; Jesus was in the desert (with the wild animals, Mark 1:13). Adam was permitted to eat the fruit of all the trees in the garden except one. Jesus **'after fasting for forty days and forty nights ... was hungry'.**[2] He was alone, facing an uncertain future, in one sense, yet, in another, one that was awfully certain. It was under these adverse conditions that Jesus did battle with the devil and won.

The first temptation: bread and obedience (4:3-4)

The tempter begins by challenging Jesus: **'If you are the Son of God, tell these stones to become bread'** (4:3). 'Think of your status; remember who you are. Why should someone like you have to suffer the pangs of hunger, when with a word you can remedy the situation?' The issue is not Jesus' divine sonship as such. He is not being tempted to doubt his position as the Son of God, but to misuse it. He is being enticed into using his divine power to avoid the path of deprivation and suffering that his heavenly Father has set before him, to disobey the Father's word.[3] This is one of many illustrations in the Gospels of Paul's teaching in Philippians 2:6-8 that Jesus, 'though he was in the form of God, did not regard equality with God as something to be exploited' (NRSV, correctly). The way of the kingdom is the way of suffering, the way of the cross. Jesus is the Suffering Servant of Isaiah 53, so he rejects Satan's suggestion out of hand, as he will also do later, in the Garden of Gethsemane (26:52-54) and then on the cross itself (27:39-40).

Christ's answer from Deuteronomy 8:3 must, as usual, be seen in its context there. In that passage Moses reminded Israel that God had led them in the desert to test them: 'He humbled you, causing you to hunger and then feeding you with manna, which neither you nor your fathers had known, to teach you that man does not live on bread alone but on every word that comes from the mouth of the LORD.' God can provide sustenance by his powerful word, by which he gave them manna in the desert, so bread is not absolutely necessary. What is absolutely necessary is obedience to the energizing word of God. If God has commanded Jesus to fast in the wilderness as part of his purpose of salvation, then he will also provide for him to live to perform that work. 'The command of God contained within it the provision of God.'[4] Essentially, therefore, Christ had to trust God — to strengthen him, provide for him and then to release him from hunger at the proper time (4:11). And this he did, unlike Israel, who complained about 'this manna' (Num. 11:4-6) and refused to submit and trust.

We must not limit ourselves to a moralistic lesson that reading our Bibles is more important than eating our food. We are in the realm of salvation here; we must see Christ's work, not our duty. The significance for Jesus is clear. 'Israel demanded its bread but died in the wilderness; Jesus denied himself bread, retained his righteousness, and lived by faithful submission to God's Word.'[5] Jesus resisted the devil's ploy to divert him from the pathway of obedience and consequent suffering. Instead he set his face steadfastly to go on towards the cross. His obedience fulfilled all God's requirements and provided a righteousness for us who believe in him.

The second temptation: promise and proof (4:5-7)

Just as we do not know exactly how 'the tempter came to him' (4:3), so we do not know whether verse 5 is to be understood in a literal or visionary manner. Certainly it was not just imaginary. The temptation was real: to **'throw'** himself down from the pinnacle of the temple and expect God's angels to save him from death.[6]

As has often been pointed out, the devil can quote (or misquote) Scripture when it suits his purposes. His interpretation and application may be plausible, but they are wrong. Failure to do proper and accurate exegesis is to play the devil's game. We must make sure that it is actually God's Word that we are trusting, not a false interpretation. Jesus' use of **'also'** in verse 7 illustrates a vital hermeneutical[7] principle: we must never interpret one passage of Scripture in such a way as to contradict other passages.

Context is vitally important. The author of Psalm 91, from which Satan quoted, refers to those who 'make the Most High [their] dwelling — even the LORD, who is my refuge' (v. 9). In verse 14 the Lord says, 'Because he loves me I will rescue him; I will protect him, for he acknowledges my name.' 'Surely,' argues the devil, 'this must apply to you, if you are the Son of God. If anyone can take this as a firm basis for throwing himself off the temple, then you can.' He, if anyone, could take this assurance of angelic protection literally.

The clue to both the nature of the temptation and the remedy lies in our Lord's counter-quotation: **'Do not put the Lord your God to the test'** (4:7, quoting Deut. 6:16). Versions which use the word 'tempt' here are unhelpful. The same word is used both for tempting to sin and for testing or trying (although the word in verse 7 is slightly different). James 1:12-14 shows the variety of meaning that is possible, from enticing to sin to proving that something is genuine. This second idea can be a good thing, as when God tries us and refines us, or bad, as here. Putting God to the test means asking him for proof of his faithfulness before you will trust him, as Israel did at Massah. Instead of relying on the God who had redeemed them from Egypt and promised to take them to Canaan, they 'tested the LORD saying, "Is the LORD among us or not?"' (Exod. 17:7). We must distinguish this from the use in Malachi 3:10, where the Lord says to Israel, 'Test me in this (prove me now, AV) and see whether I will not throw open the floodgates of heaven and pour out so much blessing that you will not have room enough for it.' This testing is not a sinful demand for further assurance. It is relying on God to keep the word he has already given, in the appropriate circumstances, not demanding proof beforehand.

So Jesus refused to demand any proof beyond what God had already promised and went on to his ministry, relying on the Lord to protect and save him as occasion arose. He did not doubt God's ability or his willingness and so did not find it necessary to put him to the test before he could launch out into the world. As the Son of God, who had come into the world to save sinners, he knew that God would support and protect him, without having to resort to a practical demonstration beforehand. God would even send his angels to sustain him when necessary, as he did in verse 11 and Luke 22:43.

We must follow this example. We must trust God, not demanding proof, even under the guise of testing our own faith. However, the real point is that Jesus, the true Israel, unlike the old Israel and unlike Adam, did trust God and showed it by his obedience. Thus he fulfilled all righteousness, defeated the devil and went on to save sinners.

The third temptation: worship and the world (4:8-11)

This time Satan did not mention that Jesus is the Son of God. Perhaps that would have been too dangerous, by reminding Jesus of his authority, but it remains implicit in the temptation. There is no mountain in Palestine which would provide this view of **'all the kingdoms of the world and their splendour'** (4:8), so we must assume that it was in vision that the devil showed them to Jesus. His amazing promise, **'All this I will give you … if you will bow down and worship me,'** has provoked many to accuse him of going beyond his rights and power. Could he really do this? The answer seems to be both 'Yes' and 'No'. As god and prince of this world, he had authority to offer in a sense; the reality of the temptation depends on this. On the other hand, the condition he attached shows that he was actually usurping the place and throne of God, which he certainly could not do. The fact is that Jesus has come to defeat Satan's kingdom and take away all his authority.

The attractiveness and power of this temptation lies in the fact that Jesus had a right to the world and its glory. One day he will achieve this, not only as God, but as God-man and Mediator. In Revelation 11:15 the angel declares, 'The kingdom of the world has become the kingdom of our Lord and of his Christ, and he will reign for ever and ever.' The way that God had ordained for this is

the path of suffering and the cross. The way of worshipping Satan
would avoid that suffering and pain. The prophets of the Old Testament had 'predicted the sufferings of Christ and the glories that
would follow' (1 Peter 1:11). Neither the Saviour nor his people
can avoid this sequence: suffering precedes glory (Luke 24:25-27;
Rom. 8:17). The temptation is of the same kind as the one that
came later through Peter, to avoid the cross, which received equally
short shrift: **'Away from me, Satan!'** (4:10; cf. 16:23).

Our Lord did not rebuke Satan for treating him as an inferior
being. Instead he quoted again from the Old Testament record of
Israel. Once again he speaks as man, the truly righteous man, the
true Israelite, the last Adam, acting on our behalf. Where Adam
went along with Satan's suggestions and, in effect, worshipped
him rather than God, Jesus says, **'Worship the Lord your God,
and serve him only'** (4:10, quoting Deut. 6:13). Jesus, as the
Son of God, had received God's promise:

> Ask of me,
> > and I will make the nations your inheritance,
> > the ends of the earth your possession
>
> (Ps. 2:8).

He trusts the Father and will worship only him.[8]

Jesus rejected the devil's offer because he trusted God the
Father to keep his promise to reward his sufferings in this way
(Isa. 53:10-12). He trusted the Father to feed and sustain him; he
trusted the Father to protect him and in due course to give him his
kingdom. Therefore he would go ahead with his ministry, no matter what it would cost, because this is the way the Father had set
before him. The devil left him for a time, defeated, and the angels,
whose help he had not presumed upon, now came to him at the
Father's command (4:11). He was given freely what he would not
take sinfully. So it will be with the kingdom.

Christians must, of course, learn to follow the example of their Lord both in content and method. We must trust and obey, trust and not test, trust and not look for pleasant shortcuts without suffering. We must use Scripture to strengthen our faith and so defeat Satan's wiles. More than this, we must fight against Satan in the strength of our knowledge that Jesus has beaten Satan once for all and that, in him, we too can be victorious. Christ, with his experience of temptation, can sympathize with us in our trials, but he does not condone our sin. On the contrary, having defeated Satan for us, he expects us to follow in his steps, without sin and assured that through him we may 'approach the throne of grace with confidence, so that we may receive mercy and find grace to help us in our time of need' (Heb. 4:16).

Jesus begins to preach the gospel of the kingdom (4:12-17)

After his successful encounter with Satan and on the basis of his victory, Jesus began his proclamation of the kingdom. Now that John the Baptist had been put in prison, Christ took over the preaching of the gospel, knowing that he would inevitably suffer, as his forerunner had done.

'**Leaving Nazareth, he went and lived in Capernaum, which was by the lake in the area of Zebulun and Naphtali — to fulfil what was said through the prophet Isaiah'** (4:13-14; cf. Isa. 9:1-2). This prophecy, which pointed to the literal place where he began his ministry, also acts as a signpost to a wider fulfilment. The Messiah has come to bring the light of salvation. This deliberate commencement of his ministry in '**Galilee of the Gentiles'** not only hints at the future calling of all nations into the kingdom. It also points out that he is coming like the dawn, bringing a '**great light'** to '**the people living in darkness'**, under '**the shadow of death'**. The Jews were in spiritual darkness —

ignorance, despair and fear. They had been living in bondage to Satan, but now that he had defeated the devil Jesus could begin to rescue them from his clutches.

The fact that **'a light has dawned'** tells us that Jesus' announcement that the kingdom of heaven is near means more than John's earlier one. The sun is no longer just below the horizon; it has risen 'with healing in its wings' (Mal. 4:2). Equally, his demand for repentance must be seen in the light of his own righteous response to Satan's temptations. Repentance means rejecting Satan and his wiles by trusting God without compromise, turning from the darkness of sin and following the victorious Saviour. We who live after the victories of the resurrection and Pentecost have a responsibility to proclaim the same gospel to a world in darkness, living in fear of death and under the threat of eternal punishment. Satan is a defeated and condemned enemy (John 16:11). Men and women must be convinced of this and turn to the Saviour.

The first disciples (4:18-25)

As a beginning Jesus called four men to follow him, both literally (4:20,22) and spiritually as disciples, or learners. It seems clear from John's Gospel that this was not their first encounter with Jesus, but until now they had not been permanently committed to him. Repentance implies instant obedience, and this they gave: **'At once they left their nets and followed him.'** The two sets of **'brothers'** deliberately left their occupations and, in the case of **'James'** and **'John'**, their father. This clearly indicates the nature of discipleship as an exclusive commitment to Christ.

The fact that Jesus promised, **'I will make you fishers of men,'** suggests that they needed to be trained, as appears later. In Jeremiah 16:16 the Lord sent fishermen to catch the wicked to be sent into exile, leading some to think that Jesus has judgement in mind, rather than salvation. Certainly the message includes judgement, as it did with John the Baptist, but it seems unlikely in the context of the good news (4:23) that this is the main point. It is more likely that Jesus uses the picture because of their occupation as fishermen. While the stress here is on the future apostles as official preachers of the gospel, it is also true that the Great Commission (28:18-20) will place the responsibility for making disciples of all nations upon the whole church.

Accompanied by the disciples, **'Jesus went throughout Galilee, teaching in their synagogues, preaching the good news of the kingdom'** (4:23).[9] The summary description of his work of healing is most impressive: **'all who were ill … various diseases … severe pain'**, etc. In the light of verse 17 it is clear that the main point was the preaching; the healings were subsidiary, but important. They were signs of his authority as God's appointed and anointed Servant. In addition they were examples of deliverance from illness and threatened death that illustrated the salvation which he had come both to announce and to achieve. Soon, however, the news about him spread much more widely: to **'Syria … the Decapolis, Jerusalem, Judea and the region across the Jordan'** (4:24,25). This was not a just local ministry to his home area, but the beginning of a widespread mission to Israel as a whole. The crowds that began to follow him were probably not committed in the same way that Peter and the others were. However, they must have understood, in some sense, that the King had come; the kingdom was beginning to be established on earth in fulfilment of prophecy.

The next chapters will explain more about this, but for the moment we readers must face up to the reality of Christ's coming and its relevance to our own day. As we look about us, we see the darkness of sin and unbelief, of ignorance and fear. Today, as then, the good news of Christ, the King, is the only hope. As we proclaim that gospel, as we try to be fishers of men in our own situation, we need the assurance of two things. First, we may be certain that Jesus is the glorious Saviour, the great light that can bring salvation in the darkness. Secondly, we must realize that this Saviour has defeated Satan, not just on one occasion in the desert, but in the whole of his life and work. We can have every confidence, both for our own lives under trial and temptation and also in proclaiming him to men in darkness. The healing of all those diseases tells us that no one today is beyond his grace and mercy. But then we must remember that the only way to enter the kingdom is by repentance.

5.
Kingdom characteristics

Please read Matthew 5:1-12

When I was at junior school, the day began with all the pupils reciting first the Ten Commandments, then the Lord's Prayer and the Beatitudes, followed by our multiplication tables. The Beatitudes, to which we now turn our attention, were thus treated as a set of beautiful sayings, not linked to anything else. In contrast to that approach we must see them in context. Jesus began his ministry by preaching the gospel of the kingdom, and 'Large crowds from Galilee, the Decapolis, Jerusalem, Judea and the region across the Jordan followed him' (4:25). It was the sight of these crowds (5:1) that led him to teach his disciples what we know as the Sermon on the Mount, which extends through to the end of chapter 7. The crowd were obviously attracted to him and his message; they found the idea of the arrival of the kingdom of God most appealing. However, it is likely that, in common with most Jews of the time, they were very mistaken as to what that meant.

For some the emphasis would be political; they were hoping for a Messiah who would drive the hated Roman overlords into the Mediterranean and free them from servitude. Others, more religious, would hope for a return to a proper observance of the law of Moses which would bring God's blessing upon the nation with deliverance from their enemies. What would Jesus say? What was the essence of the kingdom? Jesus did not address them, but rather his disciples — those who had come to believe in him and show an allegiance to him. The Beatitudes (from *beatus*, the Latin for **'blessed'**) showed that his kingdom, the kingdom of God (or of heaven), is like nothing else on earth, and certainly not like anything the crowds were looking for. It is still true that the Beatitudes show up false modern ideas of what Christianity is and describe what true disciples of Christ are like.

Blessedness (5:3-12)

In the early twentieth century it was commonplace to regard the Sermon on the Mount as a blueprint for society: 'Follow this teaching and the world will be changed.' Often the Beatitudes were ignored; all the emphasis was on turning the other cheek and so on. However, some said, 'Behave in the way the Beatitudes teach and you will be truly happy.' So one professedly evangelical author has written about the 'Be-happy-attitudes'! Actually, in the Beatitudes Jesus does not give instructions about how to live. The Beatitudes simply describe the character and characteristics of those who are blessed already, who belong to God's kingdom. This is why it is important to remember that Jesus is teaching the disciples, not the crowds. He assumes that his hearers are born again and indwelt by the Spirit. The natural man cannot live as the Beatitudes describe.

   Jesus assumes that those who believe in him as Messiah and follow him as his disciples will suffer trials and persecution. They will stick out like a sore thumb in the world and suffer accordingly, so in order to help them to persevere he assures them of God's blessing. In verses 3-12 the words that follow **'for'** sum up the gospel of the kingdom. Those who repent and believe have these privileges or blessings and must learn that these outweigh the disadvantages and trials that accompany them.

We could translate the word for **'blessed'** as 'happy', as many do. However, the usual rendering preserves the actual meaning better. Jesus is not talking about a subjective feeling of happiness — a feel-good factor — but an objective fact. Those who are Christ's disciples are under God's blessing; they benefit from his gracious favour, with all its consequences. Some would paraphrase the word as 'to be envied or congratulated', which conveys the sense of privilege. However, 'blessed' is better because it points to what God will give to the believer. To be blessed by God is to receive good things from him, and this is the destiny of Christians. Whether we feel happy or not — indeed, even if we are desperately unhappy because of our circumstances — we must believe that we are blessed. God looks upon us with favour and will pour out his blessings on us. That there is an element of feeling involved even now can be seen from the fact that Jesus exhorts them to **'rejoice'** (5:12), but that is not the main point.

This is also how 'blessed' is used in the Old Testament. For example, in Psalm 1:1 the writer describes the true Israelite:

Blessed is the man
    who does not walk in the counsel of the wicked
or stand in the way of sinners
    or sit in the seat of mockers.

David writes:

Blessed is he
    whose transgressions are forgiven,
    whose sins are covered.
Blessed is the man
    whose sin the LORD does not count against him
    and in whose spirit is no deceit
                    (Ps. 32:1-2).

The prophet pronounces a curse on

> … the one who trusts in man,
>   who depends on flesh for his strength
>   and whose heart turns away from the LORD,

but declares 'blessed'

> ... the man who trusts in the LORD,
>   whose confidence is in him.
> He will be like a tree planted by the water,
>   that sends out its roots by the stream
>
> (Jer. 17:5,7-8).

We could trace this theme all the way back to Abraham, who is promised the blessing of God (Gen. 12:2), and beyond.

This fits with other uses in Matthew's Gospel — 11:6; 13:16; 16:17, which are all concerned with a proper attitude of faith in Jesus as the Messiah, and 24:46 (NKJV), which refers to the blessing that will be received at Christ's return. In other words, the blessed man is a true believer, a Christian, who will have to suffer for his Lord, but may know that God's favour and future blessing make it all worthwhile. The opposite of blessing is cursing, as Jeremiah 17:5 made clear and as Jesus also taught in the contrasting 'woes' recorded by Luke (6:24-26).[1]

The spiritually poor (5:3)

There has been a movement in recent years, linked with so-called Liberation Theology, suggesting that God has a 'Bias to the poor',[2] as if literal, material poverty somehow has claims on God and the rich are excluded from his blessing. Thus Isaiah 61:1, quoted by Jesus in his sermon in the synagogue at Nazareth, is taken to mean that the gospel *is* providing for the poor, as propounded even by some professedly evangelical aid organizations. (This must not be confused with the perfectly valid idea that such provision is a necessary outcome or accompaniment of the gospel.)

More positively, many maintain that the phrase **'the poor in spirit'** (5:3) refers to a humble attitude, a rejection of worldly pride and aggressive self-confidence and self-reliance. This may be true, but why should this be dubbed 'poor in spirit'? The solution to this, and a vital general principle for understanding all the Beatitudes, is to consider the Old Testament background, against which Jesus himself must always be seen. Jensen and Payne write, 'The key to unlock the treasures of these well-known verses is found by looking backwards, to what came before, to the Old Testament. For these are not a new set of values. Each of the eight "blessings" echoes the teaching of the Old Testament.'[3]

These authors follow up this general principle by referring us to Isaiah 61 and the context of the exile in Babylon. There, 'The poor were the exiled people of God, who had not compromised but still longed for God to rescue them from their poverty and shame ... who, out of their poverty, longed for God to save them and establish (or re-establish) his glorious kingdom.' Ridderbos describes the poor as 'those who remain faithful to God and expect their salvation from his kingdom alone'.[4] So, says Carson, 'To be poor in spirit is not to lack courage, but to acknowledge bankruptcy. It confesses one's unworthiness before God and *utter dependence on him*.'[5]

The truly blessed are those who see that they have no riches of their own and so trust in the riches provided by Christ in his kingdom: 'For you know the grace of our Lord Jesus Christ, that though he was rich, yet for your sakes he became poor, so that you through his poverty might become rich' (2 Cor. 8:9). The New Testament states this principle in many places. Instead of putting our 'hope in wealth, which is so uncertain' (1 Tim. 6:17), we are to count ourselves rich in Christ. 'The brother in humble circumstances ought to take pride in his high position. But the one who is rich should take pride in his low position, because he will pass away like a wild flower' (James 1:9-10). Or, as James adds, 'Has not God chosen those who are poor in the eyes of the world to be rich in faith and to inherit the kingdom he promised those who love him?' (James 2:5). Truly, **'Blessed are the poor in spirit, for theirs is the kingdom of heaven.'**

Mourning, meekness and righteousness (5:4-6)

Having dealt in some detail with poverty of spirit, we may treat the rest of the Beatitudes more briefly. Why should true believers be **'those who mourn'** at that time? (5:4). Did they express grief over their sin, as some explain it? This must, indeed, be included, but the Old Testament digs deeper. The faithful remnant, grieving at the prospect of exile, had been promised that they would **'be comforted'**. God would turn their mourning into gladness: 'I will give them comfort and joy instead of sorrow' (Jer. 31:13; note that verse 15 is the one quoted in Matthew 2:18 with reference to Christ's coming). Isaiah 40:1-5 promised comfort for those mourning in exile — sorrowing because of their humiliation on account of their sin, grieving because of their bondage and suffering under the hand of Babylon, or in our Lord's time, the hand of Rome. The only solution to this was the coming of God's kingdom, the restoration of his rule in practice and their deliverance from all their enemies. This was partly realized in the return from exile, but only with Christ's coming was their real deliverance accomplished, and with it real comfort and joy granted. This began to take effect with the forgiveness of sins through the death of Christ, as the kingdom was established in principle, but this verse looks forward, like the rest of the Beatitudes, to a consummation in glory, when God 'will wipe every tear from their eyes. There will be no more death or mourning or crying or pain, for the old order of things has passed away' (Rev. 21:4).

'The meek' (5:5), like the poor in spirit and the mourners, are those who remain faithful in affliction, looking for God's deliverance. Instead of reacting with anger and resentment towards their oppressors, they put their trust in the living God and wait for him to rescue them. In this third Beatitude Jesus undoubtedly had in mind Psalm 37:8-11:

> Refrain from anger and turn from wrath;
>> do not fret — it leads only to evil.
> For evil men will be cut off,
>> but those who hope in the LORD will inherit the land.
> A little while, and the wicked will be no more;
>> though you look for them, they will not be found.
> But the meek will inherit the land
>> and enjoy great peace.

The Old Testament inheritance of the land typified the inheritance of eternal life, which includes the new heavens and the new earth. The promise that the meek **'will inherit the earth'** could be translated as 'inherit the land', as the psalm says, showing the unity of thought. In Psalm 37:5-6 we see the positive aspect of meekness, which has nothing in common with weakness:

> Commit your way to the LORD;
>> trust in him and he will do this:
> He will make your righteousness shine like the dawn,
>> the justice of your cause like the noonday sun.

This leads on to the next Beatitude in verse 6.

Again, although we must include the individual's seeking after holiness and righteousness of life, that is not the main emphasis.

Psalm 37 has shown that Old Testament believers were concerned pre-eminently with **'righteousness'** in the sense of vindication and justice. God's righteousness, they were promised, would be manifested in rescuing them from their enemies and establishing his own kingdom of righteousness, thus vindicating them:

> In those days and at that time
>   I will make a righteous Branch sprout from David's line;
>   he will do what is just and right in the land.
> In those days Judah will be saved
>   and Jerusalem will live in safety.
> This is the name by which it will be called:
>   The LORD Our Righteousness
>
> (Jer. 33:15-16).

Then righteous living, right relationships and justice would be the norm. This is linked with the individual sense, which we must not ignore. However, this was not achieved until Christ came. Through his life and death he saved his people and established his kingdom. His people were justified and vindicated; their lives were transformed and righteous living begun, but they were hardly 'filled'. That must wait until his return, when his glorious, righteous kingdom will be established in fulness. 'Then the righteous will shine like the sun in the kingdom of their Father' (Matt. 13:43). 'We are looking forward to a new heaven and a new earth, the home of righteousness' (2 Peter 3:13). Until then they **'hunger and thirst for righteousness'**. We too shall go on hungering, as we see the world of unrighteousness around us, as we fight against the private depravity and public sin of our time. But we know we are blessed; we have the hope of a better and more glorious day, with the assurance that then we shall **'be filled'** and all our longings for righteousness will be satisfied.

Mercy, purity and peace (5:7-9)

These three characteristics are different from what has gone before; they do not describe a needy condition which will be rem-
edied, but a positively godly attitude which will be rewarded,
although, of course, to **'be shown mercy'** (5:7) does assume the
need for this. This mercy includes the forgiveness of sins now but
refers more especially to the last day. This is what Paul desired for
Epaphroditus: 'May the Lord grant that he will find mercy from
the Lord on that day!' (2 Tim. 1:18). Only **'the merciful'** will
receive mercy in that day, for '... judgement without mercy will
be shown to anyone who has not been merciful. Mercy triumphs
over judgement' (James 2:13). In this sense mercy is like forgiveness, as we shall see in Matthew 6:14-15; only the forgiving receive forgiveness; only the merciful receive mercy.

To call this a reward may lead to misunderstanding, but that is
the New Testament terminology, as we shall find in verse 12. Reward here is not an extra blessing given to those who have earned
or deserved it, but the inevitable outcome of what we are doing if
it is pleasing to God. C. S. Lewis explains most helpfully: 'The
proper rewards are not simply tacked on to the activity for which
they are given, but are the activity itself in consummation.'[6] If the
student works hard his efforts will be rewarded, not by the gift of
a lump sum, but by the success for which he had been striving:
passing the examination.

Similarly, **'the pure in heart'** (5:8), those who are both 'single-
minded in commitment to the kingdom' and also 'inwardly pure',[7]
do not earn the right to **'see God'**, but give evidence of the work
of God in them that 'prepares us for the sight of holiness above'.[8]
Thus Jesus moves away from the external terms of the Old Testament types — ascending the hill of the Lord, standing in his holy
place (Ps. 24:3) — to the real destiny of the spiritual man or woman.
The requirement to have 'clean hands and a pure heart' (Ps. 24:4)
remains, but now we see what was really meant by David's

confident assertion: 'In righteousness I shall see your face; when I awake, I shall be satisfied with your likeness' (Ps. 17:15). More will be said about this as Jesus continues his ministry.

The significance of being **'peacemakers'** (5:9) must be sought, not in the context of industrial disputes or United Nations resolutions, but of salvation and the church. Peace is primarily what God makes and gives. In the Old Testament, peace is characteristic of Messiah's kingdom. Solomon's reign foreshadowed this: safety from enemies and the blessings that follow in a land at peace. Isaiah prophesies the coming of the Prince of Peace (Isa. 9:6). In the New Testament fulfilment peace begins with the reconciliation of sinners to God, peace with God, leading to peace of conscience, heart and mind, and the peace of the united church. Peacemakers are those who have entered into God's peace in every aspect, though not yet in perfection, and show this by the way they live. Peace is not to be limited to the peace of heart and mind 'which transcends all understanding' (Phil. 4:7). The New Testament lays great stress on the peace of relationships, especially in the church, which is largely ignored by evangelicals today.

The peace which is part of the fruit of the Spirit (Gal. 5:22) is peaceableness, a desire to make peace, which would be especially relevant to the strife-torn Galatian churches. 'Let the peace of God rule in your hearts,' refers to the life of the church, not personal experience, 'since as members of one body you were called to peace' (Col. 3:15; see also Rom. 12:18; James 3:17-18). In this way peacemakers show their family likeness to their Father, the peacemaking God (see 5:44-45). Therefore they will be **'called sons of God'**. Sons of God are, of course, also heirs of the kingdom and will inherit the earth. Most of all perhaps, the peacemaker longs to share in the reconciling of sinners to God, by witnessing to the gospel of peace. Whether an official ambassador or an unofficial one, he shares in the desire and appeal of his Father by imploring sinners around him to be reconciled to God (2 Cor. 5:20).

Persecution (5:10-12)

Such a commitment to righteousness, God's and their own, and to the person and gospel of Christ (see Mark 8:35) will lead to their being **'persecuted because of righteousness'** (5:10), or **'because of me'** (5:11), like **'the prophets who were before'** them (5:12). Jesus was warning them of the consequences of being his disciples: **'People** [will] **insult you, persecute you and falsely say all kinds of evil against you because of me.'** This is still true. Those who believe in Christ and serve him in this world will have to endure slander and even physical persecution such as many of the prophets experienced. But we, like the disciples, must remember that we possess the kingdom of heaven and so, even now, rejoice and be glad. Peter reminds his readers of the possibility of grief and joy at the same time, because they focus on different matters: grief because of persecution; joy because of eternal life (1 Peter 1:6). Later on he also points out that the future joy will be greater and unmixed with sorrow: 'Rejoice that you participate in the sufferings of Christ, so that you may be overjoyed when his glory is revealed' (1 Peter 4:13).

The **'reward in heaven'** (5:12), as we have seen already, is not some extra element of blessing, but reaching what we have aimed at. The true believer wants Christ to be glorified. He believes and proclaims his word and longs for the day when 'every tongue [will] confess that Jesus Christ is Lord', whether willingly or unwillingly (Phil. 2:11). How great a reward it will be for him to see Christ in his glory 'on the day he comes to be glorified in his holy people and to be marvelled at among all those who have believed'! (2 Thess. 1:10).

As with many of the apparently poetic and beautiful passages of Scripture, such as 1 Corinthians 13 or Galatians 5:22-23, the reality is both harsher and greater. This passage is startlingly relevant to the future of the disciples. Jesus is not setting forth beautiful ideals, but spiritual realities. The characteristics of those who are truly blessed are radically different from those of the world around them. They are poor in spirit, instead of self-satisfied and self-sufficient. They mourn in meekness over the state of affairs, rather than engaging in triumphalism or selfish anger. They long for righteousness, mercy, purity and genuine peace, not profit, revenge, self-indulgence and success. They belong to Christ, proclaim his gospel and teach his word, rather than following the spirit of the age and the way of the world.

This is not a blueprint for us to put into practice, but a description of what is true already of the Christian. Nevertheless, it is necessary to realize that this is what we are, so that we may live consistently with it. This will mean rejection and suffering for the present, but we shall press on, because, as Christ assures the disciples, we shall benefit in the end. So, when trials and sufferings burden us most fiercely, we must remember the Beatitudes. Then we must say with the apostle Paul, 'Therefore, we do not lose heart. Though outwardly we are wasting away, yet inwardly we are being renewed day by day. For our light and momentary troubles are achieving for us an eternal glory that far outweighs them all. So we fix our eyes not on what is seen, but on what is unseen. For what is seen is temporary, but what is unseen is eternal' (2 Cor. 4:16-18).

Most of all, we must remember, when we are rejected and persecuted as aliens in an ungodly world, that this was how they treated our Saviour himself. And when he finally enters into his kingdom, we shall be there to share his glory. We are truly blessed.

6.
A surpassing righteousness

Please read Matthew 5:13-20

One of the most difficult problems faced by theologians and preachers is the relationship between law and grace. The usual battleground is the letters of the apostle Paul, but we must not ignore the teaching of our Lord himself. The section of the Sermon on the Mount to which we now turn deals with the issue in a very practical way. It speaks of good deeds and righteousness, of the law and its fulfilment, of abolishing or practising God's commandments. And all this is in the context of God's grace in blessing lost sinners with his mercy and making them his sons and daughters, as reflected in the Beatitudes.

Jesus has already assured his disciples of their blessed position in spite of their present circumstances. The world might scorn and despise them, but they can know that God smiles upon them. The world will persecute and slander disciples today too, but the Christian looks forward to a gracious and eternal reward. However, realizing the blessedness of belonging to the kingdom of heaven does not mean inactivity. We must not hide away; on the contrary, we have work to do. Although we do not belong to the world or share its attitudes and principles, we are still living in it with a job to do. Amazingly, this unbelieving and arrogant world needs the Christians it despises.

We must live in the world and before the world. We must practise righteousness. Jesus reminds his disciples of this in verses 13-16 and then moves on to deal with a possible objection or misunderstanding in verses 17-20. Grace, blessedness and joy do not mean that we can, or may, neglect God's law. Good deeds cannot justify us before God, but righteousness is still necessary if the blessings of the kingdom are to become ours in reality.

The salt of the earth (5:13)

Salt, in biblical times, was used to preserve food from corruption, from simply going bad and becoming rotten. It could also be used as a fertilizer — 'the manure heap' of Luke 14:34 — or as seasoning, to make food more tasty and palatable (Col. 4:6), but these do not appear to be the connection here. By their presence in the midst of an ungodly society Christ's disciples are to preserve it from further corruption. The persecuting, slandering world is so rotten that without the preservative effect of Christians it would go on deteriorating until the judgement of God became inevitable, as in the days before the Flood. So, said Jesus, **'You are the salt of the earth'** (5:13).

The history of the Bible and of the church is full of this effect of God's people. Even when they are few, they may have a disproportionate effect on society in restraining sin. When they are many, as in days of revival, they can so influence the world around that public morality, if not holiness, becomes the order of the day. We must not underestimate this effect. Not only are many sinners saved and their lives transformed, but the surrounding world is put to shame. Sin is no longer so easy and so popular and the decline of society is slowed, if not halted altogether.

For this to happen, two things are necessary. First, the salt has to be applied. Meat was soaked in a salt solution or rubbed with the salt. There had to be real, close contact for the salt to have any effect. In the same way the salt of the earth must be involved with the society around. Christians must take part in the culture and structures of their day. They must not opt out by withdrawing into some kind of Protestant monastery or nunnery, or by staying in an evangelical ghetto. Some Christians seem to think that this is the only way to avoid contamination. However, while we must be careful to avoid sinful compromise and not succumb to the pressures of the world, we cannot ignore our Lord's words without being false to the ideals of the kingdom.

In the Old Testament, Joseph, Esther and Daniel all acted as salt. They lived in an alien, secular culture and, far from being corrupted themselves, had an influence for good. Another, outstanding, example is Obadiah — not the prophet, but the high official of the kingdom of Israel in Elijah's day. As King Ahab's 'prime minister' he proved so valuable to his master that he was even able to use his position to protect the true prophets from Jezebel's hatred (1 Kings 18:3-6). In more recent times, in the late eighteenth century, we have the example of William Wilberforce who, after his conversion, wrote to a friend, 'Not that I would shut myself up from mankind and immune [immure?] myself in a cloister. My walk, I am sensible, is a public one; my business is in the world, and I must mix in the assemblies of men or quit the part which Providence seems to have assigned me.'[1] John Newton had expressed the opinion that 'It is hoped and believed that the Lord has raised you up for the good of the church and *for the good of the nation.*'[2] 'God,' wrote Wilberforce, 'has set before me two great objects, the suppression of the Slave Trade and the Reformation of Manners,'[3] by which he meant public and national life. Lord Shaftesbury is another such public figure, while many more may be found in Kathleen Heasman's *Evangelicals in Action*.[4]

This is by no means limited to the past. Since writing the above words I have attended a meeting organized to encourage Christians to be involved in education, by visiting schools, becoming governors, taking assemblies, and responding to government consultation documents.[5] Writing to one's local MP or a member of the House of Lords about moral issues is also a viable option for those who care. Involvement with others in social, political and sporting connections can enable us to have an effect on the society around us.

The salt of the covenant

It is usual to insist that salt can only preserve the world from further corruption; it cannot save it or its members. Although the term we use for preserving meat is 'curing', salt cannot 'cure' the ills of society in any way. That must be left to 'the light'. However, this hardly seems an adequate explanation of Christ's exhortation in view of his stress on the coming of the kingdom. He did not come merely to make the world a better, or not so bad, place. He came to save, to rescue men from the world so as to inherit the kingdom of heaven. Surely he had something much more positive in mind for the salt. The clue to this lies, like so much else, in our Lord's constant awareness of the Old Testament background.

Leviticus 2:13 says, 'Season all your grain offerings with salt. Do not leave the salt of the covenant of your God out of your grain offerings; add salt to all your offerings.' Similarly we read in Numbers 18:19 about the people's share of the offerings, 'It is an everlasting covenant of salt before the LORD for both you and your offspring.' Salt is thus linked with positive elements: covenant and sacrifice. The covenant God made with Noah and his descendants was to continue 'as long as the earth endures' (Gen. 8:22). The earth had to be preserved until the Messiah had come to redeem sinners. Later, in 2 Chronicles 13:5, we read that 'The LORD, the God of Israel, has given the kingship of Israel to David and his descendants for ever by a covenant of salt,' pointing forward to Christ's coming and ultimately to the meek inheriting the earth. Is this why the salt is linked with **'the earth'**, not just as a stylistic variation for 'the world'?

Jesus is concerned that society be preserved from worsening corruption so that time and opportunity are given for repentance through the preaching of the gospel. For this reason we must link the salt of the earth with the light of the world, not as a contrast, but as one giving opportunity for the other. Too many feel that time spent in the world is wasted, rather than seeing it as the way in which we can increase our opportunities to witness and provide a basis for making known the gospel. The danger is, of course, that in doing this we compromise and fall into sin. It has been wisely said, 'The church and the world are like water and a boat. It is right for the boat to be in the water. The trouble comes when the water gets into the boat.' For this reason our Lord gave his warning about saltiness.

Keeping our saltiness

As well as having to be applied, the salt must be kept pure. Otherwise **'the salt loses its saltiness'**. Scientists tell us that salt cannot do this, but in biblical times salt was not the pure sodium chloride that we know and it did deteriorate because of the impurities. Jesus warns that such salt **'is no longer good for anything, except to be thrown out and trampled by men'**. We must take care that this does not happen to us. The context indicates that we cease to be salty when we lose our distinctiveness as outlined in the Beatitudes. If we do not live consistently like that then we have little influence or effect on society around us and even, perhaps, show that we are not real disciples at all. So, while we do not 'obey the Beatitudes' to become Christians, we must take care to live consistently with them.

One element that seems to be particularly important is peacemaking. In Mark 9:50 Jesus links salt and peace: 'Have salt in yourselves, and be at peace with each other.' Nothing so ruins the church's effect in the world as its constant quarrels and disputes. Again, in Luke 14, where Jesus repeats his warning about losing saltiness, the preceding parable concludes: 'In the same way, any of you who does not give up everything he has cannot be my disciple.' The salty disciple will be distinctive in his lifestyle and so demonstrate his allegiance and his convictions. Otherwise society will influence him instead! Such distinctiveness will produce the persecution of which the last Beatitude speaks, but the reward is also there.

The light of the world (5:14-16)

It is remarkable that he who is *the* Light of the world (John 8:12) should say to his feeble disciples, **'You are the light of the world'** (5:14). There is, of course, no contradiction, just a necessary awareness that the light which the disciples give is a reflection of the Saviour's light, not some independent brightness. He shines through us.

The idea of light for the world goes back to the seven-branched lampstand in the tabernacle (Exod. 25:31-40) and the succeeding ten golden lampstands of Solomon's temple (2 Chr. 4:7). These picture God's light in Israel, shining out into the rest of the world. This is taken up in Zechariah 4:2-14, which in turn points to the seven lampstands that are the seven churches of Asia in Revelation 1-3. The light is God's; the lampstands enable it to shine out.

The obvious symbolism of light is holiness and truth, in opposition to every kind of darkness (1 John 1:5-7). However, the stress here is not on the intrinsic nature of the light, though that is presupposed in the goodness of the **'good deeds'** (5:16), but on its shining forth to enlighten others. God's light is received in Christ and then sent out into the darkness to bring light and salvation. Thus David rejoices, 'The LORD is my light and my salvation' (Ps. 27:1), while the prophesied Servant of the Lord is described as 'a light for the Gentiles' (Isa. 49:6). It is noteworthy, in connection with the present verses, that in Acts 13:47 Paul can apply the prophecy of Isaiah 49:6 to his own ministry of the gospel: 'I have made you [singular] a light for the Gentiles, that you may bring salvation to the ends of the earth.'

The light of which Jesus speaks is, therefore, a light that brings salvation, not just preservation from corruption, although, as we have seen, the two are connected. We might expect him to be speaking of evangelism, the preaching of the gospel of light, but in fact he refers to their 'good deeds', their lives lived **'before men'** (5:16). In the same way, in Philippians 2:14-15 Paul explains shining 'like stars in the universe' as doing 'everything without complaining or arguing, so that you may become blameless and pure, children of God without fault in a crooked and depraved generation'. This is not to exclude witness from the picture, even if we should, with many, read verse 16 as 'holding fast the word of life', rather than 'holding out'. However, Jesus' main point here is clearly the life that the disciples live. Often in the New Testament 'good deeds' or 'works' mean acts of loving care for the poor and needy. This aspect must not be ignored here, but the main content for these good deeds is seen in the preceding verses: meekness and holiness, concern for the kingdom of heaven, creating peaceful relationships, as well as being merciful to the needy.

Because of this we must at least include conversion in men's **'praise'** or glorifying of **'your Father in heaven'** — willing praise of the God whose light they have seen. Peter makes the same point: 'Live such good lives among the pagans that, though they accuse you of doing wrong, they may see your good deeds and glorify God in the day he visits us' (1 Peter 2:12), literally 'the day of visitation'. God's 'visitation' may refer to his coming in judgement, but more often, as here, it is a visit by which he 'has redeemed his people' (cf. Luke 1:68). Indeed, Zechariah, John the Baptist's father, describes Christ's coming as:

> ... the tender mercy of our God,
>   by which the rising sun will come to us from heaven
> to shine on those living in darkness
>   and in the shadow of death,
> to guide our feet into the path of peace
>
>   (Luke 1:78).

Also, when Jesus raised the dead son of the widow of Nain, the crowd exclaimed that 'God hath visited his people' (Luke 7:16, AV).[6]

Shining before men

As with the salt, the beneficial effect of Christian living does not come automatically. The salt must keep its saltiness; the light must shine. Just as **'a city on a hill cannot be hidden'** and a **'a lamp'** is not **'put ... under a bowl'**, but displayed **'on its stand'**, so that **'it gives light to everyone in the house'**, so the disciples must ensure that men see their light. Some have felt that this sounds too much like showing off to men, 'living to be seen of them', which Jesus condemns in the following chapter, but this is clearly not his intention here. In the first place, the deeds will not be truly good unless they are done to please God, rather than men; and secondly, since they embody the righteousness described in the Beatitudes, they will often incur the wrath of men and provoke persecution.

It is common for Christians to 'admit' that they are no better than anyone else. In the sense that we are not justified or accepted by God because we are better than others, this is true. In the more obvious sense, however, it must not be true. We have God's light and salvation; we have been born again and are indwelt by the Holy Spirit; God's 'divine power has given us everything we need for life and godliness' (2 Peter 1:3). We must not make excuses for our sin. It should be obvious to all that we are better than others, even though they may not recognize this because they have a different set of values. Otherwise our light will not shine out; we shall be as dark as our surroundings, and that will bring no praise to our heavenly Father.

Our good deeds will include compassion for sinners and witness to the gospel, but this must be on the basis of a righteous life, full of good deeds. Paul instructs slaves 'to be subject to their masters in everything, to try to please them, not to talk back to them, and not to steal from them, but to show that they can be fully trusted, so that in every way they will make the teaching about God our Saviour attractive' (Titus 2:9-10). The attractiveness of the gospel of grace is not always obvious to sinful men, but the attractiveness of honest service will speak volumes to them. Peter exhorts believing wives, whose husbands reject the spoken word, to win them over by their 'behaviour', 'the purity and reverence' of their lives, 'the unfading beauty of a gentle and quiet spirit' (1 Peter 3:1-2,4).

The eighteenth-century evangelical preacher William Romaine was encountering much opposition to his appointment as rector of Blackfriars in London. To his amazement he found that one of his most active supporters was a publican in the parish. When Romaine went to thank him for this, the man replied, 'Indeed, sir, I am more indebted to you than you to me; for you made my wife, who was one of the worst, the best woman in the world.'[7] Who can argue against that? The modern Christian is tempted to think that an abrasive, forceful approach, as recommended by the advisers of the business world, is the best kind of witness. That, however, is the way of the world. Jesus makes clear that the Beatitudes describe the most effective kind of kingdom evangelism, the way that leads men to glorify our Father in heaven.

Jesus and the law (5:17-19)

The words in verses 17-20 obviously function as an introduction to our Lord's exposition of the law in the rest of the chapter. However, his words, **'Do not think that I have come to abolish the Law,'** look back as well. They may imply that some of his hearers were drawing this wrong conclusion. It would be quite natural, though totally incorrect, to assume that, since he had come to introduce God's kingdom, he was making a completely new start. Perhaps he was abolishing all previous teaching? Perhaps 'the Law' and 'the Prophets', which together probably refer to the whole of the Old Testament, were no longer relevant. Many since then have made this same wrong assumption, creating a wide rift between the Old and New Testaments, denying the continuity of the two dispensations.

On the contrary, says Jesus, his relationship to the Law and the Prophets is not one of contradiction but of continuity, not

of rejection but of fulfilment: **'I have not come not to abolish them but to fulfil them'** (5:17). He also points, in verse
18, to a time when **'everything is accomplished'**, or will actually have happened. The nature and meaning of this fulfilment are much debated, especially with respect to the continuing application of the moral law (the Ten Commandments)
as the rule of life for the believer. Some deny this; others say
that 'fulfil' means confirm or establish. They use the time-
honoured and useful, if rather over-simplified, division of the
law into moral, ceremonial and civil, and say that after Christ's
coming only the moral law continues. True though I believe
this to be, it is not really what our Lord is talking about here.

Nor is Jesus speaking of his acting in obedience to the law.
Rather he is making the point that the whole of the Old Testament directs attention to himself and his coming. Whether it
be direct Messianic prophecies, general promises of the approaching glories of God's kingdom, 'all the types and shadows of the ceremonial law',[8] even the history of God's covenant people, all speak of him (see Luke 24:27). Matthew has
already used this same word, 'fulfilled' (usually in the passive)
to show how Christ's coming has brought all these things into
actual existence (1:22; 2:15,17,23; 4:14). He is clearly referring to the whole of the Old Testament, when he says, **'I tell
you the truth ... not the smallest letter** [the Hebrew letter
yod], **not the least stroke of a pen** [probably the small "serif"
or projection that distinguishes between pairs of Hebrew let-
ters], **will by any means disappear from the Law until
everything is accomplished'** (5:18). Clearly, the whole Old
Testament will continue to witness to him **'until heaven and
earth disappear'**.

For this reason, he adds, those who practise or teach contrary to this will be **'called least in the kingdom of heaven'**
(5:19). This does not mean 'that every regulation in the Old
Testament law remains binding after the coming of Jesus. The

law is unalterable, but that does not justify its application beyond the purpose for which it was intended.'⁹ However, the
fact that Jesus refers particularly here to 'commands' indicates that his main intention is to avoid any suggestion that
God's law may be safely ignored. This is linked, as the 'for' in
verse 20 shows, with the 'righteousness' necessary to 'enter
the kingdom of heaven'. Far from abolishing the law, he has
come to fulfil it, and to ensure both that it is properly interpreted and that it can be kept by his disciples (Rom. 8:3-4).

Righteousness (5:20)

As 'Sin is any want of conformity unto, or transgression of,
the law of God,'¹⁰ so righteousness consists of conformity to
that law. Christ's followers must have a righteousness that **'surpasses that of the Pharisees and the teachers of the law'** if
they are to **'enter the kingdom of heaven'** (5:20). For this,
the depth and authority of the law must be recognized. We
must resist the temptation, to which many succumb, to interpret this righteousness as that of Christ, imputed to us through
faith. Justification, acceptance with God, of course depends
on his perfect righteousness. That is, or should be, beyond
dispute. However, that is not the topic here. This righteousness is that practical obedience to God's Word which is the
evidence of faith, that covenant faithfulness which identifies
the true child of God. We cannot earn salvation, any more
than the Pharisees could, but that does not mean we can dis-
miss the necessity of which Christ speaks here.
    Verse 20 says in as many words that the Pharisees would
not enter the kingdom, at least not unless they repented and
believed in Christ. In the later verses of this chapter Jesus will
demonstrate what was wrong with their understanding of righteousness, even apart from their failure to live up to it. For

now, we must be very clear that Jesus demands from his disciples a life of righteous obedience, keeping God's law. Mere profession of faith is not good enough. At the end of his sermon Jesus will solemnly assert, 'Not everyone who says to me, "Lord, Lord", will enter the kingdom of heaven, but only he who does the will of my Father who is in heaven' (7:21). The proper parallel to verse 20 is not Romans 3:20 ('No one will be declared righteous in his sight by observing the law'), but Hebrews 12:14: 'Make every effort to ... be holy; without holiness no one will see the Lord.'

It is vital that we take our Lord's words seriously. There are many places in the New Testament where actual righteousness is insisted on. It does no honour to the gospel of grace and imputed righteousness to ignore these passages. We are told very plainly that if we live unrighteous lives, we shall be lost, as were the Pharisees. It is Paul, the apostle of grace, the one who wrote, 'For it is by grace you have been saved, through faith' (Eph. 2:8), who also said, 'No immoral, impure or greedy person — such a man is an idolater — has any inheritance in the kingdom of Christ and of God. Let no one deceive you with empty words, for because of such things God's wrath comes on those who are disobedient. Therefore do not be partners with them' (Eph. 5:5-7).

If we ask for more details about this righteousness, Christ would refer us back to the Beatitudes, to the gracious characteristics of the blessed man. He would remind us that we must show this to the world, as we live as salt and light and do good deeds. The Pharisees were greatly respected by the common people. Our righteousness must surpass theirs. We must outstrip their equivalent today — the legalists, of whatever kind, who are so often given respect by the media and the religious world. These words challenge us to re-examine our lives. It is too easy simply to assume that we qualify for heaven, without actually checking. Is your life truly more righteous than that

of the man who is relying on his own goodness to gain heaven?
Is your righteousness superior to that of the woman who relies on her charitable giving to please God? We must not depend on our righteousness, but if it does not surpass that of
the Pharisees, we are living in a fool's paradise and will fail to
gain the real one.

7.
Christ and tradition

Please read Matthew 5:21-32

For years liberal scholars have maintained that Jesus was contradicting the Old Testament. Reams have been written and
whole sermons preached about the allegedly 'primitive' Old
Testament morality of revenge: 'an eye for an eye', etc. What
they have been unable to explain is how the Christ who spoke
verses 17-20 about the permanence of the Law and the Prophets could ever have rejected the Old Testament Scriptures.
Here Jesus contrasts what **'was said to the people long ago'**
with **'I tell you'**. In fact, Jesus is disagreeing, not with the
law, but with the teaching of the rabbis, the traditional interpretations of the elders. So he does not say, 'It is written', but
it was **'said'**. In addition, although much of what he disagrees
with actually uses the same words as the Old Testament, nowhere do the Scriptures command the Israelite to 'hate' his
enemies.

Jesus does set 'clear blue water' between his teaching and
that of the Pharisees. The seriousness of this is confirmed by
his references to **'the fire of hell'** (5:22) and to being **'thrown
into hell'** (5:29). Faith in the Messiah involves repentance
and the fruits of repentance. Without these there is no salvation, without a surpassing righteousness no entry into the
kingdom of heaven. So he does not set himself against the
teachers of the law as a new and better rabbi, but as the Prophet

and King, the one who has come to fulfil the Law and the Prophets, the Saviour of sinners. We must take his commands seriously. It is true that no one becomes a Christian by following Christ's teaching in the Sermon on the Mount, but only by faith. It is also the case that too many Christians are very limited in their understanding and lax in their practice of those teachings. If we take seriously what Jesus said in verse 20 about our need for a surpassing righteousness, we must pay attention to the following verses. In these he sets before us five illustrations of how that righteousness is worked out.

Murder and anger (5:21-22)

The elders were quite right to say, **'Do not murder'** (5:21), as the sixth commandment teaches. The trouble was that their interpretation of murder was limited and superficial, and their explanation of judgement purely temporal. Thus Jesus condemns not only literal, physical murder, but **'anyone who is angry with his brother'**, or **'who says to his brother, "Raca"'**[1] or **'"You fool!"'** (5:22). 'Brother' here must refer to a fellow-Israelite or fellow-disciple. Jesus is concerned with kingdom relationships, not with giving a blueprint for the reformation of society. Where the rabbis refer, presumably, to the **'judgement'** of the local court (5:21), his reference will be to the judgement of God (5:22). Instead of having to answer to **'the Sanhedrin'**, they are in danger of **'the fire of hell'**, the reality pictured by the constantly burning fires of the Jerusalem rubbish-dump in the Valley of Hinnom — Gehenna.

What is Jesus actually forbidding? Here we must avoid two extremes. We must not take it so absolutely that we ignore the godly anger of Jesus himself, or condemn his use of 'You … fools' in 23:17. There is a place for righteous indignation (Eph. 4:26-27)[2] and for warning about folly, the context in Matthew

23. Jesus is forbidding both the attitude and the words that lie behind, and can easily lead to, literal murder. James points out that 'The tongue also is a fire, a world of evil among the parts of the body. It corrupts the whole person, sets the whole course of his life on fire, and is itself set on fire by hell' (James 3:6). He is not referring to the effect of gossip in causing trouble in the church, although that is very serious, but to the way that if we do not bridle our tongues, we may soon find our fists or feet also out of control. Saying 'Raca' or 'fool' can easily end in killing the body. Contrary to the old saying, 'Sticks and stones may break my bones but words can never hurt me', the words are often merely a prelude to the sticks; verbal abuse leads to physical harm.

Christians must examine their hearts for hatred, contempt and abuse; they must restrain their angry words. If not, they contravene the sixth commandment and commit murder in their hearts or with their lips. When we are in the midst of theological controversy, personal disagreements about family decisions, or earnest debate in the church meeting, we must remember and deal with this.

Reconciliation (5:23-26)

Jesus is not content simply to explore and expand the application of the commandment. He goes on to give an example of how this must work out in practice, in terms of reconciliation. The best way to avoid sin is to act positively in obedience to our Lord's command. 'Love does no harm to its neighbour' (Rom. 13:10). So, far from harming him, we must show our love by seeking to establish a loving and peaceful relationship through reconciliation.

It is not enough to refrain from an angry reaction to an offence against us; we must also take the initiative if we have

offended someone else. Jesus exhorts his disciples, **'Therefore, if you are offering your gift at the altar and there
remember that your brother has something against you,
leave your gift there in front of the altar. First go and be
reconciled to your brother; then come and offer your gift'**
(5:23-24). Mere cold (armed?) neutrality is not good enough
for the disciples of Christ. Jesus is not concerned, as we so
often are, whether we are in the right or not. We must make
peace. Here, the offender must take the initiative, but in Matthew 18:15 Jesus commands the offended brother to take the
first step towards making peace by rebuking the offender, in
order to win his brother. Ideally, the offender and the offended
one should 'meet in the doorway', going to find their brother
in order to be reconciled.[3] There is no way to avoid our responsibility; reconciliation is Christ's command. Is this true in
your experience and in your church? If not, you are breaking
the sixth commandment and, in essence, committing murder.

Verses 25-26 are, in effect, a parable illustrating the seriousness and urgency with which we must seek reconciliation.
Jesus is not merely urging prudence with regard to the judicial
system. He is saying that we must be reconciled to our brother,
'your adversary', without delay, before **'the judge'** is involved. We are taken back to the danger of 'the fire of hell'.
The professing Christian who does not care about reconciliation with his brother lives in danger of the judgement. Real
repentance and faith lead to righteousness, including not mur-
dering, which includes being reconciled. We are still **'on the
way'** and have time to repent. The same kind of warning is to
be found in chapter 18 in terms of forgiving our brother. We
must not take this lightly. It is misguided, and dangerous, to
argue here in terms of justification by faith. Jesus is telling us
that justifying faith produces this kind of righteousness, that
genuine 'brothers' seek to be reconciled. The peacemakers,
who are blessed, make peace with all their brothers a prime
goal.

Adultery (5:27-30)

Our Lord begins from the seventh commandment, **'Do not commit adultery'**, as interpreted by the fathers (5:27), but goes much further. He says that his disciples must not restrict adultery to unlawful, i.e. extra-marital, sexual intercourse. We must not fall into the trap of thinking that he minimizes the physical act, as many would do today. Rather, he assumes that and then extends it to include the look and the inner attitude: **'Anyone who looks at a woman lustfully has already committed adultery with her in his heart'** (5:28). In the light of history we must note that Jesus speaks of the man's responsibility here, not to exclude women, but because so often men have thought that they were exempt. Far from accepting this, Jesus lays great stress on the man's desire and the man's heart.

The remedy for this sin is to take radical steps to achieve or maintain purity (5:29-30). The extreme language has caused difficulties for some who take it literally: **'If your right eye causes you to sin, gouge it out and throw it away.'** The right eye was generally regarded as the better one, just as the **'right hand'** is the stronger one for the majority of people. To gouge it out is a graphic equivalent of Paul's exhortation to 'put to death the misdeeds of the body' (Rom. 8:13), or to 'mortify [kill] therefore your members which are upon the earth' (Col. 3:5, AV). Either way the idea is to refrain from using those faculties or abilities for sin. This demands radical steps, such as ensuring that you cannot misuse your eyes, the source of temptation to sinful sexual thoughts, even though this may also mean depriving yourself of their legitimate use, i.e. **'throw it away'**.[4]

For instance, if you cannot watch television without being led to impure thoughts, then switch it off or get rid of it altogether, even though this means that you will not be able to watch the sport or nature programmes either. This is implicit in the contrast between losing **'one part of your body'** and the **'whole body'** being **'thrown into hell'**. Dr Martyn Lloyd-Jones sums the matter up in these words: 'He is saying that, however valuable a thing may be to you in and of itself, if it is going to trap you and cause you to stumble, get rid of it, throw it away. Such is His way of emphasizing the importance of holiness, and the terrible danger which confronts us as the result of sin.'[5]

Once again, we must take Christ's warning seriously. If we do not do this we shall **'go into hell'**. This is just another way of saying, 'Blessed are the pure in heart, for they will see God.' The impure in heart will not see God, but enter into hell. The great second-century theologian Origen took these verses literally and castrated himself. In fact, that is clearly not the meaning, for to do that still leaves the heart vulnerable. Instead of that we must follow Paul's exhortation: 'Make not provision for the flesh, to fulfil the lusts thereof' (AV), or as the NIV translates it, 'Do not think about how to gratify the desires of the sinful nature' (Rom. 13:14). This is another aspect of that righteousness which is essential for entry into the kingdom of heaven (5: 20).

Divorce (5:31-32)

Most expositors make this another distinct section, ignoring the different transition from the previous verses.[6] This not only leads to difficulties in interpretation, but also loses the important intended link with the topic of adultery. Jesus is saying that one aspect of this essential purity is faithfulness to the marriage bond. Illegitimate divorce — i.e. putting away on grounds other than **'marital unfaithfulness'** (5:32) — is a breach of the seventh commandment, as infallibly interpreted by the Saviour; morally it is equivalent to adultery. He does not discuss the teaching of Deuteronomy 24:1 that **'Anyone who divorces his wife must give her a certificate of divorce'**, which was taken by many Jews to permit divorce on very slight grounds. Instead he gives his own verdict that to divorce illegitimately — that is apart from sexual immorality — causes both parties in the new marriage to commit adultery. Given the non-literal usage of 'adultery' in verse 28, it is unlikely that Jesus means us to take this literally either. That would contradict the rest of the biblical teaching, which assumes that the innocent — i.e. wrongly divorced — party is free to remarry. It is noteworthy that the way Jesus phrases his warning, using the passive form of the verb, places all the responsibility and stigma on the guilty divorcer. Literally, the wife is 'made to commit adultery' and the future husband is 'caused to commit adultery'. '"Both have had something committed upon them." The guilt attaches to the one who broke the marriage.'[7]

Other aspects of these verses will be discussed when we come to chapter 19, which deals with the issue more fully. However, the detailed controversies and disagreements which abound here must not be allowed to obscure the fact that Jesus treats wrongful divorce as a breach of the seventh commandment, moral adultery, not just a technicality. In the light of this, we may say that gouging out the eye and cutting off the hand also apply here. In order to please God and to be pure in heart, we may have to tolerate difficulties in our marriage or continue unmarried, rather than dishonour God's holy ordinance. If we feel that we are missing out by so doing, then our Lord assures us that it is better than going into hell (5:30) or, more positively, that this is the way to enter into eternal life and see God (5:8).

Oaths (5:33-37)

The subject of taking an oath is one that has caused much controversy and divided Christians. Today, swearing has quite a general connotation: using obscene or blasphemous language, as well as the technical taking of an oath in a court of law. This last meaning is the subject here, although the passage has some relevance to the other aspect as well. Oath-taking was very common among the Jews, and the Pharisees had much to say on the matter. The basic idea of an oath, as seen in the words from which Jesus begins, is that of calling God to witness to the truth of what we say, especially of what we promise. This is on the understanding that he will know and punish if we do not tell the truth or keep our promise. Indeed, to swear by God, or a god, showed your covenant allegiance (Gen. 31:53; Deut. 10:20; Jer. 12:16).

Once again Christ begins from a saying which sounds as if it could have been Old Testament Scripture, but was in fact a rabbinical summary of verses like Numbers 30:2 and Deuter-onomy 23:21: **'Do not break your oath, but keep the oaths you have made to the Lord'** (5:33). So far there is no prob-lem, but then he not only takes issue with the methods that the Pharisees and others used to get round this clear demand for truth, but also rejects all swearing of oaths: **'I tell you, Do not swear at all'** (5:34). We must deal with the two matters separately.

The Pharisees' intention was to enable people to avoid keep-ing their promises or, indeed, being held to the truth of what they had said. They did this by subtly keeping God out of the picture. They substituted other words for the name of God. Jesus exposes the folly of this casuistry from two angles. First, he demonstrates that it is impossible to avoid the living God. **'Heaven ... is God's throne'**; **'the earth ... is his footstool'**; **'Jerusalem ... is the city of the Great King'**, i.e. God (5:34,35). The other option was to swear by their **'head'** (5:36) — a totally inadequate guarantee of truth. They, unlike God, **'cannot make even one hair white or black'**, so how can they assess, let alone punish, untruth or broken vows?

Is it, then, sinful to swear an oath when a law court requires it? Is Jesus actually abrogating this Old Testament requirement? Jehovah's Witnesses and others take the prohibition, 'Do not swear at all,' both literally and absolutely. At first sight this seems very reasonable, but the context, near and wider, is against it. In Scripture we find God condescending to swear, by himself (Heb. 6:17), not because he is untrustworthy, but because weak men need reassurance. Paul, too, when being doubted, calls God to witness (Rom. 1:9; 2 Cor. 1:23), while our Lord himself, until then keeping silent, answered when the high priest said, 'I charge you under oath by the living God' (Matt. 26:63,64).

Christ's instructions, **'Simply let your "Yes" be "Yes", and your "No", "No"; anything beyond this comes from the evil one'** (5:37), seem to indicate that in ordinary conversation we should be, and be known to be, so truthful that no oath is necessary. Only when there is some reason for doubt, such as an appearance in court or the hearer's ignorance, is an oath justified. The devil, no doubt, delights in our lies, pretence, ambiguities, broken promises, exaggerations and deceptions. He also promotes distrust by our needless resorting to oaths. Shakespeare's *Hamlet* includes a play within a play, in which the actress-queen swears she will never remarry:

> Both here and hence pursue me lasting strife,
> If, once a widow, ever I be wife.[8]

It is Hamlet's mother who comments, 'The lady doth protest too much, methinks.' So it is with superfluous oaths. The very swearing casts doubt on our veracity and breeds suspicion, distrust and disunity.

The best way to deal with questions of truth is to be positively honest and 'up-front' with our Christian brothers. The devil loves disunity and hates truth. We should be the reverse, as our Lord desires. Love 'rejoices with the truth ... always trusts, always hopes' (1 Cor. 13:6-7). The Christian is commanded to 'put off falsehood and speak truthfully to his neighbour, for we are all members of one body' (Eph. 4:25). Indeed, the unity and maturity of that body is said by Paul to come from 'speaking the truth [probably of the gospel] in love' (Eph. 4:15). To 'falsely say all kinds of evil against' someone is the mark of the persecutor, not of the Christian. If we are persecuted for telling the truth, about and because of Christ, so be it. The Lord pronounces us 'blessed' (Matt. 5:11).

Revenge (5:38-42)

Christ's exhortation to turn the other cheek is, perhaps, the most misunderstood aspect of his teaching in the Sermon on the Mount. The words to which the greatest exception is taken today, **'Eye for eye, and tooth for tooth'** (5:38), are certainly to be found in the Old Testament (Exod. 21:24; Lev. 24:20; Deut. 19:21). What Jesus is denying is the misuse of these words to justify personal retaliation and revenge. Modern writers quite rightly argue that revenge is unchristian, but wrongly deduce that the Old Testament encourages it. In fact, when Paul wants to support his command, 'Do not take revenge, my friends' (Rom. 12:19), it is to the Old Testament book of Proverbs (Prov. 25:21-22) that he turns for support. Far from permitting personal revenge, the Old Testament instructions about eyes and teeth are given to the judges. They were probably not intended to be taken in a crudely literal sense, but put simply mean, years before Gilbert and Sullivan, 'Let the punishment fit the crime.'[9] The punishment must be appropriate and measured, not excessive, as human judgement may easily become. The purpose, therefore, was to limit punishment, not increase it.

However, Jesus is not content merely to oppose personal revenge, in order to 'leave room for God's wrath', any more than the apostle Paul was when he urged his readers, 'Do not be overcome by evil, but overcome evil with good' (Rom. 12:19,21). As in the rest of these sections, Jesus is very concerned that we should live a positively righteous and godly life. A summary of verses 38-42 might be: 'Do not be content with merely foregoing revenge. Be positively loving and unselfish in spite of the cost.'

It may be necessary to remind ourselves that the context here is the kingdom of God. We are in the realm of personal relationships, not legislative theory or international politics. **'Do not resist an evil person'** (5:39) does not mean that we should condone felonies or appease dictators. It also wrong to take these words to mean that 'good men' should allow evil to prosper by doing nothing. Wilberforce was not disobeying Christ when he fought to abolish the slave trade. These words are qualified by the following ones: **'If someone slaps you on the right cheek, turn to him the other also.'** A slap on the right cheek, i.e. with the back of the hand, is an insult, a show of personal contempt, or even religious persecution, not a mugger's physical assault. In this instance, we must not retaliate. It is right to note that Jesus protested against the illegality of being struck (John 18:22-23) and that Paul demanded an apology for his false imprisonment and beating at Philippi (Acts 16:37). However, it is wrong to use this valid insistence on the rule of law to remove the force of Christ's words in the usual circumstances of personal relationships.

Jesus further illustrates his point of not demanding our rights by the case of someone being sued. We must go further than not resisting; we must voluntarily give what we are not obliged to give: not only **'your tunic, let him have your cloak as well'** (5:40).[10] Not only must we not react angrily when forced into service, as a Jew could be compelled by a Roman soldier to carry his luggage for **'one mile'**. We must carry it **'two miles'** (5:41). It is interesting that even secular writers can use 'going the extra mile' for doing good beyond the call of duty. The next requirement, **'Give to the one who asks you, and do not turn away from the one who wants to borrow from you'** (5:42), has raised problems for some. It is true, as Morris points out, that, 'If Christians took this [command] absolutely literally there would soon be a class of saintly paupers, owning nothing, and another of prosperous idlers and thieves.'[11] Jesus is not asking for that, but for a readiness to give generously, not to the professional beggar, but to the genuinely needy, even when it is risky. It is necessary to make these qualifications to Christ's seemingly absolute rules. However, the danger is that by so doing we emasculate them and blunt the sharp point of his radical teaching. He calls for real self-denial, for a willingness to put others' interests before our own.

Love your enemies (5:43-48)

This may be the most striking of a set of remarkable exhortations. The words, **'Hate your enemy'** (5:43), are not to be found in the Old Testament. Indeed, we should note the amazing requirements of Exodus 23:4-5 and Deuteronomy 22:1-4. However, the Essenes, the members of the Dead Sea Community at Qumran, explicitly required hatred for the outsider.[12] Many other Jews of Christ's day would have found his command, **'Love your enemies'**, totally unacceptable, as would many of our own contemporaries. The question is, 'Do we?' 'Love', of course, is not the same as 'like'. Christ's disciples may find their enemies highly objectionable and be unable to do anything about it. They must nevertheless seek their good and do them good, not harm, in every way. One kind, though not the only kind, of enemy is the persecutor, who is very much in Christ's mind in this chapter. **'Pray for those who persecute you'**, he tells them and us (5:44). In purely pastoral terms, when we find it difficult to desire that our enemies prosper, praying for them may be the key.

We must not be content with the world's standards. **'If you love those who love you, what reward will you get? Are not even the tax collectors doing that? And if you greet only your brothers, what are you doing more than others? Do not even pagans do that?'** (5:46-47). On the contrary, we must be like our **'Father in heaven'** (5:45). Christians are to be different, truly revolutionary! To love our enemies is to be like God: **'He causes his sun to rise on the evil and the good, and sends rain on the righteous and the unrighteous.'** There is a grace and love of God which is common to all men. We show that we are 'sons' of God when we love our enemies and do good to them, as he does.[13] Instead of sneering at 'do-gooders', we should try to outdo them in love and kindness to all men, even those who count themselves our enemies.

Verse 48, **'Be perfect, therefore, as your heavenly Father is perfect,'** is not just setting before us the aim of sinless perfection, unattainable in this life. It may include that, but it is more likely that Jesus is using 'perfect' in the sense of 'all-round' and consistent'. In connection with the immediately preceding verses, this means that his disciples must love not only one another, but also their enemies. The wider context means that, unlike the Pharisees, they must not be selective, picking and choosing which commands they will keep. Nor must they be like the worldlings, doing enough to get by, or the tax-collectors, just concerned for their 'mates'. They and we must be like the heavenly Father, loving all men, with an all-round holiness of heart, word and action. Thus we shall achieve a righteousness far exceeding that of the Pharisees and the teachers of the law.

✗ The verse is also a motivation. We must live as those who have been chosen and redeemed and called to be children of God. We must live as those who are to inherit the kingdom of heaven and see God. If we only realize what God has planned for us and given to us even now, and what lies before us in the heavenly kingdom, we shall live and love differently, radically differently, and so let our light shine before men, to the praise of God, our heavenly Father. ✗

8.
Giving and praying

Please read Matthew 6:1-10

There has been much debate in some circles as to whether it is permissible for a Christian to be an actor. The word we have here translated as **'hypocrites'** (6:2,5,16) was originally used by the Greeks for actors on the stage, from which it is an easy transition to the idea of playing a part in ordinary life. Whatever we think about the stage as a career, it is clear that Christians should not be actors in this latter sense. We cannot be sure whether the hypocrites to whom Jesus was referring were deliberately wicked or simply self-deceived; perhaps both are included. What is clear, especially in the light of chapter 23, is that he is referring once more to the scribes and Pharisees.

In verse 1 Jesus urges his disciples not **'to do your "acts of righteousness" before men'**. Literally this is simply 'do your righteousness'. Therefore, what we have in this section is a further exposition of that righteousness, surpassing that of the Pharisees, which is essential for entering the kingdom of heaven (5:20). This is worked out in terms of alms-giving, prayer and fasting.[1] Each section makes the same points: avoid doing things **'before men, to be seen by them'**; otherwise **'you will have no reward from your Father in heaven'**.

Alms-giving (6:2-4)

Jesus assumes that his disciples will **'give to the needy'** (6:2).
The question is: 'How will we perform this duty?' Will it, in
fact, be a 'performance'? There is no evidence that the Pharisees actually sounded trumpets; the language is pictorial —
strikingly so. Preachers should learn from our Lord's way with
words. The sort of thing intended is seen in Luke 18:12, where
the Pharisee announces to all in the temple that he not only
fasts twice a week (see comments on 6:16-18), but also gives
away a tenth of all he gets. However we do it, the aim is to be
noticed and praised, to gain a reputation for generosity. Sub-
scription lists and publicly organized collections, even for
missionary work, with the largest donors singled out to encourage others to give, have no place in the church of Christ.
We must not have an ecclesiastical equivalent of the gift to a
political party in the hope of receiving public recognition.

On the contrary, says Jesus, we must do our charitable giving in secret. **'Do not let your left hand know what your
right hand is doing,'** is the rule. This deliberate secrecy is the
best way to avoid the sin of ostentation. In these days of Gift
Aid, tax-deductible gifts and necessary openness in account-
ing, it is difficult to observe this absolutely. However, it is
possible to limit those who know. Church treasurers can be a
great aid to righteousness by keeping matters secret. Granted,
it is the motive and attitude that matter, but this must not be
made an excuse for slipshod behaviour, which lets the cat out
of the bag — accidentally, of course!

The matter of rewards has been dealt with already in the
comments on 5:12. The same principle of 'the activity in consummation' applies here. We are not to expect that if we give
secretly, the Lord will reward us by somehow letting our gift
become public knowledge or by enabling us to win the National
Lottery![2] The reward is not some monetary benefit, or carefully

leaked information to the religious press. Instead, if our aim is to help the needy, they will be helped. If our aim is to glorify God, he will be glorified. We shall have the God-given satisfaction of pleasing him. This should be more than enough. It is, after all, 'more blessed to give than to receive' (Acts 20:35). The satisfaction of actually helping men and women is matched only by the awareness of God's approval.

Praying (6:6-8)

Again, it is not the posture, **'standing'**, or the place, **'in the synagogues and on the street'**, that matter, but the *motive*. Doubtless the posture and place may indicate the motive, as in the contrast between the Pharisee's standing in the temple, while the tax collector stood 'at a distance' (Luke 18:11,13). Clearly Jesus is not condemning all public prayer; participation in corporate prayer by its very nature must be seen by others. In this connection it is noteworthy that the prayer outlined in verses 9-13 constantly uses **'us'**. The injunction in verse 6 is concerned with personal prayer.

How literally should we take Christ's instruction to pray in a (presumably private) **'room'**? His aim, it would appear from the context, is to give practical help towards a genuinely spiritual motivation. By this means we remove the temptation to show off, since others cannot see us praying. However, it is perfectly possible to spend so much time in our inner room that it becomes obvious to the family, if not to the larger public, that we are devoting much time to prayer. Dr John Kennedy of Dingwall, in an article attacking the campaigns of D. L. Moody, denounced the new 'habit ... of worshippers as they enter the house of God. They assume, before the eyes of hundreds, the attitude of prayer, to do, in the public assembly, what Christ directed to be done in the closet.' He describes it as 'will-worship and formality' adopted by those who neglect private prayer![3] Those of us who have grown up in a different age, with different habits, and who might consider that to omit such prayer smacks of irreverence, may regard this as somewhat extreme. However, it is possible to make much of praying before or after a service in order to show how spiritual we are.

There would appear to be no easy answer to the practicalities, but the point is clear. Pray to God for his own sake, not to impress others. Should we tell a friend that we will pray, or have prayed, for him? It depends on the motivation. Is it to encourage him in his difficult situation, or to impress him with our superior godliness? There is a world of difference between this and 'preacher's blackmail', where the congregation is manipulated into accepting a controversial sermon, on the grounds that the minister has prayed about it!

Try to establish a place of prayer where you will feel 'comfortable', not in a physical sense, but where you will be free from the distractions of people or place, where you can speak with your heavenly Father without hindrance. You must, if need be, accept that others may write you off as being prayerless, because they do not see or hear your prayers. That does not matter so long as the Lord knows. This is the Saviour's point. However, do not think that this will produce some outward reward or public acknowledgement of your prayer status. What can be a better reward than that the Father hears and approves? Others may despise you, but the Lord assures you that 'He will give you the desires of your heart' (Ps. 37:4).

Jesus also has something to say about the actual *content* or wording of our prayers. The Authorized Version's use of the phrase 'vain repetitions' has done a disservice. Repeating a prayer is not wrong; our Lord repeated himself. In the Garden of Gethsemane — and who can doubt that this was real praying? — he left his disciples 'and went away once more and prayed the third time, saying the same thing' (Matt. 26:44). The word translated **'babbling'** may be linked to the Aramaic word for 'uselessness', or may simply be mimicking mere sounds without significance. Nor are we forbidden to pray at length. Again Jesus himself prayed all night on occasions.

Jesus is condemning any attempt to manipulate God by the way we pray. Perhaps the prophets of Baal, facing Elijah on Mount Carmel, provide a good example of what 'pagans' do (1 Kings 18:28). It is not only pagans who fall into this trap. In some quarters today a prayer method is taught which involves 'visualizing' what is wanted, with the assurance that this will be forthcoming. Some even speak or write of 'ordering' your new car (or wife, or whatever) from God, giving all the details of make, colour, etc. If you follow the method the result is certain. There is even a danger in speaking of 'the power of prayer' or saying that 'Prayer changes things.' Often this is harmless. We usually know what we mean by such a state-ment, but we may be liable to forget that it is the God to whom we pray who has power and who changes things. We must never turn prayer into a method or technique and forget that true prayer is personal communion with the living God, our Father.

Have you ever been in prayer meetings where liberty in prayer seems to be equated with shouting at God? Instead of relying on a personal relationship with the living God, the heav-enly Father, we may rely upon length, volume, beauty of lan-guage, erudition or theology, trying to wear God down by constant repetition, and so get our own way. Why do some put their trust in all-night prayer meetings? Has God com-manded these? If we have so much to pray about, or so many who want to pray, then we may have to pray all night (or for a 'half-night'!). In fact, the impression is sometimes given that there is some special virtue in praying all night, when actually we may be less able to pray properly because we are too tired.

There is a danger in thinking of 'prayer support' quantitatively, almost in a mathematical way. True, it is good for many to pray, as the Bible so often exhorts us, but we must not put our trust in numbers, but in our relationship with our covenant God.

The key, according to Jesus, is that **'Your Father knows what you need before you ask him'** (6:8). This does not mean that we have no need to pray. God's omniscience is that of a father, who does not need his children to inform him what may be required or legitimate. The meaning is not that he knows what we want, although that of course is true. He knows what is appropriate; we can ask with confidence, knowing that he will make no mistakes, that he will give us what is good and necessary. Realizing this means that we shall not try to persuade him, as it were, against his better judgement! We shall not rebel against his silence or rejection of our requests, but remain confident that he knows what is best and will give us what is good. We are encouraged in Scripture to present arguments to God, to give him reasons, especially connected with his own glory, but try to manipulate God and he may give you what you want, as a chastisement. We do well to remember that when the Israelites overstepped the mark in this respect and 'put God to the test', 'He gave them what they asked for, but sent a wasting disease [AV, 'leanness of soul'] upon them' (Ps. 106:14,15). How much better simply to let your requests be made known in faith to your heavenly Father!

The model prayer (6:9)

'This, then, is how you should pray', says Jesus. The 'then' indicates that this follows on from what he has just taught about true praying. The pattern that the Lord Jesus gives them expresses properly that Godward-looking and trusting prayer.

This is a digression from the structured treatment of three aspects of piety. Jesus clearly considers it important to give an example of what he means by righteous prayer. This confirms what is implied by the word **'how'** (or 'thus' or 'in this way'), not 'what', in the command. What we have is a pattern, a model, not necessarily a form to be repeated verbatim on every occasion. This is not to deny that it may be used in that way, since in Luke 11:2 the disciples are simply told, 'When you pray, say'. However, the main aim is to provide an example, which will guide our praying.

Our heavenly Father (6:9)

As we would naturally gather from the previous verses, prayer is to be addressed to **'Our Father in heaven'**. This does not forbid us to address the Lord Jesus himself in prayer; there are examples of this in the rest of the New Testament. On the other hand, it does tell us that our normal practice should be to speak to the Father, to whom we have access through Christ in one Spirit (Eph. 2:18). Much current practice wrongly ignores this. This is not just a pedantic question of being technically correct. Our Lord's reasoning, based on the teaching in verses 5-8, seems to be that this will enable us to pray in the right way: in faith in the Father who knows our needs, who rewards our secret praying and who is able, from the throne of heaven, to grant our requests. What a privilege this is! What a blessing to be able to come with confidence to our Father and with reverence for the great God of heaven! It is this kind of approach that will enable us to pray according to his will. ✫

What that will is may be seen from the structure of the pattern that he gives. Of the six requests, three are concerned with God and three with our needs. Significantly, the first three concern God: his name, his kingdom and his will. We must also note that our needs, as distinct from what we want, are as specified by the Saviour. Having begun with a worshipping and believing address to the Father, we must remember our calling to glorify God and enjoy him for ever, by putting him first in our prayers. That does not mean that in emergencies and trials we must go through the whole system before we can cry for help, but in our regular praying, as in our living, we must observe this order of priority. The real fault with the so-called 'shopping-list' type of prayer is not that we bring specific and detailed requests, but that the list is ours, rather than God's.

Godward petitions (6:9-10)

'Hallowed be your name' is the first petition, both in order and importance. 'Hallow' is not a word that we use generally, even in Christian circles, apart from in this prayer. God's name means God himself, especially in terms of his revealed character, and thus his reputation. His name does not need to be *made* holy, only to be recognized and treated as such. If a doctor has a good name in the district, it means he is known and respected, because of his good qualities, abilities and practice. God's name deserves to be sanctified or honoured, but because of sin it is largely ignored or even despised. This is the worst aspect of the situation in the world today, not the suffering and misery of men and women. The Lord is not honoured as Sovereign or worshipped as God as he deserves.

This may also apply to God's own people. Too often we dishonour God and bring shame on his name by our sin. We cause the heathen to despise God by not living as we ought as his people, according to Paul. 'As it is written: "God's name is blasphemed among the Gentiles because of you"' (Rom. 2:24).

When Moses was told to speak to the rock so as to provide water for the children of Israel, he impatiently struck it instead. For this sin he was not allowed to enter the promised land. God explained, 'Because you did not trust in me enough to honour me as holy in the sight of the Israelites, you will not bring this community into the land I give them' (Num. 20:12). Similarly God accuses Israel of profaning his name among the Gentiles. His response to this was: 'I will show the holiness of my great name, which has been profaned among the nations, the name you have profaned among them. Then the nations will know that I am the LORD, declares the Sovereign LORD, when I show myself holy through you before their eyes' (Ezek. 36:23).

It must be our chief concern, not only to live for God's honour among the men of the world, but also to pray that he may be honoured and his name hallowed. It should grieve us immensely that the name of our Lord is not honoured, that it is, in fact, taken in vain. We were created and then redeemed to live for his glory. Therefore our chief concern and first prayer must be that he will act to glorify his name. He fulfilled his words through Ezekiel by bringing Israel out of exile in Babylon and resettling them in Palestine. It is by his actions in grace, saving sinners and causing them to live holy lives, that his name is hallowed. The next two petitions are concerned with the means by which the first comes true. God's name is hallowed as his kingdom comes and his will is done. The three petitions belong together.

The kingdom of God

The second petition, **'Your kingdom come'**, brings us back to the central theme of the Gospel. Christ has come to inaugurate God's reign on earth. The kingdom comes increasingly as more and more men willingly submit to the King's authority. God's sovereign reign in the general sense is always in operation; it does not come and go. This petition concerns the effective reign of God in the hearts and lives of men through their faith in, and service of, King Jesus. The kingdom that was typified in the Old Testament and that drew near in the ministry of John is now established in Christ's coming and grows in extent and depth as the gospel of Christ spreads and men and women submit to his rule.

Psalm 72 describes how:

> He will rule from sea to sea
>   and from the River to the ends of the earth...
> All kings will bow down to him
>   and all nations will serve him
>
>   (vv. 8,11).

So:

> Of the increase of his government and peace
>   there will be no end.
> He will reign on David's throne
>   and over his kingdom,
> establishing and upholding it
>   with justice and righteousness
>   from that time on and for ever
>
>   (Isa. 9:7).

In the context of this Gospel, and especially 5:20, the mention of 'righteousness' in Isaiah 9:7 is very significant. The kingdom will finally come in its eternal form at the end of the age, when the Saviour returns: 'Then the end will come, when he hands over the kingdom to God the Father after he has destroyed all dominion, authority and power' (1 Cor. 15:24).

We must continue to offer this second petition until that final kingdom comes. In the words of Isaac Watts's paraphrase, 'For him shall endless prayer be made.'[4] In practice this covers all our praying for the success of the gospel, the extension, reviving and building up of the church, the work of the ministry at home and abroad, the conversion of sinners and the spiritual growth of saints and, perhaps especially, the work of the Holy Spirit. Doubtless, God will be glorified and his name hallowed in the judgement of the Last Day, but primarily it will be by the coming and extension of his kingdom.

God's will

The consequence of such submission to Christ is that increasingly God's will is **'done on earth as it is in heaven'**. In one sense, of course, just as God's sovereign rule is always effective, so his will is always done. I am reminded of C. H. Spurgeon's devastating response to a lady who objected to the idea that 'What will be, will be'. His reply was: 'Well, Madam, would you prefer to believe that what will be, won't be?' That, however, refers to God's secret purpose, his sovereign plan and will in predestination. Here, on the other hand, we are concerned with his revealed will. This petition is for the actual and heartfelt doing of God's will concerning righteousness.

In heaven, the angels and archangels delight to do God's will. There is no rebellion, no hesitation, no rejection. On earth there is sin and disobedience, ungodliness and unrighteousness. The psalmist expresses his grief: 'Streams of water flow from my eyes, for your law is not obeyed' (Ps. 119:136). All around us we can see the rebellion of man against his Maker. We cannot avoid the evil-doing, the deliberate sinfulness of 'man's inhumanity to man'. On every side we see selfishness, lying, immorality and cruelty. And when we look within, the case is little better. We see society under the rule of the prince of this world: 'The whole world is under the control of the evil one' (1 John 5:19). The church is opposed and Christians are persecuted. We should pray earnestly that God's will may be done, that evil may be restrained, that sinners may be transformed, that holiness might increase in the church and that God's name may not be dishonoured. 'It is time for you to act, O Lᴏʀᴅ; your law is being broken' (Ps. 119:126) should be our prayer also.

✱ Thus the three petitions come together. As God's kingdom comes, so his will is done and his name is accordingly hallowed. How much of your praying is in this vein? How many of your petitions are about these subjects — God's glory, kingdom and will? Are we, instead, taken up with our own affairs, our own troubles? Do tears run down our faces only for the sake of ourselves and our families and friends? As we shall see, other topics are by no means forbidden, but these God-subjects are put first by our Lord. Examine your preoccupations in private prayer and the topics put forward at the prayer meeting. We must also ask ourselves whether there is a readiness to do the Father's will, to work for the extension of his kingdom and thus bring honour and glory to his name in our hearts, to back up our prayers, but here the Saviour stresses our praying. It is necessary to have right ideas about the word 'hallow', about the nature of the kingdom and the kind of righteousness that God desires. We must also want these things and pray for them, urgently and earnestly. ✱

9.
Praying and fasting

Please read Matthew 6:11-18

In a book by a well-known American preacher, who shall be nameless, we read that prayer does not include asking, that petitions are wrong. Prayer, he writes, is only about bringing our minds and desires into line with God's. Petitions are unspiritual, selfish and self-centred. Although this may sound spiritual, it is in fact a denial of Christ's teaching. The priority of prayer for God's name and kingdom does not mean that we must ignore our own needs, as these hyper-spiritual souls seem to imply. Jesus did not think so. After the three petitions concerning God, our Lord moves to petitions for ourselves. We need to remember that we began with our Father in heaven. In verse 8 Jesus made it clear that his and our Father knows what we need. Further, both here and later (6:32), he tells us that God's fatherly care is not limited to the spiritual needs of his kingdom or of his people. How foolish it would be to conclude that the creator of our bodies is not concerned for their well-being! It is wrong to seek to be more spiritual than God.

Our daily bread (6:11)

In the petition, **'Give us today our daily bread,'** the bread is traditionally, and correctly, taken to include God's provision of all the necessities of life (see 6:32; 1 Tim. 6:8; Prov. 30:8-9). **'Daily'** is difficult to define. It may refer to 'the coming day', whether referring to today when uttered in the morning, or to tomorrow when spoken in the evening, but seems to have the idea of one day at a time, like the manna (see also Jer. 37:21). As with the instructions to the disciples going out on their training mission, sufficient for our present needs is all we require; we are not to hoard out of anxiety about the future. A different culture and the use of refrigerators may work this out in a slightly different way, but the main point is the same. We must trust our Father to provide for us and pray accordingly in faith.

We must remember that the whole prayer is in the context of the kingdom of God. It is assumed that we shall use the strength gained from this bread to work for the kingdom. A right attitude to this petition will free us from undue concern with money and possessions. This is a prayer that, for most of us, is constantly granted, removing the frequent complaint of Christians about the problem of unanswered prayer. As all prayers are to be offered 'with thanksgiving' (Phil. 4:6-7), this is an appropriate point to remind ourselves that 'grace after meat' is both right and spiritually healthy.

Forgiveness (6:12, 14-15)

The prayer now moves from physical to spiritual life with the prayer that God will **'forgive us our debts'**. Debts are simply sins, as in Luke's version of the prayer (Luke 11:4), but seen here in terms of falling into arrears in the payment of our obligations to God. If the previous petition demanded a common-sense awareness of our physical needs, this one demands a common-sense realism about our relationship to God. We do need our sins to be forgiven day by day. It is quite wrong to argue that our once-for-all justification makes this petition superfluous. We must distinguish carefully between our legal standing before God as our Judge, which has been dealt with completely and finally through faith in Christ's blood, and our relationship as children with our Father, which needs constantly to be maintained through forgiveness. We must take this seriously; we must not go back under condemnation, but equally we must cherish the smile of our Father. We are not perfect. Although we have bathed, we still need to wash away the defilement of each day (John 13:10). This daily washing must not be taken for granted. Like the Puritans, we must learn to 'keep short accounts', like businessmen who pay their bills every day, not allowing their debts to pile up.

The second part of the verse, **'as we also have forgiven our debtors'**, is also to be taken seriously, together with verses 14-15. Of course, Jesus is not talking about earning forgiveness or losing it; how could he be? Equally, however, he is not saying forgiving others is optional. We shall have to consider the matter in more detail when we come to the great parable in chapter 18, but we cannot skip over the subject here. Jesus attributed enough importance to this 'condition' in his pattern prayer, to reinforce it in verses 14-15: **'For if you forgive men when they sin against you, your heavenly Father will also forgive you. But if you do not forgive men their sins, your Father will not forgive your sins.'** Mark 11:25 perhaps provides us with the clue to his intention: 'And when you stand praying, if you hold anything against anyone, forgive him, so that your Father in heaven may forgive you your sins.' An unforgiving spirit will make all our praying barren. All forgiveness, whether in justification or day by day, depends on grace. The attitude that will not forgive shows a lack of awareness of our need of God's grace. Ultimately, as chapter 18 shows, such an attitude means that we have not experienced grace at all and we shall have to pay for all our sins ourselves.

Temptation and the devil (6:13)

The third petition takes us into the realm of daily spiritual warfare. It assumes the awareness of our danger and of the opposition of the devil. Before we enter into the difficult questions involved in **'lead us not into temptation'**, it is vital to see our weakness and danger, our vulnerability, so that we call upon the Father for help without delay. It is important to see that Jesus refers to **'the evil one'**, not just to 'evil', so that we remember 1 Peter 5:8: 'Your enemy the devil prowls around like a roaring lion looking for someone to devour.' We must see ourselves with the disciples in the Garden of Gethsemane, weak and weary, in danger of letting down our Saviour and denying him before men, and hear our Lord warning us: 'Watch and pray so that you will not fall into temptation. The spirit is willing, but the body [literally, "the flesh"] is weak' (Matt. 26:41). This will give us the necessary urgency to pray for our soul's safety and also provide a clue as to the meaning of this petition.

The thought of God leading us into temptation has alarmed many. Might God tempt us to sin? How can we survive if the Father leads us into temptation? Or, if we take the word in its frequent sense of 'trial', rather than enticement to sin, ought we to ask to be delivered from that which is for our good? (see James 1:2). The New Testament speaks of 'testing', which may be translated as 'temptation' and refer to enticement to sin (James 1:13). On the other hand, it may be translated as 'trial', referring to the refining and maturing experiences of difficult situations (James 1:2-3,12). The reconciliation of this is that in any test Satan is enticing us to fall into sin, while God is pulling in the opposite direction, leading us to growth through obedience. Both aspects are true in every situation. In every examination we may pass or fail. God wants us to pass; Satan wants us to fail.

Certainly God does lead into testing: 'Jesus was led by the Spirit into the desert to be tempted by the devil' (4:1). Satan tried to make Jesus sin; God enabled him to triumph over his enemy as part of making 'the author of [our] salvation perfect through suffering' (Heb. 2:10). We, however, like Peter, are not in the same league as our Lord. Although God may test us for our good and 'will not let [us] be tempted [tested] beyond what [we] can bear' (1 Cor. 10:13), we must not presume upon his grace. Instead, we must ask to be spared from those situations where we are likely, or even certain, to fall into sin. Instead of spending our time debating the details of the doctrine, we should pray daily that he will **'deliver us from the evil one'**.

Learning to pray

This last petition illustrates one of the dangers involved in studying the Lord's Prayer — that we concentrate on its teaching rather than follow its pattern in practice. Our Lord intended his disciples to act upon his words. It is an error to say that you cannot learn to pray. In fact, in Luke 11:1-4 Jesus responds to the request, 'Lord, teach us to pray,' with a pattern prayer. It is true that we depend on the work of the Holy Spirit to enable us to pray aright (Eph. 2:18; 6:18). This does not mean that we need not think, but just hope for the best. Using the pattern only as a form is one extreme to be avoided. To ignore it is another.

Let us learn to concentrate our prayers on God's glory and kingdom, but understand that this in no way forbids us to bring our needs before the Lord. In fact, as these prayers are all expressed in the plural, using 'us', we must realize that our more personal, private devotions will include much more than is mentioned here. The function of the pattern is more to ensure that we do not omit areas of prayer than to limit them.

Here is an essential part of the regular spiritual check-up that
we all need to have from time to time. It is only too easy to
assume that we are praying properly, because we spend a certain time on our knees. We may actually be falling short by
majoring on ourselves, or despising our own needs by assuming that all is well with our attitude, or by feeling banned from
God's presence by our sins. Our Lord's wisdom in giving this
pattern is not to be wasted.

Fasting (6:16-18)

Jesus assumes that his disciples will fast. He is concerned only
that they do it properly, and so he reaffirms the principles which
he has already applied to giving alms and to praying. Their
fasting must not be like that of **'the hypocrites ... for they
disfigure their faces'** for public show. He insists that his disciples do not **'look sombre'** or 'miserable'.[1] He tells them:
**'Put oil on your head and wash your face, so that it will
not be obvious to men that you are fasting.'** Only the Father
must know they are fasting; it must be **'done in secret'** and
then the Father will **'reward'** them.

   We shall return to the subject of fasting, and particularly its
relevance for the Christian, when Jesus deals with it in chapter
9:14-17. For now we must be content to think about the manner and apply our Lord's words about ostentation. Too often
we hear it said that 'So and so must be very holy, for he often
fasts.' How can this be known if he is following Christ's demand for secrecy, as a truly holy man would? Some men have
engaged in public fasting, as if trying to put God under pressure by a hunger-strike. The same rejection of Christ's teaching is obvious in such a case. This is not a godly procedure. If
we give to charity, if we pray, if we fast, we must do it towards
God alone. We must make every effort to avoid ostentation.

Only this is righteous kingdom behaviour. Anything else smacks of trying to earn eternal life by our righteousness.

The true practice of righteousness is a response to the fatherhood of God. If we remember that he is our heavenly Father, we shall be concerned to please only him. We shall look for his reward, not man's good opinion, and we shall pray as he would have us pray. This means being eager to promote his honour and glory, his kingdom and his sovereign will. It means depending on his loving and wise care, and seeking his forgiveness above all things so that our fellowship with him may continue without shadow. His grace and strength will be our support under trial and our defence against Satan. So let us take care to understand and remember that by grace through faith we are the children of our heavenly Father and let this fact rule every part of our life and service. This is the righteousness that far exceeds that of the Pharisees and the teachers of the law.

10.
Treasure without anxiety

Please read Matthew 6:19-34

One of the most futile expressions of sympathy is: 'Don't worry. Everything will be all right' — futile, but very common. It is futile because usually no reason is given why one should not worry. Our Lord did not indulge in such useless expressions. When he said, 'Do not worry,' he backed it up with teaching that provided reasons. That is what he does here.

The earlier verses of chapter 6 have contrasted the approval and reward of men with that of God. Our Lord now continues the contrast in terms of the treasure of earth and heaven, of time and eternity. This gives a unity to the rest of this chapter, which contains two parallel sequences showing how our daily concerns and practice show our real allegiance. Serving God leads to faith, which is expressed in seeking first God's kingdom. Serving Mammon leads to worry, which is expressed in running after the things of this life. Christ begins by speaking of our treasure, which indicates where our real allegiance lies.

Treasure in heaven (6:19-23)

'Treasures on earth' are very vulnerable. In first-century terms, our enemies are **'moth and rust'** — literally 'eating',

which may also refer to rats and other vermin, or woodworm
— and **'thieves'** who **'break in and steal'**. In twenty-first-
century terms, we have to contend with other forms of corruption: dishonest institutions, computer fraud, manipulated
stock markets and financial exploitation, as well as plain old-
fashioned burglars. How many have devoted themselves to
providing for their future only find that a 'Maxwell' has robbed
their pension fund! Jesus does not mean that we should not
make adequate and sensible provision for old age, if we can;
Proverbs 30:25 commends to us the wisdom of the ant: 'Ants
are creatures of little strength, yet they store up their food in
the summer.' But Proverbs also says, 'Death and Destruction
are never satisfied, and neither are the eyes of man' (Prov.
27:20). We must always be aware of the danger of thinking
that we are only making 'sensible provision', or enjoying the
good gifts of God (1 Tim. 6:17), when in fact we are covetous
and grasping, never content, like the rich and powerful who
always want more.

To store up things and money for ourselves, to make earthly
possessions our prior or only concern, is sheer folly. The rich
fool is ever with us. Nothing is of any value if we are not 'rich
towards God' (Luke 12:16-21). What, then, are the **'treasures in heaven'**, which are safe from corruption and theft?
Jesus does not elaborate here, but the whole context, especially the Beatitudes, tells us that he has in mind the kingdom
of God, eternal mercy, righteousness and comfort, the approval
of God for his sons, enjoying and seeing the presence of God,
'an inheritance that can never perish, spoil or fade — kept in
heaven'(1 Peter 1:4). Those who hope in God alone 'will lay
up treasure for themselves as a firm foundation for the coming
age, so that they may take hold of the life that is truly life'
(1 Tim. 6:19), that is, eternal life in all its fulness. As so often,
the talk of a reward, of treasure in heaven, is intended to

counterbalance the threats of the devil. Righteousness and faithfulness to God tend to bring suffering and poverty, as the Beatitudes have already made clear. So the Lord reminds his disciples, and us, that those who set less store by earthly treasure,
and accordingly gain less of it, will be more than compensated
by the heavenly treasure that God has laid up for them.

If this is true of us, then our hearts and lives will show it:
'For where your treasure is, there your heart will be also.'
If our treasure is heavenly, so will our desires and allegiance
be. The mysterious saying of verses 22-23 makes the same
point. **'The eye is the lamp of the body,'** in the sense that we
need to see where we are going. Our feet, as it were, share in
the light of the eye. **'If your eyes are bad, your whole body
will be full of darkness.'** If you have bad eyesight your eyes
do not see where you are going, so the body will stumble and
fall. The body lives in the darkness, because the eyes are in the
dark. **'If ... the light within you is darkness, how great is
that darkness!'** That is, if our spiritual sight is fixed on the
darkness of riches and earthly treasure, then our whole life
will be dark and earthly too. If our heart is in heaven, our
spiritual eyes will be fixed on heaven, and the life we live will
show the effects of this. Jesus is not referring to a mystical,
Quaker-type 'inner light', but to the effect of spiritual desires
and true allegiance to God on our life. Paul puts it similarly
when he writes, 'Set your hearts on things above, where Christ
is seated at the right hand of God. Set your minds on things
above, not on earthly things'. He puts us with Christ at the
right hand of God, reigning in the kingdom of God, and then
shows us how this must affect the way we live, putting to
death the things that belong to the earth: 'Put to death, therefore, whatever belongs to your earthly nature: sexual immorality, impurity, lust, evil desires and greed, which is idolatry'
(Col. 3:1-2,5). What a description of 'great darkness'!

Serving God (6:24)

The reference to 'greed, which is idolatry' helps us to understand Christ's summing up in verse 24: **'You cannot serve both God and Money.'** The old translation, 'Mammon', hides the fact that the word is not an actual god, but a personification of 'money'. It is derived from the Aramaic for 'possessions', which need not have a bad sense. It is not just wrongly acquired riches that lead us astray, but any possessions that we serve instead of God. So Money, or Mammon, is set as an idol against the true God. Greed is idolatry. We cannot serve the kingdom of God and the kingdom of materialism. To serve Money is to have the bad eyesight that leads to the whole body/life being full of darkness. Truly, 'The love of money is a root of all kinds of evil' (1 Tim. 6:10). Anger, false ambition, lying, theft, murder and a host of other sins all spring from covetousness, the love of money and possessions. Less directly, a lifestyle that puts pleasure and profit before God and so leads to backsliding and absence from the means of grace comes from the same source. Of the two dangers that bedevil the church and the Christian ministry, sex and money, the latter is perhaps the more prevalent and certainly the more subtle. Beware! **'No one can serve two masters.'**

It is possible, of course, to work for two employers, but no one can belong as a slave to two masters. The Christian is a bond-slave of Christ, redeemed, delivered and called into his service. The non-Christian is still a slave of the devil and of sin, and shows this by his service of Money. Jesus is not talking simply of belonging, but of active allegiance, of **'love'**, or **'hate'**, being **'devoted to the one'**, or bound to **'despise the other'**. This teaching is not just about our attitude to possessions, but about the whole direction of our life. If we want a righteousness that surpasses that of the Pharisees (5:20), then we must not be like them in this respect either. In Luke 16 our Lord repeats his saying about God and Money. Luke records that 'The Pharisees, who loved money, heard all this and were sneering at Jesus. He said to them, "You are the ones who justify yourselves in the eyes of men, but God knows your hearts. What is highly valued among men is detestable in God's sight"' (Luke 16:14-15). So we find another link with the teaching that has gone before; as with giving, prayer and fasting, so also with our possessions, we must want to please God, not men.

Anxiety (6:25-32)

If your possessions are all that matter to you, your only treasure, then you will inevitably become worried about **'your life, what you will eat or drink'**, and **'about your body, what you will wear'**. The believer, on the contrary, knows that **'life'** is **'more important than food, and the body more important than clothes'**. The implication is that since God has given us the more important things he will not fail to supply the less important ones like food and clothes. The slave of possessions does not see this distinction and cannot take this attitude, and so he worries. No doubt he would give lip-service to the principle if it were pointed out to him, but he is so taken up with his possessions, or his lack of them, that his eye will not penetrate to the underlying, vital matters. As we have seen already, Jesus is not denying that we need to work and make provision for ourselves and our families, but we are not to be anxious about it. (The AV's 'take no thought', instead of **'do not worry'**, is most misleading to modern ears at this point.)

The key to not worrying is the realization that the man who is a slave of God, not of Money, has that God as his heavenly Father. The faith that brings us into God's service continues trusting him and thus keeps us from anxiety. So Jesus can point to **'the birds of the air'** to justify our lack of concern. They do not even **'sow or reap or store away in barns, and yet your heavenly Father feeds them'**. We should note that he is not their heavenly Father, but ours. That is why Jesus can add, **'Are you not much more valuable than they?'** In addition to this argument from faith, Jesus reminds them that such worry is fruitless and pointless: **'Who of you by worrying can add a single hour to his life?'** This could be translated, with the AV, as 'add a cubit to your stature'. However, no one is likely to imagine that he could do that. Lengthening our life is much more feasible, at least to the natural mind, and it is quite customary to use spatial metaphors to describe length of life. Psalm 39:5 says, 'You have made my days a mere handbreadth', i.e. a span of nine inches from thumb to little finger. Thus we talk of our lifespan and even refer to a birthday as passing another milestone! As Carson points out, 'Worry is more likely to shorten life than prolong it.'[1]

As he has used the birds of the air to deal with the subject of food, so now Jesus refers to **'the lilies of the field'** to deal with the matter of clothes. Flowers do not **'labour or spin'**, yet God clothes them with a glory that surpasses even that of King Solomon. So, just as men are more valuable than birds, they are also more permanent than flowers and **'the grass of the field, which is here today and tomorrow is thrown into the fire'**. In the light of this, to worry is to show **'little faith'**. In other words, it is not merely a matter of common sense or logic, but of trusting our heavenly Father. It is **'the pagans'**, unbelievers who are not children of God and who therefore do not trust him, who **'run after all these things'** — food, drink and clothing. The disciples are told that they ought to remember that **'Your heavenly Father knows that you need them'** and will provide for them.

Seek the kingdom first (6:33-34)

While we must not worry, that is not enough. We are not to
adopt a laissez-faire attitude, assuming that all will be well.
God's children must **'seek first his kingdom and his righteousness'**. Then they may be confident that **'all these things
will be given'** to them **'as well'**. This 'as well' assumes that
they will gain the kingdom, as he has already made clear. They
will inherit eternal life; they will enter the kingdom of heaven.
What is not immediately clear is what he means by seeking
God's kingdom and righteousness. At the very least he is saying that the kingdom must replace food and clothing in the list
of their priorities. Their goal in life must not be possessions,
but treasure in heaven; not earthly rewards, but divine approval
and blessing.

Thus, we must make salvation our first priority. This demands repentance and the works of righteousness which are
its matching fruit (3:8-10). Only those who hunger and thirst
after righteousness will be filled (5:6). Only those who have a
practical righteousness that surpasses that of the Pharisees and
teachers of the law will be able to enter the kingdom of heaven
(5:20). Remember, this does not mean justification by works
or deny justification by faith. That is not the issue here. Jesus
is describing the character and life of those who trust him as
their Saviour and serve him as their King. Mere claim and
profession are not enough, as he will make very clear later on.

However, this is not only an individual, personal matter.
Seeking the kingdom will mean that we seek its furtherance
and prosperity here on earth. This must and will take priority
over our own needs, possessions, property and pleasure. All
that we pray for in the first three petitions of the Lord's Prayer
must also be our aim in practice. We must seek to be the answer
to our own prayers, at least in part. God's saving reign, his

coming kingdom, with its salvation — forgiveness of sins and eternal life for all nations — must occupy our thoughts and desires. The spread of the gospel and of the kingdom is not an optional aspect of our life, but at its very heart. Those who trust Christ and look to their heavenly Father for sustenance must make it their life's work to promote the kingdom and spread his reign in practice here on earth. We must aim to see his righteous will done here on earth as it is in heaven, for the hallowing of his name.

What do you discuss when you meet a fellow-Christian, or talk together after the service? Is it food and drink and clothes? Is it house prices and furniture? Is there a difference from the pagan world, or are you bothered about the same things as they are? Or are you concerned about the progress of the gospel, the growth of the church and the extension of the kingdom? What troubles you? Is it the decline in the standard of living, or the decline of righteousness in the church and in the world? If you feel pressure, is it on your own account or, like Paul, because of a 'concern for all the churches'? (2 Cor. 11:28).

Verse 34 is not a facetious comment, when he says that **'Tomorrow will worry about itself'**, that **'Each day has enough trouble of its own,'** but a clear statement of the futility of worrying about what we cannot change. There is a sense in which 'It may never happen' is a Christian sentiment. Our efforts are better expended on what we can change, by the grace of God, in our present situation in the work of the kingdom, rather than in worrying about tomorrow before it comes. This is the way to have treasure without anxiety, for we need not worry about God's kingdom. His purpose is sure and will not fail. The ark of God does not need the hand of Uzzah to keep it safe (2 Sam. 6:1-7). The kingdom of God does not need our worrying to enable it to prosper. Worry, whether about our own needs or about the state of the kingdom, only paralyses us. We must trust our heavenly Father for the one and thirst for the other. The way of the kingdom is to seek it with all our hearts and to practise righteousness with all our God-given strength.✠

11.
Judging and being judged

Please read Matthew 7:1-29

We live in a world that uses slogans all the time — in advertising, politics, and even religion. This chapter has as many striking sayings as the previous ones — sayings easily turned into slogans. The trouble with slogans is that, while they fix an idea in the mind, that idea can often be misleading and convey a completely wrong impression. That is certainly the case here. Christ's injunction against judging (7:1), the so-called 'Golden Rule' (7:12) and building on the rock (7:24) have all been used to support wrong and dangerous teachings. Therefore, it is vital that we continue to read Christ's sermon as a whole and take these verses in their context.

The first few verses, about judging, strike a very different note from chapter 6, with its stress on God's care for his children, although this subject soon returns (7:11). It is best to see them, not as just another aspect of the righteousness that the kingdom requires, but as an introduction to the conclusion about judgement, at the end of the chapter. That will distinguish between true and false disciples, genuine believers and hypocrites like the Pharisees. The first six verses warn us against various errors in preparation for this.

Do not judge (7:1-2)

One of the dangers that threaten the sincere seeker after God's 'kingdom and his righteousness' is that of looking down on others who do not do so. Righteousness can easily become self-righteousness, so Christ begins by warning his disciples not to think that they stand in God's place as judges. On the contrary, they too are subject to judgement and must act accordingly. **'Do not judge, or you too will be judged,'** Jesus warns. Contrary to much popular opinion, Jesus is not forbidding them to exercise discernment or to assess the position of others. Verses 5 and 6 command exactly that. We must understand men's position and needs if we are to help them: to evangelize them, counsel them, or exercise church discipline with regard to them. These are not the issues here. Certainly we must not be over-critical or censorious, but Jesus is saying more than that. The real fault is when we see ourselves as being in God's place, to judge, to refuse forgiveness, to pass sentence and punish.

Instead, we should always be aware that we too are sinners, that we need forgiveness and that, if we have received mercy, we must show it to others in our turn. Jesus will have more to say on this subject in chapter 18. For the present, he is content to warn his disciples that they must see themselves in the light of standing before him on the judgement day. Then they will be judged **'in the same way as [they] judge others'**, and **'the measure [they] use'** will be used on them (7:2). As another puts it, 'Speak and act as those who are going to be judged ... because judgement without mercy will be shown to anyone who has not been merciful' (James 2:12-13). If we are conscious of our own need for forgiveness, we shall not lightly condemn others. We shall be longsuffering with people, instead of writing them off as useless and hopeless. We must take Paul's warning not to 'judge someone else's servant'

(Rom. 14:4). Our righteousness must surpass that of the Phari-sees, who condemned the common people who believed in Jesus as 'this mob that knows nothing of the law — there is a curse upon them' (John 7:49).

Specks and planks (7:3-5)

Jesus then takes the matter further. How much easier it is, he says, to see others' faults, **'the speck of sawdust in your brother's eye'**, than your own! So often we have worse sins ourselves, but are ignorant of them. We feel justified in trying to correct others by removing the speck, **'when all the time there is a plank in [our] own eye'**. Perhaps the best example of this is King David. When Nathan the prophet told his par-able about the poor man's ewe lamb, David was able to see the speck of a rich man stealing another's animal, but unable to see the plank of his own adultery with Bathsheba and mur-der of Uriah (2 Sam. 12:1-7). The self-righteousness of the **'hypocrite'** always leads to hardness and harshness. If we examine ourselves before God, we shall become aware of our own sin and this should soften our hearts. How can we insist on the strictest of rules for others, when we ourselves fall so far short? We are not judges of others, but fellow-sinners.

There is, of course, a further and different danger. This Jesus also deals with. The aim of taking **'the plank out of your own eye'** is to **'see clearly to remove the speck from your brother's eye'** (7:5). We must not seek safety in isol-ation; we have a responsibility to each other. Note that Jesus refers to one's brother, a member of our heavenly Father's family. This is not easy. Many do not welcome such 'help', which they see only as criticism. However, if we love one an-other, we shall do our best to enable one another to walk in righteousness. When Paul deals with the same issue he reverses the order, but makes the same point: 'Brothers, if someone is caught in a sin, you who are spiritual should restore him gently [remove the speck]. But watch yourself [look for the plank in your own eye], or you also may be tempted. Carry each other's burdens, and in this way you will fulfil the law of Christ' (Gal. 6:1-2). Judges merely condemn and punish; brothers will want to help, to restore and change for the better.

Dogs and pigs (7:6)

Verse 6 reminds us that some may well not be willing to be helped, but will turn on us.

> Whoever corrects a mocker invites insult;
>   whoever rebukes a wicked man incurs abuse.
> Do not rebuke a mocker or he will hate you;
>   rebuke a wise man and he will love you
>   (Prov. 9:7-8).

The contrast between brothers and pigs or dogs is probably significant. We may expect a fellow-Christian to welcome our help and profit from it, if wisely and lovingly done. Unbelievers, however, when offered **'sacred'**, or precious, things (**'pearls'**), may **'trample them under their feet, and then turn and tear you to pieces'**. Jesus appears to be referring here to the holy gospel of the kingdom of God, the pearls of eternal life and a promised inheritance. His disciples must be careful in their preaching. Those who reject them and their message must be left alone; they must shake the dust of such homes and villages off their feet (10:1-16). In those verses he adds wolves to the description of dogs and pigs here in chapter 7. This is not a description of all Gentiles (cf. 15:26, where a different word is used), but of people of any race who show scorn and hatred towards the messengers of the gospel, whether official or otherwise. Thus we find an Old Testament prophet facing and rebuking Amaziah, King of Judah. The king rejects the prophet's warning in violent and threatening terms: 'Have we appointed you an adviser to the king? Stop! Why be struck down?' The prophet wisely stops, after giving a final warning (2 Chr. 25:16).

It is clear, then, that not judging does not exclude a sane and charitable assessment of our hearers' state, so as to treat them wisely and correctly. Paul warns his readers: 'Be wise in the way you act towards outsiders; make the most of every opportunity. Let your conversation be always full of grace, seasoned with salt [suited appropriately to their taste], so that you may know how to answer everyone' (Col. 4:5-6). Paul's exhortation to make the most of every opportunity warns us against writing people off too soon. We must not give up preaching, witnessing and, especially, living godly lives before 'ordinary' unbelievers (1 Peter 3:1). Nevertheless, due caution is in order; it is not wise, or even loving, to provoke 'mockers' with our words. +

Good gifts from the Father (7:7-11)

Jesus follows this warning with more teaching about prayer, not from the angle of duty, but of assurance. Such an absolute promise as those given in verses 7-8 may seem to require quali-fication, as elsewhere, but the context provides sufficient here. We must ask why Jesus adds this teaching. The answer ap-pears to be that he has come to the end of his description of the content of the righteousness of the kingdom. Now they have to put it into practice, and there is the problem. How can sinful men be righteous in the way he has outlined? How can the disciples, whom he has just reminded of their deficiencies and inadequacies before God, ever attain to this standard? They certainly cannot rely on their own strength, so he encourages them here to ask God for what they need. Since this is asking for what God wants them to be, they need have no hesitation in praying in faith; their request is according to God's will.

Jesus speaks to us, as to his disciples. Do you need grace and strength? **'Ask and it will be given to you.'** Do want the kingdom of God? **'Seek and you will find.'** Do you want to enter the kingdom? **'Knock and the door will be opened to you.'** Do not be discouraged or deterred; there are no exceptions to this: **'For everyone who asks, receives.'** It was Augustine of Hippo who said, 'Give what you command, and then command what you will,' and that is still an important principle. Christianity is not another form of legalism. After we are forgiven, God does not leave us to ourselves. The law, which could not justify us, has no power of itself to make us holy. Not even Christ's teaching can do that! Salvation is by grace from beginning to end. Those who come to Christ find grace to live as well as to be forgiven. They are necessarily born again as well as converted. They have the power of a new life to live for God, 'everything we need for life and godliness' (2 Peter 1:3). To be in Christ for justification means to be in Christ for sanctification also, both the initial setting apart and the progressive conforming to the likeness of Christ.

However, we cannot take this for granted. We go on living by faith — a faith that asks and receives, seeks and finds, knocks and finds the way open. There has to be a day-by-day reckoning of our new status in Christ, a realization that we are dead to sin and alive to God (Rom. 6:11), and a constant calling on God for strength to live as we can and must.

We must not simply assume, but we may be sure of this help and enabling. We should be convinced of God's readiness to answer our prayers, because he is our heavenly Father. Jesus uses one of his favourite 'How much more …' comparisons to drive home this point. Even human fathers do not give **'a stone'** instead of **'bread'**, **'a snake'** instead of **'a fish'** (7:9-10). He speaks to the disciples as fathers: **'If you, then, though you are evil'** — that is, sinful, not necessarily bad fathers — **'know how to give good gifts to your children, how much more will your Father in heaven give good gifts to those who ask him!'** What should we ask for? Request the good gifts he has promised to enable us to attain to the right-eousness of the kingdom and the assurance of the blessedness he has promised. The parallel passage in Luke 11:13 refers specifically to the Holy Spirit, in place of the more general 'good gifts' here in Matthew. Those who are indwelt by the Spirit do not simply assume that he will sanctify them. They must ask for and receive his continuing work in their hearts and lives. Contrary to those who deny that we should pray for the Holy Spirit, Jesus commands it and assures us of a favourable answer. This will apply also to asking for his working to revive the church. This does not imply that he is absent, or that we are not temples of the Holy Spirit. It is his increased activity that is being requested here, just as Paul writes of being given 'the Spirit of wisdom and revelation' (Eph. 1:17).

What an encouragement we have here to live our lives as Jesus has taught us, to keep the law in its spiritual depth, to perform our religious duties towards God, not men, to trust and not worry, to help our backsliding brothers! On our own we can do nothing; with the aid of the Spirit, we can attain to the righteousness that Jesus demands, the holiness without which 'no one will see the Lord' (Heb. 12:14).

The 'golden rule' (7:12)

The so-called 'golden rule' is to be found in the teaching of many religious leaders, including the Jewish rabbi, Hillel, in

20 B.C. It is said that a Gentile challenged him to sum up the law in the time that the challenger could stand on one leg. In response Hillel, like others before and after, formulated his rule negatively: 'What is hateful to you, do not do to anyone else. This is the whole law; all the rest is commentary.'[1] However, this form leaves sins of omission untouched, unlike the positive teaching of Jesus: **'So in everything, do to others what you would have them do to you'** (7:12). The following reference to **'the Law and the Prophets'** takes our minds back to the same phrase in 5:17. This suggests strongly that what we have here is a rounding off, not just of the immediately preceding verses, as a response to God's good gifts, but of the whole sermon. Whether standing on one leg or on two, we are given a summary of the will of God for our lives that is flexible enough to be applied to other situations ('everything') in addition to those explicitly dealt with in these chapters.

If this saying **'sums up'** the rest of the law, where does the love of God fit in? The similar reference to the Law and the Prophets in 22:40 includes both of the great commandments: love for God, as well as love for our neighbour. Here, Jesus is clearly only referring directly to the second commandment, but that does not mean that the first is absent from his mind. There is a personal aspect in all the teaching of the sermon; we are to rely on our heavenly Father. Prayer is to begin with the name, kingdom and will of the Father. In 6:24 serving God is explained as loving and being devoted to him. This command must not be used as a substitute for the gospel of grace. This is not a rule to obey as a means of winning salvation. Nor is Jesus saying that we should do this as a matter of self-interest, in order to have the same done to us. The Christian must be motivated by gratitude for God's good gifts (7:11) and love to the one who has first loved us. This is the natural response of one who understands the blessedness of being a child of God (5:1-12).

The trouble is that Christians have reacted so forcefully against the abuse of the verse that they have neglected to obey it. It is said that the Roman Emperor, Alexander Severus, had it written on his wall in gold.[2] Certainly, it is a good motto to have constantly before our eyes, to obey, not just admire. Let us apply it to showing mercy (5:7), being forgiven (5:23-24), giving to the needy (6:2) and judging (7:1-2). We may use this principle to illuminate the commands of Scripture, to examine our words and deeds, our reactions and responses, to stir ourselves up to action and to avoid the misunderstanding of others.

The narrow gate (7:13-14)

Christ draws his sermon to a conclusion by challenging his hearers to respond rightly to his teaching. **'Enter through the narrow gate,'** is an immensely serious demand. Jesus sets before them two gates, two roads, two destinies and, therefore, two classes of hearer. The gate and the road, or way, seem to represent a decisive act followed by a lifelong walk.[3] The end of the walk is either destruction, the hell of 5:30, or eternal life, the equivalent of entering the kingdom of heaven (5:20; 7:21). The true disciple embarks on the journey, **'the road that leads to life'** (7:14), by entering through the narrow gate. One might have expected him to say that the wicked are already on the broad way, but he does not.[4] In the words, **'For wide is the gate and broad is the road that leads to destruction'** (7:13), he is focusing on the present situation. If they turn down his offers of mercy, reject his demand for repentance and for works suited to righteousness, then they will end up in hell. All his hearers are confronted with a choice, a decision that has to be made. Decisive action is required, not admiration.

The nature of the smallness and narrowness is not stated in so many words, but the comments, that **'many enter through'** the broad gate and **'only a few find'** life, indicate something of their character. This, coupled with the fact that the word for **'narrow'** in verse 14 is related to the usual word for tribulation, points to the idea of being unpopular, liable to persecution. Going through the narrow gate and along the narrow road is the same as taking up one's cross (daily) and following Jesus. Choosing the way of righteousness in the face of persecution (5:10) is repenting, denying self and submitting to the lordship of Christ. This is the only entry to the Christian life. True evangelism must stress this. It is not legalism or works salvation, however much some may shun it. It is recognizing the saving grace of God and responding in true obedience.

Some interpreters want to deduce a permanent principle from Jesus' words about the **'few'**. For them 'small is beautiful'. If Christianity becomes popular, it must be false; revival is a dangerous delusion. At that particular time, and often since, especially today, this necessity for going the unpopular way, against the stream, results in few being saved. However, Jesus is not giving a permanent rule; chapter 8:11 speaks of 'many' coming and taking their places in the kingdom. At some times, in some places, we may expect the multitudes to be converted. Jesus is really concerned here, not with forecasting the future, but with telling his potential disciples that the way of righteousness is not optional. Instead of thinking about numbers, we should remember our Lord's response to being asked whether only a few were going to be saved. He did not feed their speculations, but told them to make every effort to enter through the narrow door (Luke 13:23,24). This must be our stress here, not asking whether many will be saved, but whether we shall be.

False prophets (7:15-23)

One reason why few are saved is the prevalence of wrong teaching, so Jesus warns his hearers to **'Watch out for false prophets'** (7:15). They must beware of these men, because they come in disguise, **'in sheep's clothing'**. They must take them seriously, because, although they appear harmless, **'inwardly they are ferocious wolves'**, malevolent and dangerous. Jesus does not tell us what their false message is, but we may assume that it contradicts the words of the true Prophet, Jesus Christ. Old Testament false prophets, according to Jeremiah, deny the necessity of repentance. ' "Peace, peace," they say, when there is no peace' (Jer. 6:14), and to those 'who follow the stubbornness of their hearts, they say, "No harm will come to you" ' (Jer. 23:17). They say what pleases sinful men. They acquiesce in the demands of the people for 'pleasant things' and 'illusions' (Isa. 30:10). Who wants to follow the narrow way, when the prophets say the broad way is quite safe?

What he does tell us is how to discern them, in spite of their disguise — that is, by their fruits. Trees and bushes bear appropriate fruit: **'figs'** come from fig trees, not **'from thistles'**, **'grapes'** from vines, not **'from thornbushes'**. **'A good tree cannot bear bad fruit, and a bad tree cannot bear good fruit'** (7:18). We must look beyond the message to the life, including both their everyday speech (not just their preaching) and their actions. Jeremiah accuses the false prophets of being 'greedy for gain' (Jer. 6:13). It is clear in the New Testament that false teaching is generally accompanied by false living (2 Peter 2; Jude). It is also true that false teaching bears the bad fruit of wrong living in the 'converts', but this is not, perhaps, the stress here.

Such false prophets will be judged by the Lord. The judgement that John the Baptist had earlier declared about unrepentant people in general is here pronounced on the false teachers: **'Every tree that does not bear good fruit is cut down and thrown into the fire'** (7:19). Jesus points forward in verses 21-23 to the Day of Judgement. On that day mere profession of faith, saying, **'Lord, Lord'**, will not guarantee entry into the kingdom. Claiming, **'Did we not prophesy in your name, and in your name drive out demons and perform many miracles?'** will not be sufficient. **'I never knew you'**, is a 'formula of repudiation'.⁵Jesus will not acknowledge them as his servants. He calls them, **'you evildoers'**.

When the Lord says that the only one qualified to enter the kingdom is **'he who does the will of my Father who is in heaven'**, he is not teaching salvation by works, as is so often assumed. Those whom the Lord knows are those who repent and believe. They give evidence of their faith by obeying God's Word. This applies not only to professing prophets and teachers, but to anyone who claims Jesus as Lord. In the same way 1 Corinthians 13:1-3 places no value on speaking in tongues or prophesying or miracles, apart from love. Merely to call formally on the name of the Lord is not the same as that calling in faith to which God promises salvation (Joel 2:32; Rom. 10:13). Real calling, real repentance and real faith lead to obedience.

The wise and foolish builders (7:24-27)

Christ's closing parable (7:24-27) is one of his most popular, especially with those who teach children, using its graphic description of the storm: **'The rain came down, the streams rose, and the winds blew and beat against that house; yet it did not fall.'** However, it is also one of the most frequently and seriously misunderstood. The rock foundation here is not the Lord Jesus Christ, as it is in 1 Corinthians 3:10-11, nor is building on that rock said to be believing in Christ. We must not allow our (correct) belief in justification by faith only to set aside the plain sense of the text. The introduction to the parable states: **'Therefore everyone who hears these words of mine and puts them into practice is like a wise man who built his house on the rock.'** Similarly, **'Everyone who hears these words of mine and does not put them into practice is like a foolish man who built his house on sand.'** The **'therefore'** tells us that Jesus is amplifying and enforcing the lesson of verses 21-23. Mere profession of faith without practical obedience to Christ's teaching is useless and hopeless, building without a good foundation. In the storm of 'that day' (7:22), such a building will not stand, but fall **'with a great crash'**.

Summary (7:28-29)

The words, **'When Jesus had finished saying these things'**, mark the transition to the next section. This one, on the righteous character of the kingdom, began with the announcement of its arrival with the coming of the King, Jesus Christ. Both John the Baptist and Jesus himself base their call to repentance on that fact. In addition, John demands righteous fruit in keeping with repentance. As he enters on his ministry, Jesus first displays his kingly power by his victory over Satan in the desert and then teaches with kingly authority, as the crowds recognized (7:28-29). His Sermon on the Mount is an exposition of kingdom righteousness, which explains what the fruits of repentance are in practice. Even the Beatitudes at the beginning stress righteousness as the guiding principle of those who are, and will be, blessed by God. The rest of the sermon builds up a picture of the required righteousness, which surpasses anything achieved by the Pharisees and teachers of the law.

He shows what the law actually requires in inward and positive respects and then what true, spiritual religion is in the sight of the Father in heaven, majoring on prayer. All this is seen as a right and righteous response to our heavenly Father, who cares for his children and removes the need to worry. The disciple's priority must be to seek first God's kingdom and the righteousness which he requires of his redeemed people. In conclusion he warns against self-righteousness, against choosing the easy and popular option and against the self-deception of depending on mere profession of faith. He demands once more the genuine fruit of doing the Father's will, which is the same as hearing and putting into practice his own words. The kingdom of God is the kingdom of Christ. No wonder **'The crowds were amazed at his teaching, because he taught as one who had authority, and not as their teachers of the law'** (7:28-29). We, for our part, must acknowledge that authority. We, too, must check whether we are producing fruit in keeping with our professed repentance and faith. To do this we must resist the temptation to write off obedience to Christ's teaching as legalism and take seriously every word of this most wonderful of sermons.

Part 3:
The work of the kingdom (8:1 – 10:42)

12.
Authority to heal

Please read Matthew 8:1-17

There is a general recognition today that we lack authority in preaching the gospel. Men seem able to ignore us and our message with impunity. We are relatively helpless in the face of public apathy and individual opposition, and there is a widespread tendency to look for a remedy in the wrong place. The previous section ended by emphasizing Christ's authority to teach, with the result that **'When he came down from the mountainside, large crowds followed him'** (8:1). Now we see that authority displayed in action, in the work of establishing and spreading the kingdom. Therefore these chapters are very relevant to the current situation.

The works that are described are mainly, but not exclusively, healings[1] — signs of the kingdom — and we are urged on many sides to make the reproduction of these today our priority. Many are influenced by the recent teaching about 'Power Evangelism' by 'signs and wonders'. However, much of the popularity of this movement lies in the ignorance of many Christians about the nature and purpose of a biblical sign. Biblically speaking, a sign has three aims and aspects. First, it arouses wonder and attracts attention by a display of divine power. Signs are called 'wonders' or marvels. Secondly, through this it attests to or confirms the authority of the one who performs it as God's servant, in this case the Messiah/

Christ (Acts 2:22), but later his messengers, the apostles (2 Cor. 12:12). Thirdly, and very significantly for our understanding of these healing miracles, it pictures and illustrates the message he brings. The word for 'healing' is the same as for saving; these physical signs tell us much about the salvation that Christ came to bring. It is tempting to describe this salvation as spiritual, in contrast to the physical healings, but that is not the whole truth. Ultimately, as this section makes clear, Christ's salvation includes both body and soul, and even the whole universe.

The man with leprosy (8:1-4)

It is considered wrong — 'politically incorrect' — nowadays to describe men as 'lepers'; hence the subtitle above. The greatly blessed 'Mission to Lepers' has been renamed 'The Leprosy Mission'. Why is this so? The reason is that an otherwise correct interpretation of the significance of leprosy[2] in the Bible has been misused to imply that present-day sufferers from that illness are somehow to be despised as literally, not just symbolically, under the judgement of God and excluded from society as morally defiled. The revised terminology and consequent change in attitude to the sufferers are to be welcomed, but the spiritual significance of the disease should not be ignored. Laws about leprosy were part of the Mosaic ritual that taught Israel about sin and salvation.

The regulations about this disease showed them how to view themselves before God. It rendered a man 'unclean' (Lev. 13:8), ceremonially defiled. This led to the sufferer being excluded from the congregation, from the public worship of God and even from the Israelite camp (Lev. 13:45-46). In the cases of Miriam (Num. 12:10-15) and Uzziah (2 Chr. 26:16-20) affliction with leprosy was an outward symbol of being under the wrath of God. In these instances the sin and guilt were real, which may have led people to regard all leprosy as the mark of God's condemnation. However, the Mosaic regulations are a better guide to the significance of the disease and to the incident recorded here.

The man who comes to Jesus is convinced that the Lord can heal him, but he puts it in terms of being made 'clean': **'Lord, if you are willing, you can make me clean.'** He keeps his distance, according to the rules, so Jesus **'reached out his hand and'**, no doubt to his utter amazement, **'touched'** him. **'Immediately he was cured'** (literally, and much better, 'made clean'). Instead of becoming defiled himself, Jesus has authority and power to make the man clean. He does not ignore the defilement, but removes it. Unlike the rabbis, who chased away such men in case they became defiled, Jesus is compassionate and graciously willing to respond to his need. Even if we look no further than the physical situation and need, we have here a wonderful example of our Lord's love, grace and compassion. When we see the spiritual significance, there are no bounds to our wonder and amazement.

The basic point is that sin defiles us in the sight of God. It shows how God loathes sin; it is repulsive to him. Sin bans us from the presence of God and outlaws us from membership of his people. He cannot and will not have sinful man in his sight and presence (Hab. 1:13; Rev. 21:27). This is not only true of sins with a sexual connotation that are normally regarded as filthy and repulsive, like dirty thoughts or child abuse. It includes all forms of disobedience and rebellion (1 Sam. 15:23); all sin is dirty to God. Like Isaiah, once we have seen something of the holiness and purity of God, we have to cry out, 'Woe to me! ... I am ruined! For I am a man of unclean lips, and I live among a people of unclean lips, and my eyes have seen the King, the LORD Almighty' (Isa. 6:5). No wonder that Simon Peter, confronted with the person of the miracle-working

Jesus, should exclaim, 'Go away from me, Lord; I am a sinful man!' (Luke 5:1-8).

We must follow the leprous man's example and come to Jesus in all our need, with all our sin and defilement. When we plead for cleansing and forgiveness, he will not turn us away.

> Come ye sinners, poor and wretched,
> Weak and wounded, sick and sore,
> Jesus ready stands to save you,
> Full of pity joined with power;
>   He is able,
> He is willing; doubt no more![3]

After healing him, Jesus, too, observes the rules and sends him to the proper authorities: **'Go, show yourself to the priest and offer the gift Moses commanded, as a testimony to them.'** In Leviticus 14:3-7 it was the priest's function to examine the recovered man and declare him clean once more. Two birds were to be brought. The priest sacrificed one as a guilt-offering and sprinkled its blood seven times on the once-diseased person, symbolizing his cleansing. 'Then he is to release the live bird in the open fields.' No longer was the man diseased and under restrictions. Now he was clean and free — free to resume his place in the covenant people, to attend the temple worship and rejoice with the congregation. What a glorious picture of the deliverance from sin that Christians enjoy!

The sacrifices, of course, point to the cross of Christ. It is from his sacrificial death that cleansing from sin comes to those who call upon him. It is through his blood that we are made clean and free from sin, able to have communion with God and fellowship with God's people. Christ's authority is exercised already in view of his coming sacrifice. The relevance of this will become even clearer later. All this, Jesus says, is to be done **'as a testimony to them'** (8:4). The 'them' may mean all the priests, or the people of Israel in general. In any case it is a testimony to us that the Messiah has come, in fulfilment of the Law and the Prophets (5:17), and that he has authority to cleanse us from the defilement of sin.

The centurion's faith (8:5-13)

The servant of the centurion was ill: **'paralysed and in terrible suffering'** (8:6). Once again illness symbolizes the power and crushing effects of sin. The stress, however, is on the authority of Jesus to deal with sin, and that not only within Israel, but in the whole world. The centurion is, of course, a Roman, a Gentile. He is humble, aware of his unworthiness **'to have [Jesus] come under [his] roof'**. In response to our Lord's reply,[4] the centurion affirms his faith in Christ's authority and power: authority to heal the illness with a **'word'**, power to do it without entering his house. Truly Christ is able to deal with the power and corruption of sin — our sin.

The centurion's justification for his faith is frequently treated as if he said, 'I am a man *in* authority.' In fact, he says, **'I myself am a man *under* authority, with soldiers under me.'** He holds his rank in the Roman army, which in turn gives him derived authority to command others: **'I tell this one, "Go", and he goes'**, etc. He trusts Jesus, not as the Son of God with his own authority, but as the Messiah, who has come at the command of God and who, therefore, exercises God's authority on earth. This fits the concept of signs that we have already seen. Jesus constantly speaks of himself as one who has come to do the Father's will, not his own. This in no way denies his deity, but it does reminds us of the transitional, historical situation. It is consistent with his statement: 'I was sent only to the lost sheep of Israel' (15:24).

This brings us naturally to the startling assertion in verse 10: **'I tell you the truth, I have not found anyone in Israel with such great faith.'** This not only demonstrates the greatness of this Gentile believer's faith, but also shows that Jesus is looking forward to a time when the gospel will spread to all nations, when the new covenant will include believing Gentiles as well as believing Jews: **'I say to you that many will come from the east and the west, and will take their places at the feast with Abraham, Isaac and Jacob in the kingdom of heaven'** (8:11). The feast is an Old Testament picture of the consummated Messianic kingdom and was well known among the Jews, but the Gentiles were not expected to share in it. All authority has been given to Christ, over all nations, but this will come into effect only after his resurrection.

The next verse (8:12) is a warning to the Jews who were listening, and to us. Faith like that of the centurion is necessary for entry into the kingdom. Mere membership of the Jewish nation, being a 'subject' (or, better, 'son') of the kingdom is not enough. **'The subjects of the kingdom will be thrown outside, into the darkness, where there will be weeping and gnashing of teeth.'** The subjects of the kingdom are those who are the covenant people of God, but who do not keep the covenant by believing the promises and so trusting in Christ. They have the privileges of the covenant — the sign of circumcision and the oracles of God (Rom. 3:1-2), the prophecies, promises and types of Christ (Rom. 9:4-5) — but do not believe.

> But from everlasting to everlasting
>   the LORD's love is with those who fear him,
>   and his righteousness with their children's children —
> with those who keep his covenant
>   and remember to obey his precepts
>
> (Ps. 103:17-18).

Jesus will return to this theme later. For now, we must take note of this warning, along with his hearers. How many are

brought up in a Christian or religious home, hear or read the
Bible, listen to sermons and Sunday School lessons, enjoy many
privileges and opportunities, but do not actually repent and
believe? They may say, 'Lord, Lord,' as the previous chapter
has warned, but they cannot assume that all is well with them.
It may be that on the Last Day they will have to watch while
those who were far less privileged, who were brought up in
utter paganism, or lived for a time in godless apathy, enter the
kingdom through faith in Christ, while they are cast out. The
great encouragement to believe is this understanding of the
glorious authority of Christ. Here is one worthy of our faith,
able to save from sin and deliver from bondage and corruption, however deep. When Jesus speaks, it is done. When he
promises, it does not fail. **'Go!'**, he says to the centurion. **' "It
will be done just as you believed it would." And his servant was healed at that very hour.'** If we believe, we shall
receive the salvation we need. He has authority to do what he
promises.

Other healings (8:14-17)

Matthew continues his record of Jesus' healings with the case
of **'Peter's mother-in-law'** (8:14-15). Like leprosy, fevers
were regarded as defiling, but once again Jesus deals with both
disease and defilement: **'He touched her hand and the fever
left her, and she got up and began to wait on him.'** Such is
his authority that she is immediately and completely restored,
so as to be able to serve at table. From Mark's Gospel we
know that this was the Sabbath, which probably explains why
it was evening when **'many who were demon-possessed were
brought to him'**. His power over Satan is demonstrated by
the fact that **'he drove out the spirits with a word'**. In his
own temptations he demonstrated his authority over Satan;

now he shows the results of his victory. The devil cannot stand
against the kingdom of Christ. We who belong to the King
need not fear the devil. Redemption from slavery to Satan is
part of our salvation, and the word of Christ is the means we
must adopt to defeat the enemy.

What an amazing ministry we see here! Jesus touches the
unclean and is not defiled; he delivers the enslaved from the
prince of this world and heals **'all the sick'**. There are no
failures, no partial or temporary healings, no ranting and rav-
ing — just his word of authority. How could this be? Matthew
informs us that this is in fulfilment of Scripture, in particular
of Isaiah 53:4, which he quotes: **'He took up our infirmities
and carried our diseases.'**

Healing and the atonement (8:17)

There is no doubt that Isaiah 53 refers to Christ's atoning death
on the cross. However, the precise nature of the connection
with disease is not generally understood. Is there healing in
the atonement, as is often claimed? Is it true that just as we
believe and are forgiven, so we must believe and be healed?
Does illness in a Christian indicate lack of faith? Does preaching the cross include the offer of healing to all the hearers?
The answer to all these questions is, 'No', at least in the way
they are meant. This teaching is responsible for many tragedies, much disappointment and even loss of faith. There is
nothing more cruel than to blame the death of a child on the
parents' alleged lack of faith. And if miraculous healings are
the proof of the truth of the gospel, as 'power evangelists'
claim, who can blame those hearers who deduce from the mini-
mal (even claimed) successes, that the gospel must only be
two per cent true?

And yet there is an important element of truth in it all. The
fact that sin's entry into the world brought illness and death on

mankind and all creation, that all suffering is caused, directly
or indirectly, by sin, means that there is some connection between atonement for sin and the healing of disease. Isaiah 53
does speak of Christ dying for our sins. The verse following
the one Matthew quotes reads:

> But he was pierced for our transgressions,
>   he was crushed for our iniquities;
> the punishment that brought us peace was upon him,
>   and by his wounds we are healed.
>
> (Isa. 53:5).

Now it is clear that the healing spoken of here is spiritual, as it
is interpreted in 1 Peter 2:24 — that is, forgiveness. Psalm
103:3, which speaks of the Lord 'who forgives all your sins
and heals all your diseases', must be understood similarly. The
Greek (Septuagint) translation of Isaiah 53:4 also speaks of
'sins', not illnesses. However, we must not remove the idea of
illness and physical disease from Matthew's use of verse 4. It
appears that Matthew is deliberately giving his own, literal,
translation of the Hebrew, instead of using the Septuagint, in
order to emphasize this connection.

So, although we cannot speak of Christ dying for our diseases in the same way as for our sins — i.e. dying as a substitute for influenza or cancer — there is a link between Christ's
death, in the context of Isaiah, and bearing and removing our
diseases. When Christ died for sin, he also dealt with all its
effects: guilt, power and corruption, and even the effects on
our bodies and the rest of creation. The point is that not all of
this comes into effect immediately. Death was defeated at the
cross, but the resurrection of our bodies awaits the Second
Coming. The healings in the Gospels and Acts are signs of the
kingdom that is to come in its fulness at Christ's return. We
are forgiven now; we are delivered from the dominion of sin
and the devil now. However, the redemption of the body, the

adoption, must await his return, when 'The creation itself will be liberated from its bondage to decay and brought into the glorious freedom of the children of God' (Rom. 8:21,23). To say that there is healing for today in the atonement is not so much wrong as premature.

This is why it is wrong to expect the signs and wonders of the New Testament to be reproduced today. They represented an inbreaking of the kingdom in advance, which was only a guarantee and foretaste of the kingdom that is to come. We must not live as if the end has already come, as if the consummated kingdom were already here.[5] Until Christ returns, illness, disease, death and all the other physical effects of the Fall will continue. Demanding today what God has promised for tomorrow can only bring the Word of God into disrepute. We shall have to see this same principle at work in the rest of the chapter; it is the explanation of both the stilling of the storm and the fate of the pigs.

For now, we must learn the lesson of Christ's kingly authority. He is already victorious over sin and Satan, over the power and dominion of sin, and the slavery of the devil. For the moment the great means through which the kingdom comes is the word of Christ (8:3,8,16). It is the preaching of the gospel which must occupy our attention and strength. This is the means upon which we must depend, by the power of the Holy Spirit, until the final day when Christ returns. The popular advance of the movement that stresses healings, exorcisms, and even resurrections, now has brought a crisis of confidence to the church. We are being tempted to desert the old ways and look for new paths, which will promise instant success. Nevertheless, we must continue to rely on the Word of God and the power of the Spirit to convince and convert sinners, as they have always done. This is how the kingdom comes in our day.

13.
The appointed time

Please read Matthew 8:18 – 9:1

Although these verses continue and extend the theme of Christ's kingly authority, especially as manifested in stilling the storm and driving the demons into the pigs, there is a new emphasis on men's response to this — discipleship. Matthew, like Jesus before him, is essentially practical. He is not interested merely in the theory of the kingdom of Christ, but in how we react to him. As we noted earlier, when Jesus was asked a theological question about how many would be saved, he urged his hearers to 'make every effort to enter' the kingdom (Luke 13:23,24). So here he requires his followers, actual and potential, to examine themselves closely as to their motives and intentions. We, for our part, must not simply read Matthew's Gospel in an intellectual manner, or even only with a devotional intent. The question is constantly asked or implied: 'What are you going to do about this? How will you respond to the claims of Christ?' There are, indeed, difficulties and problems in these verses which must be faced and answered, but the bottom line is still: 'What will you do with Christ?'

Discipleship and hardship (8:18-20)

As so often, **'when Jesus saw the crowd around him'**, he left (8:18). On this occasion he **'gave orders to cross to the**

other side of the lake', but before they could leave Jesus was approached by some potential disciples.

The first one was a scribe, a certain **'teacher of the law'** (8:19). Some have expressed surprise, not to say doubt, that such a man should come to Jesus in this way. However, not all the leaders of the Jews were opposed to Jesus and he certainly was ready to accept all who came to him with sincerity. His answer, however, raises doubts as to whether this is such an instance. The assertion is bold enough: **'Teacher, I will follow you wherever you go.'**

Perhaps we should not read too much into his form of address as 'Rabbi'; it may be that he was only intellectually interested in Christ's teaching; in doctrine, not in living. At any rate, Jesus immediately confronted him with the real nature of discipleship. It is not only following 'wherever', but also 'however': **'Foxes have holes and birds of the air have nests, but the Son of Man has nowhere to lay his head.'** Would this teacher of the law 'follow' where Jesus leads, even into the uncertainty and suffering of his destined path? Did he realize that belonging to the kingdom of heaven is not a guarantee of comfort and prosperity in this world?

Christ's use of the title 'Son of Man' is deliberately ambiguous.[1] It seems to have been very carefully chosen by him to express the true nature of his Messiahship. It was not a common or popular Messianic title, so he could fill it with whatever content he chose. Derived from the use in Daniel 7:13-14, it refers not only to his humanity, although this must be included, especially here, but also to his glorious kingship. The 'one like a son of man' in Daniel's vision was 'given authority, glory and sovereign power; all peoples, nations and men of every language worshipped him. His dominion is an everlasting dominion that will not pass away, and his kingdom is one that will never be destroyed.' But before the Son of Man can come in his glory, he must tread the path of suffering and shame that leads to the cross. So, while some of Christ's uses of the title, such as 25:31, speak of the glorious kingdom, others, such as this verse and 20:28, stress the amazing contrast, that such a king must suffer and die. Clearly, this was directly contrary to the usual Jewish expectation of an immediately victorious Messiah, sweeping his, and their, enemies into the sea.

Victory will come in God's time, but first the King and his servants must endure 'the sufferings of the Messiah'.[2] Being a disciple of Christ means sharing his pathway of suffering and rejection, denying ourselves, taking up our cross and following. The teacher of the law obviously did not have this in mind. Do we? Or are we, in the decadent West, so taken up with our plenty, comfort, leisure, hobbies and reputation that we would turn away from him in disappointment? Before the Iron Curtain came down this was an area where we had to be ready to learn from our brothers in Communist lands. Today, it seems that they are having to learn to cope with the same temptations as we are. When Joshua took over the leadership from Moses, the Israelites promised, 'Whatever you have commanded us we will do, and wherever you send us we will go' (Josh. 1:16). This is the attitude of the true disciple. We must practise, as well as sing:

> Be it ours, then, while we're here,
> Him to follow without fear;
> Where he calls us, there to go,
> What he bids us, that to do.[3]

Discipleship and allegiance (8:21-22)

A second disciple speaks to Jesus: **'Lord, first let me go and bury my father'** (8:21). We cannot be certain whether his father was already dead and awaiting burial, or if he meant that he could only follow Jesus after his father had died. The former seems more likely to Western minds, but it has been pointed out that if that were the case, the man would have been at home already, 'keeping vigil over' his father's body. Some regard the latter as an attempt to soften the harsh impact of Christ's words: **'Follow me, and let the dead bury their own dead.'** However, Kenneth Bailey, arguing from current Arab and Eastern customs, writes, 'The phrase, "to bury one's father" is a traditional idiom that refers specifically to the duty of the son to remain at home and care for his parents until they are laid to rest respectfully.'[4] The disciple is in effect insisting that the pressure of his community and family relationships will not allow him to go yet. Christ's answer is that allegiance to him must take precedence over any other.

Either way, Christ's demand tells us today that serving the King and his kingdom must come before any cultural expectations. Bailey adds, 'The present author will never forget a class of Middle Eastern seminary students who literally turned white when this text was expounded with its clear affirmation that Jesus is claiming an authority higher than the authority of ... the father.'[5] The exact form of these expectations may differ today, although not as much as many think, but the principle is clear and firm, and may be just as shocking. The wider message is that we must learn to assess our own culture in the light of Christ's teaching. The forces of peer pressure, career prospects and the employment rat race, the structures of Western society and urban culture must be rejected when they cross our allegiance to the Saviour. We often insist that converts must reject their non-Christian culture, especially if it is foreign to us. We are not so ready to go against the stream ourselves and place every other authority under that of Christ.

In a day when family loyalty and filial duty are not so highly esteemed, we may need to stress the fifth commandment, that we must honour our father and mother. This is not contrary to Christ's demand as a general rule. The words of Jesus here seem to be of the same kind as his direction to the rich young

ruler to sell all that he had and give to the poor and then follow him. This is not the duty of us all, but when it comes to the
crunch, when the alternative is disobeying Christ, we must be
prepared to do even that. Here, while the general rule is to
fulfil our family responsibilities, as themselves part of our service of Christ, when Christ calls, we must be prepared to put
him and his kingdom first.

Nothing must be allowed to come between us and our allegiance to Christ. If we have been born again and possess spiritual life, then we can and must work for his kingdom. Unbelievers cannot do this; it is beyond their abilities, so the
responsibility is ours. They are spiritually dead, so they cannot
preach the gospel and advance the kingdom. Therefore, let
them concentrate on the non-spiritual tasks, like burying the
dead. The same principle applies with regard to many good
aspects of life in this world. The doctrine of common grace
teaches us to play our part in this life and in its culture. As far
as we can, we should further men's physical and material good.
However, when the needs of the kingdom demand our prior
attention and concern, when we cannot fulfil both the spiritual
and the natural duties, then we must leave the 'dead' to bury
the dead, support relief charities, engage in politics and wel-
fare schemes. Usually there is no conflict; this should not be
made an excuse for failing in our family responsibilities or functioning as salt and light in the world. We mainly have time and
money for both, but when a choice must be made, our duty to
serve Christ and 'proclaim the kingdom of God' (Luke 9:60)
must come first.

Calming the storm (8:23-27)

The reason for crossing the lake was given back in verse 18:
Jesus was leaving to avoid the crowd. The main point of this
incident is to demonstrate Christ's authority over the forces of

nature, the created world. The situation was extremely dangerous: **'Without warning, a furious storm came up on the lake, so that the waves swept over the boat'** (8:24). Such, however, was Jesus' confidence in his heavenly Father's care that he **'was sleeping'**. The disciples did not have this faith, and so were very scared. They **'went and woke him, saying, "Lord, save us! We're going to drown!"'** In response Jesus first rebuked them and then **'rebuked the winds and the waves, and it was completely calm'**. There are two lessons for us to learn.

The minor one concerns the disciples' faith, or rather their lack of it. Jesus says to them, **'You of little faith, why are you so afraid?'** This has caused some problems because the wording is different in the other two Synoptic Gospels. Mark records him as saying, 'Do you still have no faith?', while Luke has, 'Where is your faith?' We should not make too much of these variations. We are not usually given Jesus' actual words, but a report of the sense. It is clear, therefore, that Jesus is not stating that they have no faith at all; they are true disciples. However, the faith that they have is failing to cope with their desperate situation. Great faith is not something different in kind from little faith. Faith as a grain of mustard seed is enough; it is a matter of quality, not of quantity. It was 'little' in the sense of not overcoming this great obstacle. It could be translated 'short faith'; it began but did not persevere to the end of the trial; at this point they have 'no faith'. The distinction between little or great relates to the situation and the obstacles being faced.

Great faith, like that of the centurion, believes in spite of all the difficulties of being a Gentile in dire straits. Little faith fails when confronted with small ones. The faith is the same, but the strength varies. The solution is to see the problem in relation to Christ's great authority. Great faith sees his power as sufficient to deal with all our troubles; little faith has a low understanding of his authority and so fears the outcome. The hackneyed story of the little old Scots lady and her minister is still illuminating. When he praised her great faith in times of trouble, she replied that she did not have great faith, but little faith in a great God. This is what Jesus is teaching his disciples through this frightening experience. He demonstrates his authority over all things, so that their faith may grow and become great.

If you follow Jesus on his terms, as set out in verses 19-22, as you must, you may wonder just how you will survive: without earthly security, sleeping under hedges, with the world and culture around against you. This incident in our Lord's ministry provides much-needed help and encouragement for the faint-hearted disciple. In the context of the previous section, we may learn that following Christ includes trusting him for salvation, not only from sin, but also from the dangers and trials of the way. The stilling of the storm demonstrates that he has such authority that they, and we, need fear no enemies or opposition or danger, even from the natural world around us. We do not need to allegorize the boat into a picture of the church to rejoice in John Newton's words:

> Begone, unbelief,
> My Saviour is near,
> And for my relief
> Will surely appear:
> By prayer let me wrestle,
> And he will perform;
> With Christ in the vessel,
> I smile at the storm.[6]

However, this passage has more than an individual significance. Although Jesus is a man who needs to sleep, he is also God's King, who rules over all things. No wonder, **'The men**

were amazed and asked, "What kind of man is this? Even
the winds and the waves obey him!"' The fact that he rebukes the wind and the waves need not suggest that he sees
demonic forces behind them. On the other hand, it does point
to the fact that such storms and tempests, which threaten the
Son of God, are part of a fallen world, the effects of sin. As
Genesis 3:17 tells us, the ground shares in man's cursed condition. Such 'natural' upsets are part of the creation's 'frus-
tration' and 'groaning as in the pains of childbirth' (Rom.
8:20,22). This positive comparison assures us that a birth is
coming, a day when 'the creation itself will be liberated from
its bondage to decay and brought into the glorious freedom of
the children of God' (Rom. 8:21). Christ's redemption will
finally restore not only our bodies, but even the natural order.
Resurrection bodies will be given new heavens and a new earth
in which to dwell. But not yet. We can no more claim the
healing of our bodies at the present time than we can demand
the resurrection of the body or the restoration of all things.
We must not expect to heal the sick, raise the dead, calm the
storm, or prevent earthquakes and hurricanes. Nevertheless,
Christ's miracles are signs that all this is guaranteed. He has
the authority and one day will return to finish the application
of his death on the cross, the work of redemption.

The two demoniacs (8:28-34)

This provisional perspective will also help with the problems
raised by the next incident. Once Jesus had **'arrived at the
other side in the region of the Gadarenes, two demon-
possessed men coming from the tombs met him'** (8:28).[7]
Jesus is now in the mainly Gentile country of the Decapolis;
only here would he find pigs being kept. This particularly painful
example of the devil's rule is selected to illustrate the true

extent of Christ's power: **'They were so violent that no one could pass that way.'** Jesus continues his triumphal progress, demonstrating his kingly authority by driving out the demons. Satan is being dispossessed of his kingdom; the strong man armed can no longer keep his possessions safe (12:29; Luke 11:21-22). Even the most extreme case of his evil dominion cannot stand against the King. The prince and god of this world is being shown that the time of his defeat has arrived. Although this extension into the heathen world is only temporary — Jesus returns to Jewish territory in 9:1 — we know that after the resurrection this progress will be resumed. Paul was sent to the Gentiles, 'to open their eyes and turn them from darkness to light, and from the power of Satan to God' (Acts 26:18).

So we need not fear Satan; the Son of God has come to destroy the devil's work (1 John 3:8). God 'has rescued us from the dominion of darkness and brought us into the kingdom of the Son he loves' (Col. 1:13). Christ's exorcisms were signs that the kingdom had come and that from then on the devil was a defeated enemy. Today it is popular to teach Christians to fear curses and witches' covens, to tremble because unbelievers 'pray' against Christian marriage. This passage assures us that because of Christ's victory, he has all authority in heaven and on earth and we need not fear the enemy and his servants. Where Christ reigns, in the hearts of his redeemed people, Satan has no power, demons cannot take possession, contrary to much current teaching. Christ's authority spreads and his kingdom comes not by exorcisms, but by the preaching of the gospel.

The demon-possessed men here manifest the three marks of the real thing, which are usually ignored in the modern obsession with exorcism as the panacea for all ills: supernatural power and knowledge, distinct personality and opposition to the truth and its messengers. So they shout, **'What do you want with us, Son of God?'** Their next words show that this event foreshadows the final coming of the kingdom and also explain the destruction of the pigs, which some find objectionable. They ask Jesus, **'Have you come here to torture us before the appointed time?'** There is an 'appointed time', and they know it: the time of the Last Judgement. Then the devil and his angels will be finally consigned to the lake of fire (25:41; Rev. 20:10). They will not be 'stoking the fires of hell', as in popular mythology, but being punished in them. So they acknowledge that Jesus, the Son of God, has 'come here', i.e. to earth, before the showdown, to defeat their master and introduce the kingdom that will ultimately end his reign.

Here, then, we have another aspect of the 'not yet', which we have seen applied to bodily healing and the restoration of creation. Until that day dawns the devil is permitted to continue with his evil and destructive ways, within limits. This is why the demons' request, **'If you drive us out, send us into the herd of pigs'**, was granted. So **'The whole herd rushed down the steep bank into the lake and died.'** The fact that this permission ruined the livelihood of the pigs' owners is simply 'part of larger questions as to why human beings are possessed or why disease, misfortune, or calamity overtake us',[8] the whole problem of the existence of evil. This is a fallen world and will continue to be such until 'the appointed time'. Incidentally, we may note that the incident reveals the heart-opposition of the whole community to Jesus. When the swine-herds reported what had happened, **'Then the whole town went out to meet Jesus. And when they saw him, they pleaded with him to leave their region.'** Pigs and peace were more important than the deliverance of the possessed men. This is the reaction of the world, both Jews and Gentiles, to the authority of Jesus Christ. It must not be our attitude. There is a battle to be fought, a war to be won. Sinners will not be saved without troubles and difficulties; opposition will always be aroused as men value their own peace, prosperity and comfort more than the kingdom of Christ, even though it means their eternal loss.

We are generally like the disciples, weak and fearful, but when our faith grows strong as we see the revelation of his authority, then we can go on the attack. The work of the kingdom is his work; the authority of the kingdom is expressed in the preached word. We must see the defeat of Satan as a reality, which frees us to work for the extension of the kingdom by the preaching of the gospel. Let us not be afraid but bold, confident that Christ has all necessary authority to defeat the devil, free his possessions and bring salvation to the whole world, both Jews and Gentiles. As Jesus was able to rescue this sad and desperate man, so we need not be afraid to present Christ to the worst sinners. We may be confident that he is able, as well as willing, to save all who come to him. While we remember that this is only the beginning, the end will surely come. That should give us the hope and confidence to persevere, even in the midst of discouragements, continuing sorrows and trials, knowing that 'the appointed time' will come.

14.
Authority and faith

Please read Matthew 9:2-34

The great temptation we must resist is to treat Jesus as just a healer and teacher, instead of a Saviour, to treat the kingdom as being just about healing and morality. The twin elements that prevent this serious misconception are sin and faith, which must always be at the heart of our message. This chapter contains several further accounts of Jesus exercising his authority to heal, which place great stress on the faith of those involved (9:2,22,28). Alongside these are other encounters, which introduce and elaborate the subject of sin and its relationship to illness that was raised in 8:17. The first miracle unites these two elements in such a way as to make clear which issue is the basic and more important one. It is vital to take these various incidents together, to provide the necessary balance. Otherwise we might completely misunderstand the nature of kingdom work.

Authority to forgive sins (9:2-8)

Jesus returned to the Jewish side of the lake and 'came to his own town' (9:1). Here he might expect to be understood and accepted, but that is far from being the case. Here he is accused of blasphemy and, before the chapter ends, of being in league with the devil. When the paralytic, or paralysed man, is brought to him, Jesus deliberately draws attention to his sins: **'Take heart, son; your sins are forgiven.'** At the very least this tells us that the illness and the sins are connected, whether indirectly, as in 8:17, or possibly quite directly. A sense of his sin would account for the man's need to 'take heart' and explain why Jesus chooses this occasion to make the point about sin. It may also be linked with **'their faith'**, presumably that of the man as well as of his friends. Whatever the truth about this, one fact is clear: sin is more important than bodily health. The forgiveness of sins is our real need and only Jesus can satisfy it. If we believe this is true, then we must not only come to Jesus ourselves for forgiveness, but bring our friends to him, whether by personal witness or by praying for them.

The response of **'the teachers of the law'** is that **'This fellow is blaspheming!'** — presumably by claiming to do what only God can do. This shows that they understood him to be saying, not that the man's sins had been forgiven at some earlier time, but that he, Jesus, was forgiving them there and then. Jesus, **'knowing their thoughts'**, then challenged them with a question: **'Which is easier: to say, "Your sins are forgiven," or to say, "Get up and walk"?'** Opinion is divided as to which is in fact easier. Most agree that forgiving sins is easier to *say*, as distinct from do. However, his opponents were working on the premise that forgiving is harder since only God can *do* it. Jesus seems to combine both ideas! His **'authority on earth to forgive sins'** needs proving and is, therefore, the more difficult matter. But it can be proved by the visible success of his command: **'Get up, take your mat and go home.'** Jesus, as so often, may have been trying to make them think about the real issues involved. In the light of this, we should probably not deduce from his forgiving that he is here claiming to be God, although that may be implied, especially for Matthew's readers. Rather, this is related to his

Messianic authority, 'on earth', as the crowd's response would indicate: **'And they praised God, who had given such authority to men.'** The men's faith which believed he could heal disease must be extended to include forgiveness, since this is the one who both 'took up our infirmities and carried our diseases' and also 'was pierced for our transgressions' and 'crushed for our iniquities' (8:17; Isa. 53:4,5).

Matthew and his friends (9:9-13)

Matthew, otherwise known as Levi, was a tax collector, probably 'concerned with tolls on goods crossing the frontier ... a customs official in the service of Herod Antipas rather than a collector of direct taxes'.[1] However, both occupations were despised on account of the links with unclean foreigners and of their almost inevitable corruption. Jesus was, of course, well known by now in Capernaum, so Matthew probably knew him already. In response to the Lord's call, **'Matthew got up and followed him'** (9:9).He does not record the call of any other member of the Twelve, but it may be that, rather than drawing attention to himself, Matthew is directing our thoughts to the dinner that follows, with its important lessons about sin and Christ's true mission.

Matthew appears to be celebrating his call to be a disciple and wanting to introduce his friends to his Lord. These friends are **'tax-collectors and "sinners"'**, people like himself, disreputable outcasts, prostitutes and others, who did not conform to the Pharisees' requirements for ritual purity. Predictably, therefore, the Pharisees object. Their words to the disciples, not to Jesus himself, are more a challenge than a question: **'Why does your teacher eat with tax collectors and "sinners"?'** (9:11). What they regard as a disqualification for a religious teacher, Jesus regards as a prerequisite, as he goes on to explain: **'It is not the healthy who need a doctor, but the sick.'** The right place for a healer is where people need to be healed, a hospital. The right place for one who forgives sins is with sinners. Jesus was not afraid to be called 'the friend of sinners', even though it was meant critically (11:19). If not before, we should see here the confirmation that his healings are a picture of salvation, the healing of souls.

At this point we must take care not to be misunderstood. It is common in many church circles today to regard sin as an illness in another and literal sense. Sins are not seen as wicked, a transgression of God's law, but as a weakness, something that men cannot help, a natural failing that needs help. We do not need salvation, but understanding. The right 'treatment' is medicine or counselling, not the preaching of the gospel. While this sounds kind and merciful, it is in fact quite the opposite. To call sin an illness removes responsibility and takes away hope. While doctors, including psychiatrists, have their proper place and must not be neglected, when it comes to sin they are helpless. If sin is a disease, then nothing can be done about it. If it is an offence against God, then grace, love and mercy enter the picture and there is a genuine 'cure'. Until we confess our sin and guilt, our real need, we are left on our own without help.

If the Pharisees had such a low opinion of these tax collectors and 'sinners', why did they not do something about them? Why not help, instead of merely condemning? Jesus quotes from Hosea 6:6: **'I desire mercy, not sacrifice'**, and tells them, since they are rabbis and scholars, to **'go and learn what this means'** (9:13). Instead of trying to improve these people, they simply avoid them, for fear of contamination. Such concern for ritual holiness, instead of real holiness, is not what God desires. How easy it is to be so appalled by the state of sinners that we turn away from them in their need! Matthew is an example to us. Although he is now a disciple of the holy teacher,

Jesus, he has not rejected his friends. Instead, he invites them to meet Jesus. He keeps his links with them, not because he hankers after his old lifestyle, but because he wants them to be saved too. Of course, this may be dangerous. We must be careful about where we go and with whom we mix. We must not be overconfident, and must use all the safeguards that are available to us, but fear of the opinions of the self-righteous must not keep us from showing mercy.

Jesus confirms this with one of his most glorious statements: **'For I have not come to call the righteous, but sinners.'** 'Come' refers to his Messianic role, his coming into the world as Saviour. He has come from the courts of glory to live in a world of outcasts and sinners in order to save them. 'Call' here refers not to effectual calling, as in Paul's usage, but to his invitation to follow himself and to share in the Messianic banquet. Although the best texts do not include the words 'to repentance', we may assume, from earlier references, that this is implied. Are there 'righteous' ones who are rejected by Christ? The meaning is that those who, like the Pharisees, see themselves as righteous and in no need of salvation do not qualify for an invitation. They think the Messiah will come to reward them for their faithfulness and righteous behaviour (and their sacrifices!), but he asserts that he has come to save those who need saving and to call those who acknowledge that need. It is not so much a policy as a practical fact; those who see no need will not come, so why bother to invite them?

New for old (9:14-17)

Matthew appears to be using questioning by Christ's opponents as a vehicle for making clear the nature of his kingdom authority. The scribes, or 'teachers of the law' (9:3), and Pharisees (9:11) were distinctly hostile, but now he has to face some of **'John's disciples'** (9:14). They ask him, **'How is it that we and the Pharisees fast, but your disciples do not fast?'** Just as the earlier critics had attacked him through his disciples (9:11), so John the Baptist's followers criticize his teaching through the disciples' practice. It may be that this was actually a day of fasting for the two groups and that the dinner recorded in verse 10 therefore offended them deeply. A more important question is why this discussion appears in this section of the Gospel. What is the relation of fasting to the coming of the kingdom?

Jesus uses this approach to speak of himself and his ministry and, especially, to illustrate the significant differences that his coming makes. He refers to himself as **'the bridegroom'** (9:15). The background to this includes not only John's reference to him as the bridegroom and to himself as the friend who rejoices to hear his voice, which would be familiar to his disciples (John 3:29), but also Old Testament ideas of God as the Husband of his people and the Messianic banquet as a wedding-feast. Jesus' disciples are the guests at the wedding, so **'How can the guests of the bridegroom mourn while he is with them?'** John's ministry of preparation was a time of mourning over the sins and sorrows of Israel (3:7-12). Now that Jesus has been manifested and the kingdom is present, the time of mourning is past; joy has come. Jesus quoted Isaiah 61:1-2 in the synagogue at Nazareth, with the comment, 'Today this scripture is fulfilled in your hearing' (Luke 4:17-21). The same chapter of Isaiah's prophecy continues by asserting that the purpose of his coming is

> ... to comfort all who mourn,
>   and provide for those who grieve in Zion—
> to bestow on them a crown of beauty
>   instead of ashes,
> the oil of gladness

> instead of mourning,
>   and a garment of praise
>   instead of a spirit of despair
>
>   (Isa. 61:2-3).

Because he has come to save and call sinners, a time of rejoicing has arrived.

Fasting was a mark of mourning and sorrow. Christ has come to:

> ... destroy
>   the shroud that enfolds all peoples,
>   the sheet that covers all nations;
>   he will swallow up death for ever.
> The Sovereign LORD will wipe away the tears
>   from all faces
>
>   (Isa. 25:7).

Instead:

> ... the LORD Almighty will prepare
>   a feast of rich food for all peoples,
> a banquet of aged wine—
>   the best of meats and the finest of wines
>
>   (Isa. 25:6).

In the light of this there must be joy and feasting, not mourning and fasting. True, **'The time will come when the bridegroom will be taken from them; then they will fast.'** This must refer to the period of Christ's death and resting in the tomb, which would end with the resurrection. Jesus instructs his disciples further about this in his farewell discourse: 'I tell you the truth, you will weep and mourn while the world rejoices. You will grieve, but your grief will turn to joy. A woman giving birth to a child has pain because her time has come; but when her baby is born she forgets the anguish because of her joy that a child is born into the world. So with you: Now is your time of grief, but I will see you again and you will rejoice' (John 16:20-22). Some want to defend regular fasting by Christians on the grounds that Christ's departure to heaven is meant here, but that is clearly not the case. 'No one will take away your joy'! In Acts fasting is mentioned occasionally (Acts 13:2; 14:23), when there was a special cause for humbling before God, because a solemn decision had to be made. In general, however, the New Covenant is an administration of joy, not sorrow. It is a false piety that demands regular fasting, beyond even Old Testament requirements, such as is set forth by various teachers and books on so-called spiritual disciplines. In fact these have more in common with Roman Catholicism than the Puritanism they claim. This is quite contrary to Christ's teaching here and indeed a blatant denial of the next few verses, with their stress on newness.[2]

Christ gives two illustrations of what he means. Each refers to the incompatibility of new and old, to the contrast between his teaching and that of the Pharisees and John's disciples, but they deal with slightly different aspects of the matter. First Jesus says, **'No one sews a patch of unshrunk cloth on an old garment, for the patch will** [shrink and so] **pull away from the garment, making the tear worse'** (9:16). What is needed is not a patch on an old religion, but the adoption of a new one. This is not a disparaging reference to the Old Testament, or even to John the Baptist; they are both preparatory, not contradictory, in relation to the new order. It is the legalistic, formalistic religion popular in those days that constitutes the old garment. It is not enough to add joy to legalism; they must first come to trust him and enter his kingdom, not just add a few new elements. That is what Nicodemus seems to have been trying to do when he came to Jesus by night. He knew his old religion was inadequate, so wanted to add something more from Christ's teaching. This is the spirit of the young man in Matthew 19:20-21: 'I know about all that; what else can I add on to quench my dissatisfied longings?' Similarly this is the response of some formal, nominal Christians today, who find that evangelicals have a joy that they lack. They want to add on something to change matters: new hymns, new enthusiasm and fervour, fellowship, Bible study or prayer meetings, but without repenting and being converted. They do not want to hear about the new birth. There is nothing wrong, they think, with what they have; it just needs supplementing, patching up! If you lack joy, do not try to work it up. Go to the source, to Jesus Christ, and trust him as your Saviour and King. The gospel gives new life, not merely a new look.

The other picture is slightly different: **'Neither do men pour new wine into old wineskins. If they do, the skins will burst, the wine will run out and the wineskins will be ruined. No, they pour new wine into new wineskins, and both are preserved'** (9:17). Instead of shrinking, we are now dealing with stretching. Old wineskins have stretched already as much as they can; they cannot stretch further to accommodate the new, still-fermenting wine. New wineskins can adapt to the wine that has been poured into them. In other words, this is a positive matter. The disciples, born again of the Spirit, cannot be confined in Pharisaic, or even Old Testament forms. Their inward change demands and creates new modes of expression —new-covenant forms. This is not a case of 'Anything goes'. We do not do just as we like. The shape of the wineskins will be moulded from within by the wine; the forms will be dictated by the new life. There will be an expansion in terms of Christ. It is not just that fasting is replaced by joy, although that is important. Preparation is replaced by fulfilment, Jewish exclusiveness by universal mission, Levitical priesthood by the ministry of the body of Christ, national identity by a worldwide society of believers.

We can see the danger of bursting wineskins in the New Testament. When it was thought that believing Gentiles had to become Jews, be circumcised and keep the law, trouble brewed. It was only when the new wineskin of baptism and acceptance through the testimony of the indwelling Spirit took over, that peace was restored (Acts 11:15-18). The result was not that both the old and the new wineskins survived, as some have suggested, but that both new wine and new wineskins were preserved. Today we must beware of the twin dangers: on the one hand of resisting change which arises from the inward enjoyment of New Covenant blessings, and on the other of believing that new is always good (or even best) and simply doing what is right in our own eyes. God is indeed doing a new thing in our days, but that has been true ever since Pentecost; it is not an invention of the twentieth century, as some seem to believe.

A dead girl and a sick woman (9:18-26)

The remaining events in this section concentrate on the meaning and means of faith. Christ encourages our faith by showing his authority and power to heal a variety of afflictions, starting with the greatest of all, death itself. The first necessity for faith in Christ is a sense of need — a need that we cannot deal with ourselves, but believe that Christ can. The ruler says nothing about faith, but his words are full of it: **'My daughter has just died. But come and put your hand on her, and she will live.'** Such confidence in the power of Christ lies at the heart of faith. We must believe he can save us. The woman who had been **'subject to bleeding for twelve years'** is in the same position. Obviously she has proved over this time that no one else can meet her need; she, too, has confidence that Christ can. She does not require him to touch her; it will be enough, she believes, if she can **'only touch his cloak'**.

Matthew omits much that the other Gospel-writers include. He concentrates on his main thesis: Jesus has the authority and power to heal, and faith is the key to benefiting from this. So Jesus encourages the woman: **'Take heart, daughter ... your faith has healed you.'** We may condemn her action as superstition, but Jesus calls it faith. God honours her faith, as he did that of those who arranged for Peter's shadow to fall on them as he passed by (Acts 5:15-16). We must remember, of course, that our Lord's words do not mean that the power lay in the faith; that was solely Christ's. The words, here as elsewhere, tell us that faith is the means by which Christ's power is brought to bear on our need. It is the same here as in justification: by grace, through faith.

There is more to faith than just 'believing that ...'; we have to trust *him*, not merely believe certain truths about him. We have to come to Jesus and apply to him for what we need, as the ruler did. There has to be personal contact with Christ, as illustrated perfectly by the woman touching the edge of his cloak. In each case faith was rewarded — the woman's immediately: **'And the woman was healed from that moment'** (9:22). The other request was only answered after **'Jesus entered the ruler's house'**. The formal and artificial mourning by the professional **'flute-players and the noisy crowd'** is set against Christ's confident assertion that **'The girl is not dead, but asleep.'** Doubters have taken this to mean that she was only in a coma, but the context, as well as Luke's account, makes clear that this is an actual raising of the dead (see 11:5).

Two blind men and a demoniac (9:27-34)

Matthew's concern is still with the nature of faith, and the giving of sight to these two blind men provides a further illustration of this, as well as once again demonstrating his power to heal, and therefore save. They **'followed him, calling out, "Have mercy on us, Son of David!"'**, showing that true faith perseveres until it gains an answer. Jesus checks their faith. **'Do you believe that I am able to do this?'** he asks. His words, **'According to your faith will it be done to you,'** confirm what we have already seen about faith as the means, not the power. All the elements of faith are seen again here: a sense of need, knowledge of, and faith in, his power to heal, plus an actual coming and asking. Salvation from sin comes in just the same way. We must beware of the common assertion that all we need is to believe that Jesus died for us. The New Testament never puts the issue like that. There must be a direct encounter with Christ, the Lord, a personal and living trust in Jesus, the Saviour, himself.

The reason behind our Lord's stern warning to him to say nothing to anyone, which he ignores, is seen in the reactions to his ministry that Matthew records immediately afterwards. **'While they were going out, a man who was demon-possessed and could not talk was brought to Jesus.'** Jesus, as usual, drives out the evil spirit and the crowd is **'amazed'**. **'Nothing like this has ever been seen in Israel,'** they say (9:33). This sort of attention could only hinder his real work. Thus, the Pharisees respond by saying, **'It is by the prince of demons that he drives out demons.'** This foolish criticism will be dealt with later, but Matthew introduces it here to show that the work of the kingdom and the authority of Christ are never without opposition. We need to realize that sensationalism is the enemy of faith and that uncritical acclaim only produces opposition. As we turn to Christ's training of his disciples to continue his work of building the kingdom and spreading the gospel, we must bear this in mind. The kingdom is about salvation from sin. That salvation is received only by faith, but the Saviour King is eminently worthy of our trust and devotion. ✤

15.
Workers in the harvest field

Please read Matthew 9:35 – 10:25

With chapter 10 we come to the lengthy discourse that concludes the section on the work of the kingdom. This work requires workers to carry it out, and the discourse contains Christ's instructions to those who preach the gospel: first his apostles and then those who continue the work throughout the period leading up to his return. In other words, what we have here are the marching orders of the church. While it is necessary to discern those aspects which applied only to the first generation of witnesses, it is equally important to take seriously those principles that apply to us today. First, however, we must set these instructions in their context.

The chapter divisions in the Bible, although very useful for reference purposes, are not always helpful in other ways. In the present instance, the last four verses of chapter 9 lead straight into chapter 10, provide the context for what follows and must not be kept separate. The calling of the Twelve and their appointment as apostles is, at least in part, a fulfilment of the instruction to **'Ask the Lord of the harvest, therefore, to send out workers into his harvest field.'** The field of the Lord of the harvest, God himself, cannot be limited to Israel, and the instructions that follow, therefore, must apply not just to the apostles, but to all who, after them, work for the kingdom in all parts of the world.

Lost sheep and a plentiful harvest (9:35-38)

The whole of this brief summary description of Christ's ministry sets the tone for what follows. The priority in Christ's ministry was not **'healing every disease and sickness'**, but **'teaching in their synagogues, preaching the good news of the
kingdom'**, because of the state of the people. The description
of **'the crowds'** as **'harassed and helpless'** refers to their
spiritual condition; they are **'like sheep without a shepherd'**,
lacking true leaders (Num. 27:17-23), teachers to instruct them
in the way of salvation. The Jewish leaders and teachers, the
Pharisees and scribes, are thus shown up for what they are:
learned in tradition but ignorant of the way of salvation revealed in the Scriptures; popular with the people but useless
in shepherding them. The picture given by the prophet is clearly
applicable: 'Woe to the shepherds of Israel who only take care
of themselves! Should not shepherds take care of the flock?
You eat the curds, clothe yourselves with the wool and slaughter the choice animals, but you do not take care of the flock.
You have not strengthened the weak or healed the sick or
bound up the injured. You have not brought back the strays or
searched for the lost. You have ruled them harshly and bru-
tally. So they were scattered because there was no shepherd,
and when they were scattered they became food for all the
wild animals. My sheep wandered over all the mountains and
on every high hill. They were scattered over the whole earth,
and no one searched or looked for them' (Ezek. 34:2-6).

The same chapter says that these sheep are God's flock and
he promises, 'I will place over them one shepherd, my servant
David, and he will tend them; he will tend them and be their
shepherd' (v. 23). This one shepherd is clearly the great Son
of David (see 9:27), the Lord Jesus, the great Shepherd of the
sheep. Much of what he says about his work of seeking and
saving what was lost (Luke 19:10) fits well here. It may even

be that the reference to their being scattered 'over the whole earth' points to his and the apostles' worldwide mission in the later verses of chapter 10. When Jesus **'saw the crowds, he had compassion on them'**. This is the driving force behind his own mission and his instructions to the disciples to pray for more workers, so that the sheep may be shepherded, cared for and saved.

All this is true today. **'The harvest is plentiful but the workers are few.'** There are multitudes waiting to be reaped into the kingdom — whether they are willing is another question — but few ready and able to take the gospel to them, whether at home or abroad. It is as true today as it was in the days of the poet, John Milton, that 'The hungry sheep look up and are not fed.'[1] All around we see men and women, young and old, who are harassed and helpless, bruised and battered by life, lost and alone in the world, resorting to pleasures, or drugs, or anything else that they think will make life more tolerable or death more acceptable. Sometimes they are church-goers, or those who at least look expectantly to the church for help. And all the time those who should be shepherds are feeding them nonsense, false ideas that either lead them astray or tell them they need not worry about eternity, but nothing to bring them to God and his gift of eternal life. Those who are not called to preach, like the majority of the disciples mentioned here, should nevertheless have compassion on the lost millions and show it by pleading for more messengers to go with the gospel. It is not sufficient merely to deplore the lack of new ministers and missionaries coming forward. We must pray. 'Our Father in heaven' is the Lord of the harvest and 'Hallowed be your name, your kingdom come, your will be done on earth as it is in heaven,' includes this urgent request. Let our prayer meetings take note.

The mission of the apostles (10:1-15)

From the many less committed men who followed him (9:37), Jesus **'called his twelve disciples to him'** to be **'the twelve apostles'** (10:1,2). **'First'** marks out **'Simon (who is called Peter)'** for a special, though not papal, role, while the next three constitute the inner circle with him. The identity of **'Thaddaeus'** is uncertain, but he is probably the same as Judas (brother) of James in Luke and John, while **'Bartholomew'** may be the Nathanael of John 1:45-51. The other **'Simon, the Zealot'**, is a Cananaean[2] (not a Canaanite), one who would possibly have belonged to the later nationalist political party. His presence alongside **'Matthew'**, the government employee, shows the breadth and variety of Jesus' choice. In a class of his own is **'Judas Iscariot, who betrayed him'**.

Jesus **'gave them authority to drive out evil spirits and to heal every disease and sickness'**. There is no suggestion that Judas was an exception to this, which fits with the assumption (7:22) that even unbelievers could work miracles. Gifts are not the same as graces, as Hebrews 6:4-6 may also indicate. Although this seems to be a provisional appointment, including Judas, it was nevertheless a stage in their preparation for continuing the work of the kingdom and becoming the foundation of the church (Eph. 2:20). The appointment of twelve is obviously related to the twelve tribes of Israel (see Rev. 21:12-13) and the renewal of the covenant people of God (19:28). Apostles, as well as being simply 'sent ones' (or missionaries), are elsewhere seen as representatives with full authority; they have delegated authority from Christ to work in his kingdom.

The **'instructions'** with which Jesus sent them out reflect the provisional stage of the coming of the kingdom. They are not to **'go among the Gentiles or enter any town of the Samaritans. Go rather to the lost sheep of Israel'** (10:5-6).

This not only links with 9:36, but also with Christ's own ministry at this point. His excursions into Gentile territory are the exception, not the rule, as yet. The evangelization of the Gentiles must await his rejection by the Jews. This restriction sheds light too on some of the instructions, and especially the difficult verses 22-23. They were both in training for the future and helping Christ to fulfil his initial mission, to 'the Jew first', in the light of the judgement which John has already pronounced on the nation. Like John, they must announce, **'The kingdom of heaven is near,'** and confirm their message by performing signs, as Jesus did: **'Heal the sick, raise the dead, cleanse those who have leprosy, drive out demons.'**

The custom was for travelling teachers to be provided for by their hearers and also to receive money for their teaching. Jesus' instructions to his disciples reflect this. On the one hand, they are not to make a profit: **'Freely you have received, freely give.'** The disciples, who had received the message of grace, freely, must not charge for their teaching. On the other, they are not to take with them more than the minimum necessities of life. They may expect to be provided for by their hearers, **'for the worker is worth his keep'**. They must work according to the twin principles of grace and providence.[3] Paul later applies this to the Christian teacher (1 Tim. 5:18), using the form of wording recorded in Luke 10:7: 'The worker deserves his wages.' They must try to find suitable hospitality wherever they go and then stay there, not 'shopping around', looking for something better.

The customary greeting, 'Peace to this house', will be of real value, **'if the home is deserving'**, that is, if the inhabitants welcome the gospel message. If not, then the greeting will **'return to'** them. Greetings and benedictions, like curses, only remain on the appropriate people; they are not automatic. What applies to the home is true also of the town: **'If anyone will not welcome you or listen to your words, shake the**

dust off your feet when you leave.' This was standard practice for a Jew departing from Gentile land, leaving behind its dust and so distancing himself from the pollution and consequent judgement of the heathen community. This must not be overused; we must be patient with those who are willing to listen, even though they do not believe. However, when there is rejection and a contemptuous refusal to listen, we must follow this principle. Such people are rejecting Christ, see verse 40; hence the solemnity of the language: **'I tell you the truth, it will be more bearable for Sodom and Gomorrah on the day of judgement than for that town.'**

Persecution (10:16-23)

The possibility of such rejection means that the disciples must **'be as shrewd as snakes and as innocent as doves'** (10:16). The persecution described in the following verses implies that their mission will one day be extended to all nations. They will not only be handed **'over to local councils'** of the Jews, and flogged **'in their synagogues'**, but will also **'be brought before governors and kings as witnesses to them and to the** [other] **Gentiles'**. The accompanying promise of the aid of the Holy Spirit is probably meant for all in this situation, not just the apostles. It does not forbid forethought, only anxiety. Witnessing grace, like dying grace, is given when it is needed and not before. (This is not, as sometimes thought, a promise for lazy preachers!) Many Christians down the centuries, from Stephen onward, have relied on this promise and found it to be true. In the light of the connection between the Father's care and not being anxious in chapter 6, the description of the Holy Spirit as **'the Spirit of your Father speaking through you'** is significant. They go as messengers of Christ, but that does not remove their relationship to their heavenly Father.

So, **'Do not worry about what to say or how to say it'** (10:19).

Such persecution will not only be at the hands of strangers. Members of their own families will also be against them: **'Brother will betray brother to death, and a father his child; children will rebel against their parents and have them put to death.'** More is said later in the chapter on this subject. **'All men'**, without distinction of race, will be against them. Wherever the gospel spreads, its messengers will encounter opposition and hatred: 'Everyone who wants to live a godly life in Christ Jesus will be persecuted', especially Christ's messengers (2 Tim. 3:12). As Jesus spoke of persecution 'because of me' (5:11), so here the persecution arises **'on my account'** (10:18) and **'because of me'** (10:22). This is both a caution and a comfort. We must take care that we do not arouse persecution and hatred on our own account, as evil-doers or busybodies (2 Thess. 3:11), but as those who speak and live for Christ (1 Peter 4:15). Peter goes on to confirm the encouragement given in the beatitude: 'If you suffer as a Christian, do not be ashamed, but praise God that you bear that name.'

All these instructions convey a sense of urgency and the necessity for perseverance. **'He who stands firm'** (10:22), is the one who endures or, better, perseveres. This gives the more positive idea, not only of not giving in, but of going on with the ministry of the gospel, preaching Christ and his kingdom, as he is sending them to do. **'The end'** in other contexts would mean the Last Day or, perhaps, the end of one's life. Here it may refer to the end of the present era, the end of the Jewish nation as such at the destruction of Jerusalem (see ch. 24). At this point we shall do best to take it more generally: to the end of the persecution, not giving up on their mission part way. This is confirmed by the reference to **'going through the cities of Israel'** (10:23). The task he gave them earlier was to preach to 'the lost sheep of Israel'; this is still the topic. There is no

way that these verses can legitimately be applied to the Second Coming. That will only come after the gospel has been
preached to the whole world.

This helps us to understand the controversial words, **'before the Son of Man comes'**. Some want to interpret this of
the *parousia*, the Second Coming, so that they can assert that
Jesus was mistaken about his return. Others invent a rendez-
vous of Jesus with his disciples during their travels through
Israel, like a college tutor checking up on his students. However, the phrase 'the coming of the Son of Man', based on
Daniel 7, occurs several times in the New Testament. Not all
of these instances refer to his final return. The expression may
also describe his resurrection, or his coming by the Holy Spirit
at Pentecost, or the powerful advance of his kingdom as described in Acts. In the light of John's warning of wrath (3:7)
and the message of the disciples it may be best to refer this to
Christ's coming in judgement at the destruction of Jerusalem.
That would end the period of probation during which they
could respond to the apostles' preaching of repentance, which
the present mission anticipates.[4]

The servants' calling (10:24-25)

The disciples cannot expect to be exempt from persecution
when he, the Son of Man, has to endure it. Jesus tells them,
and us, that **'A student is not above his teacher, nor a servant above his master. It is enough for the student to be
like his teacher, and the servant like his master'** (10:24).
All Christians must expect persecution. Jesus brings this out
by referring to his sufferings: **'If the head of the house has
been called Beelzebub, how much more the members of
his household!'** 'Beelzebub', or perhaps better Beelzeboul,
means something like 'head of the household'. 'Thus the real

head of the house, Jesus, who heads the household of God, is being wilfully confused with the head of the house of demons.'[5] What right have the servants to be immune to persecution if the master has had to suffer it? It can be a great consolation to the persecuted Christian that his Lord has undergone the same treatment. It is also an incentive to respond to it in the same meek way (1 Peter 2:21-23).

We need not blame ourselves, or regard ourselves as failures, but see should it as a calling and an honour. As the apostle Paul tells his young assistant, 'Everyone who wants to live a godly life in Christ Jesus will be persecuted' (2 Tim. 3:12). The encouragement is that this is a privilege, because we are following our persecuted Master. The idea of privilege is contained in the word **'enough'**. When we might be tempted to complain of ill-treatment, this idea of privilege should be 'enough' to convince us that we should not be troubled about what is happening to us. In Acts 5: 41 we read that 'The apostles left the Sanhedrin, rejoicing because they had been counted worthy of suffering disgrace for the Name.' Similarly, Paul writes to the Philippians assuring them, 'It has been granted to you on behalf of Christ not only to believe on him, but also to suffer for him' (Phil. 1:29). The idea of privilege and honour is very important for the Christian. He should not feel hard done by when he is persecuted. His Master was persecuted; so he, too, will be persecuted. It is an honour to be put in the same class as Jesus, to be treated as he was treated.

The hymn-writer John Newton warns that Christians must expect to suffer for their faith:

Why should I complain
Of want or distress,
Temptation or pain?
He told me no less;
The heirs of salvation,

I know from his Word,
Through much tribulation
Must follow their Lord.[6]

Modern Christians are not used to this idea, especially in the
West. Our forefathers knew what it was to suffer real persecution. Several of Charles Wesley's hymns record this. As they
meet on the Lord's Day, the congregation expresses its gratitude to God that he has kept them safe during another week:

All are not lost or wandered back;
All have not left thy church and thee;
There are who suffer for thy sake,
Enjoy thy glorious infamy,
Esteem the scandal of the Cross,
And only seek divine applause.

Again he writes:

What troubles have we seen,
What conflicts have we passed,
Fightings without, and fears within,
Since we assembled last![7]

The danger today is that very few enquirers are warned of
this; too many make a profession of faith without knowing
what lies ahead. Some, perhaps many, are like the people pictured in the parable of the sower, who receive the message
with joy, but give up as soon as persecution threatens (Matt.
13:20-21). We must follow our Lord's example in this also, by
making sure that enquirers and new believers know what to
expect. Jesus, however, also gives them help so that they are
not afraid of being persecuted. We must follow him in this
too.

16.
Fear and faithfulness

Please read Matthew 10:26-42

It is a common failing with Christians, as indeed with people in general, to swing from one extreme to the other. Either we do not mention persecution and taking up our cross at all, or we major on this and leave Christians without help, fearing the future, trembling in expectation of sufferings that they will not be able to cope with. Jesus falls into neither trap. He continues with the theme of persecution, but having given solemn warnings, he now moves on to motivation and encouragement. He explains how an awareness of the disciple's privilege on the one hand, and of God's greatness, especially his fatherhood, on the other, helps in this situation. Referring to their persecutors, he says, **'So do not be afraid of them'** (10:26). If we do not feel afraid, we shall continue in our witness and testimony, which is the real subject of this chapter of the Gospel, as Jesus sends his disciples out on their mission to preach the gospel to the lost sheep of Israel. We should never regard warnings about persecution as being given in a vacuum. The context is always a matter of the devil trying to prevent the message of the gospel from spreading. He will do everything he can to hinder preachers of the gospel from making known the good news of salvation. Jesus warns and encourages, and so motivates. They must not be afraid so that they will continue to do the work of his kingdom.

So he also reminds them that they have a duty to continue with their witness. Their task is to make plain to the world publicly what he has taught them privately. What has been **'concealed'** will **'be disclosed'**; what has been **'hidden'** will then be **'made known'**. What he has told them **'in the dark'**, they will **'speak in the daylight'** and what has been **'whispered'** in their ear they must **'proclaim from the roofs'**. There is a clear contrast between the position at this time and their future ministry, to which these verses refer. The time of restricted knowledge and secrecy (9:30) will have gone. Although this has sometimes been exaggerated, in terms of the so-called 'Messianic secret', there was a clear change, first after Caesarea Philippi and then after Pentecost.

The disciples' fear (10:26-28)

The disciples need help if they are to fulfil this ministry and Jesus provides it. Just as a greater affection can drive out a lesser one, so a greater fear overcomes a lesser one. Fear of man must be countered by the fear of God. Jesus exhorts his disciples not to **'be afraid of those who kill the body but cannot kill the soul. Rather, be afraid of the One who can destroy both soul and body in hell.'** The fear of the Lord is a great necessity when it comes to preaching the gospel properly (see 2 Cor. 5:11), as well as in general Christian living (see Acts 9:31). The fear of the Lord is not only awe and reverence. Verse 28 makes it very clear that there is an element of being afraid, at least when sin is involved. This does not mean that the Christian goes through his daily life feeling scared of God, who is his heavenly Father, but that godly fear serves to counteract the fear of an enemy.

This **'One'** is not, of course, the devil, but God. Moreover, **'destroy'** cannot mean annihilate here, as some assert. Just as killing the body does not mean that it is annihilated, but decays

and perishes in the grave, so destroying body and soul does
not mean that they are annihilated, but that they perish in hell.
The reference is to eternal punishment. (This passage also
makes clear, incidentally, the existence of the soul as a separate entity that survives death. Therefore, while it is true that
some preachers refer to 'our immortal souls' in such a way as
to undervalue the significance of the body and its future resurrection, and also that the Bible can use 'soul' for the whole
person — e.g. Gen. 2:7, AV ;1 Peter 3:20, AV — it is quite
incorrect to deny the doctrine of the immortality of the soul as
being mere Greek philosophy.)

This is not a reign of terror, intended to scare Christians
into obedience, as some allege. Jesus is well aware of the situations in which his disciples often find themselves, so he provides them with a weapon to use against Satan and ammunition against the fear of persecution. When the world threatens
us with the dire consequences of faithfulness to Christ, we
should remember that the consequences of disloyalty are far
worse. This is similar to the use of rewards in the New Testament. When persecutors offer us rewards for desertion, we
need to remember that the alternative is a far greater reward
from God. We do not serve out of mere terror or for mere
reward, but when the world's ideas would undermine our faith,
it is a help to have the alternative spelt out, so that we may
judge everything rightly, instead of being over-influenced by
the world's arguments. We can set one against the other. The
fear of the Lord counterbalances and outweighs the fear of
man and of the devil. We must learn to use this weapon wisely.

It is rightly said, 'Fear of man will prove to be a snare, but
whoever trusts in the LORD is kept safe' (Prov. 29:25). Also
the prophet tells us:

Whom have you so dreaded and feared
    that you have been false to me,
and have neither remembered me

nor pondered this in your hearts?
Is it not because I have long been silent
    that you do not fear me?

                                              (Isa. 57:11).

Verse 28 is not given merely to instruct us that the soul survives death, or about the fate of unbelievers in hell, although it does do that, but to encourage us and urge us to go on in our witness, no matter what the world may threaten. The words of Tate and Brady's paraphrase of Psalm 34 are still relevant today: 'Fear him, ye saints, and you will then have nothing else to fear.' The next two lines of the hymn — 'Make you his service your delight; your wants shall be his care' — lead on to the next section, where Jesus gives further encouragement, this time in terms of the Father's providential care.

The disciples' value (10:29-31)

As in chapter 6:28-31, Jesus argues from God's care over the less valuable parts of his creation. If God cares so much about the grass and the birds, then his disciples need not worry about themselves. The contrast between verse 29 and what has gone before is quite striking. It is one thing to refer to God as one able to destroy both body and soul and hell. It is quite another to speak of him as **'your Father'**. This is the other side of the coin and a very necessary one. Our relationship to our heavenly Father is vital to persevering amid persecution. In these days when self-esteem is stressed so much, we must be careful in speaking of value. Our value is not intrinsic to us, but graciously given by God. This is what Jesus refers to here when he asks, **'Are not two sparrows sold for a penny?'** and later on says, **'Don't be afraid; you are worth more than many sparrows.'** There is no cause here for pride, only for gratitude.

As a result of this we may be assured of the Father's providential care over us. Not one sparrow **'will fall to the ground apart from the will of your Father'**, he assures them. It is not just that the Father knows about the sparrow's fall, as is often said, but that the Father is in control of every matter concerning the sparrow. Every detail is in his hands, so that **'Even the very hairs of your head are all numbered'** (10:30). He does not say that all these hairs are safe from harm, that no Christian will ever go bald, but that they are numbered and therefore cared about. He is not promising safety in all circumstances for our bodies or our lives — sparrows do in fact fall to the ground — but that he watches over everything for our benefit. 'Precious in the sight of the LORD is the death of his saints' (Ps. 116:15).

There is no contradiction of this when the Christian falls ill, or dies, or is persecuted. The only contradiction would be if the Christian did not inherit eternal life. The apostle Paul had the assurance that 'The Lord will rescue me from every evil attack and will bring me safely to his heavenly kingdom' (2 Tim. 4:18), an assurance expressed in the context of expecting very soon to die: 'The time has come for my departure' (2 Tim. 4:6). The meaning, therefore, both there and here, is not at all that no harm will come to us in this life. The assurance is that the Lord will watch over us and protect us, as far as it is for our good and his glory, and will keep us safe to eternal life. Therefore we need not be afraid, for we are **'worth more than many sparrows'** (10:31).

The disciples' cross (10:32-39)

Verses 32 and 33 are linked with the previous verses. The disciple is assured that if he does not **'disown'** the Lord **'before men'** under the threat of persecution, then the Lord will never **'disown him before'** the **'Father in heaven'**. Though the disciple may have to suffer because of his faithfulness, he may be sure that the Saviour will not desert him: **'Whoever acknowledges me before men, I will also acknowledge him before my Father in heaven.'** Jesus is not saying that a true disciple can never fail, but that he has a responsibility to be faithful to his Master, and that those who are not faithful are not true disciples. He returns to the subject of persecution as a sort of parenthesis before verse 39. His mission was not to bring peace on earth. The effect of Christ's coming as Messiah is not **'peace, but a sword'**, separating believers from unbelievers. Peace there will be — he is the Prince of Peace — but not in the sense that wars will cease and tranquillity and peace will be established at this stage. That, like so much in Matthew's Gospel, awaits the final kingdom at his return.

Persecution does not come only from strangers. Their attitude to him will, in fulfilment of Micah 7:6:

> **... turn**
> **'a man against his father,**
>   **a daughter against her mother,**
> **a daughter-in-law against her mother-in-law —**
>   **a man's enemies will be the members of his own**
>   **household.'**

Jesus, and no doubt many of his disciples, found this to be true, as have thousands since that day. This division is something that has been very well known in recent years, especially behind the former Iron Curtain, where even the children of Christians were told that it was their duty to the party and to their country to betray their parents. In less strenuous circumstances in the West it is still true that families are divided and often a Christian may be the only believer in the family and finds his chief difficulties are at home. In such circumstances the disciple is encouraged not to be afraid, but to hold fast to his faith and his testimony. ⭐

It is this that forms the background to Christ's stern and much-misunderstood warning: **'Anyone who loves his father or mother more than me is not worthy of me; anyone who loves his son or daughter more than me is not worthy of me'** (10:37). The parallel passage in Luke 14:26 speaks of hating mother and father. That is the Hebrew form of absolute statement, which is here reported in a manner more familiar to us, in terms of loving more or loving less. Jesus is not advocating, or even permitting, the lack of filial or parental love, but asserting once again the absolute supremacy of his claims on his people. Nothing and no one at all must be allowed to come between the disciple and his Lord. In fact, loving Christ should never lessen our love for members of our family in terms of tender affection. However, when it comes to priorities and faithfulness to Christ, the family must come second. Actually this is the best thing that could happen to the family, because this will be a testimony to them of the greatness of God, who deserves and wins such allegiance. ⭐

Jesus then links this with a reference to taking up one's cross: **'Anyone who does not take his cross and follow me is not worthy of me'** (10:38). The believer's cross is not just coping patiently with some difficult situation, such as caring for an ill, but demanding and awkward, relative: 'That is the cross I have to bear!' Situations like this are genuinely difficult and, of course, need much 'grace to help us in our time of need' (Heb. 4:16), but taking up the cross has specific reference to persecution. It was the Lord's righteous life and commitment to the gospel that brought the suffering of the cross. Following him similarly involves suffering for the sake of the gospel. Taking up our cross is a conscious decision to follow

Christ, no matter what it may cost. It is not deliberately court-
ing persecution or martyrdom, but willingly submitting to it
when it results from our faithful discipleship.

Jesus then returns to the issue of this life compared with
eternity. When he says, **'Whoever finds his life will lose it,
and whoever loses his life for my sake will find it,'** he means
that if we are willing to lose our life in this world for Christ's
sake, we shall 'find it' eternally in the next. Life and soul are
really interchangeable in this context and the translation can
use either word. The point is that to suffer for Christ in this
world will result in eternal blessing. To concentrate on this
world, to the detriment of our service of Christ, will have the
opposite effect. Indeed, those who put this world before Christ
show that their real allegiance is not to the kingdom of Christ
but to this world, and their eternal destiny will reflect this.
What we receive in eternity is decided in this world.

The disciples' privilege (10:40-42)

The concluding verses of the chapter return to the theme of
the disciple's identification with his Master with a reassurance
that no one who helps a disciple will lose his reward: **'He who
receives you receives me, and he who receives me receives
the one who sent me'** (10:40). It does not matter whether the
believer is an apostle (**'you'**), **'a prophet'**, **'a righteous man'**,
or someone without a particular office. Those who give even
the least-regarded help, such as **'a cup of cold water'**, to
even the least-regarded disciple, **'will certainly not lose his
reward'**. How much more if the help is great! All believers
come into the category of **'these little ones'**, his lowly disciples who are apparently vulnerable and defenceless (see comments on chapter 18).

The connection with the previous verses suggests that this help is given when the prophet or righteous man is undergoing persecution. The one who acknowledges and supports the man in trouble is, of course, also in danger of being arrested, imprisoned and losing his life. So the imprisoned apostle Paul writes, 'May the Lord show mercy to the household of Onesiphorus, because he often refreshed me and was not ashamed of my chains… May the Lord grant that he will find mercy from the Lord on that day!' (2 Tim. 1:16,18). Those who receive Christ and his word and his gospel, and align themselves with his people, show that they too belong to his kingdom and so receive the appropriate reward. The relevance for the disciples is that this identification with their Master ensures that they will receive help and protection and care, not only from God but from his people in this world.

From every direction and in every way, Jesus encourages his disciples. He has warned of danger, commanded them not to fear, assured them of the Father's care and now binds them together in his service. He has called them to train them for the work of the kingdom. The future of the work lies in their hands, after he has returned to the Father. He does not minimize the difficulties and dangers, but he also assures them that they will have all needed help and care. They will not be alone. Because they believe in him, they will have the Holy Spirit speaking through them. Because they are children of God, they will know the Father's care. Because they are sent by him, others will love and serve them.

And we can take the same encouragement. Serving our Master, preaching the gospel, bearing a witness in this evil world will bring the persecution of which he warns. We should have no doubts at all about this. For only if we disown Christ and hold back from making known the truth can we live lives at peace. You may look forward to that full and final peace in glory, but to expect that here and now is to reject Christ's warnings. So we, too, must count the cost and be prepared for these troubles and persecutions, especially from our families. Nevertheless Christ's real point is that we should not be afraid, but hold fast to him and continue in his service. He gives his disciples, and us with them, every encouragement to work. How vital it is that we do not water down the responsibilities and duties of Christ's disciples! How important, too, that we do not ignore the compensations, provisions and assurances that we can place on the other side of the ledger when we count the cost of being a disciple and working for the kingdom!

We should especially remember the privilege of being treated in the same way as our Master. It is not easy to regard this as a privilege, but it is. Remember how the apostles rejoiced 'because they had been counted worthy of suffering disgrace for the Name' (Acts 5:41). To know that Christ has gone before in this way and that men are regarding us and treating us like him is to feel honoured. Add to this the awareness of God's ability and power to punish men and give rewards, together with his providential care promised to his children, and we need not be afraid, whatever may become of us in this world. And we need not be afraid, not only of the persecution, but also of our own weakness. If we entrust ourselves to the Saviour, then he will not only undertake to care for us in terms of preserving us to eternal life, but he will also strengthen us and preserve us in our faith and testimony. Since he came to bring division rather than peace, he has also made provision for his disciples in that situation.

Summary

We have come to the end of this section about the work of the kingdom. We, today, like the disciples, must realize here that belonging to the kingdom is not just a matter of obeying the rules and laws of the King, but of serving him in the extension of his reign by the proclamation of his gospel. Matthew has illustrated and explained the work of the King and shown how it centres on the salvation of the whole man. Illnesses, demonic possession and death all show the effects of sin, and Christ's healing powers demonstrate wonderfully how he has overcome the power of sin. These miracles, plus his stilling of the storm and driving out of demons, look forward to the final salvation, the day when all the effects of sin will be done away. In this confidence the disciples are called and commissioned as apostles to take the gospel first to the Jews, but by implication also to the Gentiles. The miracles that Matthew has recounted point to the great spiritual healing that Christ has won, especially the forgiveness of sins (9:2). This must be our priority in the work of the kingdom, as in compassion we call men to faith in God's Son (9:29), but also to a discipleship which we must mirror in our own lives. This kingdom will spread to all nations, foreshadowed by the centurion in 8:5-13, as Christ overcomes the powerful rule of the devil (8:28-33).

To that end we must go forward in faith, without fear, relying upon the power of one who rules the wind and waves (8:27) and on the Father's providential care. We must go out to witness, come what may, in the fear of the Lord, conscious of belonging to Christ and of following Christ in his sufferings for the gospel. If we lose our friends or our lives, so be it, for Christ has promised that we shall actually save our souls for all eternity and receive the reward prepared by his heavenly Father.

This section is one of contrasts. Salvation is both now and future. The role of the disciple is both terrifying and comforting, demanding and rewarding. It is taking up one's cross and receiving a crown. We must guard against an unbalanced view of this. Too many today see the miracles and forget that the consummation of healing and restoration is future. Others are so keen to teach the 'not yet' that they undervalue the amazing authority of Christ, by the gospel, to deal with sin in its worst forms even now. Some are so carried away with ideas of health and wealth that they forget self-denial and taking up the cross. Others appreciate that but overlook the immense provision that Christ has made for his people. We have the new wine of the kingdom; we must pour it into the new wineskins of forgiveness, kingdom joy and obedience, godly fear and confidence, sacrifice and reward. The King has come; his kingdom is coming and progressing. We, like the disciples, have our part to play. Let us set about it with all humble confidence.

Part 4:
The coming of the kingdom (11:1 – 13:52)

17.
John's enquiry

Please read Matthew 11:1-19

The first words of chapter 11, **'After Jesus had finished instructing his twelve disciples'**, introduce a new section, which culminates in the extended discourse of chapter 13. All these chapters are concerned with the way in which Christ's kingdom comes and the devil's kingdom is defeated. Here, too, we find the contrast between the 'already' and the 'not yet' which gives a clue to much of the New Testament. This may seem rather technical and involves several controversial and difficult verses, but it is, in fact, very practical. This is often the case. What many regard as technical may be very useful for the Christian life when properly understood. Here the discussion of the place of John in the coming of the kingdom provides some much-needed instruction concerning the attitude, work and motivation of those who are least in the kingdom of heaven. Matthew makes clear, not only the various stages, but also the manner of that coming. In contrast to the ways of the kingdom of the devil, Jesus is seen preaching the gospel in the way which is appropriate and powerful. It is vital not to skip over such passages.

The works of the Christ (11:1-5)

At this time John the Baptist had been put in prison by King Herod. There he heard **'what Christ was doing'** and **'sent his disciples to ask him, "Are you the one who was to come, or should we expect someone else?"'** (11:2). It would appear that John had a problem. The message he had been given to proclaim included the fact that the Messiah's kingdom was at hand and that this would be by the Spirit and with fire; he must have expected that all would go smoothly. The Messiah would establish his kingdom; his enemies would be defeated and judged, and John would have his place in the kingdom. Instead of this, he finds himself in prison, suffering for his faith, while evil triumphs. He wonders if he has got it wrong. Perhaps Jesus is not the Messiah, as he had thought. So he sends to enquire of Jesus what the position really is.

Jesus tells John's disciples, **'Go back and report to John what you hear and see.'** He lists his activities: giving sight to the blind, healing the lame and those with leprosy, giving hearing to the deaf, raising the dead and, especially, preaching the good news to the poor. By so doing Jesus refers John back to the prophecies of Isaiah (Isa. 35:5-6; 61:1-2). These are the real marks of the promised Christ. It is significant that when Jesus preached from Isaiah 61 in the synagogue at Nazareth, he omitted the final words about 'the day of vengeance of our God'. The teaching of the present passage implies the same distinction. The victory and judgement on his enemies, for which John was looking, and the kingdom of universal peace, which he desired, were still in the future. The 'already' was the presence of Jesus; the 'not yet' was the culmination of the kingdom and the vindication of God's people. It this delay before the final kingdom of God that provides a unifying theme to this section and also keeps us today from the wrong kind of expectation.

The offence of Christ (11:6)

In verse 6 Jesus pronounces a blessing on **'the man who does not fall away on account of me'**. 'Fall away' translates the word for 'offence' or, better, 'stumbling block'. The idea is that when we encounter something that we do not expect, we trip up over it; our faith stumbles and we are tempted to give up. So John finds Jesus and his ministry an offence or stumbling block. It is not what he expected; this, he thinks, contradicts what he had himself preached. So he is in a quandary.

This is a common problem for those who hear the gospel and encounter the real Christ. In 1 Corinthians 1:23 Paul refers to those who are tripped up by the cross of Christ: 'We preach Christ crucified: a stumbling block to Jews and foolishness to Gentiles.' They do not expect the Saviour to suffer on the cross; this is an offence to them. They cannot accept this and reject the gospel because of it. Today many people find other reasons for rejecting a gospel which does not fit their preconceptions. Many non-Christians think that belief in God demands that nothing evil or difficult should happen to them. They cannot believe in a God of love who allows suffering and death. The fact that there is suffering and death causes them to stumble and to reject the gospel. Many Christians hear a false gospel which promises them 'health and wealth', which speaks of a life without difficulties. They expect that becoming a Christian will solve all their problems and when this is not the case they tend to give up. They stumble and fall away on account of the real Christ and the real gospel.

The only answer to this is to be clear about what is actually promised, just as John needed to know what had actually been prophesied concerning the Messiah. If we understand that the kingdom will always arouse opposition and that serving Christ is not something to be looked at through rose-tinted spectacles, we shall not stumble when persecution arrives and we

have to suffer for our faith. For this reason it is vital that preachers of the gospel are honest with their hearers. They must demand repentance and warn of the need for self-denial and cross-
bearing. While not failing to emphasize the benefits of faith,
and the grace and strength that God provides by his Spirit,
they must not omit the problems and difficulties.

John's place in history (11:7-11)

**'As John's disciples were leaving, Jesus began to speak to
the crowd about John'** (11:7). He raises the subject of John's
character and function. John was popular; people went out
into the desert to see and hear him. What were they expecting? What did they find? Certainly John was not fickle and
changeable, like **'a reed swayed by the wind'**. Nor was he **'a
man dressed in fine clothes'**. He was a faithful prophet of
the living God. He lived in the desert, not **'in kings' palaces'**.
Jesus explains further that John was not merely a prophet like
the other prophets. He was the herald of the Messiah, the one
who fulfilled the words Jesus quotes from Malachi 3:1: **'I will
send my messenger ahead of you, who will prepare your
way before you.'** (We may note, by the way, that this quotation implies that Jesus is the LORD, Yahweh.)

The next words are very difficult and have aroused much
controversy: **'Among those born of women there has not
risen anyone greater than John the Baptist; yet he who is
least in the kingdom of heaven is greater than he'** (11:11).
Some take this to imply that John, not being in the kingdom of
heaven, was not saved. However, that is quite beside the point,
as well as untrue; 'in the kingdom' refers to his position in
time, not to his spiritual standing. Others say that every Christian, even the least important one, has greater privileges than
John the Baptist ever had. The words of 13:17 would appear
to support this: 'Many prophets and righteous men longed to

see what you see but did not see it, and to hear what you hear
but did not hear it.' However, the context here is not that of
privileges, but function. John was the herald of the Messiah
and as such could only proclaim what he knew and what was
relevant at that time. The Messiah was at hand. He spoke better than he knew, perhaps, when he referred to Jesus as the
Lamb of God, but he could not proclaim the gospel fully, or
preach Christ as the apostles would, because Christ had not
yet fulfilled his ministry and, especially, had not yet died and
risen again. Any Christian knows more than John and, more
relevantly here, can bear his testimony to more than John could.

Much of Christ's ministry involved teaching his disciples
beyond what they had learnt from John the Baptist. He could
only prepare the way to Jesus. Jesus was the way and proclaimed the truth fully. John, like the Old Testament prophets,
did not understand about the coming of the kingdom in (at
least two) stages. Jesus, particularly here in this chapter, explains about this and will do so more in the rest of the section.
In the Acts of the Apostles we find Peter explaining to Cornelius
what happened after 'the baptism that John preached'. He
speaks of the death and resurrection of Jesus and of his command to the apostles to preach the gospel (Acts 10:39-43).
Later in the story we meet Apollos, who 'knew only the baptism of John', but preached what he knew boldly in the synagogue. Priscilla and Aquila, who had learnt from Paul, heard
him and 'invited him to their home and explained to him the
way of God more adequately'. He was 'a learned man, with a
thorough knowledge of the Scriptures'. He could speak with
great fervour, and even accuracy as far as he knew. They, however, who were some of the least in the kingdom of heaven,
were greater than he, because they could tell him the gospel
more fully (Acts 18:24-26).

This is our great privilege. We may not be as bold or as
gifted as John, but if we have believed in Christ, who has now
come, died and risen again, we have a greater function than

John. We live in gospel days and must not behave or speak as if we were still in the days of preparation. Whatever our insignificance or lack of gifts, we must do our best to spread abroad the full gospel. This is our 'greater' function.

John and Elijah (11:12-15)

Jesus then continued to speak about the ministry of John the Baptist. Verse 12 is exceedingly difficult and many interpretations have been put forward. The subject is certainly force or power. The problem is deciding whether Jesus is speaking of the power of his kingdom in converting, or the evil power of opposition and persecution. Some take the verse as in the NIV translation: **'From the days of John the Baptist until now, the kingdom of heaven has been forcefully advancing, and forceful men lay hold of it.'** It seems fairly certain that 'forceful men' refers to the activities of 'violent' men, for this is the general context. John has been put in prison by a violent man. The earlier part of the verse could refer to the power of the Spirit bringing men into the kingdom of heaven, as the NIV has it. On the other hand, this part of the verse could be translated as 'has been suffering violence', which fits in with the general context of persecution. It is, perhaps, better to see this verse as including both sides of the picture: the kingdom has been advancing since Christ began to establish it, during the days of John the Baptist's ministry, but at the same time has been laid hold of by violent men. This would answer John's problem. He knows now that the kingdom of the Messiah is powerful and strong; he has also experienced suffering at the hands of violent men.

The ministry of John was the turning point (see also Luke 16:16). He has to be classified with the Old Testament **'Prophets and the Law'**, but his days saw the beginning of Christ's ministry. Since then the kingdom had been progressing much more powerfully and would continue to do so. John knew the power of the Spirit in his ministry and also endured persecution. It is, therefore, true that his ministry resembles that of Elijah, who ministered in power, so that the false prophets were defeated, and who also suffered violence from a violent man, as well as a violent woman! So Jesus says, **'And if you are willing to accept it, he is the Elijah who was to come.'** The Jews were expecting the prophet Elijah to return, in pursuance of Malachi's prophecy (Mal. 4:5-6). However, John himself had denied that he was Elijah (John 1:21). The explanation is that John was not literally Elijah, but came 'in the spirit and power of Elijah' (Luke 1:17) to prepare the way for Jesus. The need for this spiritual interpretation is indicated by Christ's warning in verse 15: **'He who has ears, let him hear.'**

Wisdom's vindication (11:16-19)

Jesus then describes the generation in which he ministered as being like children (11:16). He had clearly observed the children **'sitting in the market places'** playing games of weddings and funerals. He imagines them complaining about others that do not respond to them and play the game. In the same way the people of that generation have not responded to John, who **'came neither eating nor drinking'** and whose ministry might therefore be compared to a funeral. Nor have they responded to himself, the Son of Man, who came living a normal life, **'eating and drinking'**, as at a wedding feast, and who was **'a friend of tax collectors and "sinners"'**. Both ministries, however, were an expression of the **'wisdom'** of God; both had their place in his purposes — preparation and fulfilment.

As well as seeing God's wisdom in those days, we can learn that today also God uses different kinds of people for different ministries. We should not despise those whose approach is different from our own, so long as it is the way of wisdom and conforms to the gospel of Jesus Christ. In particular, however, our pattern ought to be Jesus rather than John the Baptist, for the kingdom has now come; the gospel is being preached in its fulness. Our way should not be that of fasting and severity like John's, but of calling men and women to the wedding feast of Jesus. We ought to be friends of tax collectors and 'sinners' as Jesus was. Not every part of Scripture is to be applied equally to our situation. We need to understand the development and progress of God's purpose. Here we must see ourselves clearly as being in the kingdom of heaven and ensure that our witness conforms to that.

Christ's kingdom is coming in power and will continue to make progress. We should be encouraged by this in spite of all the opposition that it arouses. We must have no illusions about the opposition that we shall encounter; it is foolish to be put off because the going is not smooth. Christ has made it clear that during this interim period, before the final consummation of the kingdom, opposition will continue, suffering will abound, and we must take up our cross daily and follow him. However, the assurance is there that the kingdom will advance forcefully and the final victory is certain. We must not be put off by persecution, but must follow the way of wisdom, living and witnessing for our Saviour whatever the circumstances may be.

18.
Judgement or rest

Please read Matthew 11:20-30

It used to be customary to use a carrot-and-stick technique on donkeys. Our Lord uses a similar, but more sophisticated and more kindly, method to draw men to himself. In other words, warnings and promises alternate. In this passage there are warnings, by implication, as Jesus denounces the cities in which most of his miracles had been performed, because they did not repent. Then he issues an invitation to the weary and burdened to come to him. We need to take note of the warnings and respond to the invitation. In another way this passage gives us much to think about concerning God's ways and the relationship between his sovereignty and human responsibility. However, it is no use understanding this, as far as we may, unless we respond in the right way.

Korazin and Bethsaida denounced (11:20-22)

Here, as elsewhere, we are taught that greater light brings greater responsibility. Jesus applies this to the cities of the area around the Sea of Galilee. He goes beyond the record of the Gospel, which certainly speaks of many miracles in that area, to say that most of his miracles had been performed in them. The word **'denounce'** in verse 20 means 'indignation along with ... justifiable reproach'.[1] He pronounces a **'Woe'** upon them; they are destined for judgement, for, **'If the miracles that were performed in you had been performed in Tyre and Sidon, they would have repented long ago in sackcloth and ashes.'** He contrasts Korazin and Bethsaida with the Phoenician, and Gentile, cities of Tyre and Sidon. The Galilean cities had not only had the privilege of the teaching of the law and the words of the prophets; they had had the personal ministry of the Lord Jesus Christ, the Messiah, but had not responded by repenting. Jesus could have quoted the example of the men of Nineveh, to whom the prophet Jonah went. Here was another Gentile city, which did respond to the Word of God at a time when the Israelites were rejecting it.

By the way we may notice that this assertion concerning Tyre and Sidon shows that God has what is known as 'contingent' or 'middle' knowledge. In other words, the Lord knows what *would* happen *if* certain circumstances came to pass, as well as what will in fact happen. This is often denied by modern philosophers and theologians, but nothing else fits in with the biblical teaching concerning God's omniscience.[2] It is less clear exactly what the Saviour means by this, for no one can or will repent without the working of the Holy Spirit, not even Tyre and Sidon, even though they were not hardened like the inhabitants of Bethsaida and Korazin. Probably we should conclude that Jesus is talking simply about responsibility, the use of means, not the secret workings of the Holy Spirit, which we might express as 'humanly speaking'.

He speaks most plainly of a coming Day of Judgement, when both Jews and Gentiles will stand before God. He asserts that **'It will be more bearable for Tyre and Sidon on the day of judgement than for you'** (11:22). This mention of the Day of Judgement, of course, fits in with Christ's earlier reference to Isaiah in verse 5. Messiah's coming will also involve, in due course, God coming in 'vengeance', 'with divine retribution' 'the day of vengeance of our God' (Isa. 35:4; 61:2).

Degrees of judgement and punishment will be known and seen then.

Capernaum and Sodom (11:23-24)

Capernaum seems to have been a very proud place, claiming some kind of distinction among the cities of Galilee. However, when Jesus asks the question, **'Will you be lifted up to the skies?'** he is drawing a parallel with the great pretensions of Babylon. That city, according to Isaiah 14:12-15, also had visions of glory, but was warned that it would go down to Sheol, as Capernaum is warned of going **'down to the depths'** of Hades. Not content with comparing Capernaum to Babylon, Jesus refers also to Sodom, which, with Gomorrah, was destroyed in the days of Abraham and Lot. He asserts, **'If the miracles that were performed in you had been performed in Sodom, it would have remained to this day.'** Seeing many miracles is a privilege, but it also brings increased responsibility and judgement, if there is no response of repentance and faith. Therefore, Jesus assures them that **'It will be more bearable for Sodom on the day of judgement than for you.'** Luke 12:47-48 also speaks of more severe judgement on the basis of greater knowledge. There Jesus refers to the servant who knows his master's will, contrasted with the one who does not know it, and speaks of 'many blows' or 'few blows', ending with the principle: 'From everyone who has been given much, much will be demanded; and from the one who has been entrusted with much, much more will be asked.'

The words **'I tell you'** in verse 24 remind us that Jesus is not actually speaking to Korazin, Bethsaida and Capernaum. This is a rhetorical device also used by the prophets, who addressed warnings to many nations who never heard them. The intention is to have an effect on those who do hear, and so we, too, should take notice of what the Lord says here. Great privilege brings great responsibility. Hearing the gospel week in, week out, knowing the Word of God, being taught the truth from our youth, or hearing it regularly in church — these are great privileges, but salvation cannot be taken for granted. Here is a warning to children brought up in Christian homes, to those who attend church and who are members of the congregation. They must not despise their privileges, but must make sure that they respond in repentance and faith. Otherwise there will simply be a greater and more unbearable punishment on the Day of Judgement.

Another implication, which Jesus does not actually bring out here, is that those who fail to respond to such privileges and warnings may have the gospel taken away from them. In Acts 28:28 the apostle Paul gives the warning that, since the Jews have rejected his message, he will turn from them and go to the Gentiles, who, he assures his hearers, will listen to what he has to say: 'Therefore I want you to know that God's salvation has been sent to the Gentiles, and they will listen!' He does not mean that every Gentile who hears is elect and will believe, but that a generally unresponsive audience cannot count on the message continuing to be preached to them. The Lord sends his message to responsive audiences. Here, as we have said already, we are not concerned with God's sovereign election and the working of his Spirit, but with our responsibility for making use of the opportunity to hear that God gives us and the privileges that he assigns to us. The sovereignty of God is dealt with in the next section.

Sovereign good pleasure (11:25-26)

Comparison with the other Gospels suggests that Jesus did not utter verses 25-30 immediately after verses 20-24. 'At

that time' is very general. However, Matthew has placed the two sections together to make the point that while responsibility is laid upon us because of privileges, such as the miracles performed in the cities of Galilee, there is a higher and deeper understanding which involves the sovereign purpose of God. However, this is not all he is concerned with, as he goes on to the invitation of the end of the chapter, which is once again a matter of responsibility. But first he makes it clear that the Lord is in control of all things.

One significant point is that Jesus does not engage here in intellectual speculation, or even theological discussion about the sovereignty of God. Instead he praises God. This is not a matter for debate, but an occasion for worship and adoration. Too often Christians debate these matters in a spirit utterly unlike that of Jesus. We would do well to emulate him in his humility and praise of the Father. Similarly, he addresses God as his **'Father'**, which indicates that there is nothing in this topic to disturb his relationship with him. There is no questioning or doubting. He is at one with his Father and worships and praises him before treating this great matter.

He addresses God not only as his Father, but also as **'Lord of heaven and earth'**, giving this description as the basis for God's sovereign working. It is because God is the Creator that he has the right to ordain what happens to his creatures, and to men and women in this world. When the apostle Paul has to deal with objections to the whole doctrine of election, in Romans 9, he uses the same argument, asking, 'Who are you, O man, to talk back to God? "Shall what is formed say to him who formed it, 'Why did you make me like this?'"' God is the potter; we are but the lumps of clay. The Lord of heaven and earth has the right to deal with us as he chooses. This is a yet another reason why we should emulate our Lord's attitude of praise on this subject.

The sovereignty for which Jesus praises his Father is that of hiding and revealing. He has **'hidden these things'** — the understanding of the miracles so as to be saved through repentance — **'from the wise and learned, and revealed them to little children'**. The wise and learned seem to be those who are self-sufficient in their own wisdom and knowledge, such as the Pharisees and teachers of the law, those in the cities who regard themselves as having knowledge already and not needing what Jesus can teach them. The little children are those who are humble and teachable, willing to learn from the Saviour, such as the disciples. He has already referred to them as 'little ones' in 10:42 and this will come up again in chapter 18, where entry into the kingdom is restricted to those who have become like little children. Our Lord is not saying that the little children deserve to be granted repentance, or to have these things revealed to them. He is indicating that in God's ways and purposes he requires, and in grace provides, a humble, teachable spirit in those who will be sharers in his salvation. Similarly it is noticeable that although Tyre, Sidon and Sodom will have a more bearable judgement, they will not be saved.

No one deserves to be saved, and no one is saved, apart from God's grace. The context, even when Jesus is talking about sovereignty and God's good pleasure, is still that of responsibility. If we are proud and arrogant and deny our need for teaching, then we shall not be saved. It is God's **'good pleasure'** to leave us in that situation. Those who are like little children, humble and teachable, are so because God has made them so. From our point of view it is our responsibility to be humble and teachable, so that we might understand and repent and be saved. If this does apply to us, we should not be proud, but rejoice that it was God's good pleasure to save us.

Revelation through the Son (11:27)

Verse 27 is quite remarkable in various ways. It is unique in Matthew's Gospel and very similar to Christ's teachings contained in the Gospel of John. In fact, it constitutes a major argument against those who would assert that John's record of the teaching of Jesus is mere fabrication. This verse shows that Jesus could and did teach in this manner when he so chose. The key to this is the nature of the topics he is dealing with, which are similar to the main themes of John. Here he gives a deep insight into relationships between himself and the Father and into the processes by which he brings them and us to the knowledge of God. In particular we receive some understanding of the self-awareness of Jesus, which is basic for the teaching and the invitation that follow. Only the Son, who knows and is known by the Father, could possibly invite men to himself in this way.

'All things' here are not comprehensive, but refer to the matters under discussion: authority and power to give the knowledge of the Father. All this is part of Christ's mediatorial function as Messiah and has been **'committed to'** him by the Father. But the real subject is contained in the second half of the verse, the fact that **'No one knows the Father except the Son and those to whom the Son chooses to reveal him.'** However, Jesus also asserts first that **'No one knows the Son except the Father,'** and we may wonder why he does so. Partly it will be for the sake of completeness. This is a reciprocal knowledge such as we find in John 10:15: 'The Father knows me and I know the Father.'

The work to which the last part of this verse refers belongs to Christ's prophetic office and ministry. He is not contradicting the teaching of verse 25, that it is the Father who reveals matters to the little children; they are at one in this. The Father reveals 'all things', as the Son chooses to reveal the Father.

There is no contradiction here, but a wonderful unity, as we can see elsewhere. For instance, in John 17:26 we read, 'I have made you known to them, and will continue to make you known in order that the love you have for me may be in them and that I myself may be in them.' Previously, in verse 10, he said, 'All I have is yours, and all you have is mine.' Ultimate sovereignty lies with the Father, but this works out on earth through the ministry of the Son. Since the ascension, this ministry is assigned to the Holy Spirit, who works through the preaching of the gospel to reveal the Father.

The invitation (11:28-30)

In the wonderful words, **'Come to me, all you who are weary and burdened, and I will give you rest'**, Jesus calls needy sinners to himself, to trust in him and serve him, and so receive the blessings of life. Only in this way can they know the Father (11:27). Again we see the parallels in John's Gospel where in the same context we find both Philip's request, 'Lord, show us the Father,' and Jesus' assertion, 'I am the way and the truth and the life. No one comes to the Father except through me.' Therefore, if anyone desires to come to know the Father and have the rest that goes with that, he must come to the Saviour.

When Jesus offers them rest, this is not something new. The Old Testament is full of references to the rest of God, which is pictured by rest in the promised land, which in turn points to the rest of eternal life (Heb. 4:9-11). Isaiah addresses the Israelites, who have acted like the inhabitants of the Galilean cities to whom the invitations have gone. He records that God said to the people, 'This is the resting-place, let the weary rest,' and 'This is the place of repose', but they would not listen (Isa. 28:12). Also, in Jeremiah 31:25, in the context of the prophecy of the new covenant, God could speak to Israel in captivity and promise: 'I will refresh the weary and satisfy the faint.'

However, here Jesus has a particular aspect of the rest in mind. He offers those who will come to him rest from the weariness and burden of the yoke which enslaves them. **'Take my yoke upon you'**, implies another, burdensome yoke, which they already bore. This yoke is that of the law, falsely imposed on them by the Pharisees as a way of salvation and acceptance with God. This system, with all its detailed regulations, was truly wearying and burdensome. We shall see examples of this in chapter 12:1-14.

By contrast, Christ's own yoke is that of discipleship to the Messiah, especially of his teaching. Thus he adds, **'and learn from me'**. It is wrong to regard this as something entirely new, for it is not the Old Testament itself that Jesus is criticizing, but the current interpretation of the false leaders of Israel, as was the case in chapter 5. So, for instance, Jeremiah exhorts the people of his day:

> Stand at the crossroads and look;
>   ask for the ancient paths,
> ask where the good way is, and walk in it,
>   and you will find rest for your souls.
>   But you said, 'We will not walk in it'
>
>   (Jer. 6:16).

We find constantly in the Gospels that Jesus comes to fulfil the law, not to reject it or abandon it. At the same time his yoke, his teaching, is a much fuller and more wonderful expression of what the Old Testament contains.

The words, **'For I am gentle and humble in heart'**, remind us of Old Testament prophecies which Jesus fulfilled. The king foretold in Zechariah 9:9 would be 'gentle'. Isaiah, in his prophecy of the Servant of the Lord, spoke of one who would not break a bruised reed or snuff out a smouldering wick (Isa. 42:1-4, quoted in Matt. 12:18-21). He is actually gentle and humble in heart. This is God's Messiah, come in fulfilment of Old Testament prophecies, who is calling weary and burdened sinners to himself by the gospel.

Then Jesus assures them, **'My yoke is easy and my burden is light.'** This does not mean that his standard of holiness and righteousness is lower. However, the yoke, the means of bearing a load, would be comfortable and suited to their shoulders, enabling them to bear the burdens. Similarly, the burden is light, not because it is easier to attain, but because they are able to bear it by his grace. 'Easy' means comfortable, like a literal yoke that has been planed smooth, shaped to the shoulders that have to bear it. These are truly gracious words. The apostle John in his first letter speaks of obeying the commands of God: 'And his commands are not burdensome, for everyone born of God overcomes the world' (1 John 5:3). The teachings of Jesus, like the law when it is properly understood (Rom. 7:10-12), are for our good, suited to us and our needs, so that we are able to bear the burden which they lay upon us. How different from the yoke of the Pharisees and the burdens they impose, which are unworkable and harsh and lead only to despair, not to rest!

Our responsibility

We must learn from all this, first, to share Christ's attitude to the sovereignty of God. One of the greatest tragedies of the modern Christian world is that the Bible's teaching on election and predestination, on the sovereignty of God in general, is treated as a cause for debate and argument, even for rejection. When we understand these truths and accept the teaching which Jesus sets before us here, we shall be, with various hymn-writers, 'Lost in wonder, love and praise'.[3] These teachings are given to us for our good, not for our distress or harm, but it is only when we submit to them gladly and gratefully that we gain the full benefit from them.

Secondly, we must honour Christ in his position as Son and Mediator, as described here. He has been appointed by the Father to reveal the Father to us. Here we see something of the glory of the Lord Jesus and must honour him for it.

Lastly, and most important of all, we must make sure that we have taken Christ's yoke upon us and begun to learn from him. If we go on thinking that we know all things, that we are wise and learned, that we are good, we shall remain weary and burdened. When we take Christ's yoke upon us, when we trust him and give ourselves to him, place ourselves in his hands and under his authority, relying upon his love and grace and cross, then we enjoy the rest of eternity even now. Through him we receive and rejoice in the rest of forgiveness, reconciliation and fellowship with God. We come to know the Father himself. Then we shall share Christ's attitude to the law and be ready to praise God that he has revealed these things to infants like us.

19.
The Sabbath and the Servant

Please read Matthew 12:1-21

One of the most controversial areas in church life today is the issue of the Sabbath or the Lord's Day. It was just the same in our Lord's own day, when the different schools of the Pharisees argued about exactly how the Sabbath should be observed. They had their various traditions and, of course, Jesus was bound to come into conflict with them. In this section we have two sample incidents, where Jesus clashes with the Pharisees over their Sabbath regulations, but more especially over their attitudes to the Sabbath and to him.

However, it would be a mistake to treat these simply as material for discussion about what one may or may not do on God's day. The passage concerns far deeper issues than that, however important that is in itself. In the first place, what we have here is the issue of the person of Jesus Christ himself. Matthew shows this by the passage in verses 15-21, where he gives us a quotation from the prophecy of Isaiah about the Servant of the Lord. The issue, in other words, is not merely the Sabbath, but the Lord of the Sabbath, who is the Messiah, the Lord's Servant. Bearing this in mind, we may see these verses as illustrating the two yokes which were implied at the end of chapter 11. The Pharisees' regulations illustrate their uncomfortable and burdensome yoke. Our Lord's attitude both to his disciples and to the man with a shrivelled hand illustrates his easy yoke and his light burden.

The setting (12:1-2)

Dr Francis Schaeffer wrote a book entitled, *The church before the watching world*, in which he showed how Christians are always being observed by those who would oppose their faith and criticize their lives. This is not a comfortable position, but in the end it has its uses, since in this way they can demonstrate the power of Christ in their lives. Now we should realize that Christ has gone before us in this also. He lived his life before the watching religious world of the Pharisees and the teachers of the law. So, on this occasion Jesus and his disciples were walking **'through the cornfields on the Sabbath'**. His disciples were hungry and began to pick some ears of corn and eat them. This was permissible according to the law of Moses in Deuteronomy 23:25; merely plucking and eating some ears of grain was not stealing. However, the Pharisees were watching and, as usual, chose to attack him through his disciples. **'Look! Your disciples are doing what is unlawful on the Sabbath,'** they accused.

The disciples' activity was unlawful in their eyes because it was reaping! This was one of the many categories of work which were forbidden on the Sabbath according to their regulations. This is as ridiculous as the regulation which banned moving a stool, because one of the legs of the stool might make a groove in the ground and thus constitute ploughing! However they were quite serious in their accusation. Jesus, through his disciples, was breaking the Sabbath. Jesus chooses not to attack the folly of their regulations, but digs deeper and deals with principles of interpretation and, in fact, the whole issue of their attitude to his own person.

David and the consecrated bread (12:3-4)

The incident to which Jesus refers in verses 3-4 is described in
1 Samuel 21:1-6, where David, fleeing from Saul, appeals to
the priest of Nob to provide him and his followers with food.
The only food available was the consecrated bread, traditionally known as shewbread, the Bread of the Presence, that had
been removed from before the Lord and replaced by hot bread.
According to Leviticus 24:5-9, this special bread, which symbolized the presence of the Lord with his people, was only for
the priests to eat. It was not lawful for anyone else to eat it.
We must be careful not to deduce from this that David's situation was the same as that of the disciples. Jesus is not arguing
that the disciples were in desperate need, that they were in
danger of dying, which would justify work on the Sabbath
even in the eyes of the Pharisees. His position and argument
are rather different. Reading back from verse 6, we have to
say that Jesus is arguing that David's person and mission, his
position as the Lord's anointed, even though he was not yet
actually reigning as king, justified the setting aside of a ceremonial law. This is one of the many 'how much more' passages in the New Testament. If David's position justified his
eating the ceremonial consecrated bread, how much more the
disciples of Jesus are justified in eating the grains of corn on
the Sabbath! The point is not that they *had* to eat, but that
they were his disciples. We should note that Jesus is not setting aside the law, but arguing from it, in the widest sense.

The temple service (12:5-6)

In verse 5 Jesus argues from the fact that it was recognized by
the law that the temple service took precedence over the law
concerning the Sabbath. **'The priests in the temple desecrate**

the day and yet are innocent,' he argues. The word 'desecrate' is clearly used in only a technical sense; the priests are in fact declared to be innocent. The temple and its service are more important than some of the Sabbath regulations — those that would hinder the functioning of the temple without promoting the purpose of the Sabbath. We ought to ask the question: 'Why was the temple more important than regulations about the day of rest?' The answer must be that the temple was to be seen, not as supplanting the Sabbath rest, but working towards it.

We may note also the converse application. In the context of the construction of the tabernacle, the prohibition on Sabbath work is repeated (Exod. 31:12-13). Even the building of God's house is not exempt from this law. Man needs a rest of spirit, which is part of the purpose of the Sabbath, and that was ministered to by the temple, its services and sacrifices. Like David and his position as king, the temple was serving men (as well as primarily God). Each was forwarding God's kingdom. This is not contrary to the Sabbath principle, but an expression of it. God was working in both to provide an eternal rest for men. Implicit here, but made explicit in Mark's version, is that the Sabbath was made for man, and that means for man's rest in every conceivable way.

Jesus then goes on to assert **'that one greater than the temple is here'**;[1] he is greater than the temple. In the New Testament Jesus is seen as the new temple, the new and real meeting-place between God and men (John 2:19-22). He has come to give rest to men (11:28-30). His sacrifice is far superior to those of the temple, which justified Sabbath work. His is real, not typical; once-for-all effective, not constantly repeated. Nothing must prevent or hinder his mission, his progress towards Calvary. Thus the very presence of the 'greater' Jesus justifies disregarding even a real ceremonial prohibition of the law, never mind a mere Pharisaic regulation.

The trouble with the Pharisees is not just a superficial, legalistic and hide-bound attitude to the Sabbath, but that they are blind to Christ's real identity and mission.

Mercy and sacrifice (12:7)

Jesus once again makes use of the words of Hosea 6:6: **'I desire mercy, not sacrifice'** (12:6; cf. 9:13). God was not saying there that offering sacrifice is wrong, just as here Jesus is not saying that Sabbath-keeping is wrong, but that mercy is more important. It is only the Pharisees' attitude to the Sabbath that contradicts mercy. A true understanding and practice of the Sabbath, such as Jesus has, in fact lead to mercy and express mercy. Like the people whom Hosea was criticizing, the Pharisees were substituting ceremonial regulations and their observance for true obedience to God. That is no substitute. Jesus always kept the law perfectly, so we may conclude here that his Sabbath observance is faithful to the principle of showing mercy. Again, though, we must note that Jesus describes his disciples here as innocent. He is not saying that this is a permissible sin, but that they have not sinned at all, rather like 'justifiable homicide'. They have broken the Pharisees' technical regulations, just as the priests in the temple desecrated the day, yet were innocent of any sin. What they were doing was actually lawful when properly understood.

Lord of the Sabbath (12:8)

Jesus sums up with the statement: **'For the Son of Man is Lord of the Sabbath.'** This provides the reasoning behind his arguments and his assertion that the disciples were innocent. As Son of Man, the Messiah, he is Lord of the Sabbath, not in the foolish sense in which some take this, that he had the right to abolish it, but that he is the epitome of all that it teaches. From all his practice and teaching we may, indeed, deduce that works of piety, mercy and necessity are permitted on the Sabbath or the Lord's Day, but that is not the point that he is making here. Rather he is asserting that the Sabbath points to him. His coming, his mission and sacrifice are the real substance of the Sabbath, since they go to provide the eternal rest of the eternal Sabbath mentioned in Hebrews 4:9-11. (It was not appropriate to mention the Lord's Day, Sunday, here. However, Matthew's readers, living after the resurrection, would have applied these things to the Lord of the resurrection, the Lord of the Lord's Day.) As long as Jesus is the Son of Man, and as long as men and women need rest, so long the Sabbath must continue, but under his lordship — the lordship of one who gives rest to the weary and burdened, provides eternal rest for his people, and thus shows true and glorious mercy.

Another Sabbath incident (12:9-13)

This second controversy (12:9-14) takes place on another Sabbath day, since Jesus has gone to another place.[2] In this incident involving **'a man with a shrivelled hand'**, once again we find the Pharisees (12:14). Here too we must look beyond the mere regulations, which the Pharisees were invoking. They would permit healing on the Sabbath if there was a danger of death. However, there is no suggestion that this man was in danger of dying. Jesus could have found him on the following day and healed him. That is not the point. He deliberately heals him on the Sabbath to make his point about the real purpose of the Sabbath. His argument begins from the greater value of men compared with animals, as in 6:26 and 10:31. If it is right to save a sheep which falls into a pit on the Sabbath, how much more is it lawful here to save a man from disease, or even from the pit of hell and from the bondage of Satan, on the Sabbath! The Sabbath is made for man. This is not a worldly, 'The better the day, the better the deed,' principle. He is saying that **'It is lawful to do good on the Sabbath.'** He does not assert that we must spend the whole of the Sabbath doing good; only that it is lawful. He, Lord of the Sabbath and the Son of man, has come to do good. That good he will do: giving rest, healing and salvation to men. It is this principle that justifies the healing of this man. The same principle justifies all the effort of preaching the gospel on the Lord's Day. This is the supreme good — to give salvation to men. What better occupation is there for God's day?

It is interesting that when Jesus links himself with the Father in John 5:16-18, as working on the Sabbath, either in providence or in healing, he is making the same point. Ever since God created him, man has needed rest on the Sabbath. God provided him with that rest and, since the Fall, that rest has to include salvation, for otherwise there is no true rest. This passage enshrines the whole of the biblical progress from creation through the Fall to the promises and prophecies of the coming of the Messiah, and through that to the eternal rest which will be enjoyed in the heavenly kingdom. All this centres on Christ, the Son of Man. This is how man must order his keeping of the Sabbath, in both Old and New Testaments. Once again, we must assert that to argue about what may or may not be done on the Sabbath, correctly permitting works of piety, mercy and necessity, is to miss the point. In the first incident there is a stress on his lordship of the Sabbath, the fact of the kingdom of rest and salvation. In the second incident, by his power in healing the man he stresses salvation from sin.

The healing, as so often, demonstrates his gracious authority and power to save. This is yet another mark of the Messiah who was to come. In spite of the Pharisees' opposition to him and his kingdom, he continues on his way, demonstrating that he is truly Son of Man and that he, alone, can provide salvation. This healing is remarkable in various ways. We are told that the man's hand **'was completely restored, just as sound as the other'**. The man had been deficient and is now restored and complete. It is, of course, remarkable that Jesus commands him to do something he is quite unable to do: **'Stretch out your hand.'** His hand is shrivelled and useless; the last thing he can do is stretch it out. However, there is power in the command: **'So he stretched it out.'** There is a significant and illustrative parallel here to the call of the gospel, which comes to those who are unable to repent, unable to believe. The power comes with the call. The Spirit accompanies it with his working and the elect obey the call. This is an effectual command to stretch out his hand. The gospel, when it comes according to the purpose of God, is an effectual call to repent and believe. The power is in the call and in the command.

The Servant of the Lord (12:14-21)

The Pharisees' response, predictably, is hatred; they **'went out and plotted how they might kill Jesus'**. It is remarkable how often people who can be very enthusiastic for the law, at least according to their own interpretation, are opposed to the Saviour. It is very often the most religious church-goers, particularly those of an older generation, who would not dream of doing their washing on Sunday, who react violently against the gospel of grace. Those who truly love the Saviour will interpret the law as he did and follow his example in keeping it, including the law of the Sabbath. It is no coincidence, therefore, that Matthew goes on to quote Isaiah 42:1-4, the first of Isaiah's 'Servant Songs'. In the first place, he does this to explain Christ's actions in avoiding the crowds. We are told that **'Jesus withdrew from that place. Many followed him, and he healed all their sick, warning them not to tell who he was.'** This is typical of his avoidance of the kind of popularity and stirring up of interest which might make life difficult for him and hinder his real mission.

However, the quotation also indicates that the opposition cannot hinder his mission. He has come as the Servant of the Lord and will do what he has to do. Matthew uses the Hebrew or Greek versions of the Old Testament according to how it suits his purpose in showing the character of Christ's mission. Some of the changes reflect the words of the Father in 3:17 and 17:5. Significantly, there is a stress on the fact that God says, **'I will put my Spirit on him.'** It is through him that God **'will proclaim justice to the nations'**. Justice, in this context, does not have to do with laws and judging, but is the equivalent of God's righteousness, which, in so much of the Old Testament, particularly Isaiah, is seen as effective in the fight against evil and sin in salvation. This will not be limited to the Jews. He will proclaim this justice/salvation to the nations, to the Gentiles (see also 12:21).

Verses 19-20 are, of course, particularly significant in this context. Here is the one whose yoke is easier and whose burden is light. He will not fight against the opposition of the Pharisees. **'He will not quarrel'** with the Pharisees: **'No one will hear his voice in the streets.'** Even more significantly, **'A bruised reed he will not break, and a smouldering wick he will not snuff out.'** The kind of Sabbath-keeping that he encourages, expressing love, mercy and grace, is evidence of the gentle and longsuffering spirit that deals kindly with the weak and vulnerable. This does not mean that he is weak, however, for this is only **'till he leads justice to victory'**. The weak will be defended and the feeble vindicated. Once again, we see the Son of Man dealing graciously with his people for their salvation. In verse 21 Matthew adopts the Septuagint's **'name'** instead of 'law' in Isaiah's Hebrew. This is no contradiction of the Hebrew, for the law, especially in Matthew's Gospel, points to Christ and it is Christ's name that sets forth his power, grace and mercy in which **'the nations will put their hope'**. Strikingly, in this 'Jewish' Gospel, the place of the Gentiles in God's purposes is already being stressed.

It is vital, in conclusion, to repeat that the point of these verses is not to give new regulations or to reinterpret the old regulations about the Sabbath. The aim, both of Jesus and Matthew, is to make clear how his mission fits the scheme of God's ways from the beginning of the Old Testament. Right from the beginning God provided the Sabbath for man's benefit under his lordship. It was the reminder, not just that God created the heavens and the earth in seven days, but that he was *their* creator. Similarly, after the Exodus, the restated Ten Commandments in Deuteronomy speak of remembering their redemption from Egypt, out of which God had brought them out with a mighty hand and an outstretched arm (Deut. 5:15). He had redeemed them out of slavery and bondage so that they might enter into the promised land. The Sabbath was to remind them not only of creation and redemption, but also of the rest to which they were going. Jesus now demands that his disciples follow that same principle.

The regulations of the Pharisees were enslaving the people in a new Egypt of bondage to their traditions. Jesus came to liberate them from the slavery of Pharisaic rules and the law, seen as a way of salvation. So, by his practice as well as by his teaching, he directs them to keep the Sabbath in way that brings rest, benefit for men and women, and for his disciples in particular. This benefit comes through the saving power of Christ, as manifested in the healing of the man with a shrivelled hand. It is this to which these passages point. We are to look forward to the rest which Christ provides, first in this world through faith in his name and then, finally, in the eternal rest to which he is bringing us. If we are weary and burdened, if we are weak and feeble, if we are in bondage and in need, then our faith must look to Christ. We must not get embroiled in mere sacrifice when his mercy is needed. And this mercy is to be found in the Son of Man, who was and is the Lord of the Sabbath, who gives rest, both now and in eternity.

20.
Two kingdoms

Please read Matthew 12:22-50

There is a common idea in the Christian world that being gentle and meek means being weak. Sometimes, of course, this is true, but it is not necessarily so. The Lord Jesus Christ was certainly gentle, but he was not weak. Nowhere is this clearer than in his dealings with Satan and his kingdom. According to Matthew 11:12, the kingdom was 'forcefully advancing' and this meant that Satan's kingdom was being defeated. In these verses in chapter 12 we see the contrast between the kingdom of Christ and the kingdom of Satan and the outworking of this in many ways. In particular, we see the Pharisees' opposition to him, with their demand for a sign. Matthew concludes the chapter with a brief incident showing the opposite attitude — the true mark of those who belong to the kingdom of Christ.

The two kingdoms (12:22-30)

They brought to Jesus **'a demon-possessed man who was blind and mute, and Jesus healed him, so that he could both talk and see'** (12:22). This raised the possibility for some of those present that Jesus was truly the Messiah, **'the Son of David'**. For the Pharisees the significance was entirely different. They rejected this evidence that Jesus was the Messiah.

Instead, they explained it away by saying, **'It is only by Beelzebub, the prince of demons, that this fellow drives out demons'** (12:24). Jesus demonstrates that he is not merely 'this fellow', but the Son of God, by showing that he **'knew their thoughts'**. His response is to speak of two kingdoms: his kingdom and the kingdom of Satan.

He starts from a general principle, that any **'kingdom divided against itself will be ruined'**. From this he deduces that for him to have the aid of Beelzebub, or Satan, in driving out demons would mean that Satan's kingdom was divided against itself and so would not survive. In verse 25 he adds an *argumentum ad hominem*:[1] if his exorcisms demonstrate co-operation with Beelzebub, then what about the exorcisms performed by the disciples of the Pharisees? This, however, is just by the way. His main point is that by his coming and ministry he, Jesus, is bringing in the kingdom of God and thus conquering the kingdom of Satan. By driving out demons he shows that this is happening and, from this, that he is truly the Messiah.

The New Testament is very clear that Satan rules the kingdom of this world. He is 'the god of this age' (2 Cor. 4:4). His is 'the dominion of darkness' (Col. 1:13). The conflict between him and Christ, the ruler of the kingdom of God, comes to its climax at the cross, when 'The prince of this world will be driven out' (John 12:31). Jesus tells his disciples that 'The prince of this world is coming' (John 14:30). Satan has his own servants, demons, and through their activity he rules this world, promoting sin and bringing misery to the children of men. This is not the first time that Jesus has been aligned with Beelzebub and Satan. Indeed, he had even been called Beelzebub (10:25). In contrast with their accusations, Jesus makes it very clear that it is **'by the Spirit of God'** that he is driving out demons (12:28). This is very significant in the light of the difficult and controversial reference to 'the blasphemy against the Holy Spirit' in the following verses.

Before that, however, he uses a brief parable in verse 29 to show the link between driving out demons and the coming of his kingdom. He asks, **'How can anyone enter a strong man's house and carry off his possessions unless he first ties up the strong man? Then he can rob his house.'** By his coming and ministry Jesus is defeating Satan, tying up the strong man, and thus is able to rescue men and women from his possession by demons. All this he does by the Spirit, with whom he has been anointed, as the quotation from Isaiah pointed out (12:18). The bringing of justice and righteousness is one way of expressing Christ's defeat of sin and evil in the kingdom of the devil. Jesus does not say when he tied up the strong man, but this must include his victorious encounter with Satan and his temptations in the desert. It will come to a climax at the cross and be demonstrated most clearly by the resurrection. From then on Christ's kingdom spreads to the whole world: Satan is bound and unable to prevent this (Rev. 20:2-3).

In this battle there is no neutrality: **'He who is not with me is against me, and he who does not gather with me scatters'** (12:30). Jesus is conscious of his disciples at this point and, looking to the future, speaks of gathering men into his kingdom. The opposition will seek to scatter. Jesus is not giving a theoretical account of the two kingdoms, but calling on his disciples, and us, to support him in the coming of this kingdom by the preaching of the gospel in the power of the Spirit, which rescues men from the clutches of Satan.

The two blasphemies (12:31-32)

These verses are notoriously difficult. Many Christians have taken them wrongly and been brought to despair. It is important to see them in context. **'And so'** links these verses with the general statement in verse 30. We are not concerned here with a particular statement which brings tragedy to a Christian, but with an expression of opposition to Christ which comes from the heart, as is explained in the verses that follow. Although there are clear links with the warning passages in Hebrews 6 and 10, we must not overstate them and forget to treat these verses in their context. The important question to be considered is how the blasphemy and speaking against the Holy Spirit are apparently more grievous than speaking against the Son of Man, Jesus himself. It cannot be, in the light of the rest of the Bible, that the Holy Spirit is seen as superior to the Son of God. **'Every sin and blasphemy will be forgiven men'** (12:31), but clearly not without repentance. This implies that the reason why **'the blasphemy against the Spirit will not be forgiven'** is that there is no repentance. This blasphemy is of such a character that it prevents any such repentance.

In context, therefore, we must understand the relationship in this way: the term **'Son of Man'** is regarded here as applying to Jesus as he appeared before men. They see just another man, 'a man who was humiliated',[2] who in fact withdraws from their view (12:15) and makes no obvious, open claim to be the Messiah. However, now he has driven out a demon, which makes clear his claim to be the Messiah. If, then, the Pharisees attribute this work, not to the Holy Spirit, as Jesus does in verse 28, but to Beelzebub, they are blaspheming the Spirit. 'Demons are cast out and undeniable healings are manifest. But where this indisputability is *nonetheless disputed* and the evidence of Christ is rejected, precisely there we read this unique warning concerning the sin against the Spirit.'[3]

Such a denial of what is clear and apparent must come from an obstinate rejection of the light that is clearly seen and that, therefore, precludes repentance. Repentance comes through receiving light and having the conscience convicted. If that light and that conviction are rejected there is no way to repentance. So, **'Anyone who speaks against the Holy Spirit**

will not be forgiven, either in this age or in the age to come.'
This does not imply that some sins will be forgiven in the age
to come; it is simply a strong way of saying 'never', that 'He is
guilty of an eternal sin', as we read in Mark 3:29. Since true
believers cannot be lost eternally, this means that they need
not be consumed with anxiety over the possibility of falling
into this sin. That does not, however, mean that they can treat
the whole matter casually.

Then and now

The real problem is not the interpretation of these verses in
their context, but rather how we apply them today. Debate
about whether the Pharisees had actually committed the sin or
were simply being warned that they were in danger of doing
so should warn us to be careful before making accusations
against others or worrying about ourselves. In the rest of the
New Testament we do not find the same distinction between
the Son of Man and the Holy Spirit as here. From Pentecost
on, preaching about Christ is always in terms of the Holy Spirit,
the *'proclamation of the full light of Christ'*.[4] Therefore, for
us the issue is much simpler. Do we reject Christ as the Saviour? Do we blaspheme against him as vindicated by the Holy
Spirit, or do we accept the Spirit's testimony and put our faith
in him? There does seem to have been an intermediate stage,
reflected in Hebrews 6 and 10, where men had received an
exceptional witness, as Christ was testified to by the miraculous workings of the Spirit. In Hebrews 2:4 we read that the
'salvation, which was first announced by the Lord, was confirmed to us by those who heard him. God also testified to it
by signs, wonders and various miracles, and gifts of the Holy
Spirit distributed according to his will.' It is perhaps this that
is referred to later, when the author of Hebrews says it is impossible to renew to repentance those 'who have shared in the

Holy Spirit'. These are regarded as 'crucifying the Son of God all over again' (Heb. 6:4,6). Later, those who commit apostasy after they have 'received the knowledge of the truth', are said to have 'insulted the Spirit of grace' (Heb. 10:26,29). Because of this, some maintain that the sin against the Holy Spirit is impossible now that the miraculous charismatic gifts have ceased. This seems unlikely, especially in view of the reference to 'a sin that leads to death' without any mention of these gifts (1 John 5:16), but it should put us on our guard. We must conclude that the light and conviction that are being referred to are of a very definite kind, what Berkouwer calls a conscious disputing of the indisputable, 'incontestable evidence of Christ which is nevertheless contested'.[5] In the light of all this, we find some justification for the often-stated pastoral principle that if someone is concerned that he may have committed this sin, then he need not fear that this is so. Equally, if repentance is manifested, then this blasphemy has not been, and is not being, committed. Here, as indeed with the equally difficult problem of distinguishing between backsliding and apostasy, we are given the same instruction: call them to repentance. Whatever their situation may be, whether they are unbelievers, believers backsliding, or potential apostates, there is only one thing to say to them: 'Repent and return to God.'

The two trees (12:33-37)

Jesus now speaks of judging trees by their fruit. In verse 33 he compares men to trees, good or bad, with good or bad fruit. Whereas elsewhere (7:16-20) the fruit, the evidence by which a good or bad tree is recognized, consists of actions, here it consists of speech. Once again Jesus provides a wider context and setting for the warning about the sin against the Holy Spirit. We should note that, just as in verse 32 he refers to **'Anyone** who speaks a word', so in verse 36 he refers to 'every care-less word' in the singular. The connection is clear. We must conclude that the 'careless word' for which 'men will have to give account on the day of judgement' is not just a mo-mentary, involuntary blasphemy into which a man is deceived by Satan, but the inevitable and revealing outflow from the unbelieving heart.

He is still addressing the Pharisees, it would appear, for he refers to them as a 'brood of vipers'. 'How can you who are evil say anything good?' he asks. 'For out of the overflow of the heart the mouth speaks.' However, the warning is addressed to all, for, 'The good man brings good things out of the good stored up in him, and the evil man brings evil things out of the evil stored up in him.' We, too, must not ignore this warning, for all men 'will have to give account on the day of judgement for every careless word they have spoken'. It is encouraging to read that not only may our words bring condemnation, but also that 'By your words you will be acquitted.' We are warned, not only that we must avoid blasphemy, the obvious and extreme denial of Christ when seen in his fulness, but also everything that comes from an evil heart. It may be that 'Make a tree good,' in verse 33 is not a real command, but a proverbial saying. Nevertheless, we are here urged to have our hearts right with God, renewed by the Spirit and ready to confess to Christ, not speak against him.

The sign of Jonah (12:38-42)

Then 'some of the Pharisees and teachers of the law' come to Jesus with a request, which illustrates very well their hard-ened attitude to Christ, in spite of the clear manifestations that he is the Messiah. 'Teacher', they say, 'we want to see a miraculous sign from you.' He has already given them many signs and one, indeed, in the recent past (12:22), but they have not believed what they have seen. What they mean by 'a sign' is very different from what the Bible usually means. They want something that would compel faith, what is called in 16:1 'a sign from heaven'. They have already dismissed the signs that he has given them: healings, giving of sight and driving out demons. They are demanding a sign as a condition of faith. This is putting God to the test. Before they will believe in God he must prove himself to them. No wonder Jesus calls them **'a wicked and adulterous generation'**. This is his how Israel behaved in the wilderness. God had promised; God had given them his word; but unless he did something compelling they would not believe. It is this that Jesus was tempted to do in the wilderness. He knew, because God had promised, that the Father would take care of him, but Satan tempted him to ask for a sign by throwing himself off the temple. God would have had to prove himself.

Signs were given to strengthen faith, not to convince unbelievers. In recent times we have seen a movement, the so-called Third Wave or 'Signs and Wonders' movement, which works on the basis that if we can work 'power events' or miracles before unbelievers, they will be so convinced of the truth of the gospel that they will believe. Not only is this wrong in theory, as we have just seen, but it is futile in practice. Of the many attempts to perform miracles only very few are even claimed to be successful. If this is intended to be a test of the gospel, then the unbeliever will be quite within his rights to conclude that the gospel is only five or ten per cent true! Jesus did not work on that basis. He constantly refused to give signs to persuade people. Instead he performed signs which provided evidence for those who were ready and willing to believe. We must beware of a wrong attitude to signs. The arguments based on the practice of Christ and his apostles are only superficially plausible and actually very misleading.

Jesus does promise them a sign, in fact, but it will not be one of the kind they are seeking. Apart from anything else, this sign will only be in the future. They are responsible for believing in him in the present, but if they refuse to do this, then at a point in the future they will be given a sign which will confirm his position as Messiah, or as Son of Man, and which will be given in such a way as to condemn them. The **'sign of the prophet Jonah'** was one of 'resurrection'. After **'three days and three nights in the belly of a huge fish'**, Jonah was cast up on the shore near Nineveh. To the men of Nineveh this came as confirmation of his standing as God's prophet and thus of his declaration of judgement against them. So it would be with Christ's resurrection. According to Paul, speaking to the men of Athens, God 'has set a day when he will judge the world with justice by the man he has appointed. He has given proof of this to all men by raising him from the dead' (Acts 17:31).

The sign of the prophet Jonah demanded repentance, as Jesus demands repentance of the people listening to him. However, these men refused to repent in spite of all the signs that they had seen. Jesus warns them that **'The men of Nineveh'**, to whom Jonah had preached, **'will stand up at the judgement with this generation and condemn it; for they repented at the preaching of Jonah, and now one greater than Jonah is here.'** Not only the Ninevites, but also the **'Queen of the South'**, the Queen of Sheba, **'will rise at the judgement with this generation and condemn it; for she came from the ends of the earth to listen to Solomon's wisdom, and now one greater than Solomon is here.'** Jesus repeats his claim to be 'something greater' than all that has gone before (cf. 12:6). The Ninevites responded to a mere prophet; these Israelites refused to repent at the preaching of the Son of Man, the Son of God. The Queen of the South made every effort to hear Solomon's wisdom and acknowledge it; these men will not listen to Jesus with his far superior wisdom. We, today, must realize that we have all the evidence that we need in the gospel, in the Word of God. We do not need to look for signs, nor may we rely on the mere hearing of the gospel. We must repent, believe and produce fruit, both of word and action, that will demonstrate that our hearts have been renewed.

This wicked generation (12:43-45)

The particular sign that introduced this section was the driving out of a demon from the blind and mute man. Jesus now warns that mere exorcism is not enough. He describes what happens when a demon is merely driven out, without proper repentance and faith following: **'When an evil spirit comes out of a man, it goes through arid places seeking rest and does not find it. Then it says, "I will return to the house I left." When it arrives, it finds the house unoccupied, swept clean and put in order. Then it goes and takes with it seven other spirits more wicked than itself, and they go in and live there. And the final condition of that man is worse than the first.'** This is a warning to his hearers that freedom from demon-possession is not enough. There must be repentance and faith in him.

The danger is of being possessed by nothing — no replacing of the demon by the Holy Spirit. This indwelling, by implication, is the only safeguard against a final condition which is worse than the first. The further implication is that anyone who is indwelt by the Spirit cannot be possessed by one demon, or seven of them. Christians are secure, not from the temptations of Satan, but from demon-possession, contrary to much popular teaching today.

In fact, Jesus does not apply the warning specifically to the individual case. He speaks of **'this wicked generation'**, applying it to the whole people and to his ministry. It has often been stated that the results of his ministry must have been quite remarkable, with many healed and, especially, many freed from demons. However, this kind of ministry was not enough. Unless they repented and believed in him, then even his ministry, with all its successes, would achieve nothing permanent. Indeed, the situation would be worse. There is a parallel to this in much modern evangelism. We are often told that it does not matter if there are some, or even many, false professions of faith. 'It's worth it for one soul truly saved,' we are told. But that is not the whole story, for those who make a false profession, like those who were freed from demons but did not believe, will be in an even worse situation as a result. As Peter says, it would be better for men not to have an apparent conversion than to make a profession and then desert it (2 Peter 2:20-21). Some will do this, as we shall see in chapter 13, but we must do what we can to avoid it. The best way is to have no stress on signs and miracles, but much on repentance and faith.

The family of Jesus (12:46-50)

'While Jesus was still talking to the crowd', his family came, wanting to speak to him. **'Someone told him, "Your mother and brothers are standing outside, wanting to speak to you."'** As so often, the reply that Jesus gives can easily be misunderstood, in this instance to give the impression that he did not love his mother and brothers. This is far from the case, as we may see from his care of his mother, Mary, while he was dying on the cross (John 19:26-27). What he is doing is pointing out that mere family relationships are of no consequence in the kingdom. He points to his disciples, saying, **'Here are my mother and my brothers.'** The family of God is the family of Jesus and that family consists of **'whoever does the will of my Father in heaven'**.

Far from stressing signs and wonders, Jesus lays his emphasis on doing the will of God. We have already seen this in chapter 7: 'Not everyone who says to me, "Lord, Lord," will enter the kingdom of heaven, but only he who does the will of my Father who is in heaven.' This is a recurrent emphasis in Matthew's Gospel. This is the righteousness of the kingdom, doing the will of our heavenly Father. This is not a religion of justification by works, but of genuine faith in our Saviour and Lord. By him we come to the Father. Through him we are enabled to obey the Father by the power of the Spirit. The kingdom comes, not just when signs and wonders are performed by Jesus, but when men and women are brought truly to do the will of God. This only happens when they repent and believe in Christ and become the home of the Holy Spirit.

This passage has dealt with many and varied subjects related to the coming of the kingdom, which will be illustrated and expanded in the parables of chapter 13. We must allow nothing to replace obedience to the Word of God, an obedience which does not deny faith but is based on faith, and produces appropriate works. This is how the kingdom comes.

21.
The parable of the sower

Please read Matthew 13:1-23

There is very little that is more depressing, both for the preacher and the congregation, than the lack of gospel success. Sometimes there is no response at all, but at other times there are apparent results, which never come to anything genuine and fruitful. The effect of this can be a crisis of confidence in the gospel and in the power of the Spirit, which leads to discouragement and a lack of zeal in evangelism. Even worse, it may lead to the adoption of unbiblical methods and gimmicks, in a desperate attempt to obtain 'success'. One answer to this is a proper understanding of how the kingdom of God actually comes and this is provided in this third main discourse of the Gospel, in chapter 13. Here we have seven parables (or eight, depending on one's definition), all linked with the last section of chapter 12, which occurred **'that same day'** (13:1). How is it that the disciples of Jesus came to this privileged position of being called his 'brothers'? Chapter 13 gives the answer to this and other questions.

Parables

Many children brought up in the church can define a parable, using the traditional, and indeed time-honoured, definition: an earthly story with a heavenly meaning. While this is a useful rule of thumb, it does not cover the wide range of verbal forms which come under the umbrella of the term 'parable'. Parables include proverbs, riddles, wisdom sayings and even metaphors and similes. Verse 52 would be included in such a definition, as an extended simile. Not all parables are in fact earthly stories — for instance, the story of the rich man and Lazarus includes heaven and hell — but most of the story parables are based on a wonderfully acute observation of the natural world and of human life.[1] Further, we must be more precise about the 'heavenly' meaning. It is better termed 'spiritual'; it concerns the coming of the kingdom of God in particular.

In recent years many scholars have insisted that a parable can have only one main point. They assert that anything like an allegory, with a set of parallels, is a later invention or a wrong interpretation. However, this usually comes from an unbelieving attitude to the Word of God. They would reject Christ's interpretation of the parable of the sower as a later insertion. There is no evidence to support this, so we must gratefully follow his explanation in verses 18-23, where he goes into some detail with several points of comparison — rather like an allegory. As we would expect, this interpretation makes excellent sense and is of great spiritual value!

The parable of the sower (13:1-9)

We read that **'Jesus went out of the house and sat by the lake. Such large crowds gathered round him that he got into a boat and sat in it, while all the people stood on the shore.'** The summary statement, **'Then he told them many things in parables'**, suggests that the parts of the chapter where the disciples talk alone with Jesus, asking him questions, are not, perhaps, in their chronological order. Instead, having given the first parable, Matthew finds it appropriate to insert the section about the purpose of speaking in parables. Certainly, we are told that he spoke these parables to the people in general, not just to the disciples. If they showed some puzzlement and lack of understanding, then the disciples' later question would be quite natural.

This first parable about **'a farmer'**, usually referred to as 'a sower', focuses mainly, not on the sower himself or even on the seed, but on the different kinds of soil. There are four kinds of soil: the hardened soil of the path along the edge of the field, the rocky places with only a shallow layer of soil, the area where thorn-bushes are growing, and then the good ground. Since the key to much in this Gospel is fruitfulness, we must take it that only the fourth kind of soil, which alone produced a crop — a hundred, sixty or thirty times what was sown — is the proper and approved kind of soil. **'Good'** usually means something like fulfilling its proper function. Here that means fertile.

Jesus closes the parable with an exhortation: **'He who has ears, let him hear.'** This is a challenge to his hearers and, nowadays, to the reader. This is an important subject and, by implication, not an easy one to understand. He therefore presses on his hearers the need to think clearly and respond carefully. He does not indicate at this point what that proper response should be. Before we have an explanation and interpretation of this parable, Matthew inserts the disciples' question and our Lord's answer.

Christ's purpose (13:10-12)

'The disciples came to him and asked, "Why do you speak to the people in parables?"' (13:10). The reason for this questioning is not stated. Perhaps the disciples assume that they understand all right from their privileged position, but think it a waste of time speaking to the people who do not have the same understanding. Of course, the evidence of later verses is that the disciples had not understood either. In answer to their questions, Jesus explains the rationale behind his use of parables in teaching. He begins by telling the disciples that they have a great privilege. To them has been given **'the knowledge of the secrets of the kingdom of heaven'**, but the crowds have not received this knowledge. Secrets, literally 'mysteries', are not by nature mysterious and do not remain secret. In the New Testament a mystery is a revealed secret, one of God's hidden purposes which has now been made known to his people. For Paul, the fact of the Gentiles' equal position in the church, only hinted at in the Old Testament, but revealed clearly through his ministry, is one such mystery.

Jesus does not say that the mysteries have been given to them, but the basic knowledge essential for understanding of them. What this is, again, is not stated, but it would seem to be the basic key to the teaching of Jesus and especially to his parables, that in him, the Christ, the prophesied kingdom has come. The distinction here is the same as in 1 Corinthians 2:14, where Paul contrasts those who are spiritual with others who are natural, that is, unregenerate men without the Spirit, who cannot and do not understand the things of the Spirit of God. Having this basic knowledge means that the disciples can profit from the further teaching about the mysteries of the kingdom. **'Whoever has will be given more, and he will have an abundance. Whoever does not have, even what he has will be taken from him'** (13:12). Not having this basic understanding means that they are deprived of any real profit from further hearing about these mysteries or secrets. Indeed, Jesus may be referring here to the fact that they do not even receive the further teaching. Jesus, after a certain stage, teaches only his disciples (16:21), because of God's judicial action, to which he now turns.

Isaiah's prophecy (13:13-15)

Verse 13 gives the reason why Jesus speaks to the crowd in parables. We should insert the word 'because', omitted by the NIV, before Christ's words: **'Though seeing, they do not see; though hearing, they do not hear or understand.'** These words refer to the prophecy of Isaiah 6:9-10, which is quoted in full in the following verses. The implication is that because the people do not understand, wilfully we must assume, God hardens them so that they cannot understand. He does this by giving them the teaching in this particular form. In other words, Jesus is here confirming the stress on God's sovereignty which we have seen in verse 11. Understanding is either given or not given; God either grants or does not grant this insight into the mysteries of the kingdom, according to his good pleasure (cf. 11:25-26).

It is possible that the insertion of the actual quotation from Isaiah is the work of Matthew, who lays great stress in his Gospel on the fulfilment of Scripture, but this is not necessarily so. This quotation is from the Septuagint (LXX), not from the Hebrew. In John 12:39-40 the Hebrew is used, which is even more strongly predestinarian. That version says that:

[God] has blinded their eyes
    and deadened their hearts,
so they can neither see with their eyes,
    nor understand with their hearts,
    nor turn — and I would heal them.

Although the expression is less stringent here — **'this people's heart has become calloused'** — the meaning is the same, as indicated by the use of **'otherwise'** in verse 15. In Isaiah 6 this effect is attributed to the prophet himself: 'Make the heart of this people calloused.'

Putting these various versions together, we find that in God's sovereign purpose his Word, the word of the gospel, is the efficient cause in hardening. Where men refuse to believe, God in his justice hardens their hearts in unbelief by the effect of the gospel on that unbelieving heart. There is no infusion of hardness. God does not directly harden by the Spirit, but the Word, which is intended to bring life, has a different effect on the rebellious and unbelieving heart. In this sense, it is equally true to say that a man hardens his own heart, as we find in the account of Pharaoh in Exodus. We may see a similar effect from rainfall. If it falls on good ground, it produces growth and fruitfulness. If it falls on cement, the result is hardness.

The deduction some make from all this is that we should not use the parables at all in preaching to unbelievers, but only to the saints. That is not the case. There are three possibilities when we use the parables. First, we may follow Jesus and use the parables to explain to disciples the mysteries of the kingdom. Secondly, in the wisdom of God, that same preaching can hide the gospel from the rebellious and unbelieving, as an act of justice. This is actually intended to prevent the non-elect from hearing, understanding, turning and being healed, as the end of the quotation from Isaiah makes clear. However, we must repeat that this process of hardening is judicial and only comes to those who are already opposed to the gospel. There is also a third possibility, which is reflected in verse 9, Jesus' warning to his hearers. Men's positions are not fixed. God can use this preaching to change unbelievers. There is a challenge here which, under the influence of God's Spirit, can bring unbelievers to believe and the rebellious to submit to the gospel.

Privilege (13:16-17)

Jesus tells his disciples that they are in a different position entirely from the unbelieving multitudes. He adds, **'But blessed are your eyes because they see, and your ears because they hear.'** This is not their own doing; they are the objects of God's grace and mercy. However, they are privileged to know the mysteries and, even more, to see the fulfilment of those mysteries. In verse 14 Jesus says that in the crowds, **'is fulfilled the prophecy of Isaiah'**. In his disciples also the prophecies are fulfilled as they come to believe in Jesus. He draws a contrast between them and **'many prophets and righteous men'** who **'longed to see what you see but did not see it, and to hear what you hear but did not hear it'**.

Not only the disciples, but we ourselves, ought to understand this great privilege. Amazingly we have been chosen out of the mass of mankind to hear and believe the gospel. This is an act of God's free grace. We receive because it has been given us to receive. Repentance and faith have been granted to us. We should also rejoice in the privilege of being new-covenant believers, who know and see so much more clearly than those before the coming of Christ. They were justified and saved, but by comparison knew so little. So much was unclear to them, as Peter reminds us: 'Concerning this salvation, the prophets, who spoke of the grace that was to come to you, searched intently and with the greatest care, trying to find out the time and circumstances to which the Spirit of Christ in them was pointing when he predicted the sufferings of Christ and the glories that would follow. It was revealed to them that they were not serving themselves but you, when they spoke of the things that have now been told you by those who have preached the gospel to you by the Holy Spirit sent from heaven. Even angels long to look into these things' (1 Peter 1:10-12). How thankful we should be for this great privilege!

The interpretation of the parable (13:3-7,18-22)

The intention of this parable is clearly to explain the results of gospel preaching in terms of the different responses coming from varied heart conditions. This is not, of course, just an intellectual exercise, for we remember that it closes with a challenge to hear properly. In fact, hearing properly is of the essence of the parable. Jesus indicates that we have a real responsibility in this matter. In spite of the stress on God's sovereignty and election in the previous verses, here the stress is on how we hear. Understanding is clearly the key in verse 14. The Israelites' tragedy was of 'hearing but never understanding' and in verse 19 we read, **'When anyone hears the message about the kingdom and does not understand it, the evil one comes and snatches away what was sown in his heart.'**

This is the first response. The picture is that **'As he was scattering the seed, some fell along the path, and the birds came and ate it up'** (13:4). A path, of course, is hard, because of the passing of many feet. The devil is seen in the birds, who remove the message, the seed, which has not been absorbed into the ground. This first kind of soil, then, deals with those who do not really allow the gospel, the message about the kingdom, to enter their hearts. In modern terms, it goes in one ear and out of the other. They do not retain the message in order to think about it and act upon it. They make no effort to understand it, and so lose it altogether. In terms of verse 12, they do not have the knowledge of the secrets of the kingdom. They make no effort to understand the secrets of the kingdom, and what they do have, the message of the kingdom, is taken away from them. In this instance it is the devil, the Evil One, who takes away the message.

The second category concerns the seed that **'fell on rocky places, where it did not have much soil. It sprang up**

**quickly, because the soil was shallow. But when the sun
came up, the plants were scorched, and they withered because they had no root'** (13:5-6). If the first category concerns those who fail to understand at all, this next kind of soil
describes those who fail to understand the gospel properly,
i.e. fully. True, this man **'at once receives it with joy'** (13:20).
This is surely because of the good news. In Luke 8:13 it is
described as believing 'for a while'. However, this is not real
faith, for although he has understood that this message is good
news, he has not understood what is involved. In modern evangelism this may be the fault of the preacher, who has not made
it clear that faith demands taking up our cross and following
Christ. The sower in the parable is really the Lord himself, so
there is no suggestion that the preaching of the gospel here is
faulty. Even so, anyone who has a shallow response will not
receive that part of the message. He does not count the cost
and so, **'When trouble or persecution comes because of
the word, he quickly falls away.'**

This soil does stress the importance of making this issue
clear in our presentation of the good news. We must not be so
keen to stress the salvation and the joy that we do not tell our
hearers that there is a price to be paid. This does not 'pay' for
the forgiveness, of course, but is incurred as a result of receiving forgiveness and becoming a disciple of Christ. We must do
our best to make sure that the gospel is grafted into the hearts
of our hearers, even though this may take time and effort.
Certainly there is an implied warning in the words **'at once'**.
There can be too easy a reception of the message. If a man
does not pause to think, then we have clearly not made the
implications clear enough. It follows that exerting pressure by
any form of decisionism is very dangerous and must be shunned.

The third kind of soil illustrates the failure to understand,
not only fully, but spiritually. The parable describes the seed as
falling **'among thorns'**, which grew up and choked the plants.

The thorns are interpreted to mean **'the worries of this life and the deceitfulness of wealth'**. These are sinful aspects of the heart which must be renounced if there is to be genuine repentance. There has to be a turning from this life and from materialism, as well as from outward sins, when we come to faith in Christ. If we do not do this, the word of Christ is choked. Instead of obeying in faith, men disobey because they are worried about the consequences in this life. Instead of living for Christ, men live for this world, whether riches or some other aspect of human life, and so bear no fruit. We must not make the mistake of thinking that this refers simply to an inferior Christian life, which can be dealt with by some kind of second experience. Jesus says that such choked hearing renders **'it unfruitful'**. They bear no fruit at all. This means there is no faith and no salvation.

Therefore, our proclamation must make clear the necessity for repentance. The fact that this may deter some from believing is irrelevant, for if they do 'believe' in these circumstances it will not be real faith, a faith that brings fruit. Jesus seems to be following this pattern, when he deals with the rich young ruler in 19:21-22. We must again remember that this failure to repent is not necessarily the preacher's fault. Nevertheless, we should maintain a certain reserve about accepting professions of faith, until we see whether fruit is produced, or whether worldliness continues to rule the life of the professed believer.

The good soil (13:8,23)

After three kinds of soil that bear no fruit, and so describe a continuing lost condition, we have the last kind, what Jesus describes as **'good soil'**. He gives no indication that this proportion of three to one is supposed to represent the proportion of false conversions to true. If we think of the parable, we would expect that with a good farmer most of the seed would be sown in good ground. The proportions are not part of the message. It is the response, and the nature of the response, that matters. This **'seed that fell on good soil is the man who hears the word and understands it. He produces a crop, yielding a hundred, sixty or thirty times what was sown'** (13:23). Again the stress is on understanding. He understands the gospel, the warning about taking up the cross and denying self, so he responds by repenting, not just believing, and goes on to bear fruit by obeying the Lord himself. (It may be that the varied proportion of fruit is related to the depth of understanding.) Here we must refer back to 12:50 and 7:21, with their descriptions of the true disciple as the one who 'does the will of my Father in heaven'. This stress on practical righteousness, the result of obedience to the will of God, is characteristic of our Lord's teaching, especially in the Gospel of Matthew. Righteous fruit is the only real proof of the conversion, even with proper evangelism.

The most general aspect of the teaching here is that the kingdom comes by the preaching of the message of the King. This is the key to all parables. In Mark 4:13 Jesus says to his disciples, 'Don't you understand this parable? How then will you understand any parable?' We must learn to interpret them all in terms of the kingdom, and especially of the word of the gospel. Far from being discouraged, we should be the more determined to proclaim the truth of the gospel, seeking the power of the Spirit to make it effective in the hearts and lives of men and women. Only he can give them understanding (1 Cor. 2:14) and for this we must pray. There is no point in resorting to other methods — drama, singing and other gimmicks. God's kingdom comes in God's way; the parable of the sower must be our guide.

We must, then, not be discouraged when there are superficial responses to our testimony or preaching. Even our Lord's ministry was not uniformly successful in this sense. However, we must take all necessary care to try to ensure that our hearers do understand what the gospel is all about. We must not rush matters, pressing for professions of faith and refraining from making clear the difficult elements in the message. We must not hesitate to demand repentance, because we think it implies a works salvation. All this is implied by this parable.

However, the main point is to speak to those who hear, telling them that they must listen properly and so understand. It is not merely hearing the gospel that counts; they must understand and respond deeply, fully, spiritually. The reader is urged to ask whether this has in fact been his experience. Are you merely claiming to believe the good news about salvation, forgiveness and eternal life, or have you also turned from the old life and from allegiance to this world and its goods? Have you taken up the cross, willing to follow Christ wherever he leads, whatever it costs? Have you committed yourself to obedience to his word so as to bear much fruit?

22.
More encouraging parables

Please read Matthew 13:24-52

We live in the days of 'the quick fix'. Whatever the problem, Christians expect to find a simple answer, one verse which ends the problem, an immediate solution to every difficulty. No doubt the people of our Lord's day, including the disciples, had similar expectations. Jesus, on the other hand, knew there was no substitute for gaining a proper understanding of God's ways. Where there is discouragement or perplexity, as in the case of John the Baptist, the great necessity is to know how God works. In our case, we do not need the advice of experts, whether historians, psychologists or businessmen, but the teaching of the Bible. That is what we find in the parables of this chapter. In verse 35, Matthew links these parables with what was spoken through the prophet: **'I will open my mouth in parables, I will utter things hidden since the creation of the world.'** The **'prophet'** is, in fact, the psalmist, and he is quoting Psalm 78:2. The point of the psalm is that by understanding how God has worked in the past, the next generation is enabled to put its trust in God, not to 'forget his deeds but ... keep his commands' (v. 7). The parables are part of that same method. As we understand God's ways, we are encouraged to trust even, or perhaps especially, when the going is hard, when there are disappointments and opposition, and the work of God seems small and insignificant.

The wheat and the weeds, the mustard seed and the yeast (13:24-33)

As we come to the next parables, we must remember what we have learned in the parable of the sower. The key to the coming of the kingdom of heaven is the sowing of the Word of God, the gospel. So in this parable of the weeds (traditionally known as 'the parable of the wheat and the tares'), we find sowing once again: **'A man sowed good seed in his field. But while everyone was sleeping, his enemy came and sowed weeds among the wheat, and went away. When the wheat sprouted and formed ears, then the weeds also appeared.'** In response to the questions of his servants the owner attributes the weeds to the work of an enemy. When they ask if he wants them to go and pull up the weeds, he tells them this would harm the wheat as well as getting rid of the weeds. Instead, he commands them: **'Let both grow together until the harvest.'** Then the division between wheat and weeds will take place; the weeds will be **'burned'** and the wheat gathered and brought into his **'barn'**.

Before we come to Christ's explanation of this parable, we have to mention two other parables. In the first, the kingdom of heaven is compared to a mustard seed. This is proverbially **'the smallest of all your seeds, yet when it grows, it is the largest of garden plants and becomes a tree'**. Next Jesus tells of the yeast **'that a woman took and mixed into a large amount of flour until it worked all through the dough'**. The parable of the sower warned the disciples about hearing the gospel properly. At the same time it gave them encouragement, that there would be a harvest, in spite of the many apparent failures. These next parables are intended to give further help in understanding the way the harvest comes, how the kingdom grows.

The explanation of the wheat and the weeds (13:36-43)

Jesus did not give any explanations to the crowds, but after recounting these parables, **'He left the crowd and went into the house. His disciples came to him and said, "Explain to us the parable of the weeds in the field."'** On this occasion he clearly identifies himself as the sower of the good seed, **'the Son of Man'**. The enemy, who sows the weeds, is **'the devil'**. Perhaps the most important part of the explanation, at least as far as controversy is concerned, is Christ's statement that **'The field is the world.'** The subject of the parable is the presence of the kingdom of God in the world; it is not the presence of unbelievers in the church. Too often this parable has been used to assert that the church of Jesus Christ will always be mixed, **'the sons of the kingdom'** alongside **'the sons of the evil one'**, and that therefore we should make no effort to obtain a pure church by excluding those who make a false profession. Even Calvin fell into this trap, following Augustine in his struggle against the fourth-century separatists, the Donatists. However, Jesus did not say that the field is the church, but the world.[1]

Christ's point is that that there was to be no immediate judgement with his coming. Premature judgement would ruin the crop. In fact, there would be no crop. God's way is to have the gospel preached to an unbelieving world, sowing good seed, producing the sons of the kingdom, while the enemy, the devil, does his worst. It is true that we may not expect to have a completely pure church; we cannot read hearts and although we should try to exclude those whose profession of faith is false, we shall not be entirely successful. Nevertheless church discipline is clearly taught in the New Testament as a necessity and we must not recoil from exercising it where possible and necessary.

The parable, however, is aimed at a different problem. How do we reconcile the continuance of evil and the prospering of Satan's work with the coming of the kingdom? The answer is that God permits them to 'grow together until the harvest' (13:30), to coexist for a while. He allows believers and unbelievers to live together in the world for the time being, but at the end justice will be done. A harvest will come at the end of the age, but not before. Jesus is still addressing the problem felt by John the Baptist, which was crucial for the new age. If Jesus is the Messiah, the one who was to come, why has the judgement not come also? Why do unbelievers prosper and believers suffer persecution, as John himself was doing? The answer has to be that the kingdom of heaven comes in two stages. It is inaugurated with the coming of the Son of Man, Jesus Christ. From that time on the kingdom comes, the gospel is preached, sinners are converted, the Word of God does its work. Then, at the end, the kingdom will come finally and eternally.

Jesus tells us, **'The harvest is the end of the age... The Son of man will send out his angels, and they will weed out of his kingdom everything that causes sin and all who do evil'** (13:39,41). The fate of unbelievers is to be thrown into **'the fiery furnace, where there will be weeping and gnashing of teeth'**. John need not fear that evil will go unpunished. In God's time the kingdom will be established perfectly. In God's time, also, **'The righteous will shine like the sun in the kingdom of their Father.'** The righteous will be vindicated and rewarded. Until then we must preach the gospel and suffer persecution and opposition from the ungodly, who are serving their master the devil, the enemy. We should not be discouraged by this. God's purpose is sure. His kingdom will come. We must be encouraged.

The mustard seed (13:31-32)

The parable of the wheat and the weeds focuses on the discouragement caused by the continuing presence of unbelievers and opposition to the gospel. In this next parable the discouragement comes because of the smallness of the kingdom. The mustard seed is proverbially small, especially by comparison with a tree. The minute seed grows into a shrub, which could have a height of six to twelve feet (two to four metres). Jesus encourages his disciples by telling them that the kingdom will prosper and grow, in spite of the small beginnings. The point is not size as such. The mustard plant is not large compared with a real tree, although there will be such largeness: 'For the earth will be filled with the knowledge of the glory of the LORD, as the waters cover the sea' (Hab. 2:14). It is the principle of growth from small beginnings that is important. All necessary potential for growth is there in the twelve apostles, the gospel and the future working of the Holy Spirit.

The statement that **'The birds of the air come and perch in its branches'** refers back to the book of Daniel. (It may not be without significance that our Lord's title as the Son of Man also comes from Daniel.) In Daniel King Nebuchadnezzar has a dream in which he sees a large tree in whose branches the birds of the air live. Daniel's interpretation of this is that Nebuchadnezzar's kingdom had grown until it reached the sky and his dominion extended to the distant parts of the earth (Dan. 4:22), that is, it included many nations. The same explanation applies here. The kingdom of heaven will grow until, like that of the Son of Man in Daniel 7:14, it includes 'all peoples, nations and men of every language'.

This encouragement is needed now, as often before. This is 'the day of small things' (Zech. 4:10). It is easy to despise such days and believe that nothing good can ever happen, that the work of God can never make real progress. Such an attitude cuts the nerve of our resolve and weakens our determination to preach the gospel. Jesus calls upon us to hear his parable and be encouraged. Although unbelievers will continue, and persecution and opposition will go on until the end of the age, we can expect growth and progress in the kingdom. This parable promises nothing about the conversion of the world as such, but it does encourage us to go on preaching the gospel, sowing the seed, in confidence that the kingdom is like a mustard seed.

The yeast (13:33)

This parable has aroused much controversy. In the Old Testament leaven, or yeast, is usually used as a symbol of evil or corruption. When they left Egypt, the Israelites had to remove all leaven or yeast from their houses and the apostle Paul refers to 'the yeast of malice and wickedness', contrasted with 'bread without yeast, the bread of sincerity and truth' (1 Cor. 5:6-8). In the light of this many dispensationalist expositors, following John Nelson Darby, have taken this parable as a prophecy of the corruption of the professing church. Evil, unbelief and unrighteousness will so permeate the church that it will become thoroughly corrupt. Darby deduced from this that Christendom, as he termed it, had to be deserted and a new spiritual fellowship begun. Interpreted like this, the parable is a recipe for despair, not an encouragement.

However, this is not necessarily correct. Indeed, such an interpretation is almost impossible in this context. The subject is the coming of the kingdom, not the corruption of the church. Jesus is still trying to encourage, not depress, his disciples. It is a mistake to think that biblical symbols always have the same significance. 'Lion' in the Bible may refer both to Jesus Christ, 'the Lion of the tribe of Judah' (Rev. 5:5), and to the devil, who is 'like a roaring lion looking for someone to devour' (1 Peter 5:8). In addition, it is not true that yeast, or leaven, is always evil even in the Old Testament. True, most sacrifices had to be free from leaven, but not all. In Leviticus 7:12-13 we find that it was permissible to offer either 'wafers made without yeast' or 'cakes and bread made with yeast' (see also Lev. 23:17).

Therefore, in context the parable must be taken to teach the possibility of a small amount of yeast permeating a large amount of flour. **'The kingdom of heaven is like yeast that a woman took and mixed into a large amount of flour until it worked all through the dough'** (13:33). We must not be discouraged by our smallness, but encouraged to make the gospel known. The way the Word of God works is in secret. 'Mixed' may be literally 'hid'. The word works from within, secretly. The kingdom does not come by outward means such as political action. It is the word that works as men and women are born again and begin to live according to God's will. If the parable of the sower stressed man's response to the word, these parables stress the disciples' responsibility to make that word known. There will be no instant final success, no sweeping away of wickedness and unbelief, but in spite of its smallness and hiddenness the gospel of truth, the good news of salvation, will do its work. Christ's kingdom will come on earth gradually, increasingly, thoroughly, until the end of the age when all the evil will be removed and righteousness will reign in heaven and on earth.

Treasure and the pearl (13:44-46)

Here we begin the second group of four parables. The first four gave hope in spite of the delayed consummation of the kingdom, an encouragement to any who felt like John the

Baptist did. Now Jesus concentrates on giving motivation to the disciples as they have to make known the gospel during the period while the kingdom is in its interim phase. The man who finds **'treasure hidden in a field'** (13:44) and sells all he has to buy the field, and so possess the treasure, is accompanied by a merchant who finds a pearl **'of great value'**, sells all he has and buys it. At first sight the two parables seem to be saying the same thing. The treasure and the pearl emphasize the great value of belonging to the kingdom, of possessing salvation. Whatever it may cost to possess the kingdom of heaven, the salvation that Christ gives, is worth it. The joy of possessing such a valuable object more than outweighs the cost involved in gaining it. The present and future kingdom outweigh the cross, the cost of discipleship. In the words of Paul, 'Our light and momentary troubles are achieving for us an eternal glory that far outweighs them all' (2 Cor. 4:17). The reference to joy in verse 44, as in verse 20, tells us that this is true even at present; how much more we shall consider this to be so when we 'shine like the sun in the kingdom'!

What, then, is the difference between the two parables? The first man comes across the treasure. He is not looking for it. It might be dangerous to assert that he came across it 'by accident', although the parable would probably put it like this, but he was not searching for it. This is the experience of many of God's elect. They are taken by surprise when the gospel is made known to them. Paul speaks of these when he says that 'The Gentiles, who did not pursue righteousness, have obtained it, a righteousness that is by faith' (Rom. 9:30). He later quotes Isaiah 65:2, where the prophet speaks for God, saying, 'I was found by those who did not seek me; I revealed myself to those who did not ask for me' (Rom. 10:20). C. S. Lewis was *Surprised by joy*.[2] Those who come across the gospel as they go about their normal lives are warned here to recognize the great value of God's salvation and make it their chief aim and object to possess this. Whatever trouble they have to go to, whatever striving there is to enter the narrow gate, it will be worth it for such a valuable treasure.

By contrast, the merchant is looking for fine pearls. Perhaps he has had a religious upbringing and has spiritual ambitions, or has been stirred to search by meeting a Christian. He is looking for something, for some meaning to life, for eternal life, for rescue from sin, but has never found it. When such a man, perhaps like the rich young ruler, does find what he is looking for, he must not be put off by what it will cost: humbling, repentance, self-denial, taking up his cross (see 19:21-22). On the contrary, he must be ready to give up everything for this. He must be prepared to turn his back on everything else in order to obtain Christ for himself.

Both these men illustrate, by contrast, the description of a cynic given by Oscar Wilde, as 'a man who knows the price of everything and the value of nothing'. These men know the value, as well as the cost. So great is the value that they are willing to pay any price. What a motivation this is to believe or to make known the gospel! As we proclaim it, any who were not seeking will be confronted by it; as we make it known, some who are looking for something, although they do not know what, will find that this gospel, this salvation, satisfies all their deepest needs.

The net (13:47-50)

Here the operation of the kingdom of heaven is compared to the net **'that was let down into the lake and caught all kinds of fish'**. The fishermen catch both good and bad fish. They symbolize the angels who **'at the end of the age ... come and separate the wicked from the righteous and throw them into the fiery furnace, where there will be weeping and**

gnashing of teeth' (13:49-50). The subject is quite clearly the Day of Judgement when God, by his angels, gathers together everyone to appear before him. This is not a repetition of the idea of the disciples as fishers of men in evangelism, but the gathering together of all kinds of people for judgement. We must not make the mistake of thinking that this is a case of distinguishing the naturally good and the naturally bad. The righteous are believers, the sons of the kingdom, and the wicked are those who have not been saved.

The solemnity of the fiery furnace, where there will be weeping and gnashing of teeth, links this parable with that of the wheat and the weeds. There is the same discrimination and judgement. Is this, then, merely a repetition of that earlier parable? In the first place, we must note that although the good fish are mentioned there is no mention of their destiny and reward; the stress is all on the wicked. The purpose of the parable is, therefore, different. The earlier parable mentioned the ultimate judgement of the weeds as an encouragement during the period of delay. Here the judgement of the wicked is set alongside the great value of the kingdom, shown by the treasure and the great pearl. The aim is to give warning not to neglect the great prize, however much it may cost, because the cost of not having the treasure or the pearl is beyond imagining.

The teaching of Jesus is absolutely clear; the eternal consequences of rejecting or ignoring the claims of Christ and his kingdom are horrific. **'Weeping'** conveys the great distress of those who suffer torment in hell. **'Gnashing of teeth'** is not a modern expression; it means 'grinding', and 'conveys', as William Hendriksen explains, 'excruciating pain and frenzied anger'.[3] Hatred of God continues after death. There is no repentance or acknowledgement of sin, but anger against the God who dares to judge and punish. Eternal punishment is eternal, at least in part, because the sin is eternal; it never ceases and so the punishment also continues.

When the aged Bishop of Smyrna, Polycarp, was being threatened with being burnt at the stake for being a Christian, both his friends and his enemies urged him to consider the pain and suffering of that burning. His moving reply was this: 'You threaten me with the fire that burns for an hour and in a little while is put out, for you do not know about the fire of the judgement to come and the fire of eternal punishment reserved for the ungodly.'[4] How much we need this kind of warning, when the world draws near with its threats! When the cost seems too great, we must meditate on the cost of not being a Christian, of not having this eternal salvation, the riches of Christ.

The house owner (13:51-52)

As we saw earlier, the word 'parable' can denote many and varied kinds of speech. The clue in verse 52 is the word **'like'**. Jesus compares a **'teacher of the law who has been instructed about the kingdom of heaven'** — that is a gospel preacher, a disciple of the kingdom — to **'the owner of a house who brings out of his storeroom new treasures as well as old'**. The disciples have a responsibility to do this. This links this parable with the previous ones. It is their responsibility, in the light of the importance of the word (the sower), the present delay for the preaching of the gospel (the wheat and the weeds), the potential of the kingdom to grow and to influence men (the mustard seed and yeast), the value of the kingdom and the gospel of salvation (the treasure and the pearl) and the great danger of being cast into the fiery furnace (the net) to bring out, not just the old treasures of the law, but the new gospel of his coming. It is important to notice that the old teachings are still regarded as treasures, and are not rejected, but fulfilled and supplemented.

This section has given clear teaching about the progressive coming of the kingdom and, thus, the reason for the delay before judgement comes. This is a period for the coming of the kingdom through the preaching of the gospel. That should be abundantly clear. However, there is more to it than the theory of the kingdom's coming. There is also the realization of the tremendous urgency of this. If we have been instructed about the kingdom of heaven, if we have heard and believed the gospel, if we have appreciated the treasure of the kingdom, then we have the same responsibility as the disciples to make that gospel known to those around us.

We should not be discouraged by difficulties, by smallness, opposition and persecution. We should be so encouraged by the evident power of the gospel and the declared purpose of God to bring in his kingdom by this means that we make this our priority. In days when almost anything else is being given priority in the life of the church, we must concentrate on the preaching of the gospel, the communication of the good news to others, by many varied but appropriate means. Only thus will the community of the kingdom be brought into being by the gracious working of God.

Part 5:
The community of the kingdom (13:53 – 18:35)

23.
Jesus and the world

Please read Matthew 13:53 – 14:21

The words, **'When Jesus had finished these parables, he moved on from there'**, as usual indicate the beginning of a new section. These chapters contain the only references to the church *(ekklesia)* in the Gospels, and chapter 18, in particular, is very much concerned with the life of the church. The section as a whole describes the community of the kingdom, the disciples and their ways. However, everything must not be forced into this mould. Matthew has other themes running alongside that of the kingdom. In particular, he is concerned with the revelation of the person of the Lord Jesus Christ, which comes to a climax in chapters 16 and 17.

The author does not immediately embark on a description of the community that Jesus was forming, and which would continue his work after his ascension, but approaches this gradually. Much of the section is concerned with distinguishing Christ's people from those around them, the Pharisees, the Sadducees and the crowds, and also those to whom his community would minister. It is with this relationship to the world, or perhaps his dissociation from the world, that we must begin in these verses.

The world's honour (13:53-58)

After the teachings of the first part of chapter 13, given by the lake, Jesus returned to his home town of Nazareth. There, **'He began teaching the people in their synagogue, and they were amazed.'** They could not deny his **'wisdom and these miraculous powers'**, but they were perplexed by these facts. They seemed to indicate some kind of divine or super-natural origin, but this they could not accept or allow. It may well be that some idea of his claims to be the Messiah had entered their minds, but this could not be true, because they knew him. It is often remarked how difficult it is for a man to become minister of the church in which he was brought up. How much more difficult it was for Jesus to be acknowledged as Messiah, or even as a prophet, in the town where he had grown up!

The people's questions indicate that **'They took offence at him'** (13:57). Once again, 'offence' must be interpreted in the proper sense, that they stumbled over the facts. They were caused to reject him because they could not accept such a deduction from his miracles and teaching. So they asked, **'"Isn't this the carpenter's son? Isn't his mother's name Mary, and aren't his brothers James, Joseph, Simon and Judas? Aren't all his sisters with us?"'** Then comes the clinching question: **'Where then did this man get all these things?'** In this case, certainly, familiarity bred contempt. They rejected what they could not understand. This is quite usual, as Jesus comments: **'Only in his home town and in his own house is a prophet without honour.'**

Jesus understood men, especially those of his home town, and expected nothing less than their rejection. However, the real tragedy here is that by **'their lack of faith'** they cut themselves off from blessing. There, **'He did not do many miracles.'** It is worth noting that it was not just the people of the town, but also those of his own house, who rejected Jesus at this stage (see 12:46-50).

It is clear that Jesus was not concerned with the honour of men. He said, 'I do not accept praise from men' (John 5:41) and we must follow his example. The church must follow her Master in this, as in other matters. We must not look for honour from an unbelieving world. We must not change our message, or even our approach, in order to gain honour. Many have done this. They have modified the gospel, amended or avoided certain truths, compromised their principles, in order to be respected and honoured by the world around them. It is hard to be looked down on. Jesus must have found this even more painful than we do. Here is the Lord of glory, God's chosen Messiah, and the people simply reject him. He will not do anything to gain their respect or honour that compromises his mission and his ministry.

In his first letter to the Corinthians, Paul makes this point very strongly concerning the doctrine of the cross. While the Jews look for acts of power to impress them and the Gentiles want worldly wisdom if they are to give honour, Paul has only the foolishness of God, 'Jesus Christ and him crucified', to preach. Here, ironically, the Jews were shown works of power and still rejected Christ's testimony (see 11:23-24). They could not come to terms with the union of divine and human in him, the fact that one they knew, and had known from his childhood, could also be of divine origin, the Son of God. They had some justification, because of their previous knowledge of him, as he shows by his quotation of the proverb in verse 57, but we today have no such excuse. The Scriptures make it very clear that Jesus is both God and man, however much this may upset the world around us, and we have no right to water this down. Now, as then, the result of denying this is to cut oneself off from blessing. No mighty works of conversion follow where this is denied.

Christ's method and attitude are both to be imitated by us. Seeking honour from men is a snare for us all. It may be a respectable middle-class person, who hates the idea that people regard him as a sinner as he confesses his need of Christ. It may be the biblical scholar, who knows that his academic colleagues regard him as unscholarly, obscurantist, or even unintelligent, a theological dinosaur, because he accepts the infallibility and authority of the Bible. It may be the upper-class Christian, who knows that his peers regard his membership of the church along with those of less affluent circumstances as 'slumming it'. Selina, the godly Countess of Huntingdon, experienced this to a great extent. When she invited her noble acquaintances to hear George Whitefield preach, she received a devastating reply from the Duchess of Buckingham. This referred to the Methodist preachers' 'impertinence and disrespect towards their superiors'. She continued, 'It is monstrous to be told that you have a heart as sinful as the common wretches that crawl on the earth.' She added, very significantly, 'I cannot but wonder that your Ladyship should relish any sentiments so much at variance with high rank and good breeding.'[1]

When another 'lady' attributed the countess's absence from court to her 'praying with her beggars', the Prince of Wales took her part. 'Lady Charlotte,' he replied, 'when I am dying I think I shall be happy to seize the skirt of Lady Huntingdon's mantle to lift me up to heaven.' The countess aroused the anger of some of her tenants through 'her identification with the despised Methodists'. This, she wrote, 'proves that it is the Lord that offends them and so must he continue to the unregenerate heart'.[2] Once again we must remember our Lord's words: 'A student is not above his teacher, nor a servant above his master. It is enough for the student to be like his teacher, and the servant like his master' (10:24-25).

The death of John the Baptist (14:1-12)

The description of the beheading of John the Baptist in verses 3-12 is out of chronological order. Verses 1-2 record Herod's reaction to **'the reports about Jesus'**, whom he regards as John the Baptist **'risen from the dead'**. To him this is the only explanation **'why miraculous powers are at work in him'**. Matthew uses this response by Herod to recall the circumstances of John's death. **'Herod had arrested John and bound him and put him in prison'**, because John had publicly criticized his immorality in marrying **'Herodias, his brother Philip's wife'**. Here Matthew records how, **'On Herod's birthday the daughter of Herodias danced for them and pleased Herod so much that he promised to give her whatever she asked'** (14:6-7). Matthew tells us that, even before this, **'Herod wanted to kill John, but he was afraid of the people, because they considered him a prophet.'** Now, however, he is tricked into getting rid of John, in spite of the people's opposition, in order to satisfy the revenge of Herodias.

Afterwards, **'John's disciples came and took his body and buried it. Then they went and told Jesus'** (14:12). Here is the significance. A warning is given to Jesus that if he perseveres, not only in teaching the truth, but in propounding a gospel of righteousness, he will have to suffer in the same way as John has. The inveterate enmity of Herodias and Herod is like that of Christ's opponents. This follows the rejection of Jesus by the people of his own town and we must assume that Matthew is now drawing the conclusion that the fate suffered by John will also come to his Lord (see 17:12). Once again we have a parting of the ways. Christ and his people are set in opposition to the world. John stood for righteousness against the unrighteousness of Herod. Jesus preached righteousness and his disciples must follow after righteousness.

Here we need to remember the Beatitude: 'Blessed are those who are persecuted because of righteousness, for theirs is the kingdom of heaven' (5:10). Here is a blessing pronounced on John the Baptist, on the disciples of Jesus and on all who follow after righteousness and suffer for it. As we have no right to expect honour from the world, so we cannot expect that we shall avoid persecution. Like John and Jesus, we must call for repentance and demand fruits which match repentance. We may expect persecution, but we can also trust in the work of the Holy Spirit to convict the world of sin and righteousness and judgement (John 16:8-11). What we must not do is yield to the world's threats or conform to its standards. The death of John the Baptist, as announced to the Lord by his disciples, acted as a warning that Jesus was treading the same path. The warning comes to us also and we must take it, not by running away or changing our message, but by remaining faithful by the grace of God.

Feeding the five thousand (14:13-21)

'When Jesus heard' (14:13) seems to indicate that Jesus sought solitude, perhaps in order to reflect upon what had happened to John the Baptist. This, however, would raise chronological problems. It is more likely that it refers back to verses 1 and 2. Jesus withdraws to avoid the hatred of Herod, who, believing that Jesus was a resurrected John, would do his best to get rid of him properly. Although this may have prevented Herod's revenge, it could not produce real solitude for Jesus. **'Hearing of this, the crowds followed him on foot from the towns.'** Jesus could never have avoided the people, hard as he may have tried, but once he was found he could not resist responding to their plight. **'When Jesus landed and saw a large crowd, he had compassion on them and healed their sick.'** Other accounts of the feeding of the five thousand tell us that Jesus also taught the people, as we would expect (Mark 6:34). Here, however, Matthew's stress seems to be on what he did, rather than what he taught. We must set this alongside the response of the people of his home town and of Herod. Jesus, rejected and persecuted, still has compassion on the needs of men. He does not adopt a siege mentality. Opposition and hatred from some cannot prevent his mission of mercy. He heals the sick until evening comes.

At this point the disciples come to him and, sensibly, suggest, **'Send the crowds away, so that they can go to the villages and buy themselves some food.'** In response Jesus tells *them* to provide food for the crowds, but they have **'only five loaves of bread and two fish'**. Having demonstrated conclusively that the disciples cannot provide for the crowds, Jesus takes up the responsibility himself. The disciples are told to bring the people to Jesus, who directs them to sit down on the grass. And then we read, **'Taking the five loaves and the two fish and looking up to heaven, he gave thanks and broke the loaves. Then he gave them to the disciples, and the disciples gave them to the people'** (14:19). We do not really need the interpretation provided by John chapter 6 to know that the bread and the fish symbolize spiritual food for men's spiritual needs. While we must follow the example of Christ in showing compassion to the world, providing food and other necessities of life where we can, this is not the main point of the incident. The real needs of men — salvation, forgiveness, eternal life — are to be found only in our Lord Jesus Christ. Although the disciples have a part to play in ministering this provision to the people, they have no resources of their own and cannot give salvation. Only Christ can do this. Only this one, who is despised and rejected by family, friends and enemies, can dispense to men salvation by grace.

It is important to note that **'They all ate and were satisfied, and the disciples picked up twelve basketfuls of broken pieces that were left over. The number of those who ate**

was about five thousand men, besides women and children.' Here we see the abundance of the provision as well as the adequacy of it. No one goes without and all are satisfied. The scene is like that of a great family. The father takes the lead in giving thanks and providing for his household. Here Jesus is seen as the leader and father of his people. He gives thanks and distributes his bounty to the family. Matthew makes a point of telling us that the disciples picked up twelve basketfuls of broken pieces, for the five thousand fed here point to a greater number for whom Jesus can also provide. To the disciples he brings the bread of life and to many more, who will constitute his people, his community in the world. The number twelve, of course, reminds us of the twelve tribes of Israel and the twelve apostles. Without displaying unnecessary ingenuity, this should be interpreted that the new Israel is pictured here.

As the ministry of Jesus progresses, there is an increasing polarization. His enemies become more and more opposed, while his disciples are instructed in their future mission. While the death of John the Baptist points forward to Christ's own death, the means of salvation for his people, the disciples are taught the way to go about their future preaching of the gospel. They have their place in ministering salvation to others, just as they distributed the broken loaves to the people. Confidence in the Lord's provision and compassion for the people's needs must combine to encourage and stimulate the work of evangelism, the spreading of the gospel and the establishing of the kingdom. Rejection by unbelieving men and women, and even persecution by opponents, must not be allowed to deter them, or us, from this ministry. The community of the kingdom is based on the gospel. It is only as men and women share in Christ's provision of salvation that they become members of this community. If we allow concern for popularity or fear of persecution to control our activities, there will be little gospel work done. Only as we follow Christ's example, as well as trust his saving work, will the kingdom prosper. Conviction, concern for righteousness, and compassion must unite to make known the wonders of Christ's salvation, symbolized by the all-satisfying feeding of the five thousand.

24.
Walking on water

Please read Matthew 14:22-33

It is common today to say of a leader to whom nothing seems impossible that he can walk on water. Whether such hero-worshippers realize that they are actually speaking of the Lord Jesus Christ is open to question. However, they do have the right idea. The ability to walk on water, especially disturbed water in a storm, does demonstrate an immense, even supernatural, power and authority. The disciples, having seen the miracle of the loaves and fish, would certainly have been impressed by our Lord's authority. This would increase their faith, but it still needed to grow much more. This incident appears to have been designed to do exactly that. Matthew's record of this is part of his general purpose. The opposite of the rejection and unbelief that Jesus suffered from the people he encountered is faith. Indeed, there is much in this section about the community of the kingdom that would justify us in describing that community as the household of faith (Gal. 6:10, NKJV). We submit to the King by faith and go on serving in the kingdom by faith. Growing in faith is vital for our Christian walk and service.

Christ's initiative (14:22-24)

After the five thousand had been fed, **'Jesus made the disciples get into the boat and go on ahead of him to the other side, while he dismissed the crowd'** (14:22). While the disciples did this, **'He went up on a mountainside by himself to pray.'** This lasted until evening, by which time, **'The boat was already a considerable distance from land, buffeted by the waves because the wind was against it.'** We do not know the subject of Jesus' prayers. He may have been praying about his future, about the people who had observed the miracle or, perhaps, for the disciples whose nurture was his primary concern at this time.

It seems clear that Jesus deliberately sent them ahead into a situation which would reveal their weakness and, by this means, increase their faith. Just as he was led into the desert by the Spirit to be tempted by the devil, so Christ puts them in a situation of testing through which he would bring them nearer to maturity. We must treat trials, therefore, as God's means of increasing our faith. It is for this reason that James can tell his readers to 'Consider it pure joy, my brothers, whenever you face trials of many kinds, because you know that the testing of your faith develops perseverance. Perseverance must finish its work so that you may be mature and complete, not lacking anything' (1:2-4). The apostle Paul, also, tells us 'that suffering produces perseverance; perseverance, character; and character, hope' (Rom. 5:3-4).

The way to make progress is not, as we might think, to go easily along a simple pathway. God's ways are not the same as our ways, as John Newton discovered, as he describes in his hymn:

> I asked the Lord that I might grow
> In faith, and love, and every grace,

Might more of his salvation know,
And seek more earnestly his face.

'Twas he who taught me thus to pray,
And he, I trust, has answered prayer;
But it has been in such a way
As almost drove me to despair.[1]

It is as we obey Christ that we can be sure that the storms and
trials that beset us are part of his purpose for us and our growth
in grace. We may be sure, also, that he knows and cares about
our situation, as Jesus must have seen, or simply known, their
need and 'went out to them' (14:25). We may feel, and indeed
be, isolated, 'a considerable distance from land', and buffeted
by the wind and waves, but Jesus cares, intercedes and in due
course will rescue us.

Begone, unbelief;
My Saviour is near,
And for my relief
Will surely appear.

His love in time past
Forbids me to think
He'll leave me at last
In trouble to sink;
Each sweet Ebenezer
I have in review
Confirms his good pleasure
To help me quite through

(John Newton).[2]

Christ's sovereignty (14:25-28a)

If Christ's command placed them in difficult circumstances which would test their faith and reveal its weakness, obeying it would also reveal his power and authority. So we read, **'During the fourth watch of the night Jesus went out to them, walking on the lake'** (14:25). We need not waste time considering, and answering, the foolish theories of those who cannot believe this to be literally true and invent stones projecting above the surface on which he could walk. We are told here that the boat was a considerable distance from the land. In any case, if we do not believe that Christ could do this we may as well give up thinking about him at all. These critics would be better employed considering their sin and need and asking where salvation might be found if not in trusting him.

The disciples do not seem to have put two and two together at all: **'When the disciples saw him walking on the lake, they were terrified. "It's a ghost," they said, and cried out in fear.'** Although they had been with Jesus some time and had seen his healing miracles, and had even seen his mastery of the storm in the boat on the Sea of Galilee, they still did not realize who it was who was walking on the water. This is why Jesus immediately assured than, **'It is I.'** His exhortations, **'Take courage!'** and **'Don't be afraid,'** are based on this realization of his person and presence. The power he demonstrates is that of Yahweh/Jehovah, as declared in the promise of Isaiah 43:2:

When you pass through the waters,
    I will be with you;
and when you pass through the rivers,
    they will not sweep over you.

Faith is not stirring ourselves up to hope for the best, but realizing that our God is faithful, able and willing to save. We trust Christ because we know who he is and what he can do. We do not trust just anybody, only those who are trustworthy. It is for this reason that Peter's response begins with the words: **'Lord, if it's you...'**

Christ's command (14:28b-29)

It may well be that by 'if' Peter meant 'since'. Either way his request to Jesus, **'Tell me to come to you on the water,'** links his faith with his awareness of Christ. In response to Jesus' command, **'Peter got down out of the boat, walked on the water and came towards Jesus.'** This may rightly be described as a 'step of faith': a small step for Peter's body, but a 'giant step' for his faith. The sequence is as follows: knowledge of Christ leads to faith in Christ; faith in Christ brings courage; courage produces action. Faith is exercised in response to the Word of God. We must not presume upon God by inventing our own solutions and then expecting him to fit in with our ideas. Peter's act of stepping out of the boat was in response to a command from his Lord. That constitutes faith, not presumption.

There is too much talk today of 'taking a step of faith', when it is not a matter of faith at all. It is rather a case of a looking for some great outcome, praying, acting and hoping for the best. Jesus placed Peter in a position of distress and even danger that took away his natural confidence in himself — remember he was a fisherman used to the lake — and then revealed himself to him. Knowledge precedes faith, just as faith must precede action. The action must be in accordance with God's Word, best of all in response to a command, as here. It is as we exercise our faith that it grows. So Peter puts his trust in Jesus, steps out in faith in Jesus, and is encouraged in his faith because it 'works'. Next time he will remember this.

Christ's salvation (14:30-31)

Peter made a good start, **'But when he saw the wind, he was afraid and, beginning to sink, cried out, "Lord, save me!"'** It has become a commonplace to comment that while Peter's eyes were fixed on Christ all was well, but when he looked at the wind and the waves he began to sink — common, but none the less true. We can only assume that the size of the waves and the fierceness of the wind blotted out his awareness of the power and authority of Jesus. So he 'doubted'. We may take great encouragement from the fact that Jesus did not desert him in his need. **'Immediately Jesus reached out his hand and caught him.'** Our safety and salvation depend, not on our grasp of Christ, but on his grasp of us. This in no way denies our responsibility or encourages an attitude of *laissez-faire*, but it is truly an encouragement to those of us who know that our faith is weak, or, in Christ's terms, **'little'**.

Jesus does rebuke Peter's faith. As previously, in 8:26, he describes him as **'you of little faith'**. We need to consider what constitutes a little faith. It is still faith, even though it may be like a grain of mustard seed (17:20). Our salvation does not depend on the greatness of our faith, but on the greatness of our God. This is very true, but if we are to make progress in faith, like Peter and the other disciples here, we must try to determine what is little about Peter's faith. It may be that the word could be translated 'short faith'; the prefix is often used in connection with a brief period of time. If that is so, then the point is that Peter's faith, while genuine, did not last, in the sense that he ceased to apply it to the situation. Little faith is simply faith that does not persevere in the face of obstacles, such as wind and waves. Great faith, like the centurion's in chapter 8, perseveres in spite of obstacles.

Faith demands discipline and concentration. Today is not just 'a step' of faith, but a continuing attitude of trust. The eighteenth-century preacher William Romaine wrote a book entitled *The life, walk and triumph of faith*. This is most helpful. Single acts of faith come from a consistent life and walk of faith. The outcome of such a life and walk will be triumph by the grace of God, in particular situations as well as finally. So we must go on looking at Christ, not physically as Peter did, but spiritually, remembering who he is, what he is, what he can do and, especially, what he has already done for us. 'Let us fix our eyes on Jesus, the author and perfecter of our faith, who for the joy set before him endured the cross, scorning its shame, and sat down at the right hand of the throne of God. Consider him who endured such opposition from sinful men, so that you will not grow weary and lose heart' (Heb. 12:2-3). It is in this way that we learn not to doubt, but to go on believing. James is helpful once more. The believer may ask for wisdom without fear of rebuke. 'But when he asks, he must believe and not doubt, because he who doubts is like a wave of the sea, blown and tossed by the wind. That man should not think he will receive anything from the Lord; he is a double-minded man, unstable in all he does' (James 1:6-8).

Christ's deity (14:32-33)

Having rescued Peter, Jesus climbs into the boat with his disciple. **'When they climbed into the boat, the wind died down'** (14:32). Mastery of the wind and the waves points to Christ's divine status. **'Then those ... in the boat worshipped him, saying, "Truly you are the Son of God."'** We cannot be sure exactly what they meant by this statement. We must not pre-empt the great declaration of 16:16, when Peter declared that Jesus was 'the Son of the living God'. However, this statement must not be watered down too far, for the disciples have certainly progressed beyond the mere question, 'What kind of man is this?' (8:27). After all, they did 'worship', and what lesser conclusion could they come to than that Jesus is God?

According to Dr Don Carson, the pattern of the Gospels is that 'They show the disciples coming around to the same points again and again, each time at a deeper level of comprehension, but always with a mixture of misapprehension.'[3] A notable example of this is to be found in John's account of the wedding at Cana in Galilee: 'He thus revealed his glory, and his disciples put their faith in him' (John 2:11). If we did not know better, from chapter 1, we might easily conclude that until this point they were complete unbelievers. In fact, it is clear that they believed each new revelation as it was given to them. The same principle may explain the experience of those who lived in the transition period between the old and new dispensations, such as Cornelius (Acts 11:17-18) and the disciples of John at Ephesus (Acts 19:2). As they received new information about Christ they believed it. It may also help us to understand the growing faith of children brought up in a Christian home. In this instance, the disciples have made further progress in their appreciation of the person of the Lord Jesus, as he has revealed his glory to them. Such growth in understanding leads to a growth in faith.

As we reflect on our experience, as the disciples did, as we remember what God has done, as we raise our Ebenezers,[4] so we make provision for future days and future crises. Promises are vital to our Christian living. The fault with the old promise box was not the use of promises as such, but that individuals applied promises to themselves, when their circumstances were, in fact, quite different. However, it is even better to go beyond the promises to the God of the promises, to the Lord Jesus Christ, in whom all the promises of God are 'Yes' and 'Amen' (2 Cor. 1:20). We must treat trials as God's means of increasing our faith, remembering that Christ is sovereign in every circumstance and ready to hear our cries for help. We must act on the faith that we have, keep our eyes on Christ and on his authority and power. Then, as we exercise and, as it were, practise our faith, we shall grow in grace and faith, and so be prepared, like the disciples, for further service.

25.
Clean and unclean

Please read Matthew 14:34 – 15:39

It is popularly said that cleanliness is next to godliness. It is very doubtful whether the Pharisees would have agreed with this dictum. It seems much more likely that they would have said that cleanliness *is* godliness. They were very concerned, not with hygiene, but with ritual cleanness, shunning anything that they thought was ceremonially unclean, or that might be. The last few verses of chapter 14 describe what Jesus did after he and his disciples **'landed at Gennesaret'**. Once it became known that he was there, **'People brought all their sick to him and begged him to let the sick just touch the edge of his cloak, and all who touched him were healed.'** There is no way that the Pharisees would have allowed such close proximity to people who might well be defiled. Illness in any form had to be avoided, while lepers were sometimes even stoned by Pharisees to keep them at a distance. It is this characteristic that links these verses with chapter 15, in spite of the traditional chapter division.

In Matthew 15 the Pharisees and teachers of law criticize Jesus, but find his response more than they bargained for. He distinguishes between true and ritual cleanness, and then takes the subject a stage further by going into Gentile areas and continuing his work there for a time. As so often, actions speak louder than words, but both tell us of Christ's compassion for those who are unclean in God's eyes, and his opposition to those who are clean in their own.

The tradition of the elders (15:1-7a)

While the Pharisees and the other teachers placed great stress on God's law in theory, in practice their chief concern was with **'the tradition of the elders'** (15:2). They did not usually argue from the Scriptures directly, but quoted respected rabbinic authorities such as Hillel and Shammai, comparing and contrasting their teachings. So when **'some Pharisees and teachers of the law came to Jesus from Jerusalem'** and found the disciples of Jesus ignoring the rabbinical rules about cleanness, they objected and made their objections known to Jesus: **'They don't wash their hands before they eat!'** This is not a reference to defective hygiene. They were not suggesting that the disciples' hands were actually dirty, but merely that they had not performed a ritual cleansing before eating. This cleansing usually consisted of sprinkling or, in the case of hands, pouring water over them.

Far from accepting their criticism, Jesus counter-attacks. He **'replied, "And why do you break the command of God for the sake of your tradition?"'** (15:3). He is not content with denying the validity and authority of the tradition of the elders. He maintains that the effect of this stress on tradition is to deny the authority of God's Word. Thus he refers to the Fifth Commandment, **'Honour your father and mother'**, and also Leviticus 20:9: **'Anyone who curses his father or mother must be put to death.'** He contrasts this with the Pharisees' tradition of *Qorban*.[1] This was a means by which a man could avoid his responsibility to support his parents by saying that his resources were tied up, i.e. **'a gift devoted to God'**.

According to William Lane, 'This did not necessarily mean that the object declared *qorban* had actually to be offered to God; it signified rather that it was withdrawn from its intended use and was no longer available for a particular individual "as if it were an offering". In the hypothetical situation proposed by Jesus, if the son declared his property *qorban* to his parents, he neither promised it to the Temple nor prohibited its use to himself, but he legally excluded his parents from the right of benefit.'[2] If a man decided that he ought to help his parents, the Pharisees would not even allow him to change his mind. Jesus sums this up: **'Thus you nullify the word of God for the sake of your tradition.'** What was represented as an act of devotion to God was in fact a 'pious fiddle'. The beneficiaries were not just the son, but also the religious leaders.

It is easy to condemn the Pharisees in this respect, but we must be careful to set our own house in order. It is not only Pharisees who have traditions, which may deny or nullify the Word of God. 'Tradition' may, of course, refer to what is handed down from God to his people and by the apostles to the church. This is the way that Paul uses the concept, as in 2 Thessalonians 2:15. However, these are not 'the traditions of the elders', but the traditions of God. It is fatal to confuse the two. The Roman Catholic Church actually assigns to the traditions of the early Church Fathers an authority which transcends even that of the Scriptures. Where the Fathers are in agreement, they say, then we must follow that tradition. In fact, the Fathers are rarely in agreement and modern Roman Catholics are following the tradition of the popes. Traditions about Mary — the Immaculate Conception (not to be confused with the Virgin Birth) and the Bodily Assumption of the Virgin Mary — are good examples of this. Some traditions are fairly harmless, but these strike at the root of the gospel, presenting Mary as co-mediatrix with the Lord Jesus Christ. The gospel is nullified by them.

However, it is not only the Roman Catholic Church that has traditions. Many evangelical or fundamentalist practices, hallowed by years of use, also nullify God's Word. Traditions about church buildings, clerical dress, suits and ties, may all come into this category. Some are more serious, like altar-calls, kinds of worship, allegedly worldly pastimes. Some ideas are accepted purely on the authority of men, rather than that of the Word of God. It is often said that the last words of a dying church are: 'We've always done it this way.' It is important not to leave it to this stage before examining our ways and beliefs, to see whether they have any deeper authority than our ancestors, our denominational leaders, or our favourite preacher. We must be very careful lest Christ's denunciation of the Pharisees, **'You hypocrites!'** applies to us.

Heart and lips (15:7b-9)

When Jesus called the Pharisees 'hypocrites', he was not necessarily saying that they were insincere. The apostle Paul was a Pharisee before his conversion and several times asserts his sincerity in what he said and did (cf. 2 Tim. 1:3). The contrast is rather between outward profession and inward reality and grace. They stressed circumcision of the body, but ignored circumcision of the heart and life. Because of this Jesus quotes the prophet Isaiah:

> **These people honour me with their lips,**
> **but their hearts are far from me.**
> **They worship me in vain;**
> **their teachings are but rules taught by men.**

Such worship is not acceptable to God. Isaiah makes the same point in chapter 1:11 of his prophecy, where God rejects forms

— sacrifices and burnt offerings — not because they were wrong as such, but because the hearts of the people did not accompany the externals; there was no faith or heart obedience.

As Jesus applied Isaiah's words to his contemporaries, so we must apply them to ourselves. It is easy to profess faith, especially if others around us are doing the same. It is easy, but very dangerous, to participate in the sacraments of baptism and the Lord's Supper without knowing the Lord to whom those sacraments point. It is easy to say things that we know are acceptable in our churches, but without any experience to back them up. We may sing a hymn, but know nothing of the gracious work of God to which it refers. Jesus is emphasizing heart religion: conviction of sin, despair of self, personal trust, love and gratitude, humble fear of the Lord. All these attitudes are to be found abundantly in Isaiah, but not in the Pharisees and, too often, not in our congregations either. Without the reality the forms of worship are futile and useless. But beware! It is easy to criticize others; we must apply this to ourselves.

Uncleanness (15:10-20)

Having rebuked the Pharisees, **'Jesus called the crowd to him and said, "Listen and understand. What goes into a man's mouth does not make him 'unclean', but what comes out of his mouth, that is what makes him 'unclean'"'** (15:10-11). This was taking the battle to the Pharisees with a vengeance and soon the disciples came to him and warned him that **'The Pharisees were offended when they heard this.'** Far from retracting his statement, Jesus deals with the Pharisees as false teachers, liable to be judged by God. They are teachers, but not teachers appointed by God: **'Every plant that my heavenly Father has not planted will be pulled up**

290 The King and his kingdom

by the roots.' This is a devastating condemnation. He continues, **'Leave them; they are blind guides. If a blind man
leads a blind man, both will fall into a pit.'**

There is a serious warning here to those of us who tend to
respect anyone who holds ministerial office, no matter what
he teaches. Some Christians see a clerical collar as a guarantee of orthodoxy and divine authority, but it is only God's
appointment, not human ordination, that guarantees this. This
is not a justification for going around condemning as 'blind
guides' all those who disagree with us; it is possible to be very
arrogant in this area. However, the danger is a real one and
very serious. Such blind guides endanger their hearers and
themselves. It is important for their sakes, as well as for the
people's sake, that our Lord's words are taken seriously. Too
many continue under an unorthodox, heretical ministry, where
the pulpit is filled by those who propound their own ideas, not
those of the Scriptures. To such people Jesus says, 'Leave
them.' Again, we must say that this is not to be done lightly,
but when it is clear that the preacher or teacher does not proclaim God's gospel we must take warning for the sake of our
souls' health and salvation. Leaving too late and leaving too
easily are equally bad.

Peter sees that Christ's words in verse 11 are intended figu-
ratively, so he asks Jesus to **'explain the parable'**. Jesus evi-
dently thinks that the disciples should have understood this
easily and says that they are **'dull'**. His explanation is clear
and, perhaps, devastating: **'Don't you see that whatever
enters the mouth goes into the stomach and then out of
the body? But the things that come out of the mouth come
from the heart, and these make a man "unclean".'** And he
gives a list of sins that defile us, that is, they make us unclean
in the sight of God. These sins which come **'out of the heart'**
are **'evil thoughts, murder, adultery, sexual immorality,
theft, false testimony, slander'**. We must note that not all of

these are sins that we would call unclean in the sense of open immorality. He includes evil thoughts, but also false testimony and slander. All sin renders a man unclean, **'but eating with unwashed hands does not make him "unclean".'**

The danger of the Pharisees' rituals is not just that they place men in bondage to their traditions, but that they blind them to their defilement before God, to their need of cleansing. It is this that makes blind guides so dangerous. The pit to which they lead their unthinking and undiscerning hearers is the pit of hell. Only Christ can give real inner cleansing. Only the gospel can speak of this. Christ's willingness to heal the sick and the ritually unclean, like those suffering from leprosy, speaks volumes about his power to cleanse and give salvation: the forgiveness of sins, justification, a new heart, a new birth. Jesus, it appears, was more concerned to warn the crowds about their spiritual danger than to condemn the Pharisees. We should ask ourselves, when criticizing false teachers, whether our concern is the same. Are we simply demonstrating how right we are, elevating ourselves in our own minds and in the esteem of others, or are we really concerned for the souls of the blind, the salvation of those who have been led astray?

The Canaanite woman (15:21-28)

If the Pharisees regarded the common people, who did not follow their traditions, as unclean, they despised unclean Gentiles even more. It is no accident that the sequel to this debate with the Pharisees takes Jesus into **'the region of Tyre and Sidon'**, Gentile country. Indeed, the rest of this chapter takes place in Gentile territory. We know that Jesus' prime mission was to the Jews, the lost sheep of the house of Israel, but he ventured further afield occasionally to point to a time to come, when the Gentiles would participate fully in the blessing and righteousness of the kingdom. If Gentiles in general were outcasts, how much more was this true of a **'Canaanite woman'**, a member of one of the nations that Israel had been commanded to destroy out of the land when they occupied it! One such **'came to him, crying out, "Lord, Son of David, have mercy on me! My daughter is suffering terribly from demon possession"'** (15:22). Here is a woman in need, desperate need, who believes that Jesus is the Messiah, the Son of David. What a condemnation of the Pharisees! With all their knowledge of the Scriptures and all their privileges, they still have not understood this, but this outsider asks for mercy from the Lord Jesus Christ.

Much to our surprise, Jesus **'did not answer a word'** (15:23). He must have had some special purpose in this, for the Roman centurion had received a prompt response to his similar request in 8:6. We must remember that Jesus does nothing without a reason. The disciples apparently thought that they understood him, for they **'came to him and urged him, "Send her away, for she keeps crying out after us."'** Indeed, he appears to confirm this when he answers, **'I was sent only to the lost sheep of Israel.'** However, this is not the end of the matter. The centurion was an exception, but at least he lived in the promised land. Old Testament examples like Ruth and the widow of Zarephath were exceptions more like this woman. Now Jesus has ventured outside the promised land and his actions have great significance.

The woman does not give up easily. We read that she **'came and knelt before him. "Lord, help me!"'** she insists. Jesus gives an astonishing reply, at least to us. **'He replied, "It is not right to take the children's bread and toss it to their dogs."'** It may well be that we must not interpret the description 'dogs' too severely. These are not the dogs that roam the streets, for he uses the term 'their dogs' and she refers to **'their**

masters' table'. Nevertheless, there is a clear contrast between children and dogs, which could easily have deterred her completely. Yet, to our surprise, she persists. **"Yes, Lord,"** **she said, "but even the dogs eat the crumbs that fall from** **their masters' table."** ' In the end she secures his help. Her ' **"request is granted". And her daughter was healed from** **that very hour.'** What is the secret of this? **'Jesus answered,** **"Woman, you have great faith!"** ' (15:28).

Thus, on the individual level, we can see here a contrast with Peter, whose 'little faith' drew his Lord's rebuke (14:31). His faith was little, because it did not continue in the face of great obstacles, such as wind and waves. Her faith was great because she persevered against obstacles and circumstances, which were not only not natural, but were placed in her path by the Lord himself. It was not just that the disciples tried to get rid of her. Jesus refused to answer and then went further, reminding her of her position outside the covenant of people of God. She understood and accepted his position — we cannot know how — but still persevered in trusting him and calling to him for help. When our need is great enough and our awareness of his greatness is sufficient, we can accept God's verdict on us as unclean, defiled sinners, condemned in his sight, and still trust and call. What we must do is to accept his terms and not argue. Before God 'every mouth' must 'be silenced' (Rom. 3:19).

Many object when Jesus, by his word, shows them their sin, their unworthiness, their lack of rights before him. The rich young ruler would not submit and went away (19:21-22). Sometimes, it takes time before the Spirit convinces us of the necessity of submission. Nicodemus seems to have accepted Christ's words about the necessity for the new birth, eventually, and believed in him. Naaman accepted the arguments of his servants and submitted to washing himself in the despised River Jordan (2 Kings 5:11-14). Faith, real faith, does not reject the word of Christ. When it argues, as this woman argued with Jesus, it is on the basis of the perceived love and grace of God. She could not believe that he would not help her in her need. And she was right.

More generally, we are shown here a foreshadowing of Pentecost and beyond. There is much in Matthew's Gospel about the Gentiles. This Gospel was aimed particularly at Jewish readers, but those Jewish readers had to accept that the future was bright for the Gentiles. More is said towards the end of the Gospel. Here we have a provisional mission to the Gentiles by which they are encouraged to take up the same position as this Canaanite woman, calling upon the Son of God, the Son of David, the Jewish Messiah, for salvation.

Feeding the four thousand (15:29-39)

Jesus left the area of Phoenicia and went **'along the Sea of Galilee'** (15:29). In the light of the context this must refer to the eastern side of the lake, the district of Decapolis, which was mainly Gentile. This is confirmed by the response of the **'great crowds'** which **'came to him, bringing the lame, the blind, the crippled, the mute and many others, and laid them at his feet; and he healed them. The people were amazed…'** Their response to this universal healing was that **'they praised the God of Israel'** (15:31). Such an expression could be used only by Gentiles. Like the Canaanite woman, they recognized that this was not, yet, their God, who had brought healing to them, but they were grateful for the crumbs from the Master's table.

Next, **'Jesus called his disciples to him and said, "I have compassion for these people; they have already been with me three days and have nothing to eat. I do not want to

send them away hungry, or they may collapse on the way"'
(15:32). As so often, the response of Jesus to the crowds is
one of compassion. We are told only that he healed them, but
it may be that he taught them too and thus pointed them to the
God of Israel. Certainly his action in feeding the four thousand Gentiles — **'besides women and children'** (15:38) —
shows his ability, and willingness in due course, to save the
multitudes of the world. Here is plentiful compassion and plentiful provision. Once again there is much to spare, **'seven
basketfuls of broken pieces that were left over'**. [3]

It appears that the disciples had not learned the lessons of
recent days. In spite of the feeding of the five thousand, their
response to Christ's wishes is: **'Where could we get enough
bread in this remote place to feed such a crowd?'** They had
only seven loaves **'and a few small fish'**. Jesus rebukes their
unbelief by telling **'the crowd to sit down on the ground.
Then he took the seven loaves and the fish, and when he
had given thanks, he broke them and gave them to the
disciples, and they in turn to the people. They all ate and
were satisfied.'** It is almost a carbon copy of the previous
occasion. Unbelieving critics seize on this as an example of a
literary 'doublet', thinking, or at least arguing, that Matthew
is repeating himself. This alone would give sufficient reason
for stressing that it was Gentiles who constituted the four
thousand.

It is not Matthew's mistake, but Jesus' declaration of intention to save the Gentiles that gives us the feeding of the
four thousand. Peter and the others should have learned, not
only from the feeding of the five thousand, but also from the
success of the Canaanite woman's request, that Jesus not only
could, but also would, provide for these Gentiles. Her great
faith rebukes their little, or lack of, faith, while Jesus' willingness and compassion, which probably puzzled them greatly,

points to a wider and more glorious future. The numerical symbolism of the four thousand and the seven baskets is not clear. Negatively, 'The number seven may be significant because it is not twelve and therefore not allusive to the twelve apostles or twelve tribes.'[4] The fact that the numbers are lower probably does not mean that fewer Gentiles will be saved, but that this is only a provisional mission, a foretaste of what was to come after Pentecost.

'**After Jesus had sent the crowd away, he got into the boat and went to the vicinity of Magadan**', back into the Jewish area. This has only been an excursion into Gentile territory; the time has not yet come for a full Gentile mission. That awaits Pentecost and the coming of the Holy Spirit. Nevertheless the intention is clear. Jesus can, and in due time will, call the Gentiles to himself. He has 'other sheep' which do not belong to the Jewish fold (John 10:16). They too must be called and come to make up the one flock of his community, a community of the kingdom. This community consists of those who have been made clean. It consists of those who reject human tradition and believe the Word of God. It consists of men and women from every nation, tribe and tongue. Entry is by faith, which trusts the love and compassion of Jesus, in spite of the obstacles which are placed in its way.

We must not become immersed in the details of traditions and Gentile customs, but ask ourselves whether we are truly members of this community. From our hearts come those things which defile us and bring condemnation before God. Only in Christ is there cleansing. Only by the blood of Christ can our sins be forgiven. Only by the work of the Holy Spirit can our hearts be cleansed and renewed. Whether Jew or Gentile, it is only Christ who can save us from our sins. Then we must ask ourselves also whether we share our Lord's vision of a church called from many nations, of multitudes benefiting from his grace by the gospel. Or are we only concerned with our own kind of people, neglecting and even despising these who are outcasts and far away from the church? Jesus attacked such a Pharisaic, 'holier-than-thou' attitude and went to the poor and despised, to the Canaanite and Gentile. We must follow his example and so further his gospel and kingdom mission.

26.
Son of Man, Son of the living God

Please read Matthew 16:1-23

This chapter is one of the most controversial in the New Testament. Whole volumes have been written about verses 15-19, especially on the relationship of Peter to the papacy. Sadly, this means that all the attention is concentrated on Peter instead of on his Lord, the true subject of these verses. It is true that we encounter the concept of the church here for the first time in the Gospels, at least by name, but the real stress is on the great head of the church, the King of the kingdom of heaven. The central point of the chapter is verse 16, Simon Peter's confession of Christ, the Son of God. The earlier verses, although ostensibly concerned with signs, lead up to this great declaration, and the following verses show its implications.

It is here that the great themes of the Gospel, outlined in the introduction, come together. Here Matthew shows how everything, especially the increasing opposition of the Pharisees and Sadducees, is leading inevitably to the cross. The disciples come to a significant stage of their development and training as Jesus teaches them of his impending death. The revelation of the person of Christ comes to a climax, which combines with the theme of the kingdom. God's King, the Son of the living God, is also the Head of the church, because it is the community of those who belong to the kingdom. That church is made up, not only of Jews, but also of Gentiles, that is, all who believe. It is this remarkable intertwining of the various themes that shows Matthew's mastery of his subject.

Signs (16:1-4a)

The Pharisees and Sadducees appear to have learned nothing from previous encounters with Jesus. Once again, they **'came to Jesus and tested him by asking him to show them a sign from heaven'** (16:1). On this occasion he points out to them that they already have enough signs, but they **'cannot interpret the signs of the times'**. Although they can perform a primitive weather forecast, of the kind, 'Red sky at morning, shepherd's warning; red sky at night, shepherd's delight,' they cannot draw the proper conclusion from his miracles of healing. Therefore, he refuses to give them another sign, one 'from heaven' that compels belief. The signs he has given are sufficient for those who understand prophecy and are ready to submit to the Messiah, but not for them. Hence his conclusion follows (again, see 12:39-41): **'A wicked and adulterous generation looks for a miraculous sign, but none will be given it except the sign of Jonah.'**

The yeast of the Pharisees and Sadducees (16:4b-12)

When **'Jesus ... left them and went away'**, he and the disciples **'went across the lake'** by boat to the other side (see Mark 8:13). When Jesus warned his disciples, **'Be on your guard against the yeast of the Pharisees and Sadducees,'** they thought that he was rebuking them for forgetting **'to take bread'**. Once again Jesus accuses them of having **'little faith'**. They still do not understand. The reason that Jesus considers this to be a little faith is that if they had remembered **'the five**

loaves for the five thousand, and how many basketfuls' they had gathered, or **'the seven loaves for the four thousand, and how many basketfuls'** they had gathered, they would not have worried about bread and would have known that he was not concerned about the lack of bread.

Verse 12 tells us that **'He was not telling them to guard against the yeast used in bread, but against the teachings of the Pharisees and Sadducees.'** Since the teaching of these two groups was not the same and, in any case, much of what the Pharisees taught was true, we must deduce that he was referring only to their lack of understanding about signs. Jesus was concerned that his disciples should not fall into the same trap as the religious leaders had done and reject his claims to be the Messiah, because he did not perform the kind of sign they demanded. In this way Matthew leads naturally into the next section, where Jesus introduces this very subject.

Peter's confession of Christ (16:13-17)

It seems that Jesus deliberately led the disciples away from the area inhabited by Jews to a more sparsely populated area, where those who did live were largely Gentiles. **'When Jesus came to the region of Caesarea Philippi, he asked his disciples, "Who do people say the Son of Man is?"'** (16:13). He uses his favourite title, 'the Son of Man', so as not to pre-empt the answer to his question, but his disciples must have understood that he was talking about himself. Their reply lists various options which people were giving: John the Baptist, Elijah, Jeremiah or one of the prophets. He then asks, **'Who do you say I am?'** Although this is addressed to all the disciples, it is inevitably Simon Peter who takes it upon himself to answer: **'You are the Christ, the Son of the living God.'** By 'the Christ' Peter clearly means the Messiah. Although Jesus has not explicitly claimed to be the Messiah, this must be the inevitable conclusion of anyone who treats the signs and miracles properly. It is less obvious what Peter means by 'the Son of the living God'. In the light of the disciples' earlier assertion in 14:32, 'Truly you are the Son of God,' we must give this description due, and greater, weight, going somewhat further than mere recognition as Messiah.

In any case, if it had not been accurate and full, Jesus would not have **'replied, "Blessed are you, Simon son of Jonah, for this was not revealed to you by man, but by my Father in heaven."'** It is this assertion that ought to convince us of that Peter's confession is highly significant and, indeed, the turning point in the narrative. Such a statement is deemed inauthentic by some, but it fits exactly the words of 11:25,27 about the Father, who alone knows the Son, revealing such things to little children. Therefore, we must accept that Peter's confession is just that: a personal conviction about Jesus, reflecting true knowledge of the Saviour, not just a theoretical truth. Although there is still much to be learned about the person of Christ, some of which must await the resurrection and Pentecost, this is clearly a major step in the disciples' development. This is why Jesus now feels free to make the other assertions about the building of the church, binding and loosing, and then about his impending death.

'On this rock' (16:18)

Jesus followed up Peter's confession with the words: **'And I tell you that you are Peter, and on this rock I will build my church.'** This declaration lies at the heart of the controversy between Protestantism and Roman Catholicism about Peter and the papacy. Much ingenuity has been used to avoid the obvious conclusion that Peter himself is the rock on which

Jesus says he will build his church. It may be safely asserted that if it were not for the Roman Catholic construction placed on these words, no one would ever have thought of disputing this. However, their claims that Peter was the Bishop of Rome (irrespective of the issue of whether he actually lived in Rome at some time) and that he and his successors as Bishop of Rome had infallible authority over the whole church have absolutely no biblical or historical warrant. It is false, unnecessary and dangerous to determine our understanding of Scripture by mere reaction against false ideas. The verse must be interpreted on its own merits, whatever others make of it.

It is clear that it is because of his confession of the Messiahship and deity of Christ that to Peter is ascribed this position as rock, but it is only to avoid the Roman Catholic position that some assert that the rock is the confession itself. The suggestion that Jesus was saying, 'You are Peter [*petros* = a stone] and on this rock [*petra* = a rock]' does not really stand up to closer examination. The words of Jesus do not set a contrast between Peter and a different rock, but a link between Peter's name and 'this' rock. The variation in the Greek is purely because *petra* is feminine and Peter is a man!

Peter will be the rock in a historical sense. We only have to consider his role in the book of Acts to see that Peter, believing and preaching that Jesus is Lord and Christ, establishes the church. This statement, of course, has to be qualified. It is only as an instrument that he does this work, for Jesus says, 'I will build my church.' Further, it is not Peter alone, but as first among equals, who does this work. All the disciples were asked the question in verse 15, not just Peter, and while verse 19 about the keys of the kingdom is couched in the singular, the similar words in chapter 18:18 are addressed to all the apostles. John 20:23 similarly gives authority to forgive to all the disciples.

The other option, that it is Jesus himself who is the rock, also fails to account for the text. There is nothing to suggest that Jesus pointed to himself, when he said, 'on this rock'! We also read that the temple, which is the church, is 'built on the foundation of the apostles and prophets, with Christ Jesus himself as the chief cornerstone' (Eph. 2:20). The first layer of stones in the new building consists of the apostles and prophets, believing in Jesus as the Christ. The context of Paul's assertion that Jesus Christ is the only foundation (1 Cor. 3:11) is quite different. And in any case, Jesus can hardly be seen here in Matthew 16 as both builder and foundation!

Christ's church (16:18)

The word for church *(ekklesia)*, often popularly explained etymologically as 'called out ones', is better seen in relation to the usage in the Greek Old Testament. In the Old Testament God's people were called his 'congregation' or 'assembly', the congregation of Israel, usually translated in the Septuagint by this term *ekklesia*. We even find traces of this in the New Testament, in Stephen's reference in Acts 7:38 to 'the assembly [AV, "church"] in the desert' (see also Heb. 2:12). Now, under the new covenant, Jesus calls his Messianic community, the assembly of God's people, *'my* church'. As King he will build his church; he will increase and strengthen his community. This community will embrace both Jews and Gentiles and its first stages will be built by Christ under the delegated authority of Peter and the other apostles. Some scholars treat this mention of the church as an anachronism but, 'A Messiah without a Messianic community would have been unthinkable to any Jew.'[1]

The consequence of its being built by the Messiah is that it will prevail. It is not a work of human construction or of a mere idol, but of 'the Son of the living God'. Nothing can destroy it. **'The gates of Hades will not overcome it.'** Gates in the Bible may be the place of authority (Ps. 127:5), while

Hades is the place of the departed, or death itself. Death symbolizes all the powers of evil and this may be our Lord's intention. The devil will resist Christ's building, but he cannot prevail against it. In days when the church is disregarded and
para-church organizations are much in favour, we need to remember what our Lord says. It is the church that he has promised to build; it is the church that he has guaranteed will not be
overcome by the powers of evil. The church is not finished, as
some foolishly think. It is Christ's creation, Christ's building,
and Christ will complete the structure. It is the church for
which he died and which he is currently cleansing and beauti-
fying for himself (Eph. 5:25-27).

There is no room for pessimism here. What he has established on a rock and to which he has given such a glorious
promise must prevail. This must govern our thinking about
evangelism and mission, as well as about the health and strength
of the church that exists already. The link with Peter's confession, of course, must remind us that it is the true church
that Jesus builds. The merely nominal church, the ritualistic
man-made structures, based on human ideas rather than the
Word of God, can take no such assurance for its future.

The keys of the kingdom (16:19)

As if we had not had enough controversial subjects, we must
now consider what Jesus means by saying to Peter, **'I will
give you the keys of the kingdom of heaven.'** Keys were
given to stewards so that they could administer their master's
possessions with authority (Isa. 22:15,22). It is important to
avoid two errors here. On the one hand, we must not identify
the church and the kingdom: 'The two words belong to different concepts, the one to "people" and the other to "rule".'[2] On
the other hand, they are not to be separated, as if we could
have a church age distinct from the kingdom age. The church,

as has been suggested, is the community under the reign of the King. Thus the King can give delegated authority to the apostles, in particular Peter at this stage, in order to rule and govern the church. Keys are used to admit or exclude. The rabbis used binding and loosing as alternatives to permitting and forbidding. It is, therefore, suggested that **'Whatever you bind on earth will be bound in heaven, and whatever you loose on earth will be loosed in heaven,'** refers to commands and prohibitions in the church. Putting the two ideas together, we gather that the topic being spoken of is including or excluding men and women with regard to the church, administered through teaching, not by some arbitrary idea.

The tense used here is actually the future perfect. Thus, a footnote in the NIV tells us that the translation could be 'will have been bound' and 'will have been loosed'. This is probably true and is useful for understanding what is intended. Jesus is not telling the apostles that their decisions will be automatically ratified by God in heaven. Rather, as they teach and discipline in accordance with the Word of God and the gospel, they will reflect on earth what God has already determined in heaven. God is not confirming their decision, but because they act in conformity with his word, their decision coincides with his purpose. Through the preaching of the gospel, they will admit or exclude those whom God has determined should be admitted or excluded, not indulging in personal whims or rules. In a similar manner, through the message of the gospel, they will be forgiving, that is declaring forgiven, those whom God has appointed to this (John 20:23).

The cross (16:20-23)

Jesus still does not want his Messiahship to be publicly proclaimed. This would only cause problems and, in any case, the appointed time for his death has not arrived. So, **'He warned**

his disciples not to tell anyone that he was the Christ' (16:20). However, the cross is very much in mind, as **'From that time on Jesus began to explain to his disciples that he must go to Jerusalem and suffer many things at the hands of the elders, chief priests and teachers of the law, and that he must be killed and on the third day be raised to life'** (16:21). Though the time is not yet, the disciples need to be prepared for these remarkable events. Jesus 'must' go to Jerusalem and suffer. This reflects the divine purpose and pre-destination, the will of God to which Jesus is conforming. It must be remembered that he prophesies not only his death, but also his resurrection, although the disciples do not seem to have noticed.

As a result, **'Peter took him aside and began to rebuke him. "Never, Lord!" he said. "This shall never happen to you!"'** It is amazing how the one to whom God had revealed deep truth about the Lord Jesus could now begin to disagree with God's Messiah, the Son of the living God. Although he still calls him 'Lord', he does not treat him as Lord. He presumes to know better than Jesus. We have no right to stand in judgement on Peter. How many of us would have done any better? Nevertheless we must realize that the cross was absolutely necessary. There would be no salvation without the death of Christ. It is this, presumably, that causes Jesus to rebuke Peter in such strong terms: **'Jesus turned and said to Peter, "Get behind me, Satan! You are a stumbling block to me; you do not have in mind the things of God, but the things of men."'** Peter has demonstrated, by his reaction, his lack of insight into the purposes of God. His is a purely human reaction. He cannot envisage his beloved Lord suffering and dying. We may respect this loving concern for the Saviour without agreeing with it. Furthermore, this reveals that he is still clinging to the current idea that could not envisage God's Messiah suffering. He expected instant success, just as John the Baptist did. However, there is something even worse here. Jesus sees Peter doing Satan's work. In the temptations Satan had tried to divert Jesus from the path of suffering. He offered him other ways of gaining the kingdom and glory, but Jesus would have none of it. So here he both rejects and rebukes Peter. The idea that Peter put forward would cause him to stumble, to trip up, fall into sin, deny God's ways and fail in his mission of salvation.

There is so much in this section that it is difficult to sum up what we have learnt. We have been brought face to face with the person and work of the Lord Jesus Christ. We are compelled to ask ourselves whether this is our faith and understanding. Nothing less than a confession that Jesus is Lord and Christ, the Son of the living God, will do. Nothing less than a hearty acceptance of the necessity and value of his death will bring forgiveness and membership of his community, the church. We must combine this insistence on the teachings of the gospel, which are set before us here, with a personal conviction and appropriation of that teaching. Jesus has confronted his disciples with these facts about himself: his Messiahship, his headship of the church, the necessity for being included, not excluded, the danger of putting our trust in anything apart from his death. Peter thought only of his future sufferings; we must remember that on the third day he would be raised to life. The living Saviour will ensure that his church is not destroyed, but prevails against all her enemies. Suffering is the prelude to glory, and it is to this that Jesus turns in the following verses.

27.
Suffering and glory

Please read Matthew 16:24 – 17:13

The ill-health of modern evangelicalism is seen nowhere more clearly than in the so-called 'prosperity gospel'. Its poverty appears most clearly in the message of health and wealth. One American television evangelist went on record as saying, 'I'm sick and tired of hearing about streets of gold. I don't need gold in heaven. I've got to have it now.'[1] The contrast between this and Martin Luther's theology of the cross could hardly be clearer. 'The theology of the cross', wrote Luther, 'teaches that punishments, crosses, and death are the most precious treasure of all.'[2] The last of his Ninety-five Theses says, 'In this way let them [Christians] have confidence that they will enter heaven through many tribulations, rather than through a false assurance of peace.'[3]

This is not, of course, the whole story. There is also a theology of glory. In this section, Jesus (and Matthew following him) makes clear that there is a sequence: to glory through suffering. Peter, who here shows a lack of understanding of this, writes of it later, saying that the prophets 'predicted the sufferings of Christ and the glories that would follow' (1 Peter 1:11). The apostle Paul, when speaking of Christians as 'heirs of God and co-heirs with Christ', says that 'we share in his sufferings in order that we may also share in his glory'. If this seems harsh, we must remember that Paul added that 'Our present sufferings are not worth comparing with the glory that will be revealed in us' (Rom. 8:17,18). He even makes the amazing statement that 'Our light and momentary troubles are achieving for us an eternal glory that far outweighs them all' (2 Cor. 4:17). Both these themes are to be found in this next section.

Taking up the cross (16:24-26)

Immediately after telling his disciples that the Son of Man must suffer and die, Jesus warns his disciples, **'If anyone would come after me, he must deny himself and take up his cross and follow me'** (16:24). The servant is truly not greater than his master. The pattern for Jesus is also the pattern for his disciples. Peter, again, warns his readers that they may have to suffer for doing good, adding, 'To this you were called, because Christ suffered for you, leaving you an example, that you should follow in his steps' (1 Peter 2:21). There is more to this than following an example. There is a union between Christ and his people, which means that they share in his suffering that they may share also in his glory (1 Peter 5:1). In Luther's words, 'Christ is a bloody partnership for us.'[4]

Denying ourselves means setting aside our rights and preferences for the sake of Christ — saying 'No' to ourselves and our wishes. We must be ready to sacrifice anything in order to live as Christ's disciples, whatever the cost may be. This is a deliberate choice, not just an inevitable consequence, for those who believe in Christ. Similarly, taking up our cross means deliberately following Christ, knowing that this may, almost certainly will, involve us in suffering persecution for him (2 Tim. 3:12). It does not mean looking for trouble, nor is it referring to any and every kind of suffering endured by a Christian. It is suffering incurred because we follow Christ. Jesus has already made this point in the Sermon on the Mount, when he referred to those who are 'persecuted because of righteousness' and those who endure all kinds of slander 'because of me' (5:10-11). Jesus adds the other half of the equation in verse 25: **'For whoever wants to save his life will lose it, but whoever loses his life for me will find it.'** These paradoxical statements rest on the double reference to physical and spiritual life. If we deliberately try to keep what we have, physical life and its benefits, we shall lose everything of real value, spiritual life. If we are ready to give up everything for Christ, including life and possessions, we shall find that we receive or keep (= find) what really matters, our souls or eternal life. The apparent contradiction here is typical of the gospel. Appearances are deceptive. The Christian seems to be giving up everything, but in fact is receiving and gaining everything. Life in this world may be poorer and harder, but eternal life, the riches of salvation, more than compensate for this.

Many people have been brought to conviction and to faith by a proper realization of the meaning of the next verse: **'What good will it be for a man if he gains the whole world, yet forfeits his soul? Or what can a man gave in exchange for his soul?'** ('Life' and 'soul' are often virtually interchangeable in the New Testament.) Gaining the whole world, whether by working, inheriting, gambling, playing the lottery, is the aim of many without Christ. Possessions, riches, ambition, pleasure and comfort control their lives. The outcome is eternal loss. Others, true Christians, aim to please Christ, whatever it costs, and appear to suffer for it. The end result, however, is eternal happiness and blessing, the riches of heaven, the unsearchable riches of Christ, glory for ever.

The comings of the Son of Man (16:27-28)

The confirmation of all this, the basis for embarking on such a course of living for Christ, is that **'The Son of Man is going to come in his Father's glory with his angels, and then he will reward each person according to what he has done'** (16:27). Although Christ has to suffer, he will rise again on the third day. He will ascend to heaven, reign with his Father and one day return in glory, accompanied by the holy angels. Those who see only the cross and suffering are ignorant of the whole picture. This is a fatal misunderstanding of the cross of Christ; suffering leads to glory, for him and for his people. The original Son of Man in Daniel 7 is a glorious figure and he has a glorious and everlasting kingdom. In the usage of the Gospels, when Jesus, the Son of Man, suffers it is an apparent contradiction of his heavenly and glorious status. One day this will all be put right. The Suffering Servant will return as the King of glory. His people who have suffered with him and for him will share in it all.

There will be a conformity between what we have done and what we receive, not in terms of merit but of appropriateness. Those who have suffered for Christ will receive glory from Christ. Those who have refused his way will suffer loss. In terms of Christ's parable of the rich man and Lazarus, those who in their lifetime have sought and received good things will be in agony. Those who have received bad things, because of their allegiance to Christ, will be comforted (Luke 16:25), as the Beatitudes have already made clear (5:4).

This emphasis on the future return of Christ appears, at first sight, to be contradicted by verse 28: **'I tell you the truth, some who are standing here will not taste death before they see the Son of Man coming in his kingdom.'** If we identify this coming with the one in verse 27, we are faced with a clear contradiction. It is many years since Christ made this claim and not just his disciples, but many others, have tasted death while the Son of Man has not returned in glory. This is not a problem to some, who believe that Jesus was mistaken about many things, but those of us who honour his truth and authority cannot take that easy way out. The basic understanding that we must have is that there are various comings of Christ mentioned in the New Testament. We have seen this already in 10:23, which must refer, as we have seen, to his coming in judgement on Israel. We shall have to return to this topic in commenting on chapter 24.

It seems unlikely that the coming in verse 28 is the same as either verse 27 or as in 10:23. In context Jesus, seeking to help his disciples come to terms with his theology of the cross, is reminding them that the crucified one will rise and will establish his kingdom in the near future. They do not have to wait until the Second Coming to see his vindication and glory. His kingdom will come, his reign will be established, as the gospel is proclaimed. As the kingdom comes gradually, so the Son of Man can come gradually, or exercise his authority continually, as the gospel is preached in the power of the Spirit. So it becomes evident to the world that he is king and his disciples increase in number, both of Jews and Gentiles. This has to be set alongside the suffering and persecution, the self-denial and losing of life. Ultimately the compensation will be that Christ will come again and reward his people, but in the meantime they may take comfort in the growth of the church, the establishment of his kingdom.

Some have interpreted this coming as the transfiguration, recorded in the next verses. There is clearly a link with the transfiguration, but it is not clear how this can be referred to as a coming and, in any case, it would seem somewhat extravagant to refer to some not tasting death when a gap of only six days has intervened! Remembering that James would soon be martyred (Acts 12:2), it is better to refer this to the advance of the kingdom in the days leading up to the destruction of Jerusalem. The transfiguration will then fulfil the function of confirming Christ's glory, in spite of his impending crucifixion, thus guaranteeing his return in his Father's glory with his angels.

The transfiguration (17:1-13)

We cannot be certain which mountain was the site for the transfiguration. Traditionally it has been taken to be Mount Tabor. Others prefer Mount Hermon. The one appears to be too low and the other too high to fit the picture in Matthew. The Gospel does not tell us which, if any, is correct. What it does tell us is that **'He was transfigured before them. His face shone like the sun, and his clothes became as white as the light'** (17:2). No interpretation of this is given, but the context points to a transient revelation of Christ's true glory, shining through his humanity. There is the contrast implied between Jesus, on the one hand, and Moses and Elijah, who appeared **'talking with Jesus'**, on the other. The glory manifested here is not that of saints in glory, but of Jesus, the Son of the living God. It is pointless to try to analyse what happened; this is beyond both experience and understanding.

However, it is clear that, whatever the implications for Jesus himself, it is primarily for the sake of the disciples that the transfiguration occurred. We are told that **'Jesus took with him Peter, James and John the brother of James, and led them up a high mountain by themselves'** (17:1). We are told that he was transfigured **'before them'** (17:2) and that Moses and Elijah appeared **'before them'** (17:3). In addition, the words of the voice speaking from the cloud are in the third person: **'This is my Son'** — not 'You are my Son' — and the disciples are told, **'Listen to him!'** (17:5). Although this is the case, Peter misunderstands the indications when he says, **'Lord, it is good for us to be here. If you wish, I will put up three shelters — one for you, one for Moses and one for Elijah.'** In the first place this is not intended to be a lasting experience, a permanent situation, requiring shelters. Nor is it appropriate to place Moses and Elijah on the same level as Jesus, as his words imply.

The **'bright cloud'** which **'enveloped them'** points to the Shekinah glory and the presence of God, whose voice it is that declares, **'This is my Son, whom I love; with him I am well pleased.'** Just as the voice at the baptism of Jesus testified to his Messiahship, so here Jesus and, especially, his disciples are assured of his divine glory. Whatever the future holds by way of suffering and death cannot remove this. Whatever happens to Jesus, they are still to listen to him, serve him and obey him. Suffering, especially the suffering of Christ, does not contradict glory. He is the Son of the living God. He will come in his kingdom soon and one day will return in his Father's glory with his angels and reward his faithful people. The theology of the cross, his and ours, must always be held together with the theology of glory. The one leads to the other. It is just as wrong to limit our ideas to the theology of suffering as it is to limit them to the theology of glory. What is important is to get the order right: suffering leads to glory.

The disciples' fear is removed when Jesus comes and touches them, telling them, **'Get up'** and **'Don't be afraid.'** Only Jesus is present now. Moses and Elijah have gone. These representatives of the Law and the Prophets, examples of suffering for the sake of the Messiah in the Old Testament, have departed, leaving Jesus and his disciples to go forward. All this has been shown to them to give them strength in suffering and especially during the experiences of Christ's passion. It is not for general consumption, so Jesus instructs them, **'Don't**

tell anyone what you have seen, until the Son of Man has been raised from the dead.' Like his Messiahship (16:20), the revelation of Christ's glory was not to be known yet.

It seems almost incredible, but still the disciples' attention is fixed on Christ's prophecy of his death. In spite of his reference to the Son of Man's being raised from the dead, they are still perplexed by the idea of the Messiah suffering and dying. It may be the appearance of Elijah on the mountain that sparks off their question: **'Why then do the teachers of the law say that Elijah must come first?'** The apparent contradiction for them is this: if Elijah was to come and **'restore all things'**, as Malachi prophesied, then how is it that Jesus will still suffer? Restoring all things seems to imply justice and righteousness, not the persecution of God's Messiah. They appear to misunderstand the extent of Elijah's mission.

Jesus tells them that **'Elijah has already come, and they did not recognize him, but have done to him everything they wished.'** He is clearly referring to John the Baptist, as the disciples come to see in verse 13. This is not a literal coming of Elijah, which would contradict John's own denial in answer to the scribes and Pharisees (John 1:21), but a figurative one, as we might refer to God raising up a Whitefield or a Spurgeon to preach the gospel today. His function, as the angel pointed out to Zechariah, was to 'go on before the Lord, in the spirit and power of Elijah, to turn the hearts of the fathers to their children and the disobedient to the wisdom of the righteous — to make ready a people prepared for Lord' (Luke 1:17). This coming of Elijah and the treatment he received confirms to Jesus and his disciples that **'In the same way the Son of Man is going to suffer at their hands.'** The theology of the cross applied to Moses and Elijah in the Old Testament, to John the Baptist in the preparation for the coming of the Messiah, to Jesus himself as he came to lay down his life as a ransom for many, and to his disciples as well.

We must apply it to ourselves also. This message is as important today as it has ever been, particularly in the light of the unbiblical teaching about prosperity, health and wealth that is so popular today. Of course, such a teaching appeals to the natural man. None of us wants to suffer. We would all like to be healthy and wealthy, but since sin entered the world this is impossible as a rule. Such teaching appeals to those who are in need, but leads them sadly astray. How anyone can preach this message to the poverty-stricken and ill escapes my understanding. While the unbelieving description of the gospel as 'pie in the sky when you die', intended as a way of keeping the lower classes in order, is utterly false, there is nevertheless a tremendous truth in the words. All the treasure does not await glory and heaven. Forgiveness of sins, reconciliation to God, adoption into his family, the indwelling Spirit, with all the blessings of joy, hope and peace, are ours here and now. Nevertheless when persecution comes and suffering appears overwhelming, it is vital that we remember that, just as the Son of Man suffered, died, rose again and was taken up to heaven, so if we suffer we shall enter into glory to be with him for ever.

28.
The disciples' failure and privilege

Please read Matthew 17:14-27

Preachers often point to the contrast between the 'mountain-top experience' of the transfiguration and the immediately following valley of failure. Times of intimate communion with God are frequently followed by disappointment and depression, but we must be very careful in applying this to the present passage. While Jesus was certainly disappointed in his disciples, to speak of failure in connection with Jesus is quite wrong. As he nears Jerusalem and the time of his death, there is an increasing emphasis on the opposition that surrounds him, the weakness of his disciples and his own determination to go forward. In these three sub-sections, however, we see not only the failure of the disciples, but also Christ's encouragement of them. While not uncritical of their lack of faith, he gives grounds for future hope and, through Peter's encounter with the temple officials (17:24-27), alerts them to their privileged position in him.

In this whole section on the community of the kingdom, and particularly after Peter's confession, Matthew gives great prominence to the disciples and the subject of faith. Already several incidents — the feeding of the five thousand and the four thousand, Jesus walking on water, the Canaanite woman — have pointed out their weakness. This highlights their need to progress and, indeed, the fact of their progress. If the church is to fulfil Christ's commission, given at the end of the Gospel, then its members must grow in faith and learn to exercise faith. Therefore, while the disciples' weakness is stressed, there is also mention of increase of faith and what can be achieved through faith. At the same time, lest they should be discouraged, their privileged position as Christ's disciples and sons of God is also made clear.

The disciples' failure (17:14-18)

On coming down from the mountain with the three disciples who were closest to him, Jesus finds the other disciples in a difficult situation. They have been confronted by a man whose son, he says, **'has seizures and is suffering greatly. He often falls into the fire or into the water.'** He complains to Jesus, **'I brought him to your disciples, but they could not heal him.'** He pleads with Jesus, **'Lord, have mercy on my son.'** At this point we must remember that the disciples had previously been given authority to heal and cast out demons (10:1), but here they were unable to exercise that authority effectively. In response to this, Jesus demonstrates his own unfailing authority and power. He **'rebuked the demon, and it came out of the boy, and he was healed from that moment'** (17:18).

Before doing this Jesus expresses his grief over the unbelieving condition of the world. It is not only the disciples who are unbelieving, but all those whom he encounters. So he cries out, **'O unbelieving and perverse generation … how long shall I stay with you? How long shall I put up with you?'** This is not a condemnation of the disciples alone, nor of the whole of Israel, but of the unbelieving character of those who surround him. His actions show that unbelief cannot thwart his purposes, but it does grieve him greatly. We see his love and readiness to sacrifice his own comfort, in that he is ready to 'put up' with them. His forbearance and longsuffering were truly remarkable.

The disciples, too, after the resurrection would have to exercise this same longsuffering and we must follow in their steps. We must remember the exhortation: 'Consider him who endured such opposition from sinful men, so that you will not grow weary and lose heart' (Heb. 12:3). We should not be overwhelmed by the unbelief and opposition of the world around us. They are enslaved by sin and the devil, as we once were, and we must exercise patience with them. The apostle Paul tells Titus, 'Remind the people ... to be ready to do whatever is good, to slander no one, to be peaceable and considerate, and to show true humility towards all men,' even the wicked and unbelieving, because, 'At one time we too were foolish, disobedient, deceived and enslaved by all kinds of passions and pleasures. We lived in malice and envy, being hated and hating one another. But when the kindness and love of God our Saviour appeared, he saved us, not because of righteous things we had done, but because of his mercy' (Titus 3:1-5). If we are not to grieve our Lord, we must not only exercise faith, as he instructs his disciples, but also follow his example of forbearance with unbelievers around us.

Faith like a mustard seed (17:19-20)

As so often, **'The disciples came to Jesus in private and asked, "Why couldn't we drive it out?"'** (17:19). They had not realized that gifts of the Spirit do not work automatically. They seem to have thought that, having been given this authority, they could not fail to cast out demons, not realizing that such gifts have to be exercised in faith. As Paul writes, 'We have different gifts, according to the grace given us. If a man's gift is prophesying, let him use it in proportion to his faith' (Rom. 12:6). So Jesus gives his disciples the explanation: **'Because you have so little faith.'** He is not condemning them as unbelievers, but reminding them that service and the exercise of gifts depend on faith for their effectiveness. As we have seen, 'little faith' is not a description of the amount of faith, as if we had to summon up strength and make an effort to believe, but of its quality. Little faith does not persevere against obstacles. Their faith had been sufficient to cast out demons on their training mission, but now they are confronted by a particularly difficult situation, a particularly strong demon, and they are unable to cope. Their faith disappears before such a great obstacle.

So as not to discourage his disciples, Jesus goes on: **'I tell you the truth, if you have faith as small as a mustard seed, you can say to this mountain, "Move from here to there" and it will move. Nothing will be impossible for you.'** This confirms what we have seen about 'little faith'. Even faith as small as a mustard seed, if it is real and true, is effective because it lays hold of the power of God. Nothing will be impossible for them, because nothing is impossible with God (cf. 19:26). True faith relies on God and his great power to do what is humanly impossible. Throughout the Scriptures God is seen doing what is impossible for men. It is not only Abraham and Sarah who need to know that nothing is 'too hard for the LORD' (Gen. 18:14).

> Faith in thy power thou seest I have,
> For thou this faith hast wrought;
> Dead souls thou callest from their grave,
> And speakest worlds from nought.
>
> Faith, mighty faith, the promise sees,
> And looks to that alone;

> Laughs at impossibilities,
> And cries, 'It shall be done!'[1]

This is not wishful thinking, like that of the White Queen in Lewis Carroll's *Alice Through the Looking-Glass*, who says, 'Why, sometimes I've believed as many as six impossible things before breakfast.' These things are impossible only to men; God is able to do everything he has purposed and promised (Rom. 4:21). Jesus is not talking about the removal of a literal mountain. 'Moving mountains' was a common expression for overcoming great obstacles. When we think of what lay ahead of the disciples, we can readily see that a mountain is a suitable picture for the obstacles and difficulties that would face them. The difficulties that faced Zechariah and his colleagues after the return from exile were similarly great. The opposition of surrounding enemies combined with their own weakness to discourage them greatly. How could they cope with this situation of rebuilding the city and temple, of making, as it were, bricks without straw? God gives them encouragement: 'This is the word of the LORD to Zerubbabel: "Not by might nor by power, but by my Spirit", says the LORD Almighty.' The prophecy continues: 'What are you, O mighty mountain? Before Zerubbabel you will become level ground' (Zech. 4:6-7).

Faced with the task of evangelizing the world, the twelve apostles, or even the 120 disciples of Acts 1:15, must have quailed. However, they were given the Holy Spirit at Pentecost. The knowledge that Christ had promised that the Spirit would 'convict the world of guilt in regard to sin and righteousness and judgement' (John 16:8), was the necessary foundation for the faith, as small as a mustard seed but real faith all the same, which would enable them to do God's work. Nothing would be impossible for them. The evidence of this is seen in the Acts of the Apostles, not to mention the work of God spread around the world since then. The disciples had been assured that they would see the Son of Man coming in his kingdom (16:28). As they believed the word of Christ, trusted in the power of the Spirit and went forward, so they did see this coming to pass.

Another passion prediction (17:22-23)

Matthew keeps mentioning the fact that Jesus warned his disciples of his coming death, to impress upon us the inexorable character of the Jewish leaders' opposition, as well as the certainty of God's purpose. On this occasion there is no 'must', but Jesus is very definite: **'The Son of Man is going to be betrayed into the hands of men. They will kill him, and on the third day he will be raised to life'** (17:22-23). Such a warning of opposition, including betrayal this time, can only have increased their sense of being faced by a mountainous obstacle. However, the fact that Jesus prophesies this should assure them that everything is under control; it is God's purpose that is being worked out through 'the help of wicked men' (Acts 2:23).

Matthew does not have to comment that the disciples did not understand. That is evident because they **'were filled with grief'**. The prospect of Jesus' death overwhelms them. Once again, they do not notice the prophecy of his resurrection, which should at least have comforted them, however little they understood it at this time. Christ's approaching death is the constant context of every other incident, including the next one.

The temple tax (17:24-27)

This is one of many occasions when we have to distinguish between the uniqueness of Christ and his actions, on the one hand, and his example, on the other. In chapter 16 the cross was both his unique means of saving sinners and also an example for his disciples. It is the same in this matter of the temple tax. Christ is both example and Redeemer. The origin of the tax is found in Exodus 30:12-16, where the Lord instructs Moses to take a census of the Israelites. As they were being counted, a ransom price of a half-shekel had to be paid for each person, lest a plague strike him. Later on, the proceeds were devoted to the needs of the temple and its services. In the time of Jesus the equivalent amount was two drachmas, although such a coin was not readily available and usually two people joined together to pay the tax with a four-drachma coin.

'**The collectors of the two-drachma tax came to Peter and asked, "Doesn't your teacher pay the temple tax?" "Yes, he does," he replied**' (17:24-25). Peter has clearly, and understandably, not grasped the significance of the situation. So Jesus takes him aside, apparently knowing supernaturally what has happened, and asks the question: '**From whom do the kings of the earth collect duty and taxes — from their own sons or from others?**' (17:25). Peter's answer, naturally, is: '**From others.**' '**Then the sons are exempt**', is Jesus' response. This general question and answer conceal deeper principles and some great truths.

The first element is the implied assertion that God is King, that the tax is God's tax and that therefore Jesus, as God's Son, is exempt. Why, then, does Jesus pay the tax? He explains to Peter: '**But so that we may not offend them, go to the lake and throw out your line. Take the first fish you catch; open its mouth and you will find a four-drachma coin. Take it and give it to them for my tax and yours.**' He was exempt from the tax, but acknowledges that since his sonship is somewhat hidden, the collectors would not know this and would regard him as sinful if he refused to pay the tax. We may imagine their reaction to this 'ungodly rabbi' who refuses to pay the temple tax. Not understanding why, they would reject him and his ministry because of his apparent sin. So he gives Peter and us an example of being ready to give up our rights and liberties when the good of others is at stake. We have here an example of Paul's teaching in Romans 14 and 1 Corinthians 9, where, in things indifferent, we should give up our liberties for the sake of others. This does not mean, of course, that we should sin in a mistaken attempt to help others. However, there was no sin involved in paying this tax, just the concession of a liberty. He was exempt but not forbidden to pay.

There is a further element here. By doing this Jesus was again identifying himself with his people. His whole life consisted of this. He was not unclean, but he was circumcised. He did not have to repent, but submitted to John's baptism of repentance. He was not liable to keep the law, but he did. He observed the Sabbath and many other aspects of the Old Testament law. He was not in need of redemption and ransoming, as the original tax implied. Nevertheless he identifies himself with his people, with sinners, by paying Peter's tax as well as his own, and shows that his purpose in coming was to ransom others. His obedience counts for others; his suffering ransoms others. What condescension we find here beneath the apparent simplicity of the incident!

Jesus uses the word 'we' to make the point that Peter also is exempt. In one sense Peter was not yet exempt, for freedom from the ceremonial law actually follows the cross. Nevertheless, in principle Peter is already free, because he is in Christ. In him he is a son of the King and, in him, is fully redeemed and has no need pay this tax. The whole incident foreshadows the transition to the new covenant. Those who are in Christ no longer come under the condemnation of the law. 'But when the time had fully come, God sent his Son, born of a woman, born under law, to redeem those under law, that we might receive the full rights of sons' (Gal. 4:4-5). Since we are free from condemnation those aspects of the ceremonial which point to Christ, especially to his cross, no longer apply. Peter's freedom is ours also.

Once again, much critical ink has been expended (and wasted) on this allegedly 'trivial' and 'fanciful' miracle. This is far from being the case. The whole point of the incident rests on the fact that Jesus is the Son of the King who is ruler of heaven and earth and everything in them. He demonstrates this sonship by his mastery of the elements, of the lake, the fish and the coins. The miracle is not irrelevant. It demonstrates that Jesus is what he claims to be and that his work is effective, as he claims it to be.

So this incident instructs the disciples, although they would hardly understand it at the time, in their privileged position as adopted children of God. In the context of weak faith and impending 'tragedy', they have their spirits raised by an awareness of the power and majesty of Christ, the strength of God on which their 'mustard-seed faith' must rely and their highly privileged position as sons of God. It would have been easy to discourage the disciples by his rebuke of their little faith, and to depress them by the repeated prophecies of his coming death. Instead, Jesus links both of these with this demonstration of his power, authority, condescension and grace, which they would later appreciate and which we may appreciate today.

As well as realizing what it taught about the greatness of Christ and about our privileges, we must also learn to follow his example. We are surrounded by an unbelieving and perverse generation. In the face of this, we must go on believing, trusting in the power of God, which will move mountains for us. As we seek to witness to a world lost in sin, as we face the immense task of preaching the gospel and making disciples of all nations, we must not only realize that God is able to do this great work; we must also be ready, like our Lord, to put up with the opposition, persevere through the persecution, and take care not to cause others to stumble by insisting on our liberties. Our liberty of conscience must often be restrained voluntarily. We must be ready to 'pay', not just with a four-drachma coin, but with restricted liberty, so that others may not be put off, but encouraged to enquire further. Indifferent matters, harmless ceremonies and reasonable expectations of unbelievers must all be seen in the light of the needs of others. Christ, for our sakes, 'did not please himself' (Rom. 15:3). We must be ready not only to rely on the Messiah, the Son of God, but also to follow in his steps.

29.
Christ's little ones

Please read Matthew 18:1-14

Actors are often warned of the danger of appearing on stage or film with animals or children. They are very likely to be upstaged and ignored, while the animal, or, especially, the child receives all the attention. Many expositors think that this chapter has the same sort of attitude to children. We must be especially careful when dealing with them lest we get into trouble or difficulty. While we must not fail to take care of children, that is not the topic that Matthew and our Lord are addressing. As we have already seen (10:42), 'little ones' are not literal children or infants, but Christ's disciples. The fact that Jesus **'called a little child and had him stand among them'** does not alter this fact. The child is an illustration; the topic is disciples. Indeed, 'little ones' is a term of endearment from Jesus for his followers — all of them, not just a few who were particularly close to him.[1]

Applying these verses to little children leads to a romantic and sentimental attitude to children which is far removed from the Bible's teaching. There is no trace in the Bible of a view of children as innocent and humble. David's testimony applies to all children, including ourselves: 'Surely I was sinful at birth, sinful from the time my mother conceived me' (Ps. 51:5). In spite of the Old Testament's inclusion of children in the covenant relationship with God (cf. Gen. 17:7-14; Ps. 103:17-18), we must not treat children as if they needed no salvation or automatically possessed it. They are all 'by nature objects [or children] of wrath' (Eph. 2:3). This chapter is dealing with disciples, the members of Messiah's community, the church, and we must understand it accordingly, or we shall miss much vital teaching.

Becoming little ones (18:1-4)

Jesus' teaching about the little ones comes in response to a question from his disciples: **'Who is the greatest in the kingdom of heaven?'** (18:1). In response he uses a little child and says, **'I tell you the truth, unless you change and become like little children, you will never enter the kingdom of heaven. Therefore, whoever humbles himself like this child is the greatest in the kingdom of heaven'** (18:3-4). In the light of much sentimental teaching, we must examine these verses carefully. What exactly is the point of comparison between a little child and the disciple who will enter the kingdom of heaven? For many, children are innocent and unspoilt. Therefore, to enter the kingdom of heaven we must be like that. This is a complete denial of the Gospel's teaching, indeed of all the Bible. As mentioned already, children are not innocent but sinful. There is, of course, a difference between the child growing up in a Christian family and an adult, hardened in sin, embittered by experience and resistant to every gospel approach. However, even such children are not innocent. They all need salvation, which is the meaning of entering the kingdom of heaven.

Others seize upon the words **'humbles himself'** in verse 4 to insist that children have a humility, a childlike trust, which enables them to enter the kingdom. There is an element of truth in this, but the point has been missed. The change that is required is not to become humble, but to humble ourselves to

become like a little child. Humility is what it takes, not what
we become. We must humble ourselves from our self-sufficient
position to become 'nothing', as Paul writes of Christ himself
(Phil. 2:7-8). We must realize that we have no rights, no ability to save ourselves. A similar reference to this (Luke 18:17)
speaks of *receiving* the kingdom of God like a little child. This
is the point. We cannot work, earn, achieve, or do anything
else to gain entry to the kingdom. We can only receive the
kingdom as a gift. Children are dependent beings, receiving
everything that they need. To take up such a position of de-
pendency, receiving salvation, forgiveness and eternal life as a
free gift, is to become like a little child. It takes humility to
adopt this position, a low position where we can only receive.
Children in New Testament times were neither seen nor heard,
and to take this position is not easy for proud and sinful men
and women.

   It is impossible to come to this position apart from the grace
of God. We have already been told that it is the Father who
reveals the hidden things of the kingdom 'to little children'
(11:25). In spite of the AV translation 'be converted' — however theologically correct that may be — the responsibility
here is actually laid upon the hearer of the gospel to **'change'**.
He must change radically. Those who do this, by the grace of
God, are the greatest in the kingdom of heaven.

Accepting little ones (18:5-9)

Jesus is here elaborating the teaching of 10:40-42. His disciples are his special care, and no one can claim to welcome
Christ who does not welcome one of his disciples: **'And whoever welcomes a little child like this in my name welcomes
me.'** We must repeat, he is not talking about the child standing
among them, but 'such a little child' as described in verse 4,

one who has humbled himself to receive salvation, from a position of inferiority and need. This is made clear in verse 6 when
he refers to **'these little ones who believe in me'**. It is believers, true disciples, who have this special relationship with the
Lord. In this reference to welcoming or causing to sin, he appears to be referring to those who surround his people, the
world. Many oppose Christians and persecute disciples. Jesus
warns that **'If anyone causes one of these little ones who
believe in me to sin, it would be better for him to have a
large millstone hung around his neck and to be drowned
in the depths of the sea.'** Drowning was a recognized form
of execution in the Greek and Roman world, but Jesus, of
course, is comparing or contrasting that fate with suffering
the punishment of God. The severity of punishment described
here is because the rejection and ill-treatment of the little ones
means a rejection and ill-treatment of Jesus himself.

Jesus goes on to draw conclusions from this. He pronounces
a **'Woe'** of judgement on those who **'cause'** the little ones **'to
sin'**. Literally he says, 'Woe to the world because of stumbling blocks.' He is not talking about **'people'** in general, but
still has his disciples in mind. The fact that **'such things must
come'** in no way takes away the responsibility of **'the man
through whom they come'**. Jesus envisages the usual situation for his people, surrounded by an unbelieving world, where
many circumstances and trials will tend to cause them to sin.
Such trials and opposition are inevitable. He has already warned
that his disciples will be persecuted. God has ordained that
this is the way his people journey through the world to glory.
Here, however, the warning is issued to **'the world'**, thus giving an encouragement to his little ones, the disciples. They are
assured that he cares for them and will judge those who oppose them.

It is not all encouragement for his disciples, for Jesus warns
them about their own attitude and practice. Those who are

true disciples will care for other disciples and will show this by a radical breach with sin. Salvation by grace and justification by faith give no grounds for careless living. Jesus warns them solemnly, as he has already done in 5:29-30, that only those who deal drastically with sin are real believers and will enter into eternal life. **'If your hand or your foot causes you to sin, cut it off and throw it away. It is better for you to enter life maimed or crippled than to have two hands or two feet and be thrown into eternal fire'** (18:8). Similar warning is given about the use of our eyes (18:9). We must not behave like the world. If we do we shall suffer the fate of the world, because we have shown that that is where we really belong.

It is significant that Christ's exhortations about loving and caring for disciples are given in the context of the world's opposition. It is easy enough to deal kindly with God's people when everybody else is doing the same. The mark of the true Christian is that he cares for Christ's other little ones when the world is throwing stumbling blocks in their path. The apostle John gives love of the brothers as one of his marks of a true believer: 'We know that we have passed from death to life, because we love our brothers' (1 John 3:14). The context there, too, is the hatred of the world: 'Do not be surprised ... if the world hates you' (1 John 3:13). It is easy to love our brothers when we are shielded from the world's enmity, when we are in the fellowship of the church. It is not so easy to stand up for and love our Christian brothers when they are the objects of persecution by a hostile world.

The little ones' angels (18:10)

Verse 10 pursues the same theme. It is not only the world that is warned against ill-treating Christians. Jesus also warns his disciples concerning their fellow disciples: **'See that you do not look down on one of these little ones.'** He has already given a great motivation for this by associating himself with the little one (18:5). Now he goes even further and speaks of their relationship to God the Father: **'I tell you that their angels in heaven always see the face of my Father in heaven.'** This verse has often been cited as proof of the existence of guardian angels, specific messengers of God assigned to protect individual believers. The fact that they see the Father's face is taken to imply that their great privilege extends to the ones for whom they care. However, this does not really follow. The privileged position of guardian angels can hardly be extended to the disciples. Further, as has been pointed out, if they are guardian angels for believers on earth, what are they doing in heaven? In fact, while we are told that angels are 'ministering spirits sent to serve those who will inherit salvation' (Heb. 1:14), there is nothing in the Scriptures about individual guardian angels. (Usually, of course, it is said that these are guardian angels for literal children, which we have seen is not the case here.)

A better explanation, though not without its own difficulties, is that 'angel' here refers to the disembodied spirit of the disciple.[2] Jesus would then have been reminding his disciples that God's care of them now is such that when they die they will see God's face (5:8). Support for this idea is found in the incident recounted in Acts 12 in which Peter, having been released by an angel from prison, goes to the house where the church is praying for him. The servant, Rhoda, leaves him at the door while she goes to tell the rest about him. Having recognized his voice, she exclaims, 'Peter is at the door!' Not believing that God has answered their prayers, they reject her claim and say, 'It must be his angel' (v.15). If we were to interpret this of Peter's guardian angel we would be left with the problem of why the guardian angel should speak with

Peter's voice! It is more likely that the church is assuming that Peter has been put to death and that it is his disembodied spirit that has come to them.

This view is not be confused with the idea that when we die we become angels, like the other angels, in heaven. True, Jesus does teach that believers who die neither marry nor are given in marriage but 'will be like the angels in heaven' (22:30), but this is not the same thing. There is little other evidence to support the idea that 'angel' here means disembodied spirit, but this explanation fits the passage better than any other. Whatever our conclusion about this particular term, the implication is very clear. Christians are the object of the Father's special care and to ill-treat them is to incur the Father's wrath. We must not look down on, or despise, any fellow-Christian. That is the world's way; ours must be different.

The lost sheep (18:12-14)

Not only must we not look down on these little ones, we must positively care for them. Jesus tells a parable about a lost sheep to make this point:. **'If a man owns a hundred sheep, and one of them wanders away, will he not leave the ninety-nine on the hills and go to look for the one that wandered off? And if he finds it, I tell you the truth, he is happier about that one sheep than about the ninety-nine that did not wander off. In the same way your Father in heaven is not willing that any of these little ones should be lost'** (18:12-14). Although the parable is similar to the one in Luke 15, the context is completely different. These sheep are 'little ones', believers, who have gone astray. The lost sheep in Luke are sinners who need to repent. Jesus was perfectly able to use the same story to inculcate different lessons at different points; there are two different audiences. Sadly, too many have interpreted this parable as if it were the same as the one in Luke 15 and thus an important lesson has been missed.

Jesus is saying that we must share the Father's concern for all his people by caring for, and even going in search of, lost sheep. We must be very troubled when believers go astray, for whatever reason, or we are not like our Saviour. It is a basic principle of Christ's church, of Messiah's community, that we care for such lost sheep. It may be that such wandering sheep are a nuisance, the cause of difficulty and division in the church. Nevertheless, to say, 'Good riddance!' or speak of 'blessed subtractions' is quite unacceptable. These are little ones who belong to our Father in heaven. He is not willing that they should be lost. He rejoices when they are brought back. Our responsibility is to care for these little ones, not to give them up.

In the following verses Jesus goes on to deal with the subject of church discipline. It is very significant that before he does so, he lays down these general principles of care and concern for his people. It is easy to forget that the church is Christ's church and that these members are his little ones, to be treated with love and consideration. It would transform our church meetings and, perhaps especially, our elders' meetings if we were to work on these principles. We should no longer speak dismissively of those who do not pull their weight or who take up a disproportionate amount of our time and energy. We should no longer rejoice when difficult customers leave and take their problems elsewhere. On the contrary, we would grieve with our Lord over wandering sheep, straying children, and do our best to win them back. Winning back our brothers is the key to the next section.

We should remember, when we are speaking of discipline for those who offend against the letter or spirit of the church's constitution, that the Lord holds us responsible also. He speaks in the most solemn terms of judgement against those who put stumbling blocks in the way of young believers, or older ones for that matter. He speaks of millstones hung around the necks of those who do such things, and we must include looking down on our brothers in that category (18:10). Let us remember these things, and our churches will be different places, different communities, displaying much more of the qualities of our Lord. We shall shepherd the flock like the Good Shepherd, discipline the little ones like our heavenly Father, bring up these spiritual children in the nurture and admonition of the Lord, and so produce a community that shows forth his love, grace and mercy to the world.

30.
Discipline and forgiveness

Please read Matthew 18:15-35

Too often verses 15-20 are treated in isolation as the classic passage about church discipline, given to provide rules for running the church and principles for applying church discipline. While that is, of course, one aim of these verses, it is important to see them in relation to the parable of the lost sheep that has preceded them. This procedure is not a mere matter of church regulations and constitutions. These directions are not provided to give us the means of getting rid of recalcitrant sinners. The aim here is to recover our lost sheep or, better, the Lord's lost sheep. The key words are: **'You have won your brother over'** (18:15). That must always be the aim of church discipline, not to deliver excommunication by due process, but to recover the lost, to rescue the straying sheep. The attitude and aim are of prime importance for a correct application of the passage.

The issue here is a sin which has led to a breach with a brother. It is not certain whether the words **'against you'** are in the original, or whether all sins are included, but in any case the same general principles will apply. Jesus is not giving mere good advice. These are definite commands which we ignore at our peril. Those who have any experience in the church, and especially in the ministry, will be able to testify just how hard it is to get churches to put these principles into practice.

How much easier it is simply to ignore the problems and hope that they will go away! Or if the problem does not go away, perhaps the problem people will! So, many sins are tolerated, backsliding sinners left isolated and divisions left unresolved, because the teaching of Jesus is ignored in practice. Simple adherence to these principles, beginning with verse 15, would deal with many of the church's problems and difficulties.

Stage one (18:15)

Jesus begins with the simple command: **'If your brother sins against you, go and show him his fault, just between the two of you.'** It is clear that the result of the sin has been division. In such a case the individual's responsibility is to take the initiative and approach his brother. It is noteworthy that when the position is reversed and our brother has something against us, it is still our responsibility to take the initiative (5:23-24). It has been quaintly, but very truly observed, that when there is sin between brothers, they should meet halfway, physically, as each takes the initiative in approaching the other! The aim is not to show that you are right or justify yourself, but to win him back. This is to be done for his sake. We must not despise him (18:10), but long for his return to the fold. Even Leviticus 19:17 does not go quite this far: 'Do not hate your brother in your heart. Rebuke your neighbour frankly so that you will not share in his guilt.' That is true and necessary, but here we are exhorted to help him for his own sake and because of his and our Lord. The aim is to bring him back through repentance to forgiveness, reconciliation and restoration.

Doing this in private will tend to avoid escalation into a full-blown quarrel, making it easier for him to admit his fault, just to you. It will also remove the temptation simply to get one's own back or prove him wrong. The spirit of Galatians

6:1 is vital here: 'Brothers, if someone is caught in a sin, you who are spiritual should restore him gently. But watch yourself, or you also may be tempted.' Although Jesus does not state it explicitly, we may assume that he would expect us to pray for the Spirit's help, for grace for ourselves to approach in the right manner and for our brother, that he may be convicted of his sin. This is not a question of simply following the formula and all will be well. A spiritual approach is necessary. Nevertheless, we should not make this an excuse for ignoring our Lord's clear instructions in favour of a vague desire for reconciliation.

Stage two (18:16)

It is quite possible, even likely, that this will not be successful. If this is the case, continues Jesus, **'Take one or two others along, so that "every matter may be established by the testimony of two or three witnesses".'** The first aim here is further persuasion, because **'he will not listen'** just to you. Perhaps he will listen to the two or three, where a single approach is rejected. This, of course, assumes that you are correct. Indeed, the prospect of having to make the case before these brothers tends to make us more cautious about accusing the sinning brother. Many issues will be seen to be 'not worth the candle' if we have to do this.

It is assumed that the companions will have reasoned and pleaded with the sinning brother. If this is unsuccessful, then the presence of the one or two others has a second function. They are to be witnesses for the next stage, as our Lord's quotation of Deuteronomy 19:15 shows. This united testimony to the facts may avoid much trouble. The guilty party might easily not only deny his sin, but even make false accusations in return. Sometimes the situation becomes hopelessly complex and no one knows where the truth lies. The result is that the quarrel continues and is even made worse. Our Lord's instructions are very wise, as we would expect.

Stage three (18:17)

Sadly, it is often necessary to go on to the next part of the process: **'If he refuses to listen to them, tell it to the church.'** The whole church is involved, although the repeated 'listen' probably implies that some, presumably the elders, will take the lead in urging him to repent. Although some would limit this final hearing to the 'court of elders', it is more likely that the congregation is involved as a whole. After all, if it comes to the worst, the whole congregation will have to put the disciplinary measures into effect, not just the elders. Paul urges the Corinthian church to exercise discipline, 'when you are assembled in the name of our Lord Jesus'. Once again the aim is to win him back, that he should listen to the combined testimony and urging of his Christian brothers. In the phrase, **'if he refuses to listen even to the church'**, the word 'even' is significant. The knowledge that all the church is united, both in condemning him and in wanting him to repent, should exert considerable influence on him, if he is a true believer.

Stage four (18:17)

The final stage is commonly referred to as excommunication. This may easily be misunderstood. The communion from which he is excluded is not just the Lord's Supper, as practised by some. The impenitent sinner is to be excluded from the communion or fellowship of the church. The individual believer is exhorted, **'Treat him as you would a pagan or a tax**

collector.' He is to be treated as if he is an unbeliever, although
this may not actually be the case; that remains to be seen,
according to his response. This may explain what it means to
be delivered to Satan (1 Cor. 5:5; 1 Tim. 1:20). He is to be
regarded and treated as belonging no longer to the church,
but to the world, over which Satan is prince and ruler. The aim
is still to bring him back by bringing him to his senses.

How awful for a true believer to be treated as an unbeliever!
How painful for the Christian to be rejected and even ignored
by those with whom he has worshipped and prayed in previous days! Surely, if he is a genuine believer this will have an
effect! We cannot assume that this will be the case, but we
must be ready to receive him back in repentance. We must
learn from Paul's words to the Corinthians: 'The punishment
inflicted on him by the majority is sufficient for him. Now instead, you ought to forgive and comfort him, so that he will
not be overwhelmed by excessive sorrow. I urge you, therefore, to reaffirm your love for him' (2 Cor. 2:6-8).

Authority (18:18-20)

This is more than good advice, more than mere rules and methods. Verses 18-20 add both validity and solemnity to the process. If this matter has been pursued in a godly and biblical
way, then God's authority confirms the action of the church.
'I tell you the truth, whatever you bind on earth [i.e. exclusion from the congregation] **will be bound in heaven**
[actually 'will have been bound', as in 16:19], **and whatever
you loose on earth** [i.e. readmission] **will be loosed** ['will
have been loosed'] **in heaven.'** If this has been done biblically, spiritually and carefully, with a desire for the restoration
of the sinner, then both procedure and verdict will reflect the
previous heavenly verdict. This is far from the often cruel and

harsh treatment of offenders, which is not limited to the medieval Roman Catholic Church, but can easily be true of evangelical and reformed congregations if they are not careful. Rightly understood and practised, it is the outworking of the care of the Good Shepherd and the desire of the heavenly Father that none of these little ones should be lost.

Verses 19-20 are often quoted in relation to prayer and, indeed, there is undoubted, if indirect, relevance to that subject. Verse 20, **'For where two or three come together in my name, there am I with them,'** is sometimes used as a definition of the church. Again this is not wholly untrue. However, the context is still that of church discipline and should only be applied more widely as an extension of that. That is, if Christ is in the midst for purposes of discipline, then we may assume that he will be in our midst for other purposes also. If verse 19 should be applied to prayer — **'If two of you on earth agree about anything you ask for, it will be done for you by my Father in heaven'** — then it may refer to a prayer for wisdom and for the restoration of the sinning brother. It seems more likely, however, that 'anything' refers to a 'judicial matter'. The word is used in this way in 1 Corinthians 6:1, which is a similar context to the present one. It may be that these words confirm verse 16. The individual brother must take another with him, at least, so that two may pursue the case. If this is done properly — they must be in agreement — then it will be done by the Father in heaven, not just these individuals.

It is vital to remember the qualification, **'in my name'** (18:20). We are concerned here with the new Messianic community, 'my church'. How much more spiritual this situation is than what has preceded it in the Old Testament! This is the church of Christ. His concerns must be our concerns. The earlier verses of the chapter must all be remembered as we try to apply these principles of church discipline. Our fellow church members must always be seen as Christ's little ones. We must remember Christ's concern for them and the love of his heavenly Father as well. We must also remember our own responsibility to act in a spiritual and godly manner. It is far too easy, when considering someone who has offended us and the church generally, to take up a wrong attitude. We must remember that it is better to enter life maimed or crippled, by mortifying our desire for revenge or justification, than to have two hands or two feet and be thrown into eternal fire. When we seek to remove the splinter from our offending brother's eye, we must also examine ourselves to see whether we are doing this in a spiritual, kind and compassionate manner (Matt. 7:3-4).

How much better our churches would be in general, and in particular our church meetings, if we followed not merely the stages of discipline commended by Christ, but also the spiritual attitudes he requires! These verses are not just good advice for church leaders, but ways which promote health and holiness in the church, and increase a good testimony to the world. We must not despise one another, or feel superior to one another. It is only the one who humbles himself to take the position of a lowly and guilty sinner, receiving grace and forgiveness as a free gift of God, who is to regard himself as one of Christ's little ones, a true disciple, a candidate for heaven and eternal life.

Forgiven and forgiving (18:21-35)

Peter's question, **'Lord, how many times shall I forgive my brother when he sins against me?'**, is asked in the context of the previous teaching about church discipline. Since the previous verses are concerned with the winning back of the erring brother, the church is understood as forgiving the one who repents. Surely there must be limits to the church's readiness to accept someone back into the fold, thinks Peter. He deals with this on the personal level, for the church is made up of individuals. The rabbis taught that a repentant offender should be given three chances. Peter offers the opinion: **'Up to seven times?'** Jesus replies, **'I tell you, not seven times, but seventy-seven times.'** The traditional translation, 'seventy times seven',[1] would make no difference to the meaning, for it is not to be taken literally, as imposing a limit, but saying that we must always forgive. This must have amazed Peter, so Jesus enforces his command with a parable.

He compares the principles of the kingdom of heaven to those of **'a king who wanted to settle accounts with his servants'** (18:23). One of the king's servants was **'a man who owed him ten thousand talents'**, a huge amount by any standards. Since this man **'was not able to pay, the master ordered that he and his wife and his children and all that he had should be sold to repay the debt'**. When this servant asked for time to pay, the master, knowing that this was not a possibility, **'took pity on him, cancelled the debt and let him go'**. This servant had a colleague, **'who owed him a hundred denarii'**, a trifling amount by comparison. He demanded repayment from him, but when his fellow-servant begged for time to pay, he refused. **'Instead, he went off and had the man thrown into prison until he could pay the debt'** (18:30).

The other servants were distressed by what had happened and informed the master. He called the first man, addressed him as, **'You wicked servant'**, and reminded him of his debt that had been cancelled. Then, since this servant had not **'had mercy'** on his fellow servant, **'In anger his master turned him over to the jailers to be tortured, until he should pay back all he owed'** (18:34). Verse 35 draws the 'moral' of the story: **'This is how my heavenly Father will treat each of you unless you forgive your brother from your heart.'**

The Christian's duty to forgive his brother, even repeatedly, is quite clear. The context implies that the brother has
repented and wants the relationship to be restored. Real forgiveness does not ignore the sin, but does respond to repentance. It does not simply say, 'Never mind,' or 'Forget it.' Only
through repentance and real forgiveness can genuine fellowship be renewed. The fact that such forgiveness is to be repeated raises the whole question of sincerity. If we are told to
forgive **'from your heart'**, must not the offender repent from
the heart also? Jesus does not deal with this here, but a similar
passage in Luke 17:3-5 is instructive: 'If your brother sins,
rebuke him, and if he repents, forgive him. If he sins against
you seven times in a day, and seven times comes back to you
and says, "I repent", forgive him.' The apostles' amazed response to the Lord on that occasion was: 'Increase our faith!'
Seven sins in a day must cast doubt on the sincerity of repentance. However, Jesus does not make any allowances for this.
There is, of course, a danger of encouraging a light attitude to
sin and repentance, and if such a superficial attitude is clear
the Christian is bound in love to deal with that also. This is not
our Lord's point here. He is concerned to remove any imagined justification for withholding forgiveness.

Again, this raises the issue of 'forgive and forget'. Many
will say that that they are willing to forgive but cannot forget.
While this is literally true, for we are only human, the essence
of forgiveness is that we forget in practice. We do not act on
the basis of the forgiven sin; we do not hold it against our
brother or raise the matter again. We are told in Jeremiah 31:34
that God does not remember our sins any more. Here, too, we
cannot imagine God actually forgetting anything. What we
are told is that he will not hold the sins against us, or act upon
them. The relationship continues irrespective of the forgiven
sin.

Our Lord's sanction, expressed in verse 35, is that if we
refuse to forgive, God will withhold his forgiveness. What can

this mean? It may refer, in the first place, to that day-by-day forgiveness referred to in the Lord's Prayer (6:12), but the terms of the parable and its application demand more than that. If our settled attitude is one of refusing to forgive a sinning Christian brother, then it casts doubt on the reality of our experience of God's forgiveness. Jesus is not saying that God will withdraw his forgiveness; that is contrary to the whole teaching of the Bible. However, as is taught in many other verses in the New Testament, the verdict of the Day of Judgement will be decided on the evidence. Those who refuse to forgive will not be forgiven. Those who live like the world will be judged like the world, whatever their claims, whatever their profession.

We must take Christ's words seriously. In fact, our churches seem to be full of professing Christians who will not be reconciled to their fellow church members, refuse to speak to them or acknowledge them, refuse to forgive and make a point of remembering sin. Such people are in a very dangerous position. The sentence pronounced by the master in the parable of being turned over to the jailers to be tortured should make us very sensitive to this and aware of our danger.

The way the parable unfolds seems to be aimed more at moving us to forgiveness than at threatening us with not being forgiven. The parable gives a wonderful picture of God's grace and forgiveness. **'The servant's master took pity on him, cancelled the debt and let him go'** (18:27). This reminds us of the many verses in the Bible, particularly in the Old Testament, which express God's forgiveness in the strongest language:

As far as the east is from the west,
so far has he removed our transgressions from us
(Ps. 103:12).

You will again have compassion on us;
    you will tread our sins underfoot
    and hurl all our iniquities into the depths of the sea
                             (Micah 7:19).

I, even I, am he who blots out
    your transgressions, for my own sake,
    and remembers your sins no more
                             (Isa. 43:25).

I have swept away your offences like a cloud,
    your sins like the morning mist
                             (Isa. 44:22).

Such statements both give us the pattern for forgiveness and the motivation for it. This came first and should have moved the first servant to forgive his fellow-servant.

When we are approached by a penitent sinner, desiring forgiveness and reconciliation, we should work on this basis. First, we should see ourselves as fellow-sinners, not as judges. We have no right to sit in judgement on anyone and our experience of the grace of God should convince us of this. Secondly, we should see ourselves as repeated sinners. Even if our friend comes to us seven times in a day seeking forgiveness, we sin against God many more than seven times a day. Thirdly, we should see ourselves as greater sinners. He has only sinned against us — his sin against God is not our concern in this context — but we have sinned against God. Our sin is truly a huge amount, whereas his is but a trifling one. If we have really seen our offence against God and truly regret it, then we shall be in a frame of mind to forgive also. Broken hearts cannot refuse forgiveness.

The church consists of forgiven sinners. The fact that we are saints by God's grace can never remove this and we should always be conscious of it. Our Lord's concern is that the church should also consist of *forgiving* sinners. This consciousness provides the right context for concern for a lost sheep. The words of Psalm 119:176 should stay with us:

> I have strayed like a lost sheep.
>> Seek your servant,
>> for I have not forgotten your commands.

The consciousness of being ourselves wandering sheep, going our own way only too often, should equip us to go in search of the one lost sheep. We are not really part of the ninety-nine or, at least, not permanently so. This is the right context for church discipline. We are not priestly judges handing recalcitrant heretics over to the secular arm to be burnt at the stake. We are forgiven sinners, wanting to be reconciled to our brothers, to win them back into a loving and fruitful relationship. If this seems too hard for us, then the apostles' cry in Luke 17 should be ours: 'Lord, increase our faith!'

Part 6:
The grace and judgement of the kingdom
(19:1 – 25:46)

31.
Marriage and the kingdom

Please read Matthew 19:1-12

If there is one topic that can be relied upon to provoke disagreement and even division among Christians it is that of divorce and, especially, remarriage. Including chapter 5 and the verses under consideration here, Matthew records more of Christ's teaching on this difficult subject than the other Gospel-writers. It appears that he regards it as particularly important, as if he were writing his Gospel in today's climate. We should be very grateful that God has provided such relevant teaching for us in our need. However, some do not regard the teaching as being clear, so this passage in Matthew 19 is the subject of much debate and controversy.[1] One source of help for us is to see the passage in context.

The words, **'When Jesus had finished saying these things'**, indicate the beginning of a new major section. The contents of the usual discourse at the end (24:4 – 25:46) give a clue as to the subject of the whole section. The discourse concerns judgement and the final coming of the kingdom. Much of this section is related to these areas, including the requirements for final admission to the kingdom, but it also, and especially, explains the grace of God which alone can enable us to enter the kingdom. In the light of this, it may seem strange for Matthew to begin with the subject of divorce. However, a closer look shows the connections, both with what precedes it and with what follows. We must not allow the beginning of a new section to deny or obscure all other connections. The attitude of the Pharisees to divorce was hard and harsh, quite unlike the forgiving attitude that Jesus had inculcated in chapter 18 and which we must continue to bear in mind.

Then we are told that Jesus **'left Galilee and went into the region of Judea to the other side of the Jordan'** (19:1). The place is significant. Jesus is entering the area which was governed by Herod Antipas. Antipas had recently divorced his wife in order to marry Herodias, who had left her husband in order to join him. It was John's condemnation of this 'marriage' that brought about his imprisonment and execution. It seems very likely that the Pharisees hoped that they could trap Jesus into supporting John and thus make him liable to the hatred of the tetrarch. This section, therefore, records the increasing hardening of opposition to Jesus, which would lead to his crucifixion.

Further, the teaching on divorce is not to be seen as some form of legalism, the mere giving of rules for Christians. The fact that Jesus directs his questioners to the original situation, before the Fall, and refers to the necessity for sacrifice in the service of the kingdom (19:12), indicates that, in his mind at least, the subject of divorce is connected with the coming of the kingdom, with its requirements and demands, not to mention the need for grace. Seen like this, divorce functions as a crucial test case for measuring the disciples' commitment to the kingdom.

The Pharisees' question (19:3)

As we have seen already, the Pharisees belonged to various schools of thought, depending on which rabbi's teaching they followed. On the issue of divorce, some followed Shammai, who had a relatively strict view. In their understanding of Deuteronomy 24:1, the followers of Shammai interpreted 'something indecent' as 'gross indecency, though not necessarily adultery'.[2] The disciples of Hillel, on the other hand, extended this offence to include all sorts of real or imagined ones, including, notoriously, burning the toast! By their question the Pharisees are intending to place Jesus in a cleft stick. Whatever he says will offend someone, preferably Antipas. As today, it is virtually impossible to make a clear statement on the subject of divorce and remarriage without offending some party in some church. Many churches are divided over this issue and many Christians live in bondage because of the lack of a clear agreement on the subject.

Today we live in the midst of a multitude of reasons and arguments for divorce, which in Britain have more recently been codified in civil law in terms of 'no-fault divorce'. Adultery, desertion, mental cruelty, or a simple assertion that 'I don't love her any more', are seen as sufficient reasons for giving up on a marriage. Alongside the abandoning of marriage altogether, we find that many of those who do embark upon married life do so without any real intention of persevering in it. If all goes satisfactorily, well and good; if not, then you can easily get out of it.

God's institution (19:4-6)

Jesus is too wise to get embroiled in the debates between schools of rabbis. He simply refers to God's original ordinance, asking, **'Haven't you read ... that at the beginning the Creator "made them male and female", and said, "For this reason a man will leave his father and mother and be united to his wife, and the two will become one flesh"? So they are no longer two, but one. Therefore what God has**

joined together, let man not separate' (19:4-6). This was, we must note, a creation ordinance. God's words do not apply only to Christians, but to all men. This is something that Christians sometimes do not acknowledge. They seem to think that a marriage is really a marriage only if it was solemnized in a church building and that getting married in a civil ceremony, in a registry office or elsewhere, does not qualify. They are greatly mistaken. There is a vast difference between cohabitation and marriage, but it does not consist in the religious aspect. Marriage is not, as is sometimes asserted, just about 'a piece of paper'. In marriage, as distinct from living together, there is a public commitment before witnesses to living together as man and wife on a permanent basis. Where this is done, it is a real marriage, whether the couple are Christians or not. In these circumstances 'the two will become one flesh'. This means that the prohibition on divorce, 'What God has joined together, let man not separate', applies generally. It has the sanction of God, not just of man's laws.

The principles reasserted by Jesus are of vital importance. While we cannot expect non-Christians to take notice of them, they should do. Christians must surely take them very seriously indeed. Marriage is between **'male and female'**; there is no place here for homosexual marriage. The man is said to **'leave his father and mother and be united to his wife'**. Nor is there a place for parental interference in a marriage, which too often makes difficulties in practice. The one-flesh union, though not limited to the physical union of sexual intercourse, must include that, as an honourable part of marriage.

In the present climate of religious opinion on the subject of divorce, perhaps the most important fact to be seen is that **'let ... not'** does not mean 'cannot'. Jesus is saying that men *must* not separate, that is divorce, those whom God has joined together. He is not saying that it is impossible, but that it is wrong.

Divorce is real, a fact of life, but a sinful fact, like murder. Men *can* and do commit murder, but they *may* not; it is not permissible. (The question whether divorce is always sinful is considered below.) Equally, it is not enough to maintain the mere form of marriage. The couple must continue to be one flesh in practice as well as in theory. When it is argued that it is better to break the marriage than to continue in a state of disharmony and hypocrisy, the Christian will answer that these are false alternatives. The real option is to continue the marriage truly before God by the grace of God.

Moses' certificate (19:7-9)

As they pursue the subject the Pharisees quote the authority of Moses. This was often the crux of the matter for them. They refer to Deuteronomy 24:1: **'Why then ... did Moses command that a man give his wife a certificate of divorce and send her away?'** This apparently contradicts the plain assertion of Genesis 2:24 and commands divorce. This shows a misunderstanding both of the text and of man's nature. The simple fact is that men do separate; they do divorce their wives. Jesus says that Moses took this into account: **'Moses permitted you to divorce your wives because your hearts were hard.'** Since the Fall sin has ruined marriages; men and women do not persevere in marriage, but seek a divorce.

In fact, however, the Pharisees were wrong. Perhaps, technically, their statement was not an error, but the way they put it gives completely the wrong impression. Moses did not command the divorce, only the certificate of divorce. The situation was that men were determined to divorce their wives. If they did so, then Moses insisted on the giving of a certificate to defend and protect the wife. As well as meaning that there was time for reflection, this ensured that the reason for the divorce was made clear, so that the woman's reputation did not suffer wrongly.

Moses' practice may be sufficient warrant for modern government regulation of divorce, but it will not do for the people of God, says Jesus. **'It was not this way from the beginning.'** So he asserts his own principle, which applies after the Fall, even though men's hearts are sinful and hard, giving the one exception to his previous blanket assertion in verse 6: **'I tell you that anyone who divorces his wife, except for marital unfaithfulness, and marries another woman commits adultery.'** Most of the modern debate concerns the 'except' in our Lord's words, the so-called 'exceptive clause', but the disciples would have taken that for granted.[3] What amazed and alarmed them was his assertion that this was the only right basis for divorce. This necessarily involves the right to remarry. In spite of the sophisticated arguments of some, it is quite clear that Jesus is talking about divorce and remarriage. Unless there is remarriage, there is no adultery. The implication, supported by Jewish practice and by the Old Testament, was that divorce ended a marriage. Those divorced were able to remarry. This does not mean that it was necessarily right for both parties to do so; the guilty party would have been sinning, because of his or her sinful divorce. There is again a clear difference between 'can' and 'may' here, just as there is between 'let not' and 'cannot'. These are not hair-splitting distinctions, but valid and important ones. Both 'can' remarry; only one 'may' do so.

The meaning of the word which the NIV translates as 'marital unfaithfulness' has also been disputed. The word, often translated 'adultery', is much more general than that. Some assert that it must mean 'fornication', as the AV has. It would certainly include that, but since the context is marriage it is wrong to insist on it alone. The word is used within the New

Testament to indicate various kinds of 'sexual immorality', which would perhaps be a better simple translation, as in the new English Standard Version (ESV). Stephen Clark argues that it includes all situations described in Leviticus 18.[4] Anything that breaks the one-flesh union is to be included.

Many problems arise in our modern situation because marriage has become a legal and ecclesiastical matter. In the Bible a man banished, excluded, or deserted his wife, and this constituted a divorce. In some countries the reverse was true also; the woman divorced her husband. The biblical language of 'separate' and 'loose' means divorce.[5] The idea of a legal separation, short of actual divorce, is unknown in the Bible and contravenes 1 Corinthians 7:5. It seems to be the resort of those who are unhappily married but believe that Scripture forbids divorce or, perhaps, simply want to avoid the stigma. The additional necessity in our society of a legal formalizing of this must not obscure that simple fact. This is more important in the related passage in 1 Corinthians 7. Since I have asserted that sexual immorality is the only valid reason for divorce, it is necessary to add that the so-called 'Pauline privilege', an alleged ground for divorce based on desertion (1 Cor. 7:15), is a misunderstanding of what Paul is saying. In fact, the apostle is giving pastoral advice to those who have been wrongfully deserted, i.e. actually divorced in practice, not giving an additional ground. In the light of this, in our changed legal situation it is not sinful for a wronged Christian even to take the initiative in making the *de facto* divorce a real one in terms of local law and ecclesiastical practice.[6]

Remarriage

In the light of this there are several deductions to be drawn. It is time that Christians returned to the old concept of 'the innocent party'. While acknowledging that no one is entirely

358   *The King and his kingdom*

without fault, there is usually a clear case to be made that one partner has in fact broken the one-flesh union and thus given grounds, valid grounds, for divorce. Within the church this needs to be recognized. Church discipline has to be practised and that cannot be unless there is a consideration of guilt. Once this is done, there is no good reason why the 'innocent party' should be disciplined by, or feel excluded from, the church. Such people are, truly, more sinned against than sinning.

This has ramifications for the issue of remarriage. Much of the debate today about remarriage is carried on in the context of the Roman Catholic view of the indissolubility of marriage, whatever the actual church affiliation of the one who holds the view. This regularly makes news, whenever the Anglican Church refuses remarriage 'in church', and especially when a member of the royal family is involved. The correct view is that of sanctity, not indissolubility. The divorced man or woman is not 'still married in the eyes of God'. Divorce is real. If the marriage is ended, then those who are divorced are 'free' to remarry. That is, they are able to do so and, in the case of the innocent party, free to do so without sin. This is not the place to consider all the many and varied scenarios that can be found, but true pastoral care will not only acknowledge our Lord's clear teaching, but also practise the compassion and forgiveness spoken of in chapter 18.

The claims of the kingdom (19:10-12)

The disciples' words in verse 10 can be read in various ways. The most likely response is one of cynical dismay: **'If this is the situation between a husband and wife, it is better not to marry.'** They consider that marriage under these restrictions can be a bondage. Remaining unmarried at least gives the option of marrying at a later stage. If you marry, you are bound and cannot get free. The answer that Jesus gives is interpreted in at least two different ways. He says, **'Not everyone can accept this word, but only those to whom it has been given.'** Is 'this word' his teaching in verse 9, or the disciples' reaction in verse 10?[7] Many maintain that it is the disciples' reaction, saying that the following verses give three examples of those who find it better not to marry: **'For some are eunuchs because they were born that way; others were made that way by men; and others have renounced marriage because of the kingdom of heaven.'** The concept of the 'eunuch', literally a man who has been emasculated, occurs in each of the cases, contrary to the NIV, which paraphrases 'made themselves eunuchs' as 'renounced marriage'. The third category then refers to 'disciples, who possessing the necessary gift from God, choose to forgo marriage for the sake of the kingdom of God'.[8]

However, 'this word' implies something taught, something to be accepted, which could refer to verse 9, but hardly fits the disciples' cynical reaction. Also, the first two categories of 'eunuch' do not think it 'better not to marry'; they have no choice. Similarly, our Lord's words seem to refer to the ability to accept the teaching being given, not a gift of continence. If this is the case, Jesus is saying that only true disciples of the kingdom can accept his teaching at this point. He knows that the hard-hearted world will reject it, but expects better things of those whose eyes have been opened, whose hearts have been changed. It is the same distinction that he has drawn in 13:11: 'The knowledge of the secrets of the kingdom of heaven has been given to you, but not to them.' Indeed, Christ's final words, **'The one who can accept this should accept it,'** are very similar to his conclusion to the parable of the sower: 'He who has ears, let him hear' (13:9). They sound more like an injunction to all the disciples, all of them, to observe his teaching in verse 9 than a commendation of celibacy or continence.

The third use of 'eunuch' is clearly a very strong figure of speech, rather like our Lord's references in chapter 5 to cutting off hands and feet and plucking out eyes. This is not commending self-castration, such as performed by Origen, the third-century scholar and theologian, in his sad misinterpretation of this verse. Rather Jesus uses the expression as a vivid description of one who has renounced marriage to devote himself to the work of the gospel, to building and spreading the kingdom of heaven. Some, though not all, of his disciples will renounce marriage because of the kingdom of heaven. It may refer to one like the apostle Paul, who asserts that he has not insisted on his right to marry (1 Cor. 9:5).

While the instruction about divorce is certainly helpful and very important today, the real point of this section, as it is found in the Gospel and in the development of its argument, is that Jesus is setting before his disciples the absolute demands of his kingdom. Nothing is exempt from the principles and ethos of the kingdom. Our attitude to marriage must be that of the kingdom, not of the fallen world. Only in Christ and in the kingdom can the original ordinance of marriage be fully practised and enjoyed. He then adds that, for some, the needs of the kingdom will override their rights and privileges in terms of marriage. He himself, it would seem, had adopted this position, not marrying for the sake of the kingdom, although he was in this respect, as in all others, truly human. It has been the case in the history of the church that some have indeed made themselves eunuchs, renouncing marriage for the sake of the preaching of the gospel, especially as pioneer missionaries. Not all have to do this, but we must all accept the principle that the kingdom has the supreme right to our allegiance, that all aspects and areas of our life must yield to the authority of our King and that, even if not in the case of marriage, there will be other rights that we have to give up, gladly, for the sake of serving him. As this major new section begins, looking forward to the consummation of the kingdom, the demands are set before us, but Christ's grace is sufficient us, as the next chapters will make clear.

32.
Grace, not status

Please read Matthew 19:13-26

It is usual among those who reject the authority of the Bible to see a contrast between Jesus and Paul. It is alleged that Jesus has a simple message of love, while Paul indulges in intellectual ideas and complicated doctrines such as justification. Paul, it is said, has perverted the simple gospel of love into a complicated and barren system of metaphysics. Nothing could be further from the truth. A careful reading of the apostle's writings shows him to be a man of love and compassion, with a message of grace and holiness. Similarly, when we look properly at the teaching of Jesus we find much about grace. So Carson can write, 'Without ever using the word "grace", Matthew returns to this theme repeatedly.'[1] This is nowhere clearer than in the passage from 19:13 to 20:16. The message is given repeatedly: salvation is by grace, not according to merit, privilege or status. Twice Jesus tells us that 'The last will be first, and the first will be last.' Human judgements and categories are turned upside down. The incidents of the children being brought to him and the coming of the rich young man both make this point: contrary to the disciples' expectation, salvation is not on the basis of status or ability. It depends on the gift of God.

The little children (19:13-15)

There is no particular chronological link with the preceding verses, but the topical connection between marriage and the family is clear. We read, **'Then little children were brought to Jesus for him to place his hands on them and pray for them.'** The account in Luke's Gospel makes clear that these were infants, babes in arms. This is why the NIV reads, **'The disciples rebuked those who brought them,'** interpreting the 'them' of the original. It would appear that the disciples shared the common attitude to children, that they were of little or no importance and that their Master should not be troubled with them. Jesus shows by his rebuke that their attitude is wrong and that the little children are very important to him.

The understanding of his words, **'Let the little children come to me, and do not hinder them, for the kingdom of heaven belongs to such as these'**, has been much clouded by the issue of infant baptism. Although there is no mention at all of water, the passage is clearly relevant to discussion of the status of children in the church. This same issue has caused some to assert that Jesus is not talking here about literal children, but about those who believe like little children. It is true that Mark's account includes words teaching this, but although that point was made in 18:4 Matthew does not include them here. The words 'such as these' do not refer to those like children, but to those of the same class, that is these particular children and others like them. This is asserted by both David Kingdon (Baptist) and John Murray (paedobaptist)! The former writes that the Greek word here 'by no means implies the exclusion, but rather the inclusion of the one mentioned. The child is one of the class it represents ... our Lord must mean that the kingdom belongs to these children and all others like them.' Similarly Murray argues that Jesus 'is not speaking of the class resembling little children but is referring to little children themselves'.[2]

The next question to be settled is what Jesus means by belonging to such as these. The original could mean either that the kingdom belonged to them, or that they belong to the kingdom. It could, therefore, either mean that they had a special privilege in relation to the kingdom, or that they were actually members of the kingdom. The form is strictly the same as in 5:3,10, except that 'of such' here replaces 'of them', in the Beatitudes. The earlier words must mean that the kingdom of heaven belongs to them, as it is usually translated: 'for theirs is the kingdom of heaven'. Here this cannot mean that Jesus is affirming the salvation of these children, but that because of their privileged position they must not be hindered from being brought, or coming, to him. It is implied that they have been brought to him to receive salvation, for he places his hands on them, prays for them and thus blesses them. This implies that they are capable of being saved by him and that his concern is for their blessing and salvation.

This may, indeed, give grieving Christian parents hope concerning the salvation of those dying in infancy. It is argued by some that nothing is said about their being children of believing parents, but these are Jewish children, children of the covenant, children of Israelites who have at least enough faith to bring them to the Saviour. Their position is that of those to whom Peter preached, describing them as 'heirs [literally "sons"] of the prophets and of the covenant God made with your fathers' (Acts 3:25). Nothing is being taught directly about other children. Aside from all debates about baptism, the point being made is that salvation does not depend upon status. The disciples were quite wrong to bar little children from the presence and blessing of the Saviour. Although they were just children, without rights or standing in society, Jesus demands that they be allowed to come to him. It is grace, not merit or status, that opens the door to the Lord Jesus Christ.

The rich young man (19:16-19)

The same teaching is embodied in the account of this young man who **'came up to Jesus and asked, "Teacher, what good thing must I do to get eternal life?"'** The reply of our Lord has evoked much controversy, much of it coming from a desire to deny the sinlessness of Jesus. His reply, **'There is only One who is good'**, is not intended to say anything directly about his holiness or lack of it, although by implication believers may deduce that he is to be identified with the one who is good, namely God. His real intention is to deal with the young man, who clearly believes that Jesus can shed new light on the issue of eternal life, different from what he has already learned. He appears to be rather like Nicodemus, expecting some special teaching that will ease his passage into the kingdom. Jesus, therefore, is refusing to dissociate himself from God, and directs him back to the written Word of God. Nothing in the teaching of Jesus contradicts what has already been stated by God in the Scriptures. The newness of his teaching consists of a new depth and its relationship to him and his work (see 1 John 2:7-8). It is not essentially new. The young man cannot avoid the demands of the Old Testament by appealing to the teaching of Jesus. Nor can we today.

Therefore Jesus refers him back to the law of God: **'If you want to enter life, obey the commandments.'** In response to the man's further enquiry, Jesus specifies, **'Do not murder, do not commit adultery, do not steal, do not give false testimony, honour your father and mother,'** and adds **'love your neighbour as yourself'** (19:18-19). It is essential to see this in its proper context. Jesus is not debating with legalistic Pharisees or Galatian Judaizers. He is dealing with an enquirer, who wants to know the way of salvation. We, in such circumstances, would almost certainly direct the person to faith in Jesus Christ. Why does Jesus not do that here? It is often asserted that he is just testing the man, assuming that he believes in salvation by works and wanting to show him how impossible this is. There is certainly something of this as the conversation continues, but at the beginning we have no right to take our Lord's words at any but their face value.

As with the children in the previous incident, this young man is one of the covenant people. The Old Testament has already made it clear that salvation and justification are by faith, although not in quite the specific terms that Paul would use. Those who were God's people in the Old Testament had to believe the promises. On this basis they were forgiven and accepted by God. However, those who trusted in God's covenant promises had to demonstrate their faith by obedience to the Word of God, as we read in Psalm 103:17:

> But from everlasting to everlasting
>   the LORD's love is with those who fear him,
>   and his righteousness with their children's children —
> with those who keep his covenant
>   and remember to obey his precepts.

Jesus is not telling the young man to keep the commandments in order to earn salvation, but describing the faithful Israelite's way to eternal life as one of obedience to the commands of God. What we have here is a combination of the stress of Paul with that of James. True faith leads to true holiness and righteousness; faith produces works.

This is not the right way to evangelize Gentiles, but for a Jew it was the appropriate method. Jesus uses exactly the same method with the expert in the law who tests him in Luke 10:25-28. There, too, the question is, 'What must I do to inherit eternal life?' Again Jesus refers him to 'what is written in the Law'. When the legal expert replies with the two great commandments — love for God and love for our neighbour — Jesus answers, 'Do this and you will live.' Here too Jesus is not teaching salvation by works, but reminding the man that the way to eternal life is paved with obedience and godliness. In the parable of the Good Samaritan that follows, it is the Samaritan who demonstrates his faith by caring for the robbed and wounded man. The priest and the Levite, although they are nominally children of the covenant, show by their failure to help, their failure to love their neighbour, that they are not true Israelites. The Samaritan puts them to shame. He illustrates the words of Romans 2:27: 'The one who is not circumcised physically and yet obeys the law will condemn you who, even though you have the written code and circumcision, are a law-breaker.'

The same principle applies under the new covenant also. The apostle Paul, in a different context, makes the same point. 'For if you live according to the sinful nature, you will die; but if by the Spirit you put to death the misdeeds of the body, you will live' (Rom. 8:13). There are those who accuse Paul of teaching justification by works, but he is not saying that mortification earns eternal life, but that the pathway to it is one of dealing with sin and living in holiness. The promises of the new covenant include not only God's assertion that he will not remember our sins any more, but also the writing of his law on our hearts (Jer. 31:31-34; Heb. 8:8-12). Forgiveness from God leads to a life of pleasing him in obedience to that law. Jesus is making the same point here, at least to begin with.

The one thing lacking (19:20-22)

It is at this point that the young man demonstrates that he is not in fact a believer, not a true member of the people of God. He is one who enjoys the privileges and knows the oracles of God, but he has not truly trusted in the promises of God. Otherwise his response to Jesus' further exhortation would be different. From his facile claim, **'All these I have kept'**, Jesus deduces that his spiritual condition is unsatisfactory. So when the man asks, **'What do I still lack?'** Jesus gives him an instruction which will reveal the inadequacy of his obedience. It is probably significant that our Lord had omitted, from his list of commandments, the tenth: 'You shall not covet.' It is this commandment that relates to the exhortation: **'If you want to be perfect, go, sell your possessions and give to the poor, and you will have treasure in heaven. Then come, follow me.'** Obedience to this would have shown that he was born again, that he had a new heart, which put Christ before everything else. Covetousness or 'greed ... is idolatry', says Paul in Colossians 3:5. This is not something extra, as he perhaps expected, but the essence of real repentance and genuine godliness.

We are told that **'When the young man heard this, he went away sad, because he had great wealth.'** As he often does, Jesus pinpoints the very place where the man is lacking. This command is not intended to be a universal one. We do not all have to sell up everything to give to the poor. However, for this young man this was the 'crunch' issue. He was covetous. His faith in, and love for, Jesus was not genuine, so he clung on to his riches and lost the Saviour — and riches in heaven.

This method of Jesus illustrates the second function of God's law. It was originally given to show God's people, redeemed from Egypt, how their Lord wanted them to live. As such it was not a covenant of works, but the rule of life for those had been redeemed, the so-called 'third use'. Those who believed the promises and received forgiveness, and wanted to serve God in gratitude, knew how to please him — by keeping his commands. However, many did not believe, but misinterpreted and misused the covenant as one of works, in which they would earn their salvation by keeping the commands. Then, in the wisdom of God, that same law became a means of conviction of sin, the schoolmaster, or pedagogue, to lead them to grace and to Christ (Gal. 3:21-24). It is this difference between those who hear in faith and those who hear in unbelief that explains the apparently ambivalent attitude to the law in the New Testament. Where there is faith in the promises and in the Christ of the promises, the righteousness of the law will be fulfilled through the working of the Holy Spirit (Rom. 8:4). Where there is no faith, but a desire to justify oneself by works, the law is found to bring condemnation and the great need is to be redeemed from it in that way (Rom. 6:14; 7:6).

The eye of the needle (19:23-26)

Jesus draws a very sad conclusion from the man's departure: **'I tell you the truth, it is hard for a rich man to enter the kingdom of heaven. Again I tell you, it is easier for a camel to go through the eye of a needle than for a rich man to enter the kingdom of God.'** Much misplaced ingenuity has been displayed in an attempt to find a natural explanation of 'the eye of a needle'. Some have written of a kind of rope or cable called a camel. Others have invented a gateway in the wall of Jerusalem, allegedly called 'the eye of the needle', through which a camel could go only if it was unladen. This is supposed to represent the young man getting rid of his possessions and so entering the kingdom unladen. However, all these efforts to find a feasible explanation completely miss the point. Jesus is not saying only that it is difficult, but that it is impossible. The disciples clearly understood this, and **'were greatly astonished'**. They asked, **'Who then can be saved?'** If the rich and privileged cannot be saved, then there is no hope for anyone.

The issue here, once again, is that of merit, ability and privilege. The disciples had assumed that because this young man had all the natural advantages of riches, class and knowledge of the law, he was a good candidate for eternal life. While we must not deny the value of privileges (Rom. 3:1-2), we must always remember that privileges have to be used, and the proper use is to believe the promises of God and, in this case, to trust Jesus as Saviour and Lord. In this instance riches were only a hindrance. They promoted self-confidence and self-satisfaction, not to mention self-righteousness. It is these characteristics that prevent, not just hinder, a man from entry into life. However, the situation is not absolutely hopeless.

'Jesus looked at them and said, "With man this is impossible, but with God all things are possible."' It is only God who can enable us to reject our human abilities and assets in order to receive salvation as a free gift. For this young man it was riches. For another it may be intelligence or upbringing. Anything that keeps us trusting in ourselves prevents us from trusting in Christ. What every man lacks is the ability to repent of his own abilities and righteousness and trust in the Saviour alone. The 'crunch' issue will vary from person to person, and the wisdom of the evangelist or personal worker lies in discerning what it is for any given individual, as our Lord did. Of course, they cannot do it infallibly, or indeed nearly as well as he did, but the effort has to be made.

The important thing is to realize that verse 26 is not intended to be negative and discouraging, but to encourage us. The disciples, full of disappointment, are being assured that, in spite of the enslaving power of riches in particular and of unbelief in general, men and women can be saved. God can do what is impossible for men, and indeed has often done so. The God who provided a son for Abraham and Sarah can work in the hearts and minds of sinners to bring them to repentance. He can cause them to leave their sin and their reliance on all human matters and come to Christ. He did this for Saul of Tarsus, who trusted in his own righteousness and had to give this up in exchange for Christ (Phil. 3:6-8). If there is some barrier holding you back from coming to Christ — riches, pride, an unwillingness to forgive, fear about the consequences — then rely on God to remove it, to do for you what you cannot do for yourself. Then come and follow the Saviour, the Lord Jesus Christ.

33.
The last will be first

Please read Matthew 19:27 – 20:16

It has been said that the present section, especially the parable of the workers in the vineyard, is contrary to natural human justice. Far from being a criticism of our Lord's teaching, this gives a valuable clue to the understanding of these verses. God's ways are not the same as our ways and his thoughts are not the same as our thoughts (Isa. 55:8-9). It is God's prerogative to raise up and cast down. In many verses of Scripture this is asserted, from Hannah's prayer to the letter of James.

> The LORD brings death and makes alive;
> he brings down to the grave and raises up.
> The LORD sends poverty and wealth;
> he humbles and he exalts
>
> (1 Sam. 2:6-7).

Similarly Proverbs asserts that God 'gives grace to the humble' (Prov. 3:34); this is also quoted in James 4:6. Mary's song, the Magnificat, tells us, 'He has brought down rulers from their thrones but has lifted up the humble' (Luke 1:52).

All these are reflected in Christ's teaching here, especially in the concluding verses of the two sections (19:30; 20:16). The only difference is that here Jesus is not only asserting God's sovereign disposal of men, but also telling us that the basis for this is grace. We do not earn our raising up by being humble. It is God who graciously gives us what we do not deserve. A proper understanding and acceptance of this principle is essential to a right attitude to judgement and salvation, which will vitally affect the way we live.

Peter's question (19:27-30)

Peter has just seen a rich man go away sad because he has great wealth. He has rejected our Lord's instruction to sell his possessions and give to the poor as the only way to have treasure in heaven. When Jesus asserts that it is impossible for such a man to enter the kingdom of God, Peter is moved to wonder about his own position and that of the other disciples. If a refusal to leave all for Christ bars a man from entry into the kingdom, what about those who obey? So he says, **'We have left everything to follow you! What then will there be for us?'** It appears that, what was impossible, God has caused to happen in their case. What then about the treasure in heaven? Peter is often criticized as being mercenary at this point, but Jesus does not take him to task severely, although there is an element of rebuke implied in his reply.

Jesus assures Peter of the blessings of the kingdom. He refers to the coming **'renewal of all things, when the Son of Man sits on his glorious throne'**, using a word for 'renewal' which elsewhere in the New Testament refers to the new birth (Titus 3:5). The day of his return will be a day of regeneration for the world; there will be new heavens and a new earth. This gives support to the belief that the new heavens and earth will not be entirely new, but the old creation redeemed and renewed from all the effects of sin (Rom. 8:20-21), like the regeneration of individuals. On that day, says Jesus, **'you who have followed me will also sit on twelve thrones, judging**

the twelve tribes of Israel'. This remarkable statement must
be taken to link the twelve apostles with the twelve tribes (cf.
14:20), but the reference to the Last Day implies that these
twelve tribes are not to be taken literally. As in James 1:1, the
twelve tribes represent the true Israel, consisting of both Jews
and Gentiles, as will be made clear later in the Gospel (see
also Luke 22:30).

The reference to the Son of Man takes us back to the prophecy of Daniel, where thrones are set and the kingdom is given
not only to the Son of Man, but also to 'the saints of the Most
High' (Dan. 7:9,13-14,22). In the light of this it is better to
take 'judge' in the Old Testament sense of governing or ruling, as in the book of Judges. As Herman Ridderbos writes,
'Here the translation should not be "judging", but "governing." The metaphor refers to the future glory of the twelve
tribes under the rule of the twelve apostles and, therefore, can
only be understood as indicating the glorified Church. The
expression "the twelve tribes of Israel" denotes the coming
Church by the name of the old people of God. It is the con-
tinuation of the latter and its fulfilment.'[1] While the rich man
fails to enter the kingdom, the poor disciples, having 'left everything', will rule in it.

While Jesus thus reassures his apostles, he is concerned
also for all his people, so he continues: **'And everyone who
has left houses or brothers or sisters or father or mother
or children or fields for my sake will receive a hundred
times as much and will inherit eternal life.'** Jesus assures
all believers that, whatever the cost of following him, it will
pale into insignificance compared with the treasures that he
bestows. When we speak, naturally perhaps, of giving up positions or possessions to follow Christ, we are not actually
speaking correctly. There is simply no comparison. The benefits of belonging to Christ, even in this world, are 'a hundred
times' greater than anything we give up.

The details of verse 29 are obviously, like the twelve thrones, not to be taken literally. Who wants a hundred brothers (or sisters for that matter!)? Jesus simply means that the compensations are much greater than what we give up. He uses the same concepts so as to make clear the relationship to what we 'lose'. However, some idea of what he is talking about may be gained by taking certain terms literally. Those who find that becoming a Christian involves a breach with their brothers will enjoy fellowship in the kingdom with many Christian brothers instead. Those whose family rejects them when they come to Christ find that many another home is open to them. Property (**'fields'**) may have to be left, but the Lord will provide for our needs, often in amazing ways. It is not being mercenary to remember all this. Our Lord's aim is to give us ammunition to use when the way seems hard and we are tempted to give up. This is the way with all the warnings and rewards in the Bible. We need something to strengthen us to persevere.

That is not all. Jesus adds that these true disciples will inherit eternal life. As if it were not enough to receive so much to compensate for the 'sacrifices' involved in becoming a Christian, he assures us that heaven and eternity will more than make up for anything else that still bothers us. In fact, 'sacrifice' is not the right word at all. When Dr Martyn Lloyd-Jones, who left a most promising medical career to enter the ministry, was asked about the sacrifice involved, he replied simply, 'I gave up nothing.'[2] The privilege was such that success, money and fame meant nothing at all by comparison. That is the true position, as the words of the apostle explain: 'For our light and momentary troubles are achieving for us an eternal glory that far outweighs them all' (2 Cor. 4:17). It may be that Jesus has particularly in mind persecutions that come to us after the initial leaving, as is suggested by the parallel passage in Mark 10:30.

Both the reigning and the enjoyment of compensating bless-ings illustrate the principle Jesus announces in verse 30: **'But many who are first will be last, and many who are last will be first.'** This proverbial expression sums up the lessons of the previous verses. Those who are first, in riches and rule (although it is only Luke 18:18 which designates the man a ruler), have no guarantee of God's blessing. Poverty is not a good thing in itself, but if it is the result of confessing Christ, **'for my sake'**, then it leads to rule and riches, treasure in heaven. However, we must not think that there is some strict proportionality between suffering and treasure. The parable that follows will show that all is of grace. It is essential not to separate the two passages.

The workers in the vineyard (20:1-12)

Here our Lord cautions Peter and the others against thinking in terms of merit and deserving where the kingdom of heaven is concerned. It **'is like a landowner who went out early in the morning to hire men to work in his vineyard'** (20:1). Much of the parable follows the customs of the day. It was usual to hire workers in this manner and **'a denarius for the day'** was the usual wage. We are not told why the owner returns at **'the third hour'** and **'the sixth hour'** and **'the ninth hour'** (20:5). It seems simply to divide up the day; all these workers really constitute one group contrasted with the last set of workers: **'About the eleventh hour he went out and found still others standing around.'** He asked them why none of them was at work. They replied, **'Because no one has hired us.'** So **'He said to them, "You also go and work in my vineyard."'** When it comes to payment the procedure is in reverse. Those **'who were hired about the eleventh hour came and each**

received a denarius'. In fact, no amount had been agreed with them. Presumably the same applied to them as to those hired at the third hour, that he would pay them **'whatever is right'** (20:4). No one seems to have objected until the foreman comes to those who had been hired first. **'They expected to receive more. But each one of them also received a denarius. When they received it, they began to grumble against the landowner.'** They think that because they **'have borne the burden of the work and the heat of the day'**, they ought to receive more instead of being paid an equal amount.

Grace and sovereignty (20:13-16)

The landowner's answer is most significant: **'Friend, I am not being unfair to you. Didn't you agree to work for a denarius? Take your pay and go. I want to give the man who was hired last the same as I gave you. Don't I have the right to do what I want with my own money? Or are you envious because I am generous?'** There are two points being made here. First of all, by implication, he asserts his sovereignty; he may use his money as wishes. He has a right to do what he wants and no one can make any objection. In terms of the parable the employer was completely justified. Where he had made an agreement he kept to it. The others, who had no agreement or contract, received an amount which was more than reasonable. We are not here in the realm of trade unions and written contracts and it is simply foolish to raise objections in those terms. The parable is not intended to be true to life in that respect. God's ways are not our ways. While we must, of course, acknowledge the sovereignty of God in every respect, we must be careful not to interpret the kingdom in terms of working and earning.

All is of grace, whether we receive much or little. The kingdom is not to be judged by the working practices of the world.
Nor are we to think of the kingdom in terms of wages. The
point being made is that God is not bound by our position or
status. Though we may be first in our own eyes, we may be
last in God's. Though we suffer more or less than others we
shall receive the same eternal life. Some have drawn a wrong
conclusion from this. 'Earlier Jesus taught that there are degrees of punishment in hell (Lk. 12:47-48); now he makes
plain that there are no degrees of reward in heaven.'[3] This is a
failure to distinguish things that differ. The reward of eternal
life is the same for all, but a later parable, that of the talents
(25:14-30), will paint a different, but complementary picture.
The important thing is to understand the biblical idea of rewards, which does not involve merit.

The second element is generosity as opposed to envy. Peter
and the others were being told not to think about other people.
If the Lord ordained that they should bear the heat and burden
of the day and others be let off lightly, they could have no
complaint. They had not been promised an easy time.

Why should I complain
Of want or distress,
Temptation or pain?
He told me no less.[4]

They must be concerned only for their own duty and not be
envious about others. God is generous and often we receive
more than we expect. In fact, we have no right to expect anything at all. Jesus is not talking about different degrees or levels
within the kingdom here. Those who are the last are lost, like
the rich young man. Though they may have had status and
privilege and imagined that they had merit, they will not enter
the kingdom of God. The rich young man thought he was

first, and the disciples would have agreed, but because he preferred riches to Christ he was last. He went away sad and would regret this eternally.

The original workers wanted justice, believing that this would give them more than the one denarius for the day's work, since they had worked much longer than those who received a denarius for one hour's work. If we look for justice, we shall not receive anything except punishment. All that we receive is of grace and we must be content with this. Indeed, we should be most grateful! We must not look at others and think that we serve and deserve more than they do. We may reject the whole possibility that we might envy others, until we think of concrete instances.

How many there are who think it is not really fair that the thief on the cross should gain heaven, just the same as we do. He did nothing for the kingdom; he did not work for Christ, and his suffering was not for Christ, but for his crimes. Jesus would say, 'Are you envious because I am generous?' His sovereignty determined that this man should be saved. We may feel the same about Saul of Tarsus. Why should such a man as he describes himself to be in 1 Timothy 1:13 — 'a blasphemer and a persecutor and a violent man' — not only be 'shown mercy', but be given such a prominent position in the church? Why should people be allowed to make a deathbed repentance? Many of us must sympathize with the feelings of Corrie ten Boom, when she came across one of the guards who had oppressed and mocked her and her sister in the concentration camp at Ravensbruck. When he thanked her for her message and professed that Jesus had washed away his sins, she found it almost impossible to forgive him and accept him as a brother in Christ.[5] And many of us feel some misgivings when we hear of Nazi war criminals finding forgiveness and salvation after the Nuremberg trials.

Too many of us are like the prodigal son's elder brother. While we claim to believe in salvation by grace and justification through faith, we nevertheless have a sneaking suspicion that we deserve rather better than others. This is dangerous. We must do our very best to deal with such feelings of envy, and simply acknowledge that we deserve not the least of God's blessings. Jesus' rebuke of Peter, if it was a rebuke, was very mild. He really wanted to know what the position is for those who have left all and followed Christ. If he had gone further and implied that he and the other disciples had some special merit, that justice demanded that they receive special consideration, because they had followed Christ, then the rebuke would have been much more severe. When we start thinking about others in this way, we need to remember Christ's words to Peter, after the resurrection, concerning John: 'If I want him to remain alive until I return, what is that to you? You must follow me' (John 21:22).

Jesus closes the parable with the very solemn words: **'So the last will be first, and the first will be last.'** This reverses the order of 19:30. That verse was directed to those who think they are first, warning them that position, status and riches guarantee nothing in the kingdom of heaven. This later verse aims to comfort and encourage those like Peter and the other disciples, who are last in the eyes of men, with the knowledge that God's generous grace is what counts. We must be thankfully content with that, not envious of those whose path seems easier than ours.

34.
True greatness

Please read Matthew 20:17-28

It ought to be beyond debate that the cross of Jesus is the centre of the Christian faith. However, simply to assert this is not sufficient. There are many aspects to the cross and we must include as many as we can. Evangelicals are sometimes accused of thinking only of substitution at this point. That should not be true. This is, of course, the heart of the matter: his sacrifice, dying to pay a ransom price for sinners. This is made very clear in verse 28. Nevertheless that is not the whole truth. As well as other elements relating to the atonement and salvation, in terms of justification, reconciliation, victory over the devil and sanctification, we must also reckon seriously with Christ's death as a pattern and example. We have already seen something of this in our Lord's injunction to take up our cross and follow him. In 1 Peter 2:21 Christ's example is applied to unjust suffering. Here the pattern applies to a life of service. This is not to say merely that there are two aspects to the cross. The fact is that they are closely linked and only those who appreciate both can be said to understand the cross.

There is no contradiction, of course, between these two aspects. There are some who see only the example of the innocent sufferer, not reacting angrily against his persecutors. Others are so narrowly insistent on Christ's death as a substitute that they treat any idea of its being an example with

The King and his kingdom

contempt. Our Lord links the two aspects very closely. In fact, by his whole literary structure Matthew requires us to link the two themes. The major issue in this passage is humility and service as true greatness. This is framed by the cross: at the beginning Jesus' awareness of his approaching death, by his clear intention to go to Jerusalem as well as by a prediction, and then at the end of the passage by the reference to his death as a ransom (20:28). The common literary convention of an *inclusio* (or inclusion) is used here to tell us that the whole of our life and every attitude should be seen within the framework provided by the cross.

Christ's sufferings predicted (20:17-19)

It is significant that Matthew tells us that this prediction was given **'as Jesus was going up to Jerusalem'**. This focus on Jerusalem fits in with the increasing opposition that we have seen from the Jewish leaders and points to the inevitability of his death through their plotting. This prediction is fuller than the previous ones in 16:21-23 and 17:22-23. For the first time Jesus mentions the manner of his death, by crucifixion, and the necessary involvement of the Gentiles, the Romans, the only ones able to perform this. Once again there is only a brief mention of the resurrection. It is this prediction that sets the scene for the discussion about position in the kingdom of heaven. This displays not only the blindness of the disciples, but also the hardness of their hearts. How was it possible for them to debate about having positions of privilege and authority in the kingdom, when their Master had just told them that he was going **'to be mocked and flogged and crucified'**? We find the same inappropriate attitude in Luke's account of the Last Supper where, immediately after the institution of the Lord's Supper and the warning by Jesus that he is going to be betrayed, 'A dispute arose among them as to which of them was considered to be greatest' (Luke 22:24). There is a warning here to those of us who pride ourselves on understanding the death of Christ. Is this more than an intellectual appreciation? Is there also a real understanding of what it cost Jesus to come and redeem sinners?

The mother's request (20:20-25a)

There has been some debate over whether the request came from James and John, or only from their mother. Matthew tells us that **'Then the mother of Zebedee's sons came to Jesus with her sons.'** Although she voices their request, it is quite clear that they are involved, for Jesus speaks **'to them'** in verse 22 and his rebuke applies mainly to them. When asked **'a favour'** Jesus wisely responds, **'What is it you want?'** Her answer is: **'Grant that one of these two sons of mine may sit at your right and the other at your left in your kingdom.'** They have already been assured of high position in the kingdom of God, for the apostles would 'sit on twelve thrones, judging the twelve tribes of Israel' (19:28). Here, however, is something more. The right hand is the position of favour and, presumably, a higher position than that possessed by the other disciples. In the light of their regular behaviour in this connection, we may doubt whether the one who was occupying the left side would be content with that!

Jesus tells them, **'You don't know what you are asking.'** When he adds, **'Can you drink the cup I am going to drink?'** he is pointing out what we have already seen on several occasions, the inevitable link between suffering and glory. To share such a glorious position of authority they must first share his sufferings. And this, he implies, they are not able to do. They answer, **'We can,'** but they speak with little understanding. Drinking the cup refers at the very least to the task put into his hands by God. In the light of Scripture in general and the specific context here of his death we must go further. He is referring to the suffering of God's judgement and retribution, which he later asks to be removed in chapter 26:39. Sometimes in the Old Testament it is Israel or Jerusalem that has to drink 'from the hand of the LORD the cup of his wrath' (Isa. 51:17). More usually it is the nations which have persecuted Israel who are addressed. The prophet is told, 'Take from my hand this cup filled with the wine of my wrath and make all the nations to whom I send you drink it. When they drink it, they will stagger and go mad because of the sword I will send among them' (Jer. 25:15-16). At first, then, it refers to Christ's unique redemptive work and the two disciples are wrong to believe that they can share in this drinking.

Then, however, Jesus changes tack and answers them according to their own understanding. **'You will indeed drink from my cup'**, he says, **'but to sit at my right or left is not for me to grant. These places belong to those for whom they have been prepared by my Father'** (20:23). In these words he lowers his sights, as it were, and accepts that the disciples, James and John in particular, will share in his suffering in one sense. We must be careful to defend the uniqueness of Christ's sufferings, but also to remember that when Christians suffer they are sharing in Christ's sufferings. The apostle Paul, indeed, tells us that this sharing is a filling up of the sufferings of Christ. He says, 'Now I rejoice in what was suffered for you, and I fill up in my flesh what is still lacking in regard to Christ's afflictions, for the sake of his body, which is the church' (Col. 1:24). These are not redemptive, expiatory sufferings, but part of the sufferings involved in bringing in the kingdom, the so-called 'woes of the Messiah'.[1] These not only may, but must, be shared by those who belong to the Saviour.

He then makes it very clear that decisions about special honour in the kingdom are not determined by him, the incarnate Son of Man, but by the Father who sent him into the world. There is surely no clearer indication in the Gospels than this, apart from the declaration of his ignorance of the time of his return (24:36), of our Lord's self-humbling in his incarnation. It is his kingdom, secured through his death, but he submits to the Father and obeys his will. Therefore it is the Father who will determine who will occupy these positions of honour in the kingdom. We must not judge James and John too harshly, as if they were unique in this attitude. We read that **'When the ten heard about this, they were indignant with the two brothers.'** This indignation, judging by later, continuing disputes, is caused not simply by the sons of Zebedee's ambition, but by the fact that they have got in first! The other ten disciples shared in the ambition to have authority and position in the kingdom. Therefore Jesus calls **'them together'** when he instructs them in true greatness.

The greatness of serving (20:25b-27)

First, Jesus refers them to the world's ideas on this subject. Greatness consists of having authority and exercising it: **'You know that the rulers of the Gentiles lord it over them, and their high officials exercise authority over them. Not so with you.'** The NIV probably goes too far in using the expression 'lord it'. 'Jesus is not criticizing abuse of power in political structures — the word never has that meaning ... and should be translated "exercise lordship over," parallel to "exercise authority over" in the next line.'[2] He is not criticizing worldly or human authority or its exercise, but insisting that this cannot be transferred to the kingdom of heaven. To do that is real worldliness. It is essential that we see and understand

the basic difference between the world and the kingdom, between men in general and the church.

Jesus gives us no excuse to refuse submission and obedience to those with authority in this world (Rom. 13:1; 1 Peter
2:13-14). However, we must not think about the kingdom in
worldly terms. The Gentiles are not to be our pattern. Worldliness does not consist merely in entertainments, as is often
thought, but in standards, methods and mindset. It is when
Jesus stands before Pilate that he insists that his kingdom is
not of this world. He tells Pilate that if it were his servants
would fight to prevent his arrest. 'But now my kingdom is
from another place' (John 18:36). Transferring that to this
context, we might say that since his kingdom is a heavenly
one, from a different place from earth, his disciples will not
seek after authority and power. They will not work according
to the principles of this world. In modern political terms they
will not be concerned with 'spin', numbers, sensationalism and
market forces. Their concerns will be spiritual and not worldly.

What, then, is to be our principle? Jesus replies very clearly:
**'Instead, whoever wants to become great among you must
be your servant, and whoever wants to be first must be
your slave.'** It is not wrong to want to be great, but kingdom
greatness is something very different from worldly greatness.
Jesus insists that serving is greatness, being a slave of others.
He is not saying, as he is often interpreted, that the way to
achieve greatness is as a reward for service. No! In God's
eyes it is the service itself that constitutes greatness. God looks
at the servant, the slave, and regards him or her as being great.
It is service that pleases God, whatever men may think. The
world is impressed by status and power, by the trappings of
success and authority. It despises those who, in its view, become doormats, allowing others to trample upon them and
their rights.

Richard Hobson was an evangelical minister of the Church in England in late nineteenth-century Liverpool, a contemporary and friend of the great Bishop Ryle. He ministered in a very poor and rough area of the city, where he did a great work. In his autobiography he recounts how, when going to church one Sunday morning he overtook 'Johnny', a poor cripple who was getting along very slowly on his crutches in an attempt to get to the service on time. Hobson could see that a heavy shower was imminent so, in spite of the man's protests, he put him on his own back, giving him a 'lift' to church. He records that 'It certainly brought down on me, from certain quarters, censure and scorn, as being *infra dig.*, and unbecoming "the cloth".' His critics thought he had demeaned himself by doing this, but he was conscious that this was pleasing in the Lord's eyes and 'as nothing in comparison with even the smallest portion of what has been done for each of us by Him who gave His back to the smiters and His face to them that plucked off the hair'.[3] Serving is greatness in God's eyes.

This does not mean that authority as such is wrong. Jesus did speak of the twelve thrones and appoints officers in the church with authority. However, authority is not to be sought for its own sake. The authority of elders and overseers in the church is given to them only to enable them to serve properly. It is a ministerial authority in the proper sense of minister, that is 'servant'. There are some who resent such authority, who may be surprised to learn that they are rejecting Christ's teaching. Their reason for denying this authority is that they want it for themselves. That is just as bad as wanting authority for its own sake. How sad it is that the church has often, too often, been taken up with rivalry and jockeying for position! The other side of the coin is that of James: 'Not many of you should presume to be teachers, my brothers, because you know that we who teach will be judged more strictly' (James 3:1).

Christ's pattern (20:28)

Jesus does not leave them with a vague idea of the necessity of service, but refers them to his own example: '**... just as the Son of Man did not come to be served, but to serve, and to give his life as a ransom for many**'. The whole point of the incarnation was to serve mankind by saving them. The Son of Man came as the Servant of the Lord, and as such humbled himself, taking the form of a slave, becoming nothing in the eyes of the world, not exploiting his position as Son of God, but always taking the position of service (Phil. 2:5-9). It is significant that Jesus uses here his title as 'Son of Man'. As Son of Man he certainly had the right to be served. We must not be misled by the use of 'man' here. This is not an assertion of his humanity, although that must be included. It is a divine title; the one 'like a son of man' in Daniel 7:13-14 is a heavenly, divine figure. He was 'given authority, glory and sovereign power; all peoples, nations and men of every language worshipped him'. That, however, looks forward to the future. For the moment he has come to serve, in spite of his rights.

Nowhere is this seen more clearly than in Christ's washing of the disciples' feet. It is important to remember that his adoption of the slave's position in washing the feet of those who had come for a meal involved no denial of his own position and genuine authority. We read, 'Jesus knew that the Father had put all things under his power, and that he had come from God and was returning to God; so he got up from the meal, took off his outer clothing, and wrapped a towel round his waist' (John 13:3-4) in order to wash his disciples' feet. Jesus was always aware that he was the Messiah and the Son of God, the Son of Man, with authority over his kingdom. It was right for the disciples to call him 'Lord' and 'Teacher' (John 13:14). Nothing, however, would prevent him from serving and so saving. It was not a glamorous task to wash the dirty feet of his disciples. It was even less glamorous to die on a

Roman cross, but this Jesus did when he gave his life as a ransom for many. He took the lowly place, a place in which he had even given up the right to determine who would be at his right or left in the kingdom.

It was a shameful place (Heb. 12:2). When we think of what he endured in terms of betrayal, desertion, paying, suffering and the wrath of God, as well as the scorn of men, we can see something of the true greatness of our Lord. It is when we see Christians doing similar things in the service of their fellow-Christians that we may understand true greatness in the kingdom of God. There is a real sense in which the purpose of our existence, especially our existence in the church, is to be servants and slaves. Jesus 'came' to serve, not to be served. We have been redeemed to serve, not to be served. The more we see this, the better we shall fulfil our function as members of the body of Christ. It is not the job of others to serve us. In the church we should be ready to take the lowly position and serve others. We must look for their good, not ours. The pattern of Jesus, who 'did not please himself but, as it is written: "The insults of those who insult you have fallen on me"' (Rom. 15:3), must control our living. This is not a small matter. It is not a side issue in the church. If only we all took the place of servants, ministering to one another's needs instead of insisting on our own rights, the church would be very different. It is, of course, easy enough to assert that we will serve the Lord. Jesus insists that serving him means serving one another, and that we do not find so easy. We must be prepared to follow Christ's example, whatever it costs.

The ransom (20:28)

Verse 28 gives us a wonderful insight into the purpose and effect of Christ's death. Here is the work of the Messiah, the Son of Man. He became man, took a human life in order to lay it down, in order to give it for sinners. This was not something forced upon him; his death was not merely the result of opposition and hatred. He tells us that he 'gave' his life and that 'The reason my Father loves me is that I lay down my life — only to take it up again. No one takes it from me, but I lay it down of my own accord. I have authority to lay it down and authority to take it up again. This command I received from my Father' (John 10:17-18). There is no greater gift that a man can give than his own life. It was his own life that Jesus gave on the cross for our salvation. The words, 'Jesus Christ laid down his life for us. And we ought to lay down our lives for our brothers' (1 John 3:16), appear extreme to some people, but they are saying no more than these verses in Matthew 20. There is a difference, of course, and we must ask what it meant to give his life **'as a ransom for many'**. There are various clues here, which instruct us about the substitutionary death of Jesus: the words 'cup', 'for' and, especially, 'ransom' all point us to his sacrificial death.

We have already seen that the idea of a cup points to the wrath of God. A death that averts God's wrath is a sacrifice of propitiation. 'For', the Greek word *anti*, means 'in the place of', as a substitute. It looks back to the Old Testament sacrifices in which the worshipper brought an animal on which he placed his hands, showing that it stood in his place. This was killed and had its blood sprinkled, indicating that it had died in the sinner's place to atone for his sins before God. That, of course, was type and picture; here we are concerned with the reality. Christ was the true Lamb of God, who died in the place of sinners, taking the punishment they deserved, so that they might be forgiven and reconciled to God.

The word **'ransom'** also has an Old Testament background. There are many examples of payments that freed from slavery and bondage. Redemption is deliverance by the paying of a price, a ransom. The bondage could be that of slavery or imprisonment, debt or liability to death. Israel was said to be redeemed from bondage in Egypt, where there was no obvious price paid, unless we see this in the Passover lamb. In the law the payment was often literally made, as in the half-shekel paid to deliver the Israelite from threat of death, because of his sins in the sight of God (Exod. 30:11-16). (We have already seen this in the background to 17:24-27.) The next of kin was known as the kinsman-redeemer, because his task was to rescue his brother from bondage of various kinds, usually by paying a ransom price (Lev. 25:24-55; Ruth 2:20; 3:9-13; 4:1-6). In the gospel we are redeemed by the blood of Christ (Rom. 3:24-25) from the guilt of sin (Eph. 1:7) and from bondage to sin (1 Peter 1:18-19), from the curse of the law (Gal. 3:13) and all the effects of sin, even upon our bodies (Rom. 8:23).

As well as having an Old Testament background, ransom points us to the slave market of our Lord's own day. Once again a price had to be paid to purchase a slave and thus, by a complicated procedure, secure his freedom. The price, which the slave may have saved up himself or may have been paid by a well-wisher, was given to a temple. In a kind of legal fiction the slave was being bought by the god of the temple, who then allowed him to go free. This reminds us of the other aspect of redemption. It is not only redemption *from*, but redemption *to*. It is purchase from bondage to sin to belong to the Lord Jesus Christ. Too often we forget that we have been redeemed, not only from sin, guilt, death and hell, but also into the service of the living God. If we have been 'redeemed from the empty way of life handed down' to us from our forefathers (1 Peter 1:18) it is that we might enter into a new way of life in the service of the Lord Jesus Christ. We must live as those who are not their own, but have been 'bought at a price' (1 Cor. 6:19-20). The Son of Man is 'our great God and Saviour, Jesus Christ, who gave himself for us to redeem us from all wickedness and to purify for himself a people that are his very own, eager to do what is good' (Titus 2:13-14). This new life is, of course, a life of service, of ministering to others. Jesus has redeemed us from the world's ways as well as from the world's condemnation so that we may live not like the world but as true members of the kingdom, serving one another in the service of Christ.

The word **'many'** must not be neglected. It is significant that not all are ransomed or redeemed, except in the sense of all kinds and conditions of men: Jews and Gentiles, men and women, masters and servants, kings and their subjects (1 Tim. 2:3-6). The word 'many' would remind Jewish readers, and should remind us, of Isaiah 53:11-12. There God's righteous Servant (and the term 'servant' is significant) is said to justify 'many', whose iniquities he bears, for, 'he bore the sin of many'. In Jewish thought the many are God's elect, God's own people. What we have here, therefore, is a restatement of 1:21, that Jesus came to 'save his people from their sins'. We should take this term, not in a restricted sense, but to indicate that God truly has a great people, all redeemed by the precious blood of Christ. We are told here that there are many of God's people. Even when it is a remnant that is being saved, it is a remnant of many.

It has been said that there was one penitent thief next to Jesus on the cross, saved at the last minute, so that no one should despair, but only one, so that no one should presume. In the same way it is true that many are said to be ransomed, so that no one should despair, but only many, not all, so that no one should presume. The Christian delights in this verse, which tells him that his Saviour gave his life as a ransom for many, for the elect, and thus for him personally and individually. Christ was a substitute for me, for my sins and my guilt and my deliverance and my salvation.

Understanding this verse in this way, with some fulness, takes us a stage further in the application of the passage. We are not only being told of Christ's service and ministry as the Saviour. We are also having his example set before us as a pattern. However, when we link the two we can go even further. It is not only that Christ's cross is a pattern for us and our service, but a motivation also. Why should we follow his example and pattern? It is not merely because this is a good and great example. It is not merely that it is so admirable and wonderful, worthy of imitation. The fact is that his service has saved us and rescued us from hell. We belong to him and in gratitude and love we should serve him by serving one another. When Saul of Tarsus persecuted Christians, he persecuted Christ (Acts 9:5). When we serve Christians we serve Christ, who loved us and gave himself for us (Gal. 2:20).

At this point various questions press themselves upon us. Do we understand the centrality of the cross of Christ? Do we understand that he died as a substitute to pay the price for our sins, not just as an example and as a demonstration of his love? Do we see that being redeemed has positive indications, that we are saved to a life of service, not just from our life of sin? Are we ready to serve one another, to seek true greatness by being true slaves, not just of Christ but of others too? Are we ready to put their interests before our own, instead of seeking prominence for ourselves? Those who know that Christ has given his life as a ransom for them, even though as Son of Man he had a right to our service, will have hearts full of gratitude and devotion. They will long to demonstrate their allegiance and love by living as Christ both commands and exemplifies, as servants ready to lay down their lives for one another.

35.
The declaration of kingship

Please read Matthew 20:29 – 21:22

Christ's triumphal entry into Jerusalem constitutes his first open and plain declaration of kingship. The details given by Matthew explain something of the nature of that kingship: its spirituality and its strength. The account itself is surrounded by an *inclusio* once more, this time related to blindness. It begins with the account of two blind men who receive their sight (20:29-34). Then towards the end we are told that the blind and the lame came to him at the temple and he healed them (21:14). If we wonder why the blind and lame are singled out for attention here, the answer lies in the history of King David. David's first act, once he was made king over all Israel, was to capture the city of Jerusalem so that it could become his capital. This was a difficult task and the Jebusites, who lived there, taunted him saying, 'You will not get in here; even the blind and the lame can ward you off.'¹ When David succeeded in capturing the fortress by using a water shaft, he referred to the 'lame and blind' as his 'enemies' (2 Sam. 5:6-8). From that time the blind and lame seem to have symbolized the success of David and his kingdom. The fact that Jesus heals the blind and the lame when he enters Jerusalem tells us that he has come as a victorious king to his capital, but that his victory is one of showing mercy. The rest of the account makes this even clearer.

Two blind men (20:29-34)

We are told that it was **'as Jesus and his disciples were leaving Jericho'** that they encountered **'two blind men'**. When these men, **'sitting by the roadside ... heard that Jesus was going by, they shouted, "Lord, Son of David, have mercy on us!"'** There is a slight problem here in that Luke tells us that Jesus was entering, not leaving, Jericho when this happened. Various suggestions have been made for reconciling this apparent contradiction, for we know that Scripture does not contradict itself. While some have maintained that there were two Jerichos and that Jesus was leaving old Jericho and entering new Jericho, there is little evidence to support this. It is more likely that Jesus first encountered the blind men as he was entering the city but actually healed them on his way out. Luke, having mentioned the first encounter, simply goes on to complete his account, while Matthew only describes the culmination of the event. This fits the method frequently adopted by the two Gospel-writers.

It is more important to see the significance of this healing. The blind men identified Jesus as 'Lord' and 'Son of David', the Messiah. In spite of the crowd's rebuke, telling them **'to be quiet'**, the two men **'shouted all the louder'**. When Jesus asked what they wanted him to do, they answered simply, **'We want our sight'** (20:33). They know who Jesus is, the promised Saviour, and obviously believe that he is both able and willing to save, as the hymn-writer puts it, 'full of pity joined with power'.[2] The crowd's rebuke has no effect because they believe that the Lord Jesus will welcome their request, and so it proves. **'Jesus had compassion on them and touched their eyes. Immediately they received their sight and followed him.'**

This sign has all the same significance as previous ones. In this miracle we see a testimony to the authority and power of the Messiah, as indicated by the prophet Isaiah: 'Then will the eyes of the blind be opened' (Isa. 35:5). This gives a picture of what his work is — to give light, spiritual sight and salvation — and also the means by which we may benefit from this: faith. The blind men illustrate the nature as well as the importance of faith. They believe in the power and mercy of Jesus, but they are not content with that. They resist all efforts to hinder them and keep them away, and persevere in their request. Such faith receives the mercy and salvation of Christ. We must identify with them, not with the crowd, which seems to have taken the view, like the disciples at an earlier stage, that the blind were not worthy of his attention. Jesus sees their need, has compassion on it and deals with it. They show the reality of their faith, not only by receiving sight, but by following Jesus, which is intended to indicate discipleship, or at least illustrate it.

The triumphal entry (21:1-11)

Every element in this account has its significance for our understanding of the nature of Christ's kingship. The decision to enter Jerusalem in this way means that Jesus is claiming kingship and demanding acceptance and submission. We can see from later verses that he does not expect to receive this, but he claims it all the same. Such an open claim could only provoke his opponents and so he is quite deliberately looking towards his crucifixion and death. Some, however, do accept his authority, so he sends **'two disciples, saying to them, "Go to the village ahead of you, and at once you will find a donkey tied there, with her colt by her. Untie them and bring them to me"'** (21:1-2). We read in verse 6 that **'The disciples went and did as Jesus had instructed them.'** It is not only the disciples who acknowledge Jesus' authority. He provides them with an answer in case anyone challenges their right to take the donkey and the colt: **'If anyone says anything to you, tell him that the Lord needs them, and he will send them right away'** (21:3). Jesus clearly knows what is to happen — whether by divine insight or by human arrangement is not made clear. What is evident is that the owner of the donkey acknowledges him as Lord. Jesus' use of this title for himself is very unusual and a clear claim to deity.

It is just possible that the reference to Zechariah's prophecy (21:5, quoting Zech. 9:9) was spoken by Jesus himself. This is not definite, but certainly we must see this quotation and its fulfilment as giving clear teaching concerning the kingdom and the King. Not only had the blind men referred to Jesus as 'Son of David', but now we have Zechariah's reference to **'your king'**. Jesus is seen as King of Israel, described here as **'the Daughter of Zion'**, waiting for her king to come to her. If, as is usually the case, we must bear in mind the context of the original prophecy, we shall see that the king is not only **'gentle'**, but also, in Zechariah's words, 'righteous and having salvation'. The context of the previous chapter not only points to Christ's future suffering, but also explains that this involves humble service that brings salvation as the King gives his life as a ransom for many.

Jesus, it would appear, sat on **'a colt, the foal of a donkey'**, according to the prophecy, not on the mother. Using a donkey's colt for his entry does not deny his kingly position; in the Old Testament donkeys were sometimes ridden by rulers (Judg. 10:4). However, it does mark him as a king of peace (Zech. 9:10). A warrior-king, of the kind expected by many of the Jews, would have ridden a warhorse. Further, Mark and Luke tell us that this colt had never been ridden, which has its own significance. 'In the midst, then, of this excited crowd, an unbroken animal remains calm under the hands of the Messiah who controls nature (8:23-27; 14:22-32). Thus the event points

to the peace of the consummated kingdom (cf. Isa. 11:1-10).'[3]
The Son of David announces and demonstrates his authority.
He demands obedience, requires submission and foreshadows
his final, glorious kingdom.

> **The crowds that went ahead of him and those that
> followed shouted,**
>
> **'Hosanna to the Son of David!'**
> **'Blessed is he who comes in the name of the Lord!'**
> **'Hosanna in the highest!'**
>
> (21:9).

Granted that 'Hosanna' was just an expression of praise by
this time, its original meaning of 'Save!' is still significant.
The King's coming is in order to show mercy and bring salvation. The kingdom of Christ is not just a matter of rules and
regulations, but of redemption from sin. Too often his kingdom has been interpreted merely in terms of obeying his rules,
bringing his law to bear on the world, and waiting for his judgement. All these are included, but at this stage particularly the
heart of the matter is salvation. Before the King reigns over
his people, he has to rescue them from their, and his, enemies
(Luke 1:68-71). Before his people can serve him, 'eager to do
what is good', they have to be redeemed from all wickedness
(Titus 2:14). The kingdom is dynamic and saving, not just static
rule.

The response when Jesus enters Jerusalem, that **'the whole
city was stirred and asked, "Who is this?"'** shows that this
understanding was generally lacking. The crowds who had
accompanied Jesus, many of them probably from Galilee, show
that they have little more comprehension, for they answer only,
'This is Jesus, the prophet from Nazareth in Galilee.' In
the previous verses it has become clear that Jesus is much

more than just a prophet. He is the Lord, the Messiah, the anointed King of Israel, the Son of David. He is gentle and merciful, bringing salvation, and demanding both faith and then obedience from his potential subjects. Sadly, they do not know the time of their visitation (Luke 19:41-44).

At the temple (21:12-17)

If we needed to be informed of the fact that King Jesus, though meek, is not weak, the next event would make this clear: **'Jesus entered the temple area and drove out all who were buying and selling there. He overturned the tables of the money-changers and the benches of those selling doves. "It is written," he said to them, " 'My house will be called a house of prayer,' but you are making it a 'den of robbers'."'** The King expresses his righteous anger. His entry into the temple constitutes a claim to be not only prophet and king, but also priest with authority for the temple. The quotation from Isaiah (Isa. 56:7) occurs in the context of 'all nations'. It is not only the defilement of the temple by dishonest commerce that angers Jesus, but the fact that the gospel message contained in the temple structure and services is hidden, not only from the Jews, but also from the Gentiles. This comes from his concern for salvation — salvation for all nations. Where that is hidden or compromised his anger is manifested.

This theme is developed in the next verses. We have already seen that **'The blind and the lame came to him at the temple, and he healed them.'** Jesus by his coming has transformed the position of these outcasts. Where David regarded them as his enemies, at least symbolically, and the Jewish authorities forbade them to enter the temple, Jesus treats them as his subjects and those who may receive his healing and saving

grace. Although the Day of Judgement is to come, at present
this is the day of salvation and Jesus is making that very clear.
The Jewish leaders, on the other hand, show plainly that they
do not understand this, for **'When the chief priests and the
teachers of the law saw the wonderful things he did and
the children shouting in the temple area, "Hosanna to the
Son of David," they were indignant.'** What Matthew describes as 'wonderful things' they appear to regard as sacri-
lege and blasphemy. How blind they were! So Jesus answers
them by quoting from Psalm 8:2: **'From the lips of children
and infants you have ordained praise.'** The psalm refers to
the praise of God, but Jesus refers it to the children's praise of
himself. He has courted this praise deliberately. He allows the
children to give it and defends them now against their critics.
It is no wonder that one who made such claims was crucified.

We, too, are confronted by the kingship of Jesus. Our understanding is challenged. We must realize that the kingdom
of God and Christ is not a matter of rules and regulations, a
case of trying to better social and material conditions on earth
in the name of God. His kingdom, as prophesied in the Old
Testament and fulfilled initially in the Gospels, consists of God's
King, gentle and righteous and having salvation, coming to
earn and bestow that salvation. His kingdom is established on
earth when men and women submit personally to the King and
share in his mercy and salvation, like the two blind men. Both
his righteous anger and his gracious healings foreshadow the
consummation of that kingdom. Then all those who oppose
and deny his kingship, who attack those who honour and praise
the King, will be judged. At that time all illness, sin and death
will be banished. The blind and the lame coming to the temple
foreshadow the King's final triumph.

Understanding, however, is not enough. We are faced personally here with Christ's demand for complete submission
and instant obedience. Like the disciples and the owner of the
donkey and its colt, we must be ready to worship him as Lord

and obey his instructions without question. We, too, must be angry with those who hide the gospel and hinder the conversion of the nations. The temple, which is the church, must be constantly a house of prayer, not a commercial enterprise, a source of gospel knowledge and salvation for the nations of the world. The various stages of the kingdom are here set before us: the enjoyment of mercy and forgiveness, the spread of the gospel of the kingdom to all nations and the consummation when all God's people will dwell with him in the new heavens and new earth. By his entry into Jerusalem the King has announced his claim to the throne, and he will ascend it, despite the enmity of men, despite the hostility which will take him to the cross and thereby, ironically, ensure his final victory.

The fig tree (21:18-22)

After spending the night in Bethany, Jesus returns to Jerusalem. '**Early in the morning, as he was on his way back to the city, he was hungry. Seeing a fig tree by the road, he went up to it but found nothing on it except leaves. Then he said to it, "May you never bear fruit again!" Immediately the tree withered.**' We are told that the disciples '**were amazed**' when they saw this. They are not alone in this. Many have questioned this miracle, attributing it to the Lord's alleged ill-temper, especially as they claim that he had no right to expect figs on the tree at this time of year. The sign is, indeed, unique. No other miracle is destructive of life as this one is. Even the fate of the Gadarene swine was incidental to the positive healing of the man possessed by a legion of demons. No explanation is actually given, so we must interpret it according to its context.

The Bible generally uses fruit as a symbol of an obedient and righteous response to God's Word and covenant. John the Baptist, whose own ministry will be discussed later in this same chapter, has already accused the Pharisees and Sadducees of not producing 'fruit in keeping with repentance'. He warned them that 'Every tree that does not produce good fruit will be cut down and thrown into the fire' (3:8-10). What we have here is an application of this general principle to the Jewish leaders and, perhaps especially, to Jerusalem. The context of the temple reminds us of the privileged position of the Jews. God had made his grace and mercy known to them down the centuries, 'for salvation is from the Jews' (John 4:22), but all they have done is turn this witness to the gospel into a 'den of robbers'. Like the fig tree, they have many leaves of privilege and profession. The Lord has a right to expect to be received and honoured as King and to be given the submission and obedience that are his due. However, he finds no fruit on the fig tree, just as he has found only unbelief and opposition in the capital city.

The words of the prophet were perhaps in his mind:

> What misery is mine!
>   I am like one who gathers summer fruit
>   at the gleaming of the vineyard;
> there is no cluster of grapes to eat,
>   none of the early figs that I crave
>
> (Micah 7:1).

This reference to 'early figs' may incidentally help in the supposed problem of the fruitless trees. 'Fig leaves appear about the same time as the fruit or a little after. The green figs are edible, though sufficiently disagreeable as not usually to be eaten till June. Thus the leaves normally point to every prospect of fruit, even if not fully ripe. Sometimes, however, the green figs fall off and leave nothing but leaves.'[4] This miracle displays not bad temper, but grief mixed with anger. Once again the sign calls attention to Christ and authenticates his

Messiahship. It does more. It points to and illustrates his wrath against, and judgement upon, those hypocrites who, while they profess to be his people, his covenant people, do not produce the fruits of praise, worship, submission and righteous obedience. This cursing of the fig tree points forward to the destruction of Jerusalem to be described in chapter 24 and beyond that to the final judgement. Further illustration will be seen in the parables later in the chapter.

The disciples appear to be amazed more by the power that Jesus has displayed than by any meaning they discern in the sign. ' **"How did the fig tree wither so quickly?" they asked.**' In reply Jesus says, '**I tell you the truth, if you have faith and do not doubt, not only can you do what was done to the fig tree, but also you can say to this mountain, "Go, throw yourself into the sea," and it will be done. If you believe, you will receive whatever you ask for in prayer.**' The promise about moving mountains has been given already (17:20). There it seems to refer to the future great task of the apostles in preaching the gospel to the world. Here that task is seen to be even greater than they thought. Even the Lord has been rejected by Jerusalem. He has apparently 'failed'. What hope is there for the disciples? The answer is that they will not only have power, by faith, to administer judgement — we may think of the fate of Ananias and Sapphira (Acts 5:1-11) — but they will also be able to spread the gospel, overcoming mountains, to make the new temple, the church, a house of prayer which will bring light to the nations.

In this way Jesus rounds off his arrival in the city. The 'wonderful things' of the kingdom, the receiving of sight and the healing of the lame, the glories of the gospel, are paralleled by the darker side of the message. The King requires faith and obedience, fruit and righteousness, not just form and profession. It is not enough to call him, 'Lord, Lord'. They must do the will of his Father in heaven (7:21-22). We must ask ourselves which category we belong to. Are we those who worship and praise him, with the children of Jerusalem, or do we side with the Jewish leaders, who reject him and ultimately crucify him? As we look to the future we are called to believe and trust and pray, so that, by the power manifested in cursing the fig tree, he will be able to make his gospel effective for the salvation of sinners and the coming and establishing of his glorious kingdom.

36.
By what authority?

Please read Matthew 21:23 – 22:14

A young man once took his parents to a carol service at an evangelical church. His parents were exceptional people — exceptionally moral, exceptionally nice, exceptionally good in their treatment of a handicapped son. However, when the gospel was preached, their reaction was to say of the preacher, 'Who does he think he is?' The preacher had dared to suggest that Christ had come to save sinners and that they, as part of the congregation, were such sinners. The charge is made against the authority of the preacher, as if he were claiming something for himself, but in fact the objection is against the authority of God and his Word. Resistance to authority is one of the chief marks of unbelief and frequently this is expressed by the objection: 'Who does he think he is?' Mrs Mary Whitehouse, the heroine of the fight against pornography in the British media, was often attacked in this way and entitled her autobiography, *Who does she think she is?* Whenever sin is rebuked in the name of Christ, the same objection will be made. Whenever there is a suggestion that respectable people are sinners and need to be saved, the same response will occur. In these days, as in our Lord's day, evangelical religion is denounced by the followers of institutional religion. Wherever there is something that does not fit into their preconceived notions, which causes them to think about their own position before God,

their reaction will be to challenge the authority of those who
speak.

Christ's authority (21:23-27)

In Christ's case it was **'the chief priests and the elders of the
people'** who challenged his authority, not only to speak, but
also to act as he did. They objected to his entry into Jerusalem
on a donkey and, perhaps especially, to his cleansing of the
temple. If they knew about the cursing of the barren fig tree,
that also will have been included as they asked, **'By what
authority are you doing these things? ... And who gave
you this authority?'** In reply, Jesus refused to answer their
questions, unless they first answered his question. **'If you
answer me, I will tell you by what authority I am doing
these things. John's baptism — where did it come from?
Was it from heaven, or from men?'** This really put the Jewish leaders on the spot. If they said, **'From heaven'**, he would
ask them why they not believe him. If they said, **'From men'**,
they would offend the people, for they all held that Jesus was
a prophet. **'So they answered Jesus, "We don't know."'**
Therefore he refused to tell them what his authority was.

This response is sometimes thought to be just a clever ploy
on the part of our Lord, a way to avoid answering the question. That is far from being the case. The point was that his
authority was the same as John's authority. Both came as messengers of the true and living God; their authority was God's
authority. Those who rejected John's authority, as these leaders had done, would inevitably reject his authority. Those who
accepted John's authority would accept Christ as Messiah too,
as some of his disciples had done. The same link is obvious a
few verses later (21:32). We have seen already in 19:17 how
Jesus refused to distinguish between his authority and God's

authority. The Word of God, whether from prophets, John the Baptist, or his own beloved Son, always has the same authority, divine authority. There is, of course, something very special about the revelation that comes through Jesus Christ: a new depth, a fresh breadth, fulfilment and consummation of revelation. However, the authority is the same. It is this that is denied, presumably unintentionally, by those who print the words of Jesus in red in their Bibles. All Scripture is God-breathed (2 Tim. 3:16).

However, the opposition which we see here in Jerusalem is neither unintentional nor superficial. They would not, and indeed could not, accept the authority of Jesus, because he condemned their sin and denied their standing before God. He had asserted his kingship and authority by actions, even more than by words up to this point. The tragedy is that they would not submit to his authority and thus they excluded themselves from his gospel and grace. They were rebels and would not have this man to rule over them (see Luke 19:14). They rejected the King and so did not enter his kingdom. Jesus proceeds to amplify and apply this principle by the use of three parables, each of which takes up some aspect of this debate.

The two sons (21:28-32)

The first parable refers to the leaders' treatment of John the Baptist and contrasts them with the outcast sinners. It refers to **'a man who had two sons'**. The father asks his sons to go and work that day **'in the vineyard'**. One of them at first refuses but **'later he changed his mind and went'**. The other son is the reverse; initially he agrees to go, but **'he did not go'** in fact. The application to the historical situation is clear. The first son, says Jesus, represents **'the tax collectors and the prostitutes'**, who at John's coming were rebels and strangers from the kingdom. Until that time they had refused God's authority, which called them to work in his kingdom. Then, **'John came to you to show you the way of righteousness'** (21:32). They changed their minds, repented and believed him, and so entered the kingdom of God. The second son represents the rulers who at first sight seemed to be obedient sons, willing to work for God, but also changed their minds, rejected John and did not believe him. We are not told in the parable whether the rebellious son changed his mind after seeing his brother's repentance, but Jesus points out that the Jewish leaders had not benefited from the example of the tax collectors and the prostitutes: **'And even after you saw this, you did not repent and believe him.'**

When first John and later Jesus preached, the common people, the sinners and outcasts, heard them gladly. Many, it seems, repented and entered the kingdom of God. They began as 'outsiders', but repented and believed. The various members of the ruling class began as 'insiders', committed to the kingdom, at least in their own minds, but rejected the demands of both John and Jesus for true repentance and faith. The application to the rest of us should be equally clear. It does not matter whether we begin as insiders, apparently righteous and good, or as outsiders, openly sinful and rebellious. What counts is our final position. Do we actually obey the authority of the king? Those brought up within the church community must beware of rejecting their heritage. Those who are outside the fold completely are encouraged to repent and come inside. Do we receive the message of God from his Son, his prophet, his preacher? As a result, do we enter by the way of righteousness?

It is important to remember that 'the way of righteousness' is not a way of simple obedience to the Ten Commandments by which we earn our own salvation, but a way of faith in God's appointed Saviour, which is demonstrated by obedience to his Word. It is just as wrong to ignore the way of righteousness that must follow on from genuine faith as it is to believe in a righteousness of our own will, that we think will bring us acceptance with God. In Matthew's Gospel this idea of righteousness, doing the will of the Father, is of prime importance. We have already seen in the early chapters that kingdom righteousness is vital. This emphasis continues to the end. Again we must repeat, this is not a way of salvation by works, but a way of salvation by faith that produces works of righteous obedience.

The tenants (21:33-46)

The second parable expands on the historical situation. The picture is that of **'a landowner who planted a vineyard. He put a wall around it, dug a winepress in it and built a watchtower. Then he rented the vineyard to some farmers and went away on a journey. When the harvest time approached, he sent his servants to the tenants to collect his fruit.'** The parable is based on the prophecy in Isaiah 5, which gives a clue to its meaning. The vineyard represents Israel. In Isaiah too the owner has been careful to provide everything necessary for the vineyard, expressing his love and concern for it. We read, 'Then he looked for a crop of good grapes, but it yielded only bad fruit' (Isa. 5:2). The identification is clear in verse 7:

> The vineyard of the LORD Almighty
>   is the house of Israel,
> and the men of Judah
>   are the garden of his delight.
> And he looked for justice, but saw bloodshed;
>   for righteousness, but heard cries of distress.

The picture in Christ's parable is very similar, even down to the cries of distress over the death of God's Son.

The link with Isaiah makes clear the nature of the fruit God expects from us. God speaks to his covenant people and, in return for his grace, mercy and kindness, requires the fruit of covenant obedience. This has been a recurrent theme in this Gospel, from the ministry of John (significantly) to here. The barren fig tree gave an object lesson concerning the same idea and, indeed, this whole section is really an exposition of that dramatic event. This fruit is not only obedience to God's law, the fulfilling of his commands. There is a more general commitment to him, to his love and service, involved. This becomes clear when we see a further element in the parable which is lacking in Isaiah's prophecy, although in fact Isaiah the prophet has his own place in the parable.

When the landowner sends his servants to collect the rent, the tenants react viciously. The Lord tells us, **'The tenants seized his servants; they beat one, killed another, and stoned a third. Then he sent other servants to them, more than the first time, and the tenants treated them in the same way.'** Jesus does not identify the servants, but throughout the Old Testament prophets there are references to 'my servants, the prophets' and it is clearly the prophetic messengers who are intended here. The account of the decline and fall of the southern kingdom of Judah includes very similar words: 'The LORD, the God of their fathers, sent word to them through his messengers again and again, because he had pity on his people and on his dwelling-place. But they mocked God's messengers, despised his words and scoffed at his prophets until the wrath of the LORD was aroused against his people and there was no remedy' (2 Chr. 36:15-16). It is noteworthy that the messengers are sent out of pity, not in a grasping fashion. Many of the prophets suffered at the hands of the Jews, as our Lord makes clear specifically in 23:35. In this context we must assume that John the Baptist is included with the rest: rejected, ill-treated and eventually killed.

The identity of the last messenger to be sent and the description of his reception constitute a moving conclusion to the parable: **'Last of all, he sent his son to them. "They will respect my son," he said. But when the tenants saw the son, they said to each other, "This is the heir. Come, let's kill him and take his inheritance." So they took him and threw him out of the vineyard and killed him.'** These words are almost too awful to contemplate in view of our knowledge of what was to follow in the life of Jesus. Christ's coming is seen as the supreme example of God's loving concern for his people. Christ's death is the ultimate rejection of the Saviour and a terrible insult to the living God. It is not clear exactly what lies behind the idea of taking the son's inheritance. Some refer to a particular law of the time, which enabled the state to take over an inheritance if the natural heir was killed, but this seems to have little relevance to the parable. What does have relevance is the reaction of the owner of the vineyard.

Jesus raises the question of what his response will be and his hearers provide the answer: **' "He will bring those wretches to a wretched end," they replied, "and he will rent the vineyard to other tenants, who will give him his share of the crop at harvest time." '** This would indeed be the natural reaction of such a man, and even God's patience comes to an end. The ministry of the prophets throughout the Old Testament has culminated in the coming of the great forerunner, John the Baptist, and then of the King himself. If these ministries of mercy are rejected, there remains no way of salvation. Jesus builds on his hearers' conclusion and, referring to Psalm 118:22-23, prophesies a threefold judgement. He quotes:

> **The stone the builders rejected**
>   **has become the capstone;**
> **the Lord has done this**
>   **and it is marvellous in our eyes.**

The first consequence of the tenants' action will be a vindication of the final messenger, which condemns them and their
attitude. Although the Jews, and particularly their leaders, have
rejected God's Son, the Lord will vindicate him. The resurrection is clearly in view here. God's building of his kingdom
will continue and, while the Jews consider Jesus unworthy of
even a place in the building, God will raise him and establish
him as Lord and Christ, the capstone, the chief cornerstone of
the building.

This is not all. Just as the crowd concluded that the owner
would rent the vineyard out to other tenants, so Jesus speaks
of the kingdom of God: **'Therefore I tell you that the kingdom of God will be taken away from you and given to a
people who will produce its fruit'** (21:43). This judgement
must be understood carefully. Much grief has been caused by
a misunderstanding of it. Much anger has been raised by what
some Jews and others call 'replacement theology'. Some have
suggested that the Jews are 'replaced' by the Gentiles as God's
people. The complaint is then made that this means that the
Gentiles enjoy the promises while being absolved from the
judgements. This false idea, and also the false accusation, come
from a misreading of the text. Jesus does not say that the kingdom will be taken away from the Jews and given to the Gentiles, but taken from those of them who reject him and given
to those who trust him and bring forth the proper fruit of service and obedience. The way of righteousness is once again the
criterion. It is not all Jews who are rejected, but those who
reject Christ. It is not all Gentiles who are accepted, but those
who believe in Christ. There is a continuing, true Israel, which

replaces nominal Israel. The Old Testament principle, which is summed up by Paul as 'Not all who are descended from Israel are Israel' (Rom. 9:6), is illustrated here. True Israel is established in the kingdom of heaven on earth in the new-covenant people of God. In Romans 11:16-24 we have an olive tree, which has its roots in the patriarchs, but continues through the Old Testament into the New. Unbelieving branches are broken off and believing branches grafted in. The olive tree is not exclusively Jewish, but consists ultimately of those who believe and live in righteousness.

The third result, of course, is the final judgement, the 'wretched end' of those who reject the gospel of the kingdom and refuse to submit to God's Son. Jesus takes up the description of himself as a stone and concludes: **'He who falls on this stone will be broken to pieces, but he on whom it falls will be crushed.'** Those who find him a stumbling-block will come to grief and those who persist in rejecting him will be punished. The picture is horrific. No wonder **'the chief priests and the Pharisees ... looked for a way to arrest him'**. Jesus had used his parable to speak of them without their realizing it until the end, but then **'they knew he was talking about them'** (21:45). Their anger could not find expression at this stage: **'They were afraid of the crowd because the people held that he was a prophet.'** Soon, however, their hatred would find an outlet.

The wedding banquet (22:1-10)

The first two parables have stressed repentance, righteousness and judgement. Jesus adds a third in which the stress is more optimistic. Judgement and repentance have their place, but the essence of the parable is an exposition of the people to whom the kingdom is given, those who will produce its fruit.

The Old Testament contains references to a Messianic banquet. When the Messiah comes he will entertain his people at a feast:

> On this mountain the LORD Almighty will prepare
>   a feast of rich food for all peoples,
> a banquet of aged wine —
>   the best of meats and the finest of wines
>   (Isa. 25:6).

Jesus has already referred to this in 8:11. Now he extends his reference by telling this parable. **'The kingdom of heaven is like a king who prepared a wedding banquet for his son.'** The banquet is to be given in honour of God's Son, the Messiah.

The parable follows the normal pattern for such a banquet. Invitations are issued and then notice is sent that the banquet is ready. Dinner is served. Many are invited to this banquet. The initial guests refuse to come. **'Then he sent more servants and said, "Tell those who have been invited that I have prepared my dinner: My oxen and fattened cattle have been slaughtered, and everything is ready. Come to the wedding banquet"'** (22:4). The invitation to the wedding banquet was issued initially by John the Baptist and then in the ministry of the Lord Jesus himself. However, the rejection and refusal continue: **'But they paid no attention and went off — one to his field, another to his business.'** The next two verses are parallel with the second parable, with their reference to the seizure of his servants, their ill-treatment and death, and then of the judgement by the king. We are told that **'The king was enraged. He sent his army and destroyed those murderers and burned their city.'** The judgement is made more specific this time by the apparently gratuitous reference to their city. This must look forward to the destruction of Jerusalem in A.D. 70. Those for whom the banquet was

intended will not come and will be judged instead. John tells
us in his Gospel that Jesus 'came to that which was his own,
but his own did not receive him' (John 1:11).

So far the parable mainly follows the same pattern as before. However, the king has not finished. He is determined to
have guests at his banquet. **'Then he said to his servants,
"The wedding banquet is ready, but those I invited did
not deserve to come."'** Later Paul tells the unbelieving Jews
of Antioch, 'We had to speak the word of God to you first.
Since you reject it and do not consider yourselves worthy of
eternal life, we now turn to the Gentiles' (Acts 13:46). So
here the king issues his instructions: **'Go to the street corners and invite to the banquet anyone you find.'** There is
no specific definition of these guests. The general context of
the Gospel would suggest that the first ones are the Jewish
leaders who claimed to be waiting for the Messiah. The further guests are the outcasts and sinners, the tax collectors and
the prostitutes of 21:31 and, in the light of 21:43, even Gentiles. **'So the servants went out into the streets and gathered all the people they could find, both good and bad,
and the wedding hall was filled with guests.'** The exact
identity of these guests is not important for the parable. What
is important is the conclusion that the king will have his guests.
The banquet will be filled. There will be a people who will
produce the fruit of the king. God's purpose will be fulfilled
and his kingdom will come.

The wedding garment (22:11-14)

Jesus has not finished. He concludes the parable with the man
who is not wearing a wedding garment: **'But when the king
came in to see the guests, he noticed a man there who was
not wearing wedding clothes. "Friend," he asked, "how**

did you get in here without wedding clothes?"' The man was speechless; he had no excuse. He was sentenced to be tied up and thrown outside, **'into the darkness, where there will be weeping and gnashing of teeth'**. In terms of the parable he is clearly rejected. In terms of reality he is an unbeliever, sentenced to eternal punishment. Why is he rejected? This is clearly of great importance to us all. The first lesson is, of course, that we must not make assumptions. We must not assume that we are eligible to partake of the King's banquet. The question is, though, 'What are the wedding clothes?'

For many the issue is very simple. The wedding garment must be the robe of imputed righteousness. The only dress which can stand up to the scrutiny of God is the righteousness of Christ, imputed to us through faith. It is argued that the wedding garment was provided by the host, just as Christ's righteousness is given by God, but the guest has not bothered to put it on. This is certainly sound doctrine, but it has no support in the parable or in the context. This is not one of Paul's epistles. The whole context here is of the way of righteousness, the fruit which is righteousness. Faith and repentance must be included, but so must obedience, covenant faithfulness. Merely to hear and receive the invitation is not enough. True reception is by faith and repentance which produce fruit.

Our Lord's conclusion is: **'For many are invited, but few are chosen.'** The word for 'invited', usually translated 'called', has caused confusion. In the rest of the New Testament to be called is the result of being elect or chosen. There is no separation between the called and the elect, see 1 Corinthians 1, where those who were called in verse 26 are said in verse 27 to be chosen. Here, however, it is possible to be called but not chosen. The mark of being chosen, of being elect, is not hearing the gospel, but believing and obeying. The wedding garment which marks out the truly believing, the true member of the kingdom of heaven, is righteousness.

Jesus has not only answered the question about his authority for doing these things. He has also expounded the nature of a true acceptance of his authority. All three parables assume that Jesus is the Messiah who has come to bring in the kingdom of God. The Jewish leaders, who rejected John the Baptist, have also rejected him. Even after they saw the outcast sinners believing the message of John, they did not believe the Saviour's own message. While they claim to be God's people, they refuse him his rent, the fruit from his vineyard, the obedience of the covenant. While they have heard the invitation to the Messianic banquet, they prefer their own ways, their fields and businesses, and even plot to kill the Son of God himself.

As for us today, the key verse is the one that speaks of 'a people who will produce its fruit' (21:43). We are not the Jewish leaders of Jesus' day, nor the outcasts of his day. However, the gospel message comes to us, inviting us to believe in the Son of God, to repent of our sin and come to him, to enjoy the promises of the covenant by faith and obedience to his commands. We must not fall into the error of the Jews and assume that because we hear we are saved, that because we know about the kingdom, we have entered it. How sad to be like the man without the wedding clothes, or the man described in 7:21, who says, 'Lord, Lord', but does not do the will of the Father! He is like the foolish man who builds his house upon the sand. When the rain comes, the stream rises and the winds blow, his house will fall. The Lord, who sent his prophets time and again to call his people to repent, would far rather that he turn and live (Ezek. 33:11) and enjoy all the blessings of the Messiah's banquet.

37.
Kingdom controversies

Please read Matthew 22:15-46

The four controversies included in this section are to be taken as a whole, as is indicated by the links: **'That same day ...'** (22:23); **'Hearing that Jesus had silenced the Pharisees ...'** (22:34); **'While the Pharisees were gathered together, Jesus asked them ...'** (22:41). The three questions posed by Christ's opponents are all trick questions similar to the modern, 'Have you stopped beating your wife?' They think that there is no answer which can avoid getting Jesus into difficulties with someone. These are not honest seekers after truth, but enemies looking for a way to condemn Jesus. So we read, **'Then the Pharisees went out and laid plans to trap him in his words'** (22:15). Similarly, in verse 35, the expert in the law **'tested him'**. Jesus, however, is not to be tricked or deceived. He answers the questions in such a way as to avoid their traps, but also provide helpful teaching for those who follow him. The consequence is that, after his own question to them, **'No one could say a word in reply, and from that day on no one dared to ask him any more questions.'**

Caesar and God (22:15-22)

The first question comes from the Pharisees through **'their disciples ... along with the Herodians'**. Normally the

Pharisees were opposed to the Herodians, supporters of King Herod and the Roman occupying power. The Herodians would be in favour of paying taxes — in this case the poll tax — while the Pharisees, like the Zealots, regarded this as treason. They begin with flattery: **'Teacher ... we know you are a man of integrity and that you teach the way of God in accordance with the truth. You aren't swayed by men, because you pay no attention to who they are.'** After this ingratiating opening comes the dagger thrust: **'Is it right to pay taxes to Caesar or not?'** If Jesus answers in the affirmative, then the Pharisees know that the people will object to this, not only on the grounds that most people object to paying taxes, but especially because this involves paying tax to the hated Romans. If, on the other hand, he supports non-payment, then he is likely to be in trouble with the authorities.

Jesus, **'knowing their evil intent,'** calls them **'hypocrites'** and refuses to fall into their **'trap'**. He says to them, **'Show me the coin used for paying the tax.'** When they bring him a denarius he pursues the subject: **'Whose portrait is this? And whose inscription?'** There is only one possible answer: **'Caesar's'**. The image of Caesar on the coin demonstrates his right to be paid tax. The use of his coins was one of the benefits of his rule, however much they resented this. The fact that they have a coin in their possession, and thus in use, shows that they are accepting Caesar's rule in practice. Therefore, they should pay the tax. Jesus draws the proper conclusion from this: **'Give to Caesar what is Caesar's.'** The rest of Scripture is in line with this. Paul refers to the function of those in authority: to rule, reward and punish. He draws the conclusion: 'This is also why you pay taxes, for the authorities are God's servants, who give their full time to governing' (Rom. 13:6). Christians must not engage in tax evasion. This is not the same as (legal) tax avoidance, but even the latter may raise questions.

The crucial part of Christ's answer, however, is the second half: **'Give to Caesar what is Caesar's, and to God what is God's'** (22:21). God, too, has his rights. It is not clear whether the fact that men are made in the image of God — that is, that they have his image upon them, just as Caesar's image was on the coin — is relevant or not. What is relevant is God's covenant with Israel. Since they have all the privileges of the covenant they ought to give God his due. This refers back to the parable of the tenants. The owner of the vineyard sent his servants to collect his fruit, his rent, that was due to him because of the benefits he bestowed upon the tenants. The tenants in the parable refused to give him his due. Those questioning Jesus, whether Pharisees or Herodians, are refusing to give God his due.

While we must take account of the basic teaching here, about taxes and the functions of government, the more important aspect is God's right to be served and obeyed. This is the issue. It is not only the Jews, who were in covenant with God, who had this responsibility to serve God. Even those outside the covenant receive many benefits from God and are responsible to serve their Creator in return. Having religious privileges, such as being brought up within the covenant community and having 'the very words of God' (Rom. 3:2), as well as natural, material benefits, imposes a great responsibility on us too. It is typical of Jesus that, in addition to dealing with the trick question posed to him in a way that avoids getting into difficulties, he can also give positive teaching and warning to them. In effect, he is preaching the gospel to these opponents. They should not try to trick and trap him, but think of their own souls, which are in danger because they have failed, and continue to fail, to give God his due. No wonder we are told that **'they were amazed'**.

The resurrection (22:23-33)

His next opponents are **'the Sadducees, who say there is no resurrection'**. They envisage a situation, technically possible but utterly unlikely, based on the Old Testament levirate law (Deut. 25:5-6). This states **'that if a man dies without having children, his brother must marry the widow and have children for him'**. They postulate **'seven brothers'**. Each brother in turn marries the same woman and dies without having children, **'right on down to the seventh'**. Eventually the woman dies, having been married to all seven brothers. The problem raised is: **'At the resurrection, whose wife will she be of the seven, since all of them were married to her?'** On their basis, there would appear to be no sensible answer to the question. However, Jesus denies the whole foundation of their test, not by denying the law of Moses, but by rejecting their understanding of the resurrection. In fact, of course, this was complete hypocrisy on the part of the Sadducees, since they did not believe in the resurrection, or even spirits, at all (Acts 23:8). Jesus, however, did.

His response is definite and devastating: **'You are in error because you do not know the Scriptures or the power of God. At the resurrection people will neither marry nor be given in marriage; they will be like the angels in heaven.'** There are two allegations in his reply. First, the Sadducees are condemned for not knowing what is taught in the Bible. Jesus knows what they believe, or rather do not believe, about the resurrection, and he also knows that the Old Testament clearly teaches the resurrection of the body, for example in Daniel 12:2. Even the Pharisees knew and believed this, as the apostle Paul, a Pharisee himself, asserts in Acts 23:6-8. Secondly, Jesus understands the thought behind this, that God is not able to raise the dead. In fact, in the New Testament, it is this ability to raise the dead that categorizes the power of God (Eph.

1:19-20). It must be noted that Jesus does not say that they
will become angels in heaven, in spite of many a sentimental
gravestone, but that there will be no marriage in heaven. The
lesson for us is that any continued happy relationship with
husband or wife in heaven will be on the basis of our shared
faith. It is sad, and somewhat worrying, to find so many more
concerned about reunion with their partner in heaven than about
communion with the Lord Jesus Christ.

So far our Lord's answer is easy to understand, but the
next two verses are more difficult. Jesus adduces proof from
the Old Testament, which we would probably not have seen
for ourselves. He quotes the words spoken by God to Moses
at the burning bush: **'I am the God of Abraham, the God of
Isaac, and the God of Jacob.'** He asserts that the Lord is
'not the God of the dead but of the living'. It is no wonder
that **'When the crowds heard this, they were astonished at
his teaching'** (22:33). The nature of Christ's proof is often
misunderstood. It is assumed that he is saying that since
Abraham, Isaac and Jacob are spiritually alive in the presence
of God, this proves that he is the God of the living. That,
however, would only be a proof of immortality, not of the
resurrection of the body, which is the doctrine in dispute. We
need to understand that, in biblical terms, while the body is
dead, we are dead.[1] Therefore, for the Lord to be God of the
living, Abraham, Isaac and Jacob must be raised from the dead.
God's commitment in this covenant promise to be their God
must include the resurrection. For him to be regarded truly as
their God, they must enjoy his presence and blessing in full, in
body as well as in spirit.

It is important that modern Christians should not be
Sadducees. Too often the whole idea of the resurrection of
the body is unknown to them. Salvation is thought to be complete once we go to heaven when we die. The body is left
under the power of the death; salvation is incomplete. On the

contrary, the body is to be raised and must even now be treated with the appropriate consideration because of that. Paul argues against defiling the body by sexual immorality, on the grounds that 'By his power God raised the Lord from the dead, and he will raise us also' (1 Cor. 6:13-14). We must also guard against any temptation to doubt the resurrection, because of the obvious difficulty involved. We must not deny 'the power of God', as the Sadducees did. This, of course, fits in with the general theme of this section, which relates to the kingdom in its consummation. Jesus not only defeats and corrects the Sadducees, but also calls the rest of his hearers, and us, to make sure that we live with God in eternity.

The greatest commandment (22:34-40)

It is now once again the turn of the Pharisees. **'Hearing that Jesus had silenced the Sadducees, the Pharisees got together. One of them, an expert in the law, tested him with this question: "Teacher, which is the greatest commandment in the law?"'** This was quite a common question debated among the Jewish experts: which of the 613 commandments thought to be included in the law was the most important? This hardly seems a subject for getting Jesus into trouble, so perhaps the questioner is not so opposed to him as previous ones. Once again, in his reply, Jesus demonstrates his superiority to them in every way. His answer is in accordance with the Old Testament (Deut. 6:5; Lev. 19:18). It answers the question without giving them any opportunity to make trouble. It also presses upon them their own responsibility. He does not allow them to remain in the theoretical realm. He replies, **'"Love the Lord your God with all your heart and with all your soul and with all your mind." This is the first and greatest commandment. And the second is like it: "Love**

**your neighbour as yourself." All the Law and the Proph-
ets hang on these two commandments.'**

Where the Pharisees place their stress on detailed rules and
regulations, Jesus insists that the true response to God's love
and grace is one of wholehearted devotion. Giving God what
is his due and enjoying God as the God of the living involves
loving and serving him with all that we are and all that we
have. Every other duty, including the second commandment,
is deduced from the first. It may well be that the mention of
the second commandment, to love one's neighbour as oneself,
is aimed precisely at the hatred and opposition of both the
Pharisees and the Sadducees. Once again there is an important message for today's Christian. Too many of us base our
lives on observing the rules of our church, on giving up this or
that, refraining from this or that kind of behaviour, when what
is really needed is wholehearted devotion to him who loves us
with an everlasting love.

David's Lord (22:41-46)

**'While the Pharisees were gathered together, Jesus asked
them, "What do you think about the Christ? Whose son
is he?"'** Jesus regards this as an opportunity, having silenced
the Pharisees, to turn defence into attack. He knows that they
will give the orthodox answer, that the Messiah, or Christ, is
'the son of David'. He then sets them a problem. Referring to
a psalm of David, he asks, **'How is it then that David, speaking by the Spirit calls him "Lord"?'** The words of Psalm
110:1 are:

> **The Lord said to my Lord:**
>   **'Sit at my right hand**
> **until I put your enemies**
>   **under your feet.'**

The problem for the Pharisees is this: a father does not call his son 'Lord'. Why then does David refer to his son, the Messiah, as 'my Lord'? Again it is no wonder that **'No one could say a word in reply, and from that day on no one dared to ask him any more questions.'** For them this was a devastating question. On their assumptions there was no answer. The son of David is only a man. There is no way David could refer to him as his Lord. Yet here the Lord himself (the Hebrew is Yahweh / Jehovah) actually refers to his sitting at his right hand and having his enemies placed under his feet. Properly, the Pharisees should have joined the disciples who, after the calming of the storm, exclaimed, 'What kind of man is this?' (8:27). The only possible answer is that the Messiah is both God and man. He is, as man, the son of David. As God, his eternal being is such that even David must regard him as Lord and call him 'Lord'. The apostle Paul puts the two aspects together when he describes Jesus Christ as 'his [God's] Son, who as to his human nature was a descendant of David, and who through the Spirit of holiness was declared with power to be the Son of God' (Rom. 1:3-4).

Jesus has exposed the Pharisees' unfaithfulness to the covenant, demonstrated the Sadducees' ignorance and pointed them all to their real duty, to love the Lord their God with all their heart, soul and mind. The real issue, it would seem, is that, in fact, the Lord could not truly be described as 'your God'. If they reject the Son, then they reject the Father. The root of all their problems is their attitude to the Lord Jesus Christ. It is only when they recognize him as God's Messiah, God's Son, God's Saviour, that they will be able to submit to the Word of God in all its aspects. Then they will begin to keep covenant with God. They will believe in God's power, as well as knowing the Scriptures. They will obey God's law from their hearts, not as a burden, but as a delight. Until then, they are his enemies and can look forward to nothing but defeat and humiliation under Christ's feet at the last day.

We, today, should learn about our duty to the state in the matter of paying taxes. We must believe properly in the resurrection of the body. We need to understand the relationship of the great commandments to all the rest, putting the stress where it ought be placed, as Jesus taught us, on the love of God. Most of all, however, we must make sure that we are Christ's people, not his enemies. We must believe in the person of Christ, both God and man. We must trust him as Saviour, relying on his grace. We must not assume that, because we have the outward characteristics of the people of God, we are truly his people. 'For many are invited, but few are chosen.' Those few demonstrate their election by their faith in Christ and their allegiance to him as their Lord and God, by loving and serving him, submitting to him and to his teaching, not testing him and trying to trap him as the Pharisees did. Those who behave like that demonstrate that they are enemies, and his enemies will be judged and punished at the Last Day. How great the danger is of being hypocrites is seen in the next chapter.

38.
Hypocrites!

Please read Matthew 23

This chapter contains one of the most severe denunciations in the whole of the Bible. We must, therefore, remember that the speaker is the sinless Son of God. While the teaching and implications of these verses must control our thinking and practice, they do not justify us, sinful mortals, in engaging in such devastating declarations of judgement. This is not to say that people today, especially false teachers, do not deserve such condemnation, but rather that we must exercise due caution in how we apply these verses to them. We cannot read hearts and are not ourselves beyond criticism. In addition, we must always remember the compassion demonstrated in the last three verses of the chapter, so that we may have the proper balance in attitude. It is also true to say that the best safeguard is to apply these verses to ourselves, taking care to learn the positive lessons given to us about how we should follow Christ.

The Pharisees' teaching and practice (23:1-12)

Jesus is speaking **'to the crowds and to his disciples'**. Some of the following verses are addressed more particularly to his disciples and some to **'the teachers of the law and the**

Pharisees',[1] while the crowds are intended to hear all that is said. Jesus begins with a quite amazing statement: **'The teachers of the law and the Pharisees sit in Moses' seat. So you must obey them and do everything they tell you.'** This is hardly consistent with the radical criticism that Jesus has made earlier of the Jewish leaders' teaching. It is, therefore, better to take these words ironically. Jesus is saying that the teachers of the law and the Pharisees have seated themselves in Moses' place, usurping his authority and requiring the people to obey them. Jesus now points out that the reality of their practice should not be followed, **'for they do not practise what they preach'**. He accuses them of burdening the people with their **'heavy loads'**, while not being **'willing to lift a finger'** to help those who find this crushingly burdensome. This is in direct contrast with Christ's easy yoke and light burden (11:30). They use their pretended authority to impose upon men, while Christ uses his genuine authority to bring ease and rest to the weary and burdened.

Why do these teachers do this? Jesus gives the answer: **'Everything they do is done for men to see'** (23:5). Their great aim is to be noticed, praised and applauded. For this they make a great show of their religion: **'They make their phylacteries wide and the tassels on their garments long.'** The phylactery was a box, usually quite small, containing appropriate scriptures (Exod. 13:2-16; Deut. 6:4-9; 11:13-21), which was worn on the forehead or arm. This was in any case a literalistic and incorrect interpretation of verses that were intended metaphorically (Exod. 13:9; Deut. 6:8) and, moreover, the Pharisees made their phylacteries large and obvious. All Jews wore tassels on the corners of their outer garments (Num. 15:37-41; Deut. 22:12), but these leaders made theirs longer than usual. Everybody could see that they were very religious! In addition, says Jesus, **'They love the place of**

honour at banquets and the most important seats in the
synagogues; they love to be greeted in the market places
and to have men call them "Rabbi".' It is not hard to see
parallels in the modern day. It is easy for those in authority in
the church, especially preachers, to do things for show. Prominent, often larger and more comfortable, seats in the services,
clerical dress, a desire for promotion, a false status, may all be
manifestations of the Pharisaic spirit.

Jesus then addresses his disciples, telling them that their
attitude and spirit must be directly opposite to that of the Pharisees. They are **'not to be called "Rabbi"'**, for they **'have
only one Master'** and **'are all brothers'**. He directly opposes
any idea of superior authority among the apostles, whether
Peter or John, or among the teachers in the church. No one
can demand absolute obedience as a **'father'**. This appears to
be a reference to earlier authoritative teachers of the law. Only
God can demand such obedience; they have only **'one Father,
and he is in heaven'**. While the Bible clearly teaches that
there are to be teachers in the church, no one is to claim this
title for himself alone (23:10), for only Christ occupies this
position: **'You have one Teacher, the Christ.'** The issue is
one of serving, as Jesus confirms in words reminiscent of 20:26:
**'The greatest among you will be your servant. For who-
ever exalts himself will be humbled, and whoever humbles
himself will be exalted.'** The Father and the Son will approve
of those who exercise their ministry rightly, honouring the
authority of God and speaking only as his servants. Those
who demand recognition of their own authority and speak as
dictators in the church will be humbled. The teachers of the
law and the Pharisees have their modern successors. We must
be careful not to follow them instead of following Christ. Jesus
then elaborates on the faults of the Jewish leaders in seven
woes.[2]

The first three woes (23:13-22)

'**Woe**' can be a lamentation or, as here, a declaration of judgement. The earlier verses of the chapter have described the teachers of the law and the Pharisees as hypocrites and now Jesus applies the term explicitly to them: '**Woe to you, teachers of the law and Pharisees, you hypocrites!**' The first charge is, perhaps, the most serious. They are accused of shutting '**the kingdom of heaven in men's faces**'. Not only do they refuse to enter themselves; they will not '**let those enter who are trying to**'. This assumes that entry to the kingdom is available in the person of Christ. Those who want to enter believe in him. The Pharisees refuse to accept Jesus as the Messiah, the Christ, and also do all they can to prevent anyone else from recognizing him and believing in him. Is this not typical of the false teacher? They will not believe the gospel and do their best to dissuade others from believing it. Not content with rejecting Christ crucified for themselves, they guide their congregations in a different direction and thus hinder or prevent them from entering the kingdom of God.

The second 'Woe' provides the other side of the coin. If the Pharisees will not encourage people to believe in Jesus, they certainly make every effort to win disciples for themselves. Jesus says, '**You travel over land and sea to win a single convert, and when he becomes one, you make him twice as much a son of hell as you are**' (23:15). We do not usually associate missionary zeal with the Pharisees, but there is evidence to suggest that during this whole century they showed tremendous zeal in seeking proselytes, converts to Judaism, who would be circumcised and undertake to keep the law of Moses fully. When they were successful, the result was that the new converts had an even greater zeal for the law than their teachers, thus making them twice as lost as they were themselves. It is well known that the adherents of modern false cults and sects are often even more zealous than the leaders, and that converts to these religions are more in earnest than those brought up in them, and are thus even more firmly entrenched in their false ideas. Woe, indeed, to those who bring this about!

The next 'Woe' is longer and more detailed, showing how the Pharisees pervert the Word of God. They claim to be guides, but are **'blind guides'**, as Jesus describes them here (23:16), **'blind fools'** (23:17) and **'blind men'** (23:19). They are unable to lead men into the truth, because they do not know it for themselves. They trivialize the law, distinguishing between oaths made **'by the temple'** and those made **'by the gold of the temple'**. They distinguish between one who **'swears by the altar'** and one who **'swears by the gift on it'**. The latter **'is bound by his oath'**, but the former's oath **'means nothing'**. All this is sheer folly. Jesus points out that it is the temple **'that makes the gold sacred'** and **'the altar that makes the gift sacred'**. You cannot avoid the consequences of your oath by this false and futile distinction. Even more importantly, those who swear by the temple swear **'by the one who dwells in it'**, and, similarly, **'He who swears by heaven swears by God's throne and by the one who sits on it.'**

Jesus is expanding the teaching he gave on this subject in chapter 5:33-37. There his stress was on the necessity for speaking the truth without having to resort to an oath to confirm what we say. Here he destroys the pretended distinctions of the Pharisees, which could be used to avoid keeping an inconvenient oath. Surely these are blind guides, who encourage their disciples to offend against the living God by ignoring his knowledge and willingness to judge those who break their word. Jesus cuts through the verbiage and false distinctions and confronts men with the living God. This particular form of avoidance may not apply so much to us today, but there are

other forms of unstated condition that we may be guilty of.
Christians may not resort to the heathen device of crossing
their fingers behind their backs, to ward off bad luck when
telling a 'white lie', but how many of us have consoled ourselves with the thought that 'I didn't actually tell a lie', when,
in fact, we intended to deceive?

The fourth woe (23:23-24)

This woe is central to our Lord's condemnation of the Pharisees. On the surface he is criticizing the hypocritical inconsist-
ency that tithed spices — **'mint, dill and cummin'** — but
**'neglected the more important matters of the law — jus-
tice, mercy and faithfulness'** (23:23). He accuses them of
straining **'out a gnat'**, but swallowing **'a camel'**. At this stage
in the development of God's purposes the details of the law
were still relevant. So he can say, **'You should have practised the latter'** (the important matters of the law), **'without
neglecting the former'** (tithing spices). With the coming of
Christ the detailed laws about tithing became obsolete, but
that is not the point here. Jesus is pointing to the necessity for
true godliness and righteousness at the heart of our religion.
The law is not a matter of mere details and regulations, but of
serving our covenant God from our hearts. This is nothing
new. The prophet Micah, centuries before, rejected a stress on
outward ritual, which was used as a substitute for true holiness. He asks:

> With what shall I come before the LORD
>   and bow down before the exalted God?
> Shall I come before him with burnt offerings,
>   with calves a year old?

Will the LORD be pleased with thousands of rams,
with ten thousand rivers of oil?
Shall I offer my firstborn for my transgression,
the fruit of my body for the sin of my soul?
He has showed you, O man, what is good.
And what does the LORD require of you?
To act justly and to love mercy
and to walk humbly with your God
(Micah 6:6-8).

Here already we have justice, mercy and faithfulness, shown in a humble walk with God, not just faithfulness to men.

The fifth and sixth woes (23:25-28)

Having moved from the rejection of the kingdom, through a false and superficial understanding of the Word of God, to the heart of the matter, Jesus now reverses the process. He deals again with mere externalism of various kinds, moving back to the crucial rejection of God's Word, especially seen in their attitude to himself. First, he accuses them of being concerned only with the outward. When he says, **'You clean the outside of the cup and dish'**, we may imagine that he is simply referring to the Pharisees' concern with outward, ritual cleansing. However, when he continues with a combination of **'greed and self-indulgence'**, we can see that he is speaking in pictures. The cup and dish represent the man, the Pharisees themselves. They are content with cleansing their lives externally, without dealing with inward sin. No wonder Jesus says, **'Blind Pharisee! First clean the inside of the cup and dish, and then the outside also will be clean'** (23:26). If the heart is renewed, then the life also will be renewed in holiness. If the heart is changed, the life will be changed. If there is a new birth, there will also be new conduct. The Pharisees reversed the order or, rather, ignored the inward.

Jesus continues his attack on their hypocrisy by comparing them to **'whitewashed tombs, which look beautiful on the outside but on the inside are full of dead men's bones and everything unclean'** (23:27). There is some disagreement about the nature of Christ's reference here. Some refer to the custom of whitewashing tombs and graves during the Passover period. This was a warning to pilgrims coming to the feast, so that they might avoid defilement by contact with death. However, this does not really fit this verse, since such tombs were hardly beautiful; they were intended to warn people off, not attract them. So others take the picture to refer to monuments of beautiful construction or ossuaries (bone containers), which were beautified with a marble and lime plaster.[3] This combines attractiveness and defilement. It is noteworthy that the Pharisees appeared to the common people **'as righteous'** (23:28). They had an excellent reputation and, indeed, attracted many disciples. However, the reality, as Jesus points out, was that **'on the inside'** they were **'full of hypocrisy and wickedness'**. The result was that contact with them harmed and defiled the Jews, which is perhaps a parallel with the idea of making men proselytes and thus twice as much sons of hell as they were.

The last woe (23:29-36)

This final woe is extended into a warning to the Jews in general. Jesus begins by referring to the fact that the Pharisees **'build tombs for the prophets and decorate the graves of the righteous'**. He then takes up their proud assertion: **'If we had lived in the days of our forefathers, we would not have**

taken part with them in shedding the blood of the prophets.' He points out that by so saying they admit to being **'the descendants of those who murdered the prophets'.** Jesus is affirming that they are truly sons of their forefathers in more than one way. They are not only descended from them, but also share their nature and attitude and, therefore, will **'fill up ... the measure of the sin of [their] forefathers'.** Like father, like son, is the lesson here. They are truly 'chips off the old block'. Just as their forefathers murdered the prophets, they are planning to murder him. He does not state this, but the implication is clear.

He goes on to address them as **'snakes'** and a **'brood of vipers'.** He warns them that they will not **'escape being condemned to hell'.** He implies his deity when he says, **'I am sending you prophets and wise men and teachers. Some of them you will kill and crucify; others you will flog in your synagogues and pursue from town to town.'** This elaboration and extension of the words of the parables of the tenants and of the wedding banquet points to the future ministry of the apostles. We do not know for certain that any of them were crucified, but the idea may simply be that they were to follow in the steps of their Master. Jesus is saying that this generation of Jews, especially the leaders, will bring to culmination the process of opposition to God and his Word, the full measure of sin. There is a final point which, when it is reached, means that God's patience and longsuffering will end and his judgement will fall. In an earlier day, the Canaanites had ultimately arrived at this point; the entry of the Jews into the promised land was delayed, 'for the sin of the Amorites has not yet reached its full measure' (Gen. 15:16). Now the coming of the kingdom in power has to await a similar stage of filling up.

So Jesus prophesies that **'Upon you will come all the righteous blood that has been shed on earth, from the blood of righteous Abel to the blood of Zechariah[4] son of Barakiah,**

whom you murdered between the temple and the altar. I tell you the truth, all this will come upon this generation' (23:35-36). All the prophets had warned the Jews for centuries. The servants of Jesus, whom he will send to them, 'the prophets and wise men and teachers', will tell the Jews about their responsibility to believe in the Messiah, Jesus Christ, and of the consequences of rejecting him. When this process comes to an end, the judgement will fall upon the nation, the city and the temple.

Lament over Jerusalem (23:37-39)

How important it is not to separate the lament of verses 37-39 from the rest of the chapter! Any impression of hardness and harshness is removed as we consider these words of the Son of God: **'O Jerusalem, Jerusalem, you who kill the prophets and stone those sent to you, how often I have longed to gather your children together, as a hen gathers her chicks under her wings, but you were not willing.'** At this point we must set aside as irrelevant any consideration of the doctrine of election. The stress is on their responsibility: 'you were not willing'. Questions about how Christ could long for something which was not actually possible are equally out of place. What we have here is the heart of Christ's humanity, showing compassion and longing for the sons of men. He grieves even over those who have killed his messengers. How much more does he sorrow over those who are merely misled! Here is what Calvin describes as 'an amazing and unparalleled instance of love'. How different is the attitude of some today, who seem to delight in denunciation and the declaration of God's righteous judgement, apparently gloating over those who are destined for hell. The example of Jesus is a rebuke to us all and to our cold hearts.

Jesus finishes with yet another warning: **'Look, your house is left to you desolate.'** This may refer to the temple or, perhaps, to Jerusalem as a whole. Either way he is pointing them to their hopeless position. He is leaving them. He has nothing more to say to them. He is going to be crucified, rise again and ascend to his Father's side. The day of salvation is ending for Jerusalem. So he warns them, **'You will not see me again until you say, "Blessed is he who comes in the name of the Lord."'** This further reference to Psalm 118:26 points to the Last Day, when all will see him and all will bow the knee to him, whether willingly or unwillingly. These Pharisees and those who remain impenitent like them will nevertheless acknowledge him in that day.

How can we profit from this awful series of denunciations and woes? The story is told of a lady whose minister preached nothing but heresy and false ideas. When asked how she survived in this situation, she replied, 'I simply put a "not" in each sentence and take that to heart.' The practice cannot be recommended, but it does have an important lesson for us as we consider this chapter. One safeguard against becoming experts in denunciation with cold hearts and unforgiving attitudes is to treat the chapter positively. We must be the opposite of the teachers of the law and of the Pharisees. As Jesus exhorts his disciples in verses 10 and 11, we must follow him in humble service. He is the one teacher, the only one with real authority. So we must humble ourselves before him, love and serve him with all our hearts. If we do this, then we shall find that it is possible to exercise real authority, from the Lord, without selfish arrogance like the Pharisees. We must avoid the quest for status and public approval, finding our satisfaction only in God's 'Well done'.

Our great desire must be to enter the kingdom and encourage others to enter. We shall not be without zeal to win converts, but careful that they are converted not to us, but to our

Saviour. They will thus become the sons of heaven, not sons of hell. Instead of using our teaching position to help men avoid their responsibilities to the Lord, we shall encourage them to see God in all things. Our efforts, both for ourselves and others, will not be to avoid serving him, but to serve him with all our hearts. Instead of concerning ourselves with the minutiae of Christian doctrine or, worse, denominational distinctives, we shall major on the more important matters of the law: justice, mercy and faithfulness. Like the Scottish Covenanting field-preacher, Donald Cargill, we shall be 'most in the main things'.[5] Christmas Evans, the great Welsh preacher, was for a time taken up with the Sandemanian teaching. One of the divisions produced by that heresy was over the question of whether the bread broken at the beginning of the Lord's Supper should be raised from the table or broken on the table.[6] The Pharisees had nothing to teach such people. We must be careful not to be like them.

The heart of the matter is that our hearts are what matters! Cleaning up our outward act ministers only to pride and arrogance. If we concern ourselves with an inner godliness and holiness, our relationship to God and our walk before him, then our lives will be clean and holy and glorifying to him. We must guard our attitude to the Word of God. It is not enough to honour the prophets and apostles, or even our Lord, in name. What matters is whether we obey God's Word. It is possible to honour the Bible, good theologians and faithful preachers, even our Lord himself, and yet effectively persecute them by refusing to obey and put their teaching into practice. Such dishonouring of the Word of God brings the wrath of God upon any generation, not just that of the first-century Jews.

Above all, we must take note of our Lord's lament. First, we must take note for ourselves. Have you listened to his longings and pleadings, through his servants, that we come and take shelter under his wings? Have you responded to the voice of the gospel and found rest, reconciliation and salvation in him? This, not the observance of law, must be our first concern. Then, secondly, we must share our Lord's concern and longing for the salvation of others. How many there are around us whose houses are left desolate, who go on in an empty life, void of the presence and blessing of God! How sad if we rejoice in what we know of God's salvation and simply ignore those who are truly lost and bound for hell!

39.
The end of the age

Please read Matthew 24:1-35

There is so much in this passage that is difficult and even controversial that it is easy to ignore the most important issue of all. That is the infallible authority of the Lord Jesus Christ. It is this that makes the careful interpretation of the passage vital. Jesus says in verse 35, **'Heaven and earth will pass away, but my words will never pass away.'** On some views of these verses that assertion would be quite untrue. Indeed, even some supposedly evangelical authors have said that Jesus was mistaken, particularly with regard to verse 34. This will not do. Whatever our opinions on the interpretation of prophecy and on the return of the Lord Jesus Christ, nothing compares with the importance of our Lord's inerrancy. If he was mistaken about this, then he could be mistaken about anything. The whole gospel is at stake here. We must be able to depend upon Christ's teachings about the purpose of his coming, the way of salvation and the privileges and blessings of the kingdom.

If verse 35 shows us the supreme importance of the correct interpretation, verse 34 gives us the clue to that interpretation. Here Jesus imposes a time-frame on his discourse: **'I tell you the truth, this generation will certainly not pass away until all these things have happened.'** Apart from a couple of verses which are explicitly excluded from 'these things', everything else in this passage must occur within the lifetime of the generation then alive. It is true that some have tried to avoid this conclusion by asserting that the word 'generation' should be translated 'nation' and arguing that it refers to the continuing existence of the Jewish people. Linguistically that is just about possible, although very rare, but in the context, especially of 23:36, it cannot be accepted. That passage refers very clearly to a judgement on Jerusalem and the temple, and this must be the judgement which Jesus has already asserted 'will come upon this generation'. This must fix the meaning of the word 'generation' in 24:34 too. The following exposition is based on this assumption that, with the exception of the two verses already mentioned, everything here is concerned with the destruction of Jerusalem in A. D. 70. Our Lord's prophecies about his return do not begin until verse 36.

The setting (24:1-3)

We are told at the beginning of the chapter that as **'Jesus left the temple ... his disciples came up to him to call his attention to its buildings'**. In response he asked them, **'Do you see all these things? ... I tell you the truth, not one stone here will be left on another; every one will be thrown down.'** This clear assertion that the temple was to be destroyed clearly shocked the disciples, who then came to him privately, saying, **'Tell us ... when will this happen, and what will be the sign of your coming and of the end of the age?'** It is possible to interpret their question as being about one or more actual events. It may well be that they did not know exactly what they were asking about. Certainly the basic question was about when the destruction of the temple would occur. It is most likely that they mistakenly linked this with his return[1] and the end of the age, probably the end of the world, as in 13:49.[2] Jesus' answer, however, is limited, in the light of verse 34, to the events surrounding the Romans' capture of Jerusalem.

Warning about deception (24:4-8)

Before he speaks about the actual events, Jesus gives the disciples a double warning. First, he warns them of the possibility of being deceived: **'Watch out that no one deceives you. For many will come in my name, claiming, "I am the Christ", and will deceive many.'** We know from history that there were many false messiahs who appeared, perhaps like Simon Magus (Acts 8:9-10), just as there were false apostles within the New Testament period. The particular ones to whom Jesus refers seem to have been claiming that they were the returning Christ. The disciples are warned that this will happen but also assured that these are false Christs.

Jesus then refers to other events, natural catastrophes, which might seem to indicate that his return is near. He refers to **'wars and rumours of wars'**. He specifies that **'Nation will rise against nation, and kingdom against kingdom. There will be famines and earthquakes in various places.'** Such things have happened in every generation, both before and since A.D. 70. They have no real significance for that event, never mind for the Second Coming. **'Such things must happen, but the end is still to come,'** says Jesus. On many occasions I have been greeted at the door, after conducting a service, by someone who confides that he believes that the coming of Christ is near. 'Wars and rumours of wars,' he will say. He will point to recent earthquakes and disasters. The very things that such a person is suggesting are 'signs of the times', warnings of the imminence of Christ's return, Jesus himself affirms are no such thing. 'The end is still to come.'

In this passage several words are used in differing ways from what we might expect. We have to ascertain in what sense words like 'coming' and 'end' are used. The disciples referred to 'the end of the age' and Jesus uses the term **'end'** here and again in verses 13 and 14. Remembering the situation in which Christ speaks, we may conclude that the end is not the end of the world, but, as he says, the end of the age. Jews thought in terms of two ages: the pre-Messianic age and the Messianic age. Jesus will be referring to the former of these: the end of the period dominated by the children of Israel, the period preceding the establishing of the kingdom of God. After this end of the age, a new age begins. So Jesus, referring to the false messiahs, wars and earthquakes says, **'All these are the beginnings of birth-pains.'** These events, while they signify the end of the departing age, have a positive function; they introduce the 'birth' of a new age, the age of the church, of new life and the worldwide kingdom.

Persecution (24:9-14)

Jesus warns his disciples: **'Then you will be handed over to be persecuted and put to death, and you will be hated by all nations because of me'** (24:9). On many occasions he warned his first disciples of impending persecution. If the Master is hated, the servants will be hated too. These will be difficult days as the gospel is preached and the kingdom of God spreads: **'Many will turn away from the faith and will betray and hate each other, and many false prophets will appear and deceive many people.'** Opposition from both Jews and Gentiles characterized the period of the Acts of the Apostles. The apostolic letters, too, reflect a period of persecution and false teaching. We have only to read the letters to the seven churches in the book of Revelation to find evidence that **'Because of the increase of wickedness, the love of most will grow cold'** (24:12; cf. Rev. 2:4). Those who love and protect the persecuted themselves become the objects of hatred and are tempted to draw back. However, there is an assurance given that **'He who stands firm to the end will be saved'**

(24:13). Jesus has already given this promise in 10:22: 'All men will hate you because of me, but he who stands firm to the end will be saved.' The 'end' here may refer to the end of the age, but is perhaps more likely to describe persevering as long as is necessary.

Verse 14 has often been taken as a sign of Christ's return. Jesus says, **'And this gospel of the kingdom will be preached in the whole world as a testimony to all nations, and then the end will come.'** As an incentive to volunteer for service abroad, we are told that once the missionary movement has extended to all nations of the world Christ will come back. Therefore, helping in foreign missions will bring about the return of Christ. This is different from 2 Peter 3:11-12 and a difficult concept in practice. Does it mean that the nations are fully converted, or that a few have found the Saviour, or simply that the gospel has been made known? Actually, taken in context these words are talking about something completely different. Jesus is looking forward to the time when, instead of being restricted to the Jews, the gospel will be preached to the Gentiles, not to every single nation in the world, but to the nations of the world in general.

This began to happen with the ministry of Peter to Cornelius and then, especially, with Paul's turning to the Gentiles. The Acts of the Apostles records the spread of the gospel 'in Jerusalem, and in all Judea and Samaria, and to the ends of the earth' (Acts 1:8). The apostle Paul could write, 'This is the gospel that you heard and that has been proclaimed to every creature under heaven' (Col. 1:23). This is not to be taken in a literalistic sense, for we know that was not literally true. Paul is saying the same as Jesus, referring to the spread of the gospel beyond the confines of the Jewish nation. These sufferings are the birth-pangs of a new stage in the kingdom of God, the spread to all nations. Once this worldwide proclamation is under way, the new age is beginning. Then the end, the final destruction of the Jewish state, will occur.

The abomination of desolation (24:15-20)

The words inserted in the middle of the next sentence, probably by Matthew, rather than by our Lord, **'Let the reader understand'**, indicate the difficulty of the reference to **'the abomination that causes desolation'**. This expression is borrowed from Daniel 9:27 and has caused much discussion. Many refer it to an alleged coming of Antichrist to the (rebuilt) temple in the last days of the world, but that is to wrench the whole idea out of its context. Luke, interpreting for Gentiles, gives us some help here. He records the words as: 'When you see Jerusalem being surrounded by armies, you will know that its desolation is near' (Luke 21:20). There, as here, this is the signal for **'those who are in Judea'** to **'flee to the mountains'**. Whether **'the holy place'** refers to Jerusalem or to the temple itself does not matter. What we have here is the Roman armies invading the land, bearing their sacrilegious banners, or eagles, to defile the holy place.[3]

It is worthy of note that Jesus expects these events to be seen and clearly understood — signs which may be acted upon. This is completely different from the prophecies concerning his Second Coming, given later in the chapter. In that instance there is no warning; there are no signs. Always there is surprise. Here we have signs which the Christians can observe and from which they can take warning. The historical record is not clear, but there is what Carson calls 'reasonably good tradition that Christians abandoned the city, perhaps in A.D. 68, about halfway through the siege'[4] and took refuge in the mountains. Jesus then gives detailed instructions — instructions which could not be followed in time, if the return of Christ was in the picture. These are actions which belong to Palestine and indicate that these verses belong to this period before A.D. 70. It was in Palestine that men would be on the roof of their house and needed to be warned not **'to go down to take anything out of the house'**. Those in the field are

warned not to go back to get their cloaks. **'Pregnant women
and nursing mothers'** would suffer in such circumstances.
Most clearly, we read, **'Pray that your flight will not take
place in winter or on the Sabbath.'** The reference to the
Sabbath, especially, demands the context of first-century Palestine. If they fled on the Sabbath, they would find no help
from Jews, eager to keep the Sabbath and unwilling to help
those in need.

Great distress (24:21-22)

Whole libraries have been written on the subject of the so-
called 'secret rapture', debating whether this will take place
before or after 'the Great Tribulation'. Will the church go
through the tribulation or will it be taken away before, or even
during, this worldwide trial? Will Christ's secret return for his
church be 'pre-tribulation', 'post-tribulation' or 'mid-
tribulation'? Remembering that all these things were to happen before that generation passed away, we may say that that
this whole concept of the Great Tribulation is unbiblical. What
Jesus is referring to is the sufferings of the Jews under the
Roman attack, and particularly those of the inhabitants of Jerusalem during the Roman siege. It was not so much their
treatment by the Romans as the internecine quarrelling and
fighting of the Jews that caused such great distress and suffering. When he eventually entered Jerusalem and saw the evidence of fighting and suffering, the Roman general, Titus, called
God to witness that this was not his doing. The Jewish fac-
tions had ill-treated and killed each other. This is worthy of
the description of Jesus of a **'great distress, unequalled from
the beginning of the world until now — and never to be
equalled again'** (24:21).[5] In God's mercy the day's were **'cut
short ... for the sake of the elect'**. It may be that Jesus is

referring to those as yet unconverted, who would not have
fled but would survive to believe in the Saviour. More likely is
Kik's suggestion that a longer war would have spread to the
whole land and so engulfed the Christians too.

False Christs (24:24-28)

It was inevitable that during such a crisis **'false Christs and
false prophets'** would appear. They would **'perform great
signs and miracles to deceive even the elect — if that were
possible'**. Again this is not referring to the appearance of
Antichrist, working miracles and deceiving mankind. This
warning is given to the disciples about the immediate future:
'See, I have told you ahead of time.' It is these men listening
to him who are in danger of being deceived. However, they
are elect and God will preserve his chosen ones from this. Part
of God's method of doing this is, of course, the Saviour's
warning. Therefore, if they are confronted with these false
claims to be the Christ, they can know it is not true. The time
has not yet come for Christ to return. **'So if anyone tells you,
"There he is, out in the desert," do not go out; or, "Here
he is, in the inner rooms," do not believe it.'** Such a coming
in the desert or in the inner rooms is private and secret. Certainly it does not accord with what will be true when Christ
really does come (24:27).

This does not contradict the principle from verse 34, because Jesus is stating that this will *not* happen during this period.
On the contrary, when Jesus does return, it will be obvious
and clear to everyone: **'For as the lightning that comes from
the east is visible even in the west, so will be the coming of
the Son of Man.'** He will say more about this in the second
part of his discourse, but for the moment his concern is that
his disciples, first-century Christians, should not be deceived

by false claims. When Christ does come there will be no question, no doubt. It will be obvious to all. He will be seen by everyone. Furthermore there will be no time then to come down from the roof, collect a cloak or take flight, whether in winter or summer. For now, just as the presence of a dead body is known because **'the vultures ... gather'**, so the signs will be undoubted evidence of the corpse of the Jewish nation.

The coming of the Son of Man (24:29-31)

The heavenly signs spoken of in the next few verses constitute the most difficult aspects of our Lord's discourse to fit in with the time-frame of verse 34. However, our Lord's words leave no room for doubt. These events occurred in the first century, the period around A.D. 70. There are two keys to the understanding of these words. The first is the realization that our Lord is using prophetic language — language similar to and based upon that of various Old Testament prophets. It was natural for him, bearing in mind that his ministry was placed within the age that was nearing completion, to use the same poetic terms that the prophets had used before him. Secondly, we must remember that that the word 'coming' does not always refer to the Second Coming. There is a special word, *parousia*, which was used in verse 27, which consistently in the New Testament refers to our Lord's coming again, his final appearing at the last day. It describes the coming, and often the residence, of a ruler or high official at which he is welcomed and honoured. The word that is used in verse 30 is different, the ordinary word for coming, which also occurs in 16:28. We have already seen that this coming is not the Second Coming, but occurs in the immediate post-resurrection period. It is not a literal appearance of Christ, but an event which must be interpreted in accordance with Old Testament usage.

Having established that **'the distress of those days'** refers to the end of the Jewish state and the fall of Jerusalem, it is clear that the heavenly happenings described in verse 29 must also be at that period, for they occur **'immediately after the distress of those days'**. At first glance it does seem incredible that

The sun will be darkened,
    and the moon will not give its light;
the stars will fall from the sky,
    and heavenly bodies will be shaken

does not refer to the Second Coming. However, we may consult the prophets.

In Isaiah 13:10 we read:

The stars of heaven and their constellations
    will not show their light.
The rising sun will be darkened
    and the moon will not give its light.

This refers to the day of the Lord in his judgement on Babylon (Isa. 13:1,10). Also in Isaiah's prophecy we find the words:

All the stars of the heavens will be dissolved
    and the sky rolled up like a scroll;
all the starry host will fall
    like withered leaves from the vine,
    like shrivelled figs from the fig tree.

Isaiah is describing God's judgement on Edom, not the last day (Isa. 34:4,5).

The words of Joel 2:30-31 are, of course, familiar from Peter's reference on the Day of Pentecost: 'This is what was spoken by the prophet Joel' (Acts 2:16). Earlier in the chapter, however, we read:

> Before them the earth shakes,
>   the sky trembles,
> the sun and moon are darkened,
>   and the stars no longer shine.

The reference is to a plague of locusts advancing like an army in judgement on Israel, not to literal events in the sky. According to these precedents, our Lord is referring to the judgement of God upon a nation. Undoubtedly here the nation is that of Israel, which had rejected him.

The same principle of interpretation must apply to the words: **'At that time the sign of the Son of Man will appear in the sky'** (24:30). In fact, the Greek behind 'sky' is the singular 'heaven', not 'heavens', and the word order indicates that a better translation would be: 'At that time the sign of the Son of Man in heaven will appear.' The Son of Man, having been raised and having ascended to heaven, reigns on the throne of his kingdom. The sign that this is so, that his kingdom has been established and that he now reigns in heaven, is that Jerusalem is judged. We shall be wasting our time if we look for a flaming cross in the sky, such as the Roman emperor, Constantine, is supposed to have seen. The sign has already appeared. Jerusalem and Israel have been judged and the point has been made very clear that the Son of Man is now on the throne in heaven. As a result of this **'all the nations of the earth'** (better, 'all the tribes of the land') 'will mourn', whether because of the judgement or, possibly, because some at least are being brought to repentance (see Zech. 12:10-14; Rev. 1:7).

In the light of the above discussion, the reader will not be surprised to find references in the prophets to **'coming on the**

clouds of the sky' or 'of heaven'. They speak of the Lord's coming in judgement. For instance, we find 'one like a son of man, coming with the clouds of heaven' (Dan. 7:13), who in the following verse is 'given authority, glory and sovereign power', a clear prediction of the reign of Jesus Christ. In an oracle concerning Egypt, Isaiah says:

> See, the LORD rides on a swift cloud
> and is coming to Egypt.
> The idols of Egypt tremble before him,
> and the hearts of the Egyptians melt within them
> (Isa. 19:1).

There was no literal appearance, but coming on the clouds refers to judgement on Egypt. We shall see this usage again in Matthew 26:64.

Many use their imagination, linked with 1 Thessalonians 4:16, to envisage angels sounding trumpets and gathering God's people together at Christ's return. However, in the context, it is more likely that verse 31 refers to the trumpet call announcing the year of jubilee, the year of liberty and redemption (Lev. 25:8-10). The New Testament applies the year of jubilee to the time of the preaching of the gospel of liberty (Isa. 61:1-3; Luke 4:17-21). This will be the fulfilment of Isaiah's great prophecy: 'In that day ... you, O Israelites, will be gathered up one by one. And in that day a great trumpet will sound. Those who were perishing in Assyria and those who were exiled in Egypt will come and worship the LORD on the holy mountain in Jerusalem' (Isa. 27:12-13). Here in Matthew, **'his angels with a loud trumpet call'** are simply God's 'messengers', who will preach the gospel and so **'gather his elect from the four winds, from one end of the heavens to the other'**.

The fig tree (24:32-35)

The use of the symbol of **'the fig tree'**, **'its twigs'**, **'leaves'** and imminent **'summer'** fruitfulness, confirms what we have seen here. Bearing in mind the parable that Jesus has told about the vineyard and its fruit, and the acted parable of the barren fig tree, we are pointed forward here to a time of hope. This is not the end of the world that is under consideration, but the time when summertime begins and fruitfulness comes, birth following birth-pangs. In other words, included by Luke, 'Even so, when you see these things happening, you know that the kingdom of God is near' (Luke 21:31). The barren fig tree has been judged. The nation which bears fruit (21:43) will come into its own. The worldwide spread of the gospel is at hand. It only awaits the judgement of the Jewish nation, the end of the age, for the latter days of the Messiah to begin. **'When you see all these things, you know that it is near, right at the door.'** 'These things' are not signs of the final end, but of the beginning, not of the close of the gospel day, but of its full opening — the coming of the kingdom in power. They are words of optimism, not pessimism. Once again it is significant that Jesus refers to the disciples seeing all these things. This happening is not without warning, unlike his Second Coming. So he concludes with his assertion that **'This generation will certainly not pass away until all these things have happened. Heaven and earth will pass away, but my words will never pass away.'**

The immediate reference of these warning verses is for the disciples and the early church. They are warned to be on their guard, so that when the Roman armies appear they may escape across the Jordan into the mountains and be kept safe. However, there is much more to this warning. Jesus will continue his discourse by referring to the certainty of his literal coming again in glory. The guarantee that this will actually happen is that the earlier event came to pass. He foretells the destruction of Jerusalem, so that we, as well as those who were present when these things were happening, may be assured that the Second Coming will also happen. His words about Jerusalem will never pass away; equally his words about 'that day' are utterly reliable.

There is more than warning here, however. There is also encouragement. How must the disciples have felt, knowing that the Jewish leaders were rejecting their Master, the Messiah? We know that they became utterly discouraged. The disciples on the road to Emmaus had thought that Jesus had come to redeem Israel, but now they have changed their minds. This prophecy, particularly when it was fulfilled and remembered, would convince some of them that, far from being defeated, the kingdom of God was just beginning to triumph. Now, with their task of discipling the nations clearly in their minds, they could be encouraged that the kingdom was coming, that the elect were going to be gathered from the four winds, from one end of the heavens to the other, that the fig tree's summertime was coming and fruitfulness would be the order of the day. The same encouragement should be ours today. We should be optimistic about the future prospects of the kingdom of God. For us too, the end of the Jewish era brings certainty that Christ is in heaven on the throne and that his kingdom is coming and will come. We are pointed to our responsibility to make known the gospel in our own generation. The warnings which Jesus gave his disciples about the period before Jerusalem was attacked and destroyed are not pointless for us either. The necessity for not being deceived by foolish claims that the Messiah has come, the need to stand firm to the end, the danger of false prophets and deception — all these things are always relevant. Indeed, many of these warnings will apply as we seek to understand Christ's further prophecies, which are about his Second Coming.

40.
That day

Please read Matthew 24:36 – 25:13

There are two basic errors concerning prophecy. The first is to deny that there is any element of prediction. Many modern scholars insist that prophecy is only forth-telling, not foretelling. Others, more traditionally, insist only on foretelling and forget that prophecy was a message from God to the people who heard it. The first error simply ignores the evidence of the prophecies in the Bible. As the first part of Matthew 24 makes clear, the prophet, whether servant or Master, speaks of the future, predicting what will actually happen. The second error simply encourages curiosity and speculation without obedience. There is only an earnest desire to know when and how the prophecy will be fulfilled. Is it now? Is it still to come? We must resist both errors.

Christ's prophecy of the destruction of Jerusalem was clearly a prediction, but a prediction for a reason. Those who believed Christ's words were to obey his instructions. They were to flee, without trying to rescue goods from their homes, even a cloak. Similarly, when Jesus moves on to speak of his Second Coming, the purpose is to provoke action, not satisfy curiosity. So we find imperatives, commands, in this passage: **'keep watch'**, **'understand'**, **'be ready'**.

The difference between these sets of commands shows the difference between the two subjects. It is this that rules out the common idea that the first part of Matthew 24 will receive a double fulfilment: first in the destruction of Jerusalem and then in the Second Coming. The same words cannot refer to two different events, because they are utterly different in character. In fact, the approach in the two sections is radically different. In the first, as we have seen, Jesus prophesies certain things which his disciples will see and note, and in the light of which they will take action. In this section we are now to consider, there is no possibility of acting on what is seen. Nothing will be seen until it is too late to do anything about it. Once Jesus has come it will be too late to repent, prepare, or do anything else. They will not, and cannot, correctly predict or expect his return (24:44). All the commands are to be fulfilled in advance so that whenever Christ returns they are ready to face him.

The unknown day (24:36)

Jesus begins his prophecies about his return with a remarkable sentence: **'No one knows about that day or hour, not even the angels in heaven, nor the Son, but only the Father.'** The sentence actually begins with the word **'but'**, wrongly omitted by the NIV. This sets off these verses in contrast to what has gone before. Those events, 'these things' (24:34), will be known, but no one knows about 'that day or hour'. 'That day' is almost a technical term for the Last Day, the Day of Judgement. Jesus uses it in this way in 7:22, when he speaks of professing disciples appearing before him 'on that day'. That day is the day of the Second Coming, the *parousia*. No one knows when that will be. We should simply ignore the foolish quibble that says that although we do not know the day or the hour, we may know the month or year! Its time is altogether unknown.

Even the Son is ignorant of this. Only the Father knows when it will be. This is the most obvious example of our Lord's ignorance while here on earth. Ignorance, of course, is not the same as error or mistake. He made no mistake about the fall of Jerusalem. He did not know the time of his return. During his ministry he knew what he needed to know, knowledge ministered to him by the Holy Spirit. He did not need to know the time of his return. Nothing could impress upon his disciples, and us, the unknown and unknowable quality of this so much as the fact that he himself did not know. His assertion that no one knows must be taken seriously. It is nothing short of amazing that so many agree that we do not know, but then speak of the signs of the times, say that the return of Christ is imminent, that because certain things are happening in the world we know that he is near. The contrast with the earlier verses, it is true, means that his return will be after the destruction of Jerusalem. Similarly the apostle Paul tells us that it cannot happen 'until the rebellion occurs and the man of lawlessness is revealed, the man doomed to destruction' (2 Thess. 2:3). Apart from this we do not know, and we must refrain from inventing signs that we hope will give us a start on others in the search to know.

As in the days of Noah (24:37-44)

When Jesus says, **'As it was in the days of Noah, so it will be at the coming of the Son of Man,'** he uses the special word, *parousia*, for that 'coming'. Christ's return will occur like the Flood, when daily life is going on as it has done for years. The King will return, and return to rule as king, when people are going about their ordinary affairs: **'For in the days before the flood, people were eating and drinking, marrying and giving in marriage, up to the day Noah entered**

the ark; and they knew nothing about what would happen until the flood came and took them all away. That is
how it will be at the coming of the Son of Man.' Noah
believed the prophecy and made ready; he was prepared. No
one, however, knew the day or the hour of the flood's coming.

The following words have been taken by many, who hold
to the dispensationalist position on the last things, to teach the
'secret rapture'. This teaching asserts that before (probably)
the 'Great Tribulation' and the millennium, the church will
simply disappear from the earth. Planes will crash because the
pilot has been raptured. Children will be mystified because
parents have disappeared. This strange concept is supported
from these verses: **'Two men will be in the field; one will be
taken and the other left. Two women will be grinding with
a hand mill; one will be taken and the other left.'** However, these words teach the reverse of what is claimed. It must
be granted that the word 'taken' in verse 40 is different from
'took' in verse 39, but the action is the same. It is not the
saved person who is taken away here, but the lost. As the
wicked were taken away by the flood, so the wicked will be
taken away from the field or from the grinding. The one who
is left is not the unbeliever, but the believer, left with his Lord
who has come to reign.

Jesus presses this idea on his hearers. They must **'keep
watch'**, because they do not know when their **'Lord will
come'**. He uses a brief parable to illustrate this. The thief did
not advertise the time of his coming to rob the house. Otherwise the owner **'would have kept watch and would not have
let his house be broken into'** (24:43). In the same way the
disciples must be ready, for **'The Son of Man will come at
an hour when you do not expect him.'** If we try to turn this
into a sign, that Jesus will return at the least likely time, and
concentrate on such a time, we shall tie ourselves in knots, for
by so doing we turn the time into a likely one! As we shall see,

this must not be taken literally, but spiritually. It is not a question of staying awake lest Jesus should come at night, but of being spiritually alert. 'So then, let us not be like others, who are asleep, but let us be alert and self-controlled ... since we belong to the day, let us be self-controlled, putting on faith and love as a breastplate, and the hope of salvation as a helmet' (1 Thess. 5:6-8).

Faithful servants (24:45-51)

The fact that Jesus is to come at an unexpected time does not mean that we are helpless and can do nothing to prepare. What it does mean is that there are no special preparations to be made, as if we could see him approaching and rush to make ready. Our responsibility is to be faithful and wise servants all the time. It may be that **'the faithful and wise servant'** points us to the apostles, with leadership responsibilities, who are **'put in charge of the servants in his household to give them their food at the proper time'**. If this is so, then we need also to take notice of the words that Jesus added, as recorded in Mark 13:37: 'What I say to you, I say to everyone: "Watch!"' The point is the principle of wise and faithful service. In fact, the idea of wisdom will be expanded in the parable of the ten virgins and that of faithfulness in the parable of the talents in chapter 25.

Here Jesus sets forth a contrast. We have a duty and responsibility to be found doing what we are supposed to be doing when Christ returns. Such faithful obedience will bring a reward: **'He will put him in charge of all his possessions.'** However, as in Matthew 7, Jesus also speaks of the servant who is wicked. Here is the professing Christian, or supposed disciple, who has this responsibility in the household. Jesus says, **'But suppose that servant is wicked and says to himself, "My master is staying away a long time," and he then**

begins to beat his fellow servants and to eat and drink with drunkards.' The indication is clear here, as in other parables, that a delay is envisaged before Christ returns. Just how long, of course, we do not know, but the context tells us that it is at least until after the destruction of Jerusalem.

This unfaithful, wicked servant points to professing Christians, as defined in other parables. There the contrast is not between Christian and non-Christian, but between true Christian and professing, nominal Christian. So it is here. The man who claims to be a servant of Christ, but who does not obey him beyond an initial period, will find that the Saviour returns when he is not expecting him, **'at an hour he is not aware of'** (24:50). He will be taken by surprise and judged. In passing, we should note that, for those who are not alive at the return of Christ, the same principle applies to the time of their death. We should always be living, acting and serving in the knowledge that Christ may come at any time. The 'false professor', as our forefathers used to call merely nominal Christians, will receive the punishment of an unbeliever. When Christ comes, **'He will cut him to pieces and assign him a place with the hypocrites, where there will be weeping and gnashing of teeth.'** The false disciple will take his place with the unbelieving Pharisees. The warning is clear. To **'watch'** (24:42) is not to be always looking for Christ appearing in the sky, but to be ready and prepared by fulfilling our responsibilities to him. It is to be spiritually awake, to have a spiritual readiness in the midst of normal life, so that whenever Jesus comes he will find us doing what we ought to be doing.

The ten virgins (25:1-13)

The words, **'at that time'** (25:1) show that this parable is continuing the subject of Christ's return, as does the reason given in verse 13: **'because you do not know the day or the**

hour'. Following on from the passage about servants, it seems likely that the ten virgins represent the visible church, those who profess to serve the King. The bridegroom obviously stands for the Lord Jesus Christ, as has already been made clear in this Gospel (9:15), as well as by John the Baptist (John 3:27-30), not to mention various Old Testament passages. The link with the wedding banquet (22:1-14) also supports this. The important issue here is not the numbers (although **'ten'** would suggest that the whole visible church is in view). It is not suggested that half the visible church is true and half false. The issue is one of wisdom. The customs of an Eastern wedding are observed here. These virgins are not bridesmaids, but bridegroom's maids, whose task it is to greet the bridegroom and conduct him into the wedding banquet. The fact that this is in the evening and that the bridegroom does not come until **'midnight'** proves nothing except that there is to be a delay before the Second Coming of Jesus and we must be prepared for that.

The lamps in question would be 'either small oil-fed lamps or, more plausibly, torches whose rags would need periodic dousing with oil to keep them burning. In either case the prudent would bring along a flask with an additional oil supply'.[1] **'The foolish ones took their lamps but did not take any** [extra] **oil with them. The wise, however, took oil in jars along with their lamps.'** Because of the delay the lamps would have used up all the original oil, so when **'the cry rang out: "Here's the bridegroom! Come out to meet him!" ... the virgins woke up and trimmed their lamps.'** We are not told what the oil represents. Is it the Holy Spirit, since oil does represent the Spirit in anointings? Does it represent faith, or righteousness, or faithfulness, or witness? We are not told. The fact that the foolish virgins' oil runs out suggests that none of these is correct. The point being made is simply that wisdom thinks ahead and prepares. We may then supply what we know from the rest of the Gospel is the proper preparation for Christ's return: repentance with its fruit, faith in Christ, leading to faithful service and righteous living. We must be wise, and so be prepared to face Christ at his coming.

There is an unusual stress here on the foolish virgins. When the bridegroom comes all are asleep. Clearly that is not a criticism here; being literally awake is not the point. They all awoke and the wise trimmed their lamps using the oil that they had brought with them. Then, **'The foolish ones said to the wise, "Give us some of your oil; our lamps are going out."'** We should not enter into speculations about whether the wise should have shared their oil or whether the shops would have been open to sell oil after midnight. The point being made is that this is a personal matter. We must not rely on anyone else, but must ourselves be prepared — and that in advance. There is no collective grace, no transferable faith, no inherited righteousness.

The story continues with the foolish going off to buy oil and the bridegroom arriving while they are absent. **'The virgins who were ready went in with him to the wedding banquet. And the door was shut.'** When the others return and ask to be let in, they receive the crushing and awful reply: **'I tell you the truth, I don't know you.'** We are not concerned here with differences between believers, with varying degrees of reward. These foolish virgins represent unbelievers, whatever their appearance or profession may have been. They do not belong to the King, in spite of their calling to him, **'Sir! Sir!'** and asking to be allowed in. They have not believed in him and he does not know them or acknowledge them as belonging to him. The preparation that brings such acknowledgement — repentance, faith and consequent obedience — must be made before he returns (or before death). There is no second chance.

There is no place here for speculation or curiosity about the time of Christ's return. In different ways, using a variety of pictures and parables, Jesus has made the point that all who hear the gospel and, especially, all who profess faith in Christ, must be ready for his return. We cannot make preparations when we know that he is about to arrive, because we can never know that. In the midst of the ordinary business of life, we must be about our Lord's business. We must know him, love him and serve him. To do this and to be faithful in his service is the only wise way. Jesus will go on to show what that wise faithfulness involves in the next two parables, but for now both reader and author need to consider whether they are truly prepared for Christ's coming, ready to meet the Saviour. All that has gone before in this Gospel leads up to this, whether it is the invitation to come to Jesus for rest (11:28), the command to enter through the narrow gate (7:13), or the demand for self-denial and taking up our cross (16:24), our response must be made now, before it is too late. Christ's return is certain and we shall stand before him, whether or not this is preceded by our death and resurrection. True wisdom is to know Christ as Saviour and Lord and so to be known by him.

41.
Coming to judge

Please read Matthew 25:14-46

The Rev. Rowland Hill is reported to have said that he saw no reason why the devil should not have all the good tunes.[1] Equally, the devil should not have all the best words, but in fact he has taken many of the best ones, like 'charismatic' and 'evangelical', and twisted them for his own use. We must not allow him to do this with 'talent'. Far too often the parable of the talents is wrenched from its spiritual context and wrongly applied to the use of our gifts and abilities, whatever the sphere. I remember in my school-teaching days hearing one of my colleagues using this parable to exhort the children to work hard at their studies, using whatever gifts and abilities they had. Whatever else we understand about this parable, we must know that talent does not equal ability, or even spiritual gift. It would appear that it is, in fact, a false interpretation of the parable that has given rise to the secular use of talent for such an ability. This is just one instance of the care that we need to take in interpreting these two important parables. Each of them has been twisted to teach a lesson far from our Lord's intention.

Approaching the end of this section, which has been concerned with the judgement of God, as well as the grace which is needed for any of us to face that day in peace, Jesus is continuing to expound the qualities necessary for the Christian, if he is to be saved. As we saw in 24:45 the servant must have a combination of faithfulness and wisdom if he is to be pleasing to his Master. Wisdom is shown in being prepared, as the parable of the virgins illustrated. Now faithfulness is the subject of the following parables, first in general in the parable of the talents, and then, more specifically, showing in what that faithfulness consists, in the concluding account.

The talents (25:14-15)

Once again, the setting of the parable is a man leaving his servants and going away, to return later. The kingdom of heaven is **'like a man going on a journey, who called his servants and entrusted his property to them'**. This setting, as on previous occasions, clearly corresponds to Christ's departure to heaven for a period, during which the church is built and the kingdom is spread, and which is concluded by his return at the Second Coming. The message for the disciples and for us is clear. This is how we must live our lives as Christians in the light of his return. The fact that the servants are 'entrusted' with his property immediately sets the agenda of faithfulness. As the apostle Paul writes, 'Now it is required that those who have been given a trust must prove faithful' (1 Cor. 4:2). The servants are given various sums of money; a talent was worth a considerable amount. In the parable Jesus selects three of them to be considered: **'To one he gave five talents of money, to another two talents, and to another one talent.'**

The talents do not represent gifts or abilities since they were distributed to **'each according to his ability'**; so what do they represent? The simple and obvious answer is that they stand for the responsibility of the servant to serve his master. Spiritually, they represent our individual responsibility to work for Christ's kingdom, fulfilling the tasks he has laid upon us. Such a responsibility and such tasks depend on the abilities we have. 'From everyone who has been given much, much will be demanded; and from the one who has been entrusted with much, much more will be asked' (Luke 12:48). While this is clearly a great responsibility, it is also a privilege and an opportunity. It is important to see responsibilities in this way, so that we are not deterred from working for our Lord, but encouraged to labour for the kingdom of God.

The accounting (25:16-23)

So the servants are left to get on with their work. The first two servants **'put [the] money to work'** to make a profit, in each case in proportion to the amount he was given. However, **'The man who had received the one talent went off, dug a hole in the ground and hid his master's money.'** He did not lose it, waste it, or use it for himself. He simply did nothing with it. We are not told if the servants knew how long the master was going away for, but we have no excuse. We are told that it was **'after a long time'** that the master returned. When he did he **'settled accounts with them'**. The first two servants told him what they had done and were rewarded with a commendation and a reward. Each of them was told, **'Well done, good and faithful servant! You have been faithful with a few things; I will put you in charge of many things. Come and share your master's happiness!'** (25:21,23).

The meaning of **'good'** always depends on the context. It signifies that which is appropriate. These two servants have behaved as they were supposed to behave. They have worked and made a profit. Such good behaviour is faithfulness. Even though they had only been put in charge of 'a few things', they had done what was necessary and had been faithful to their trust. The other reward that they were given is a double one.

Being put in charge of 'many things' as a reward fits what we have seen as being the usual New Testament idea of reward. It is clearly related to their efforts. The reward is not something different, but the consummation of what they have been doing. We may agree with Richard Baxter, who wrote:

> Come, Lord, when grace has made me meet
> Thy blessed face to see;
> For if thy work on earth be sweet,
> What will thy glory be?[2]

It is true that we shall rest from our labours in heaven (Rev. 14:13), but our service of the Master will continue, without the burdens and aggravations of this sinful world that turn work into toil. For this reason our Lord speaks of sharing our Master's happiness. He will rejoice in what we have done on earth, and we shall rejoice with him. These faithful servants do not share their colleague's opinion of the Master and nothing can be more delightful and joyful than to have his commendation, continue in his service and enjoy his joyful presence.

The lazy servant (25:24-30)

What about the third man? Some, who do not understand the dynamics and realities of the kingdom of heaven, have sympathized with this man, just as they feel for the prodigal son's elder brother. He does not deserve this and we shall not deserve it if we follow his example, rather than that of the faithful ones. He is a **'wicked, lazy servant'**. He has a completely wrong view of, and attitude to, his lord. **'Master,'** he says, **'I knew that you are hard man, harvesting where you have not sown and gathering where you have not scattered seed.'**

This is a travesty of the situation. The master has provided the capital for their business, has looked only for a reasonable return and has given a wonderful reward to those who have served him well. This wicked servant has no idea of his responsibility to his master and less love for him! If we transfer this to the reality of the kingdom, we have to say that he has no idea of the love of Christ or of his redeeming work, no appreciation of all that is given to those who belong to the Saviour, or of the obligation that they are under. 'You are not your own; you were bought at a price' (1 Cor. 6:19-20).

There is no way that Jesus is a hard master. True faithfulness and real service come, not from fear, but from love. There is, of course, an element of fear — and the fear of the Lord — which makes us aware of the consequences of disobedience and unfaithfulness. But that alone would not bring us to serve diligently, faithfully and even sacrificially. Only love can do this: love experienced from our Lord and love rendered to him in return. When this is so, our great delight is to please him by serving him; our great reward is that he is pleased and glorified. So the third servant wasted his opportunity and merely hid the money. He did give it back, resentfully, but even his allegation of injustice does not ring true. Jesus, speaking for the master, says, **'Well then, you should have put my money on deposit with the bankers, so that when I returned I would have received it back with interest.'** Debates about usury and the relative merits of investment are out of place here. Jesus is simply exposing the lack of understanding and sheer ingratitude of the third servant.

His punishment fits his crime: **'Take the talent from him and give it to the one who has the ten talents. For everyone who has will be given more, and he will have an abundance. Whoever does not have, even what he has will be taken from him.'** This somewhat paradoxical sentence makes very clear that, if we do not benefit from our privileges, we shall lose them. A similar statement, recorded by Luke, includes a helpful word: 'Whoever has will be given more; whoever does not have, even what he *thinks* he has will be taken from him.' He who shows no profit loses his capital. He who produces no fruit of faithfulness loses his (imagined) status as a disciple. This servant is not really a servant; he just thinks he is; he just appears to be. He is a false professor and is shown to be that by his unfaithful behaviour. The warning is issued to all those who claim to be disciples. It is not enough to profess to belong to Christ. Anyone can claim to believe and say, 'Lord! Lord!' (7:21). The test which will be made at the Last Day will unmask the hypocrites and reward the true disciples. The unfaithful will be seen for what they are and the faithful will be rewarded. The solemn last words, where 'the story has been "invaded" by its application,'[3] illustrate the truth of John Bunyan's statement that there is 'a way to hell, even from the gates of heaven, as well as from the City of Destruction':[4] **'And throw that worthless servant outside, into the darkness, where there will be weeping and gnashing of teeth.'**

Those who are occupied with serving the Lord, fulfilling their responsibilities according to their abilities, must also ask themselves whether they are truly working for Christ out of love. The parable does not explicitly show the source of the servants' faithful devotion, except by contrast with the wicked servant's opinion that the master is 'hard', but the next few chapters will tell us as they describe the Saviour's saving death. Once again the hymn-writer shows the connection clearly:

My gracious Lord, I own thy right
To every service I can pay;
And call it my supreme delight
To hear thy dictates and obey.

'Tis to my Saviour I would live,
To him who for my ransom died:
Nor could untainted Eden give
Such bliss as blossoms at his side.

His work my hoary age shall bless,
When youthful vigour is no more;
And my last hour of life confess
His love hath animating power.[5]

Sheep and goats (25:31-46)

This account describes the return of Christ, truly the end, the
Last Day: **'When the Son of Man comes in his glory, and
all the angels with him, he will sit on his throne in heavenly glory.'** It is not really a parable like the others, although
since the term includes any kind of comparison it is not entirely wrong to use it. We are here dealing with the reality, but
Jesus compares the actions of the king to those of a shepherd:
**'All the nations will be gathered before him, and he will
separate the people one from another as a shepherd separ-
ates the sheep from the goats. He will put the sheep on his
right and the goats on his left.'** The rest of the account ignores this comparison, but it may not be exactly literal either.
It is perhaps this misunderstanding of the nature of the whole
section that has caused some to misinterpret it so wrongly.
Some seize on the word **'nations'** and use this to support
their weird idea that whole nations will be judged for the way
that they have treated Israel. Others ignore the word **'brothers'** (25:40) and use it to support their own version of the
social gospel. Others go to the opposite extreme and find here
a denial of the gospel of grace and faith. In each case a careful

examination of the actual wording will keep us on the right track.

The king's division is clearly between those who are saved and those who are lost, as his verdicts make clear. The first group, those on his right. are told, **'Come, you who are blessed by my Father; take your inheritance, the kingdom prepared for you since the creation of the world'** (25:34). We have only to recall the Beatitudes to realize that these blessed ones are faithful children of God, the true disciples of Christ. They are heirs of the kingdom, the kingdom prepared in God's sovereign grace since the creation of the world. All this has to be assumed. Jesus does not include every element of the gospel in every part of his teaching. Salvation is by grace, received in faith. That we must never doubt. What we have here is the evidence of that faith. Salvation is by faith and judgement is by works. The king looks for works as evidence of genuine faith. This much-neglected truth is to be found throughout the New Testament (cf. 2 Cor. 5:10; Rom. 2:16). What we have here is a further definition of what it means to be faithful.

The particular evidence that the king cites here involves good works of compassion and love shown to him: **'For I was hungry and you gave me something to eat, I was thirsty and you gave me something to drink, I was a stranger and you invited me in, I needed clothes and you clothed me, I was sick and you looked after me, I was in prison and you came to visit me.'** These are not the actions of nations; whole countries do not go sick-visiting! These examples are not intended to be exhaustive. How could Jesus exclude works of spiritual activity like prayer or witness? These, however, are evidence that gets to the heart of faithful service. This will become clear in the following verses, as **'the righteous ... answer him,'** denying that they have ever done these things for him and to him. They are completely unaware of what they have done to deserve this commendation. The king's reply is clear and wonderful: **'I tell you the truth, whatever you did for one of the least of these brothers of mine, you did for me.'** What is he saying?

Jesus is not referring to all men as 'these brothers of mine'. It is not true that when we serve the hungry, thirsty, strangers, naked, or prisoners, we are doing it to Jesus. If that were true, then Jesus would be teaching that everyone who engages in good works, supports charities and does his bit for the needy of the world is 'righteous' and will inherit eternal life. We may expect the liberals to teach this, but sadly we find evangelicals using this passage, inaccurately and unnecessarily, to support their works of compassion. The works themselves are excellent, not to be despised in any way, but this passage is not about them. Christ's brothers are not all men, nor just Jews, but Christians, disciples. He has referred to them in this way elsewhere already in this Gospel in 12:48-50 and will do so again (28:10). Of course, we must not limit our doing good to our Christian brothers, his brothers. We are told to 'do good to all people,' although 'especially to those who belong to the family of believers' (Gal. 6:10), but such good works do not provide the necessary evidence of faith.

The New Testament lays especial stress on love of our brothers, Christian brothers. Jesus told his disciples that all men would know that they were his disciples because they loved one another (John 13:34-35). We are told that 'We know that we have passed from death to life, because we love our brothers' (1 John 3:14). Love, like charity, begins at home, in the family of believers. This is evidence of our redeemed status as the children of God. It is implied that we are doing this because they are our Lord's brothers. This shows our allegiance to him and our love for him and, therefore, our position as his true disciples. More general good works do not have this motivation and so do not provide this evidence. We should note that Jesus refers to **'the least of these brothers of mine'**.

They may be unattractive, humble or unimportant, but they are Christ's. Christian loving hospitality does not end with entertaining the nice and pleasant for a meal. It includes them, but it does not end with them. Some are very happy to entertain a group of attractive, stimulating students, but the old and infirm and those who provide no enjoyment at the time are not so welcome. Jesus, we must remember, urged hospitality for those who cannot ask us back! (Luke 14:12-14).

Our motivation must not be what we get out of it, but simple devotion to our Saviour. We cannot show our love for him directly. Like the people in this account, we cannot go to see him in prison, but we can visit him in his people. Just as Saul persecuted Christ when he persecuted the church, so we love and serve him when we love and serve his people. This will not be without cost. Those who feed strangers may sometimes be taken in. Those who visit Christians in prison may be put in prison with them, as happened to one Henry Barrowe in the sixteenth century. He visited his Christian friend, John Greenwood, who was in prison for preaching irregularly — that is, without permission from the ecclesiastical authorities – and was not only imprisoned but later executed for these alleged crimes.[6] However, Henry Barrowe has now entered into his inheritance.

The opposite is also true. Those on the left, the wicked and unrighteous, are condemned because they have failed to serve and help Christ. In their case their reply is not simply a confession of ignorance, but a denial of guilt. The solemn words of the king send shivers down one's spine, while also giving comfort to those who have suffered at the hands of the Evil One. **'Depart from me, you who are cursed, into the eternal fire prepared for the devil and his angels.'** The king's reason for his sentence is simply the opposite of verse 40: **'I tell you the truth, whatever you did not do for one of the least of these, you did not do for me.'** 'These' are presumably those on the right, who have not been recognized as Christ's people, Christ's disciples, and did not receive any consideration or help. They did not necessarily persecute them; they just ignored them and, with them, Christ. The words of 10:40-42 are relevant here.

The worst effect of misunderstanding is to send Christians out eager to do good works for the world in general. That is to begin at the end, not the beginning. We must begin with our allegiance to, and love for, our Lord Jesus Christ. It is when we understand his love, grace and compassion that we shall be moved to work for him in his kingdom and serve him in his family. We must, of course, resist the temptation to look to our service and works for justification. We are accepted by God only on the basis of what Christ has done for us, because of his death on the cross and his righteousness credited to our account. Nothing must divert us from this. The relevance of these passages is to our assessment of our position as his people now and his assessment of our claims at the Last Day. When he comes in his glory it will not be enough merely to call him 'Lord' (cf. 25:37), to claim to belong, to believe, to have been baptized, confirmed or received into church membership. The evidence alone will speak. Christ will judge according to our works and it will be clearly seen, publicly seen, whether we are truly his by the way we have lived for him and shown compassion for his people, for his sake. The conclusion is definite and clear.

The wicked **'will go away to eternal punishment, but the righteous to eternal life'**. This parallel statement is almost sufficient on its own to refute those who claim that the fate of the wicked is annihilation, not everlasting conscious punishment. While it is true that 'eternal' can refer to the quality of the age to come, the link with life in the presence of God shows that it must include the idea of 'everlasting', as God is everlasting. This should be sufficient to direct us first to Christ for mercy and then to examination of ourselves for confirmation that we have received forgiveness. Although the wicked were considered second, Christ ends his discourse with the destiny of the righteous. These are words of warning, but also of promise. His desire is that sinners should repent. Like the Father, he takes 'no pleasure in the death of the wicked, but rather that they turn from their ways and live' (Ezek. 33:11).

Part 7:
The sufferings and triumph of the King
(26:1 – 28:20)

42.
The Passover Feast

Please read Matthew 26:1-30

This new section begins with the customary transitional words: **'When Jesus had finished saying all these things'** (26:1). We may be tempted to think of these final chapters as a mere epilogue, considering the five great discourses to be the main business of the Gospel. That would be a great mistake. This is no anticlimax, but the culmination of Christ's ministry here on earth. Without the events described here, Christ's teaching, while obviously enthralling in itself, would lack power. His teaching concerning the kingdom, our entry into it and our life under his reign, depends on the facts of the gospel. There is no kingdom without salvation and no salvation apart from the cross. There is no kingdom without our living King, and no living King apart from the resurrection. So we must be careful to give these events their full weight, even though they are so familiar to us.

Jesus gives a framework to these happenings by saying **'to his disciples, "As you know, the Passover is two days away — and the Son of Man will be handed over to be crucified."'** It is no accident that our Lord was crucified at the time of the Feast of the Passover. Already Jesus is giving them a clue to the meaning of his death, which will be amplified in the account of the Last Supper. It is this emphasis upon the cross that explains the structure of these verses. Initially we

have, once again, an *inclusio.* The account of the anointing of
Jesus in Bethany is framed by two aspects of the plotting of
'the chief priests and the elders of the people'. First, we
read that **'they plotted to arrest Jesus in some sly way and
kill him. "But not during the Feast," they said, "or there
may be a riot among the people'** (26:4-5). Then, in verses
14-16, we read how Judas becomes part of the plot. In between we have the account of the anointing of Jesus, which is
placed here out of chronological order, but quite deliberately
so, because it is the approaching cross that gives meaning to
this event.

The anointing at Bethany (26:6-16)

We know from John's more precise chronology that this happened before Christ's triumphal entry into Jerusalem. It is quite
clear that there was only one anointing at this stage, recorded
in slightly varying ways by Matthew, Mark and John. This is
not the same as the anointing described by Luke in chapter 7
of his Gospel. The place is different, the host is different, the
character of the woman is different and the focus is different.
We must understand its significance in the light of Jesus' final
words: **'I tell you the truth, wherever this gospel is preached
throughout the world, what she has done will also be told,
in memory of her'** (26:13).These are not mere words of praise
for the woman. They tell us that this event is important for us
and especially for an understanding of the gospel.
   The woman, who John tells us is actually Mary, the sister
of Martha, **'came to him with an alabaster jar of very ex-
pensive perfume, which she poured on his head as he was
reclining at the table'** (26:6-7). The disciples objected to
this, because they regarded it as a **'waste'**. They remonstrated
that **'This perfume could have been sold at a high price

and the money given to the poor.' This was, no doubt, quite correct. According to John the perfume was worth approximately a year's wages for a manual worker. God's people certainly do have a responsibility for helping the poor, but the disciples had missed the point, which Jesus makes very clearly in verse 11: **'The poor you will always have with you, but you will not always have me.'**

This concern for the poor, certainly sincere in many cases, although not in the case of Judas (John 12:6), nevertheless betrays a lack of understanding both of Mary's devotion to her Lord and the impending work of atonement. Jesus defends the woman: **'Why are you bothering this woman? She has done a beautiful thing to me.'** Verse 11 is not really a contrast between himself and the poor, although that is certainly true. The point is that he is about to leave them — after he has completed his work on the cross. He regards her anointing as a contribution to his work: **'When she poured this perfume on my body, she did it to prepare me for burial.'** We cannot be sure whether Jesus means that Mary understood this or whether it was so in the providence of God. There was a practice of anointing the bodies of those who died, before their burial, but this was not permitted for anyone who had been executed as a criminal. It may be that Mary had more insight than the disciples, took his prophecies of being crucified seriously and, therefore, knew that if he were to be anointed, it had to be done now.

In the light of this, what they saw as an extravagant waste, she regarded as only his due. This lavish outpouring of perfume reflects the equally abundant outpouring of her love and devotion. It is significant that Jesus links this with the preaching of the gospel. She loved Jesus, because Jesus had first loved her. She showed her love in this act of costly devotion, because she understood something of what he was doing for her. She related this to his burial, because his love for her was taking him to the cross. Therefore, she wanted to make her contribution to his work. She could not pay even for her own sins, of course, but she could anoint his body for burial and so do 'what she could' (Mark 14:8).

We, in our turn, must not only understand the significance of Christ's death, but also give him our love and devotion in return. We must also be ready to do what we can in the service of the gospel, because of our devotion to him. Since Christ has returned to glory, we cannot show our devotion to him in person, although our words of praise and the love in our hearts perform this function. It may be that when we serve the poor, we are showing our devotion to Christ. However, it is even more important that we show our devotion to the Lord Jesus by making him known and spreading his gospel. We can do the one without neglecting the other. Like Mary we must be ready to serve Christ, not only with words of devotion, but with sacrificial acts, especially in the service of the gospel. It may be that our contribution is small and insignificant, but if it is done out of love for the Saviour, he will take notice of it and take pleasure in it. The cost to us of our service, whether in money, effort or suffering, is the measure of our love, as it was with Mary.

The contrast between this love and devotion and the Pharisees' and elders' plotting is striking. The contrast is made even clearer by the response of **'one of the Twelve — the one called Judas Iscariot'**, who **'went to the chief priests and asked, "What are you willing to give me if I hand him over to you?"'** Where Mary was willing to devote a gift of such value to the honouring and serving of Jesus, Judas receives **'thirty silver coins'** (26:15). Where she prepared him for his burial, after his redeeming death, **'Judas watched for an opportunity to hand him over.'** The contrast could scarcely be more stark.

The Last Supper (26:17-25)

In spite of some theories, it is clear from this account that the Last Supper was the Passover meal.[1] **'On the first day of the Feast of Unleavened Bread, the disciples came to Jesus and asked, "Where do you want us to make preparations for you to eat the Passover?"'** Not only does Jesus say that he is **'going to celebrate the Passover with [his] disciples'**, he also links this with the fact that his **'appointed time is near'** (26:18). Thus, in various ways Jesus, and Matthew following him, refer to the Passover as a source for understanding the meaning of Christ's death. On the afternoon of the Thursday the lambs were brought to the temple to be sacrificed by the priests. It would be after sunset, i.e., at the beginning of the following Jewish day, that the households would gather to remember the Exodus and eat the Passover lamb. So it was that after the disciples had followed their Master's instructions and **'prepared the Passover'**, **'When evening came, Jesus was reclining at the table with the Twelve.'**

Before the institution of the Lord's Supper, Jesus dealt with Judas and his betrayal. In fact, there is no actual command about future observance recorded by Matthew. We very often see what we expect to see. However, this is not to deny or even doubt the fact that Jesus did institute the Lord's Supper, but to see that this was not Matthew's chief concern in recording the event. Jesus makes the solemn and tragic assertion: **'I tell you the truth, one of you will betray me'** (26:20). This naturally grieved the disciples who began to question him saying, **'Surely not I, Lord?'** We can hardly imagine just how they felt. Although they may not have understood Mary's actions, they certainly shared something of her devotion to the Lord and the idea of betraying him was unthinkable.

In response Jesus goes further. He replies that the betrayer is **'one who has dipped his hand into the bowl with me'**. It is not an enemy, but a friend, indeed, a disciple present at that time. We are aware even today of the Eastern custom that forbade treachery where a meal had been shared. Judas is so far gone in unbelief and hatred, under the influence of the devil, that even this does not prevent him from going on with his evil work. Jesus saw this betrayal in its setting of the purpose of God: **'The Son of Man will go just as it is written about him. But woe to that man who betrays the Son of Man! It would be better for him if he had not been born'** (26:24). His death is the result of the divine purpose, according to divine prophecy. However, the sovereignty of God never removes human responsibility. He pronounces a woe on Judas, a terrible condemnation, for predestination and prophecy never remove guilt. Jesus was going to die, and be 'handed over ... by God's set purpose and foreknowledge', but it was 'with the help of wicked men' that he was put to death (Acts 2:23). Judas, no less than the Jewish leaders and the Roman authorities, was one of these 'wicked men'. There is a debate, to which there is probably no certain answer, as to whether Judas actually took part in the Lord's Supper. The answer may well be irrelevant, in any case, for he certainly appeared to the disciples as a believer and is treated by Jesus on the basis of that profession.

'My body' (26:26)

Jesus and his disciples are still eating at this point. We read that **'Jesus took bread, gave thanks and broke it, and gave it to his disciples, saying, "Take and eat; this is my body."'** What we have here is, we must remember, a Passover meal. When Jesus speaks the stress is on **'my'**. In contrast with the body of the Passover lamb, he refers to his own body. We need not enter here into the debates about whether the bread is actually turned magically into the body and flesh of Christ by these words. Clearly, the word **'this'** makes nonsense of that idea. We are in the realm of pictures and symbols. Equally, the Passover Feast was not a sacrifice; the sacrifice had been made earlier. At the feast they partook of the benefits of that sacrifice. Similarly, the Lord's Supper is not a sacrifice, as Roman Catholics assert, but a symbolic sharing in the benefit's of Christ's sacrifice. Jesus is not enacting his death and we do not re-enact it when we remember him. The breaking of the bread is not a picture of the breaking of Christ's body on the cross, as popularly understood. Indeed, we are told that not a bone of his body was broken, in fulfilment of the Passover events (Exod. 12:46; John 19:36). That many use the word 'broken' in connection with the cross is unimportant.[2] What does matter is the positive point that the loaf was broken so as to be distributed to the disciples. The emphasis is on participation, on feeding on Christ crucified, and so entering into the benefits earned by his death.

Quite clearly Christ's teaching about himself as the bread of life in John 6 is not directly linked with the Lord's Supper, which had not been instituted at that point. However, the terminology used there points to the same reality as the Supper does. He says, 'I am the living bread that came down from heaven. If anyone eats of this bread, he will live for ever. This bread is my flesh, which I will give for the life of the world' (John 6:51). Eating means believing in, coming to, and thus benefiting from, the Lord Jesus Christ's death (John 6:35). So here, eating Christ's symbolic body means trusting in his redeeming death and sharing in its benefits. It is this emphasis on faith, as symbolized by eating, that forces us to regard the Lord's Supper as more than a mere historical remembrance. It is not a sacrament in the sense that it automatically conveys grace, but it is a sacrament in that it is more than mere remembrance. It is best described as a means of grace. The grace is not automatic, but, as always, comes through faith.

The blood of the covenant (26:27-28)

It is important to note that Jesus gave two symbols with respect to his death: bread and wine. They must be considered
separately, because Christ kept them separate. The bread, pointing to Christ's suffering in death, speaks of bearing our guilt
and enduring our punishment, the wrath of God. It refers to
his death as a substitute, dying in our place, just as the Passover lamb died in the place of the first-born Israelite, and sub-
sequent lambs, bulls and goats died in the place of the sinner
who offered them. In every sacrifice there is then a second
stage. The blood of the Passover lamb had to be applied to the
doorposts and lintels of the houses. This symbolized the presentation of the offering to God for his acceptance. In and
through that acceptance, the benefits of the sacrifice are received. It is to this that the cup of wine points. So Jesus **'took
the cup, gave thanks and offered it to them, saying, "Drink
from it, all of you."'** The drinking, again in parallel with John
6:53-56, pictures our entering into all these benefits, having
Christ's death applied to us, by faith. What happens once for
all at conversion is remembered continually as we partake of
the Lord's Supper.

Jesus relates this to the covenant of grace. **'This is my
blood of the covenant, which is poured out for many for
the forgiveness of sins'** (26:28). The reference to blood being poured out concerns the presentation of the sacrifice to
God. On the first day of the Feast of Unleavened Bread the
blood of the sacrificial lambs was poured out at the base of the
altar. Contrary to popular usage, the shedding of blood does
not refer to the killing, but to the shedding, or pouring out, of
that blood before the Lord. Jewish readers, like the disciples
themselves, would link the term **'many'** with the words of
Isaiah concerning the Servant of Lord, who would 'justify

many' and 'bore the sin of many' (Isa. 53:11-12). The 'many' were the elect of God, those for whom Christ gave his life as a ransom (20:28). Christ's words inevitably recall the events surrounding the establishing of the old covenant at Sinai. Animals were sacrificed and the blood collected. Then, we read, 'Moses took half of the blood and put it in bowls, and the other half he sprinkled on the altar. Then he took the Book of the Covenant and read it to the people.' Their response to this reading was to promise obedience. 'Moses then took the blood, sprinkled it on the people and said, "This is the blood of the covenant that the LORD has made with you in accordance with all these words"' (Exod. 24:6-8) The covenant was thus inaugurated, ratified and sealed by the blood (Heb. 9:18-20).

The relevance of the blood can be seen in the promises of the new covenant. All the blessings of the covenant can only be received once our sins are dealt with, forgiven and remembered no more (Jer. 31:31-34). Thus Jesus emphasizes **'the forgiveness of sins'**. All the benefits of the new covenant depend on the cross of Christ. It is the blood of Christ that seals and ratifies the new covenant, with all its blessings: first forgiveness, then justification, reconciliation, adoption, inheritance with the saints, communion with God and thus membership of the people of God. Once again, Jesus has stressed participation by commanding them to drink. Drinking represents believing and trusting — once for all and then continually, especially as we remember Christ at his table. This reminds us that the Lord's Supper is not merely to be watched, but participated in. Just as there is no sharing in the benefits of Christ's death without faith, so there is no sharing in the benefits of the Lord's Supper apart from faith. It is as we continue to exercise our faith that we receive greater enjoyment and assurance of the benefits won for us by Christ.

The Father's kingdom (26:29-30)

Jesus warned his disciples on the occasion of his anointing that he would not always be with them. Now he confirms this by telling them, **'I tell you, I will not drink of the fruit of the vine from now on until that day when I drink it anew with you in my Father's kingdom.'** Just as the Passover itself looked forward to entry into the promised land, so this feast looks forward to entry into the consummated kingdom of God. Jesus will not drink this wine with them again, because he will have returned to his Father's side. Here they are given the assurance, not only that they will participate in the Messianic banquet, but that they will do this with him. There they will participate in the newness of the final kingdom. He looks beyond his sufferings and death to his final triumph and glory. The implication is that they will share in the Lord's Supper in the succeeding days. They will remember the Lord's death 'until he comes' (1 Cor. 11:26).

Thus the Lord's Supper has a threefold perspective. As they looked forward to the near future, so we must look back to the historic sacrifice of Christ, where he accomplished salvation and redemption for the many, for his people. We must also look up, remembering not just the events but the Lord himself, for the Supper is intended to remind us of him. We are not to go through the motions, but enjoy personal communion with our Saviour, who has promised to be with us to the end. Thirdly, we are intended to look forward to the final kingdom. What greater encouragement can there be than to know that Christ died for us, and therefore our sins are forgiven, that Christ, the living Lord, is with us, shepherding us as his flock, and that the future is guaranteed, for our Lord will drink the new wine of the kingdom with us in his Father's home?

The anointing and the Last Supper are bound together by the stress on the cross. While the Pharisees plotted and the false apostle betrayed, God was working out his purpose, fulfilling the Scriptures that had been written about the Son of Man. The centrality of the cross, especially in relation to the gospel of our salvation, is very clear. It is the great revelation of Christ's love, because by it he secured our redemption. Because of this it is the great stimulus for our love to him, which must be expressed in devotion like Mary's. The helping of the poor, while having its own importance, must yield to the primacy of the gospel and its proclamation. Once we have believed, we share in the Lord's Supper, being reminded by it of all that our Saviour suffered and all that he has secured for us, confirmed and guaranteed to us by a new and everlasting covenant. The cross is not just a historical event. Nor is it just a means of reconciliation to God. It continues to be for the Christian the prime motivating force of his life and service, pointing him to its final consummation in the presence of God and of his Son, our Saviour. How wise our Lord was to insist that we eat the Lord's Supper, constantly, to remind us of him and his cross! Otherwise we shall easily go astray.

43.
Testing times

Please read Matthew 26:31-56

The word variously translated as 'temptation', 'trial' and 'testing' is one of the most difficult terms in the New Testament to define accurately. We have already seen it in relation to our Lord's temptations in the wilderness, as well as in the prayer he taught his disciples. The first chapter of James's letter has various references to trials and testings, as well as temptations in the sense of enticements to sin. It is not always easy to disentangle these various meanings. Perhaps the best way to understand is to remember that in every time of trial and testing God is actively working for our growth in grace as we are enabled to pass the test, while the devil is actively working for our failure when we fall into sin. Sometimes the first aspect is to the fore and at other times the second is given prominence. In the present passage we are concerned with a time of testing, for Jesus himself and also for his disciples, where both aspects are in view.

Our Lord's testing, which has been going on throughout his ministry, reaches its climax in the Garden of Gethsemane. The disciples, who have had to survive their own tests during their period of training, now come to the moment of truth. In this passage we see Jesus, as we must expect, passing with flying colours, yet without finding it an easy matter. The disciples, however, especially Peter, fail and fall, in spite of their Master's warning.

The warning (26:31-35)

In fact it is not only Peter who receives the warning, but it is he who, as usual, speaks unwisely. However, we must note that he was not alone. Jesus warns them, **'This very night you will all fall away on account of me.'** Falling away, sometimes translated as being offended or stumbling, as we have seen earlier with respect to John the Baptist, means being trapped or ensnared into sinning, because of a situation with which we cannot cope. Here the situation predicted by our Lord is his impending death. He quotes the Old Testament: **'I will strike the shepherd, and the sheep of the flock will be scattered'** (26:31, quoting Zech. 13:7). In spite of Christ's predictions the disciples still have not accepted that the one they believed to be the Messiah has to be rejected and suffer death. Peter, it would seem, is still of the same mind as in chapter 16. He believes that this should not, and must not, happen to his Lord. He is still wrong. The original prophecy includes a command given to the sword: 'Awake, O sword, against my shepherd,' while in Jesus' quotation of the passage here God himself declares that he will strike the shepherd. There is no real difference. The point is that God, whether directly or through the sword at his command, is responsible for the striking of the shepherd.

This in itself is terrible to contemplate. When we say that God punished the Saviour in our place for our sins it sounds much more reasonable, more 'civilized' even. The thought of God striking and killing his own Son is beyond our imagining, and yet that is what Jesus says here.

Jehovah lifted up his rod:
O Christ, it fell on thee!
Thou wast sore stricken of thy God;
There's not one stroke for me.
Thy tears, thy blood, beneath it flowed;
Thy bruising healeth me.

Jehovah bade his sword awake:
O Christ, it woke 'gainst thee;
Thy blood the flaming blade must slake,
Thy heart its sheath must be.
All for my sake, my peace to make:
Now sleeps that sword for me.[1]

The quotation from Zechariah also includes the fact that 'The sheep of the flock will be scattered.' This is the basis for our Lord's assertion that the disciples, the sheep of his flock, will fall away on account of him. They are representatives of the Israel of whom the prophecy speaks, thus showing that they are to some extent sharing in the unbelief of the nation, at least for a time. Jesus does, however, encourage them by saying that **'After I have risen, I will go ahead of you into Galilee.'** Whether or not the idea of Jesus' going ahead refers to the customary action of the Eastern shepherd in going ahead of the sheep, this clearly refers to our Lord's meeting with them after his resurrection. Very probably, it includes the element of restoration for the scattered flock. The wider context of Zechariah's prophecy, which New Testament practice usually includes with the actual quotation, speaks of one third of the people being left in the land.

This third [God says], I will bring into the fire;
    I will refine them like silver
    and test them like gold

(Zech. 13:9).

This severe test through which they are passing will ultimately be for their good. This is the unvarying teaching of the Scriptures about trials (Rom. 5:3-4; James 1:2-4).

As with his previous predictions, this assertion that he will rise again should have helped them to come to terms with the prediction of his suffering, but they cannot comprehend this. The unexpected and unacceptable idea that the Messiah is to be struck down by God is at the root of their failure described in the following verses. For the time being, however, Peter asserts that, whatever anybody else does, he will never fall away. Jesus then goes even further. Not only will Peter stumble and fall by failing to support him, but **'This very night, before the cock crows, you will disown me three times'** (26:34). Peter makes matters worse by asserting that he is even willing **'to die with'** Jesus. **'And all the other disciples said the same.'** The following record of their failure shows that their confidence in themselves was utterly misplaced. Their self-assurance seems very foolish to us, with the benefit of hindsight, but we must not forget to honour their sense of loyalty, even while we regret their overconfidence. For who of us would have done any better?

Gethsemane (26:36-39)

Now it is time for the Son of Man to be put to the test. The time for his arrest, trial and crucifixion has come. How will he face this most severe of trials? There are some who seem to think that this was easy for the Son of God. He had no sin within, no lack of faith in his Father. Surely this was not a severe test, it is said. This shows a sad unreality. In time of war, when resistance heroes are captured and tortured, it is the bravest who hold out longest and suffer most. When Christians are tempted by Satan, is the purest who hold out longest and suffer the extremes of temptations. Since our Lord did not capitulate immediately, or at all, the tempting and trying and testing would go on and on, as indeed it has done up to this point. Because he does not give in he has to go on suffering the insinuations and accusations of Satan. Certainly he 'suffered when he was tempted' (Heb. 2:18). 'For we do not have a high priest who is unable to sympathize with our weaknesses, but we have one who has been tempted in every way, just as we are — yet was without sin' (Heb. 4:15).

When they arrive at Gethsemane Jesus takes **'Peter and the two sons of Zebedee along with him'** (26:37). The severity of the trial is shown by his very demeanour: **'He began to be sorrowful and troubled. Then he said to them, "My soul is overwhelmed with sorrow to the point of death."'** What agony and anguish there must have been for our Saviour to say that his soul was overwhelmed and that he was, as it were, at the point of death because of this! He asks his three closest disciples to **'Stay here and keep watch with me.'** We know that they failed to do this and he had to face his test without human love and support. Here, again, we see the real humanity of the Saviour. Failure to understand this reality minimizes his suffering and reduces the stature of his achievement. As man, in spite of all he faced, he nevertheless goes on.

He goes forward on his own and, falling **'with his face to the ground,'** he prays, **'My Father, if it is possible, may this cup be taken from me. Yet not as I will, but as you will'** (26:39). Expositors and preachers have often said that they hesitate to write or speak about these most holy moments. We feel we should take off our shoes, because the ground on which we are treading is holy ground. Nevertheless God has caused these words to be recorded and it is only right that we should see both the depth of the sufferings of Christ, as far as we can, and also the wonder of his love and grace. This was a test for him, of course. Would Jesus press on along the path that the Father had set before him? In the earlier temptations Satan tried to divert him from the path of obedience, but Jesus was having none of it. Now, when the cross and his sufferings were so near, when the prospect of death was actually facing him, would he still persist in obedience? Christ's obedience, the basis of the righteousness which is imputed to believers, was not limited to the law under which he was born, but especially includes the plan of salvation which he came into the world to implement. He 'became obedient to [as far as] death — even death on a cross' (Phil. 2:8). So when he says, 'Yet not as I will, but as you will,' he is not uttering words of mere resignation. It is his desire and determination that God's declared will, his command to the Son that he should die for sinners, may be actually put into effect, may take place.

All that this plan involves is clear from the use of the word **'cup'**. This, as so frequently in prophecy, is the cup of God's wrath (Isa. 51:17; Jer. 25:15-18). This further explains what it means for God to strike the shepherd. God's wrath comes upon the substitute bearing his wrath in the place of sinners.

> Death and the curse were in our cup:
> O Christ 'twas full for thee!
> But thou hast drained the last dark drop,
> 'Tis empty now for me.[2]

This is Christ's sacrifice, the substitute dying in place of the offenders. Unlike the Old Testament sacrifices, his is a voluntary sacrifice. The lambs, bulls and goats had no choice; they were simply put to death. Jesus chooses to die, determines to fulfil God's will and drink the cup of his wrath. Sometimes the question is asked whether the cross was absolutely necessary. Some great names have supported the idea that it was only relatively necessary and that some other way to assuage God's wrath could have been found. Our Lord's words, **'if it is possible'**, refute this. He was not rebelling; he was not refusing to go in God's way. However, such was his awareness of the awfulness and horror of death, not just any death, but death as a substitute bearing the Father's wrath, that he asked if some other way was possible. It was not, so he went ahead.

The disciples' failure (26:40-46)

Jesus had asked them to keep awake and thus support him. After praying, **'He returned to his disciples and found them sleeping.'** He rebukes them, more in sorrow than in anger it would appear again. He addresses his words to Peter, perhaps because it was Peter who had asserted that this would never happen, but the rebuke applies to them all: **'Could you men not keep watch with me for one hour?'** At the very moment when Jesus was passing his test, the disciples were failing theirs. He gives them a further warning: **'Watch and pray so that you will not fall into temptation.'** This, of course, is a warning we need all the time, but here it is especially appropriate. They are in a dangerous position. Everything is building up to a climax and they will be caught up in events quite beyond their understanding or ability to cope. The only way to survive without falling away is to be alert and pray for grace and strength. It is here that Peter's folly is most manifest. He thinks all will be well. He is confident of his own ability, certain that he will never disown Christ. So, it would seem, he has not troubled to pray. Falling into temptation, bearing in mind the comments with which we began this chapter, seems here to mean actually sinning — falling into temptation so as to sin.

Trials will come, testings will occur, but we must pray that we may not fall into temptation so as to commit sin. God has promised that grace may be ours: 'God is faithful; he will not let you be tempted beyond what you can bear. But when you are tempted, but he will also provide a way out so that you can stand up under it' (1 Cor. 10:13). This does not refer to a way out of the temptation, but a way out of falling, a way to stand up in the time of testing and not sin. Peter ought to have prayed for such a way out, for grace to hold fast. Our Lord acknowledges their good intentions: **'The spirit is willing, but the body is weak.'** He is aware that they are weary, lacking in sleep and so at a low point in every way — in modern terms, 'stressed out' — because of the events of a long day. Overconfidence is always bad, but especially when it does not take account of our own natural weaknesses, never mind our sin.

Jesus left them and **'went away a second time and prayed, "My Father, if it is not possible for this cup to be taken away unless I drink it, may your will be done."'** This time he does not ask for the cup to be taken from him, but acknowledges that it is not possible for it to be taken away. ('For' seems to mean 'since', as so often in the New Testament.) On his return he finds them sleeping still, **'because their eyes were heavy'**. He leaves them to sleep, goes away and prays a third time, **'saying the same thing'**. Finally he leaves them to sleep, for there is nothing more that they can do. Then, aware that Judas and 'a large crowd armed with swords and clubs' are on their way, he says to his disciples, **'Rise, let us go! Here comes my betrayer!'** He deliberately sets out to confront the crowd and do his Father's will.

The arrest (26:47-56)

The account of our Lord's arrest illustrates the determination with which he approaches the cross. His death has been purposed by God, predicted by the prophets and plotted by men. So Judas comes leading those **'sent from the chief priests and the elders of the people'**. He has a signal arranged with them: **'The one I kiss is the man; arrest him.'** He puts this into operation and Jesus, amazingly, addresses him as **'Friend'** and tells him to do what he has to. Our Lord is in control. If these words are interpreted as a question (as they may be) and thus a mild rebuke, that is the nearest that Jesus comes to being angry with Judas. Once again, there appears to be more sorrow than anger in the Saviour's response to the one who betrayed him. This does not remove Judas' responsibility, of course, but it shows what an awareness of God's sovereignty and of one's own agreement with God's purposes can do to preserve our equanimity in the face of hatred. We must learn from Jesus.

'**Then the men stepped forward, seized Jesus and arrested him.**' This produces a remarkable exchange, which again illustrates Christ's continuing readiness to do the Father's will and go to the cross: '**One of Jesus' companions reached for his sword, drew it out and struck the servant of the high priest, cutting off his ear.**' Now that it is too late, one of the disciples — Peter, as we know from John's Gospel (John 18:10) — tries to defend and rescue his Master. This is on a par with his rejection of the whole idea of the Messiah being put to death seen in chapter 16. He still does not understand that Jesus has come to die and must die, if sinners are to be saved. It is not possible for the cup to be taken from him. Peter no doubt thought that he was being faithful to Jesus, loyally defending him, but in fact he was showing once more his lack of understanding and falling away because of Jesus. It is this lack of expectation of the cross that caused him and the other disciples to despair and fall into sin when it became clear that Jesus was going to be put to death.

Jesus rebukes his would-be helper, telling him, '**Put your sword back in its place**', giving the reason that '**All who draw the sword will die by the sword.**' This has no relevance to issues of pacifism. It does have relevance, however, to the issue of defending the church and, even more, to propagating the gospel by the use of force. If Jesus wanted to be defended he had other, more effective, means at his disposal: '**Do you think I cannot call on my Father, and he** will at once put at my disposal more than twelve legions of angels?' When Paul tells the Philippians that Christ did not 'regard equality with God as something to be exploited' (Phil. 2:6, NRSV),³ he presumably had situations like this in mind. The Son of God could have availed himself of angelic help. He chose not to do so, but went the way of the servant, going to death, even the death of the cross. He refused to take that way out, because that would contradict his whole purpose in coming as contained in the prophecies of the Old Testament. So he asks, **'How then would the Scriptures be fulfilled that say it must happen in this way?'**

The fact that Jesus was obeying God's will in allowing himself to be arrested, tried and then put to death, does not remove responsibility from those who opposed him. They ought to have seen that that they were proceeding in an unlawful manner. In fact, the way that they had set out, **'with swords and clubs to capture'** one who **'sat in the temple courts teaching'** every day, shows that this was not really a legal matter at all. They were demonstrating that there was a plot, a secret plan, which had nothing to do with the law, but much to do with hatred of Jesus. Nevertheless, he did not hesitate to remind them that **'This has all taken place that the writings of the prophets might be fulfilled.'** Constantly we have this twofold explanation: the sovereign purposes of God and the responsible wickedness of men.

The last words of verse 56 sum up what has been going on with the disciples. We began with Christ's prediction that they would all fall away, that the sheep of the flock would be scattered, and now we read that **'All the disciples deserted him and fled.'** They have been tested and found wanting. They asserted much and have achieved nothing. Peter, in particular, claimed that he would never do this, that even if everybody else let Jesus down, he would not. The first stages of his disowning of Jesus are seen here. When put to the test, his assertions of loyalty and devotion are seen to be worthless. What a warning that is for us all, who do not face such stressful situations and such severe tests! It is fatal to boast that we shall achieve anything, that we shall never let the Saviour down. Determination to be loyal is one thing; assertions that we shall never be guilty of this is another.

This is seen all the more clearly when we contrast the disciples' attitude with our Lord's calm confidence. Again we must remember that it was not easy for Jesus. He was not above all such stresses and fears. He did not simply sail in calm waters in the midst of the storm. He was blown and buffeted by the winds and waves, but still remained faithful to the Father and to the Father's purpose. The prophecies of the Scriptures would be fulfilled. It was necessary that he should die; it was not possible that he should avoid drinking the cup of God's wrath. So he resisted the temptation to take an easier path, the path of avoiding suffering at all costs, and went forward to meet the betrayer and his companions. He refused proffered help which would have led him astray from the Father's will, and so went on alone to face trial, condemnation and the cross.

Contrasting the disciples' failure with our Lord's steadfastness should lead us to consider ourselves. When we remember, as Hebrews tells us, that he sympathizes with our weakness and proneness to temptation, this does not mean that he condones our sin. Instead, the fact that he was able to resist the temptation and go on in the right path tells us that he is able to give us strength and courage to do the same. Relying on this is not self-reliance, but faith in the power of Christ and in the strength that the Spirit of God can impart. In times of testing, we are too often like the disciples. We must pray for the grace of Christ, that we may be more like him and walk in the Father's ways.

44.
Crown of thorns

Please read Matthew 26:57 – 27:31

We have already seen that Christ's death was an absolute necessity. However, was it also necessary that he should die in this particular manner? Certainly many of the details of his sufferings were prophesied and these had to be fulfilled, but God could have caused different details to be prophesied, but chose not to. Jesus escaped earlier attempts on his life, because his time had not yet come. He had to die in Jerusalem at the time of the Feast of Passover. It seems that it was also necessary for his death to be public, not private; at the hands of the authorities, not of a 'Jewish gang'; and that it be should made very clear that he was actually innocent. He was crucified, not stoned, and by the Romans, not the Jews, so that he was hanged on a tree and thus regarded as cursed. The reason for all this appears to be that God had deliberately arranged that the formal and outward aspects of his trial, condemnation and execution should mirror what was actually happening in the spiritual realm. What men did to him reflected what God was doing in the pursuit of our salvation.

There is, as it were, a divine irony at work, as seen also in the words of Caiaphas recorded in John 11. The members of the Sanhedrin were worried that Jesus might become so popular that the people would rise in rebellion. Then the Romans would attack them and destroy both temple and nation. In response

Caiaphas said, 'You know nothing at all! You do not realize that it is better for you that one man die for the people than that the whole nation perish.' John points out that, in the sovereignty of God, Caiaphas was speaking in his official capacity as high priest and thus unwittingly 'prophesied that Jesus would die for the Jewish nation, and not only for that nation but also for the scattered children of God, to bring them together and make them one' (John 11:49-52). The same is true of the Jewish leaders' actions here as of Caiaphas' words in that passage. Unwittingly they act out in human terms what God is performing in his divine purpose. As the high priest's words about saving the nation are applied to the nation of God's elect people, and Christ's dying at the hands of the Romans functions as a sacrificial death for sinners, so all the other details fit in with the various elements of the gospel.

Before the Sanhedrin (26:57-68)

The first part of the trial of our Lord took place before the Jewish council at the home of **'Caiaphas, the high priest, where the teachers of the law and the elders had assembled.'** The allegations of illegality concerning Jesus' trial are very complicated. It may be that this was not a formal gathering of the Sanhedrin, although its members were concerned. 'By later Mishnaic law a capital trial could not be held during the night, and so it is possible that the "trial" took place in two stages, first an informal, hastily convened gathering to determine the charge against Jesus, followed by a more formal verdict pronounced by the full Sanhedrin in the morning. But perhaps it is more likely that Matthew and Mark are speaking of a single protracted sitting which finally reached its verdict at daybreak.'[1] In any case this was all preliminary, for only Pilate could pronounce sentence of execution and carry it out. The

Sanhedrin had many powers but capital punishment was not one of them.

We are told that **'Peter followed him at a distance, right up to the courtyard of the high priest. He entered and sat down with the guards to see the outcome.'** In a rather different way, Peter is on trial as well as his Lord. One of the aspects of the trial that is very important for the doctrine of the atonement is Christ's innocence. We know that he was sinless, completely blameless. In picture this is represented by the findings of the authorities who try him. So we read that **'The chief priests and the whole Sanhedrin were looking for false evidence against Jesus so that they could put him to death. But they did not find any, though many false witnesses came forward.'** In the end they found what they believed, or hoped, was evidence. Two witnesses, as required by the law (Deut. 17:6), accused **'this fellow'** of saying, **'I am able to destroy the temple of God and rebuild it in three days.'** This perversion of some actual words of Jesus (see John 2:19-21) could be taken literally as a threat against their sacred place. So the high priest challenges Jesus to answer **'this testimony that these men are bringing against you'**. By remaining silent (26:63) Jesus not only implies that this so-called testimony is false, but also fulfils the prophecy of Isaiah 53:7:

> He was oppressed and afflicted,
>   yet he did not open his mouth;
> he was led like a lamb to the slaughter,
>   and as a sheep before her shearers is silent,
>   so he did not open his mouth.

The high priest then goes a stage further and charges Jesus **'under oath by the living God'**. He says, **'Tell us if you are the Christ, the Son of God.'** Once again Jesus is faced with a dilemma. If he asserts that he is the Son of God then he lays himself open to the charge of blasphemy and a sentence of condemnation. If he denies this then his whole ministry is denied and his previous claims must be dismissed. The reply of Jesus, **'Yes, it is as you say'**, does not come over in such a definite form if translated literally: 'You said [it].' However this is certainly what he means.[2] Indeed, Jesus goes further with words that must surely have sealed his fate: **'In the future you will see the Son of Man sitting at the right hand of the Mighty One and coming on the clouds of heaven.'** He does not use the word 'Christ', but refers to himself as usual as 'the Son of Man', but the claim to be at the right hand of God and coming on the clouds of heaven leaves little room for misunderstanding of his claims.

There is more room for misunderstanding exactly what he did mean. Is he referring to his Second Coming, the *parousia*? Jesus is alluding to the prophecies of Psalm 110:1 and Daniel 7:13, which speak of his kingly authority. **'In the future'**, literally 'from now on', is more likely to refer to his coming in judgement on Jerusalem, as in 24:30. In any case the point for the high priest and his colleagues is that this prisoner on whom they are sitting in judgement will in the future sit in judgement on them! They conclude that he has **'spoken blasphemy'**. Blasphemy had various definitions, but according to any of them, it would seem, Jesus was guilty, unless his claims were actually true. So the Sanhedrin pronounces him **'worthy of death'**. This judicial pronouncement fits ill with their behaviour described in the next verses: **'Then they spat in his face and struck him with their fists. Others slapped him and said, "Prophesy to us, Christ. Who hit you?"'** (26:67-68). They were not asking him to predict the future, but to identify his attackers. To understand this we probably need to bear in mind the information, given by Mark, that he was blindfolded.

The Jews believed that the Messiah should be able to identify them even blindfold, for he would not 'judge by what he sees with his eyes' (Isa. 11:3).

The conclusion is very clear: Jesus is falsely accused and wrongly condemned, though completely innocent. He is not guilty of blasphemy or any other crime. This illustrates the fact that in God's court he is not guilty of any sin either. The whole proceeding mirrors the spiritual transaction before God: innocent, but condemned, in the place of sinners.

We have already referred to the fulfilment of Old Testament prophecy in his silence (Isa. 53:7). We may add the words:

> I offered my back to those who beat me,
>   my cheeks to those who pulled out my beard;
> I did not hide my face
>   from mocking and spitting
>
> (Isa. 50:6).

Linking these with the rest of Isaiah's prophecies, we may see that his innocence is a crucial part of the picture. Only if he was innocent could he bear the sins of others. His life was not already forfeit on his own account. Only so could it be true that

> ... he was pierced for our transgressions,
>   he was crushed for our iniquities;
> the punishment that brought us peace was upon him,
>   and by his wounds we are healed.
> We all, like sheep, have gone astray,
>   each of us has turned to his own way;
> and the LORD has laid on him
>   the iniquity of us all
>
> (Isa. 53:5-6).

Bearing shame and scoffing rude,
In my place condemned he stood;
Sealed my pardon with his blood:
Hallelujah! what a Saviour![3]

Peter and Judas (26:69 – 27:10)

While all this was happening, **'Peter was sitting out in the
courtyard.'** Now it is his turn to be tested further. Three times
he is challenged about his relationship to Christ. First, **'A servant girl came to him. "You also were with Jesus of Galilee,"
she said.'** Peter denies all knowledge of this. **'Then he went
out to the gateway, where another girl saw him and said
to the people there, "This fellow was with Jesus of Nazareth."'** His second denial is made **'with an oath'**. A third
denial follows when **'those standing there went up to Peter
and said, "Surely you are one of them, for your** [Galilean]
accent gives you away."' This third disowning is even worse,
as he **'began to call down curses on himself'**. Reconciling
Matthew's account with those in the other Gospels is difficult
but not impossible. Whatever the problems, the words of Jesus
were fulfilled: **'Immediately a cock crowed. Then Peter remembered the word Jesus had spoken: "Before the cock
crows, you will disown me three times."'** As a result Peter
'went outside and wept bitterly'. Before we assess what
happened to Peter, it will be helpful to consider the following
verses about Judas.

In the morning the Sanhedrin put their previous condemnation into formal effect. They had decided that Jesus must be
put to death. So, **'They bound him, led him away and
handed him over to Pilate, the governor'** (27:2). Somehow, Judas learned of this and he **'was seized with remorse
and returned the thirty silver coins to the chief priests and**

the elders. **"I have sinned,"** he said, **"for I have betrayed innocent blood."** ' The word translated 'remorse' is the same as the one used in 21:29, where it is translated 'he changed his mind', and it means 'repentance'. However, this is not repentance as properly understood and 'remorse' is a fair translation. If this is true, even though Judas confessed that he had sinned, that he had betrayed his innocent Master, how was he different from Peter?

Perhaps the crucial difference, by which we may decide that Peter was a backslider while Judas was an apostate, is that Peter, ultimately, returned to the Lord, while Judas in despair **'went away and hanged himself'** (27:5). We do not know whether Peter's bitter tears were evidence of repentance at that stage, but we do know that he later returned and, far from despairing, served his Lord as an apostle. When **'Judas threw the money into the temple'**, he was simply trying to get rid of the responsibility that he knew he bore for the death of Jesus. The chief priests rightly considered the thirty pieces of silver as **'blood money'** and used them **'to buy the potter's field as a burial place for foreigners'**. This fulfilled **'what was spoken by Jeremiah the prophet'**. The words given by Matthew include **'thirty silver coins'** as in Zechariah 11:13. In Jeremiah 19:1-13, however, mention is made of elders, priests and a potter (v. 1), 'the blood of the innocent' (v. 4), and the Valley of Ben Hinnom, which parallels 'the field', has its name changed to the Valley of Slaughter (v. 6) and is to be used as a burial place (v. 11). It is all attributed to Jeremiah, probably because he is the major prophet. This linking of quotations from different authors under one heading is also seen in Mark 1:2-3.

A comparison of Peter and Judas may be helpful pastorally. We know from other references that Peter remained a believer. Jesus promised that his faith would not fail (Luke 22:32). Judas, although one of the Twelve, was never a believer. John records,

'For Jesus had known from the beginning which of them did not believe and who would betray him' (John 6:64; cf. 6:70-71). Peter was restored. Judas, according to Acts 1:25, left his apostleship 'to go where he belongs', which implies that he went to hell. Peter was weak rather than wilful. He let Jesus down under great pressure, at the end of a long day, in a dark and dangerous situation, where he could easily have been arrested and executed with his Lord.

Many in history have done this. Notable Christians like Archbishop Cranmer and Thomas Bilney failed to hold fast to their profession, but then were restored and even died for their Saviour. While this must not make us careless, thinking that it does not matter if we fail to stand for our Lord, it is important that we do not condemn Peter, or ourselves, too easily. Too great a condemnation may even ruin our confidence and deter us from returning to the Lord. We must, however, realize that lack of prayer, lack of faith and lack of attendance on the means of grace can easily weaken us so much that we deny our relationship with Christ before men and even, like Peter, descend into false and unchristian language to defend ourselves.

Judas, on the other hand, deliberately opposed Jesus. The only clue we are given to his behaviour is that he was a thief (John 12:6), that 'as keeper of the money bag, he used to help himself to what was put into it'. It has become popular to find excuses for Judas, following the lead of Dorothy L. Sayers in her play, *Man born to be king*. There is, however, no evidence that Judas thought Jesus was himself betraying the people by not leading a rebellion. All we know, which is not very much, is that he asked for money in return for betraying Jesus. He took the initiative in approaching the chief priests. There is all the difference in the world between succumbing to tremendous pressure, as Peter did, and deliberately seeking to benefit from denying and betraying Christ. Even though we cannot insist that the word used of him means 'remorse', not 'repentance', although he did admit his sin, he did not return to the Lord Jesus Christ. There was no trust, no real allegiance, no personal love, or he would have come back.

The great warning to us today is twofold. First, we may see how high a false disciple may rise. Judas was one of the Twelve; he exercised miraculous gifts as one of those sent out by Jesus on the training mission (10:8). He deceived the rest of the disciples, who had no idea that he was doing this work of betrayal. We must take warning from this. We cannot read hearts and, while deeply saddened, we should not be utterly surprised when people give up their profession of faith and even turn into opponents of Christ. On the other hand, we should learn how low a genuine believer may fall. Peter, with all his privileges, fell into sin and disowned his Lord three times. For ourselves, we must beware lest we fall. We must not presume, fail to pray, or trust in our own abilities and steadfastness. For others, we must be ready to have true compassion and, where there is genuine repentance, be ready to welcome them back. None of us has the right to sit in judgement on others. We must be ready to forgive those whom Christ has forgiven, and restore them to their place of fellowship in the church.

Pontius Pilate (27:11-31)

While all this was happening, **'Jesus stood before the governor, and the governor asked him, "Are you the king of the Jews?"'** Once again Jesus gives his roundabout agreement to this. The chief priests and elders bring their accusations and once more Jesus will make **'no reply, not even to a single charge — to the great amazement on the governor'** (27:14). Far from antagonizing Pilate, this seems to impress him and he tries to release Jesus. The reason given is that **'He knew it**

was out of envy that they had handed Jesus over to him.'
He invokes the custom of releasing a prisoner at the Passover
Feast. The prisoner to be released was **'chosen by the crowd'**,
so he asks them, **'Which one do you want me to release to
you: Barabbas, or Jesus who is called Christ?'** Pilate has
an added reason for wanting to release Jesus. He has received
a message from his wife: **'Don't have anything to do with
that innocent man, for I have suffered a great deal today
in a dream because of him.'** This confirms Pilate's own conviction that Jesus is innocent. **'But the chief priests and the
elders persuaded the crowd to ask for Barabbas and to
have Jesus executed.'**

The weak governor cannot resist their demand. He asks
rather lamely, **'What shall I do, then, with Jesus who is
called Christ?'** (27:22). He receives the uncompromising
answer, **'Crucify him!'** Pilate asks, **'Why? What crime has
he committed?'**, but **'They shouted all the louder, "Crucify him!"'** Therefore, rather like Judas returning the priests'
silver coins, Pilate tries to absolve himself from all responsibility for **'this man's blood'** by washing his hands **'in front of
the crowd'**. **'It is your responsibility!'** he says and receives
the dreadful answer: **'Let his blood be on us and on our
children!'** We, today, cannot read these words without remembering that God's judgement did fall on Jerusalem and
the Jewish nation in A.D. 70. This, of course, provides no
excuse for anti-Semitism. Not only Matthew, but all the
apostles, including Paul, were Jewish. There was a godly remnant then and there always will be a remnant, and indeed more
than a remnant, according to Romans 11. However, it is clear
that the rejection of the Jewish nation as such, in favour of a
nation that brings forth the fruits of the kingdom (21:43), is
because of their rejection of Jesus. To speak of a curse on all
Jews as 'Christ-killers' is just as wrong as to accuse the Jewish apostles of anti-Semitic sentiments.

The great point that has been made is the innocence of Jesus. As we have seen already, this is vital to our understanding of the meaning of his death on the cross. The attitude of Pilate, not to mention his wife's message, constitutes the judicial verdict that counts. The twisted justice of the Sanhedrin and the manipulated prejudice of the crowd cannot contradict this. Jesus was not guilty of blasphemy or any other crime. He was an innocent victim. In making this clear, Matthew shows us that Jesus was not dying under the judgement of God on account of his own sins, but for ours. The point is further illustrated, probably deliberately, by the fact that Jesus is substituted for Barabbas. **'Then he released Barabbas to them.'** The guilty Barabbas is set free. (Was the third cross originally intended for him?) He was a rebel who deserved execution. Jesus could ask the crowd arresting him, 'Am I leading a rebellion, that you have come out with swords and clubs to capture me?' (26:55). He was not a rebel, but an innocent man. We who are rebels against the living God can only worship and adore when we see the innocent Son of God not only suffering the judgement of men, but suffering the judgement and punishment of God in our place.

Pilate then **'had Jesus flogged, and handed him over to be crucified. Then the governor's soldiers took Jesus into the Praetorium and gathered the whole company of soldiers round him.'** Jewish flogging was limited to forty lashes minus one (see 2 Cor. 11:24), 'but the Romans were restricted by nothing but their strength and whim'.[4] This could lead to death and Jesus must have been severely weakened even before he was led away to be crucified. The soldiers were not content with the flogging. **'They stripped him and put a scarlet robe on him, and then twisted together a crown of thorns and set it on his head.'** They mocked him and jeered at him as 'king of the Jews'. They spat on him and struck him with the staff of authority which they had previously put in his hand. Once again Matthew is showing us men who, in their dreadful cruelty, speak more wisely than they know. He is truly the King, not only of the Jews but of all his people, even though his crown is made of thorns. That in itself tells us that Christ's reign, his kingly rule, comes only through his suffering. **'After they had mocked him, they took off the robe and put his own clothes on him. Then they led him away to crucify him.'**

This account of the trial of Jesus confirms that he is the innocent substitute for sinners, the suffering Messiah, the Saviour of his people. Nothing remains for him but to die a cursed death. We can only feebly imagine what he went through during this period of time. He has endured a long and wearisome day. He has been betrayed and deserted, arrested and spat upon, struck with fists and slapped in the face, insulted and degraded. He has been flogged to within inches of death and then mocked and derided by the soldiers. The mental agony combined with the physical pain, however, is only the prelude to his deepest suffering. All this, we are told, is borne because of the sins of others, for he is innocent. He is going to die in the place of others, who deserve mercy as little as Barabbas did.

There has been much stress on the teaching of Jesus throughout this Gospel, but we must not allow ourselves to be diverted from our Lord's actions and sufferings. Without them the teaching is meaningless and pointless. Instruction about the kingdom is based on the fact that the King wore a crown of thorns. It is here that we must look to ourselves, confessing our sinning and our rebellion. We cannot wash our hands of our responsibility for the death of Christ, for he died because of us. We need to meditate on the sufferings of Jesus, that we may repent more deeply of our sins, value him more highly and serve him more faithfully. How awful were his sufferings for us! And they are not finished yet, for the actual crucifixion still lies ahead.

45.
Crucified, dead and buried

Please read Matthew 27:32-61

The crucifixion and death of the Lord Jesus Christ are described in some detail, yet there is very little information given about the physical sufferings he endured. Unlike some modern commentators, who fill their pages with medical theories as to how death actually ensued, Matthew appears more concerned with the doctrinal implications. This may, of course, be partly because the horrors of crucifixion were well known among the Jews, but it is more likely that the author does not want us to be over-concerned with the physical and so ignore the spiritual. Thus we are made very aware of who it is that is being crucified and what his death accomplished. It is not our sympathy that is required (cf. Luke 23:27-29), but our understanding, leading to faith.

Some of this is accomplished by the continuing use of irony, in the jeers of Christ's tormentors, and by the mirroring in earthly terms of what was happening before God. Most of the details reflect Old Testament prophecies, although Matthew does not add to his earlier frequent use of 'that it might be fulfilled'. In this way the death of Jesus is set firmly in the context of God's purposes of salvation. It is made clear not only that Jesus is the Messiah, but also what kind of Messiah he is. We see here that the whole of Christ's ministry has been leading up to this point. The opposition of the Jewish leaders culminates in his death. The emphasis in all the Gospels on the suffering of Christ can only indicate that his death is vital for our salvation, that there was no other way for his people to have their sins forgiven and receive eternal life. It was not only the apostle Paul who concentrated on 'Jesus Christ and him crucified' (1 Cor. 2:2).

Crucifixion (27:32-44)

It was customary for the condemned man to carry his cross, or at least the crossbeam, to the place of crucifixion. This must have been beyond the strength of our Lord after his flogging, so when the soldiers **'met a man from Cyrene, named Simon ... they forced him to carry the cross'** (27:32). It would appear from Mark's description of him (Mark 15:21), that Simon's sons became believers and were known to the church in Rome. However, there is no suggestion that Simon himself was anything but imposed upon. This was not a sympathetic volunteer. The point of mentioning this is to stress our Lord's weakness. The crucifixion took place at Golgotha, **'The Place of the Skull'**, which would be outside the city walls as a place of execution. We need not trouble ourselves with theories as to the actual place. Our concern is with the historic Christ who died for sinners, not with shrines built on the site.

'There they offered Jesus wine to drink, mixed with gall; but after tasting it, he refused to drink it.' The significance of this is disputed. Was the wine offered with the kindly intention of lessening his pain, as some suppose, or was it another form of mockery? Did Jesus reject it because he was determined to be fully conscious all the time, or because he recognized the intention, since gall is very bitter, to torment him further? It is, in fact, dubious whether the mixture that was offered to Jesus had any painkilling effects, and it seems unlikely that the soldiers who offered it to him had any interest in lessening his pain. What is beyond dispute is that this fulfilled the typical prophecy of Psalm 69:21: 'They put gall in my food and gave me vinegar for my thirst.' As usual the context is helpful, which here includes the words, 'scorned, disgraced and shamed... I looked for sympathy, but there was none, for comforters, but I found none' (Ps. 69:19-20).

'**When they had crucified him, they divided up his clothes by casting lots**', according to the usual custom and, more importantly, according to the amazing account of sufferings in Psalm 22:18. The soldiers, having crucified him, sat down to keep watch so that no one could interfere. For some reason there are people, such as the Jehovah's Witnesses, who count it important to assert that Jesus was crucified on a stake, rather than the traditional-shaped cross. The fact that '**Above his head they placed the written charge against him,**' shows that the traditional concept is correct. Again, more important than the shape of the cross is the content of the charge: '**This is Jesus, the King of the Jews.**' Just as those responsible for his crucifixion would not let the ground of his condemnation be forgotten, so Matthew wants us to remember that this is our King who is being crucified, not the traditional King of the Jews, but God's Messianic King of his people.

Matthew tells us also that '**Two robbers were crucified with him, one on his right and one on his left**' (27:38). He concentrates at this stage, however, on '**those who passed by**' and '**hurled insults at him, shaking their heads and saying, "You who are going to destroy the temple and build it in three days, save yourself! Come down from the cross, if you are the Son of God!"**' Thus the passers-by align themselves with the devil in calling upon Jesus to prove that he is the Son of God by disobeying the Father's command. As Son of God he could have come down from the cross. Nothing could have prevented him, except that this was the way to which he was committed, the way of salvation for sinners. Unwittingly, of course, they confirm what is actually the case, that his body is the temple of God (John 2:20-21), the meeting-place of God and man, and that he is truly the Son of God.

'In the same way the chief priests, the teachers of the law and the elders mocked him.' In their own way they too point to the reality of Christ's work: **'He saved others ... but he can't save himself!'** How true it was that, if he was to save others, he could not save himself! They demanded that he should come down from the cross if they were to believe in him: **'Let God rescue him now if he wants him, for he said, "I am the Son of God."'** At this point **'The robbers who were crucified with him also heaped insults on him.'** Matthew does not tell us that one of them repented and was saved, as Luke does (Luke 23:39-43). His stress is on the mockery and insults endured by our Lord in fulfilment of Psalm 22:6-8.

In the providence of God the mocking and insults, the challenges to his divine sonship and claims to be the Saviour all serve to show what was happening on the cross. It was because he was saving others that he could not save himself. It was because he would not come down from the cross that we do believe in him. It was because he trusted in God that he stayed on the cross and because he was the Son of God that he suffered and died for us. And it was because God did delight in him that he rescued him from death in the end and raised him to life. While they mocked and insulted him, we who owe everything to him and to his death can only worship, adore and love.

Death (27:45-50)

Christ's death, at the end all these sufferings, was preceded by a significant event: **'From the sixth hour until the ninth**

hour darkness came over all the land.' For the three hours after noon the land was darkened. We are not interested in theories about the scientific reasons for this event, but the theological reasons are important. Darkness indicates judgement, as it did during the plagues on the land of Egypt at the time of the Exodus. The prophet Amos provides a likely background to the darkness:

'In that day,' declares the Sovereign LORD,

'I will make the sun go down at noon
  and darken the earth in broad daylight.
I will turn your religious feasts into mourning...
I will make that time like mourning for an only son
  and the end of it like a bitter day'

(Amos 8:9-10).

The land which has rejected God's Son and crucified its Messiah is shown to be under judgement. No doubt the people were filled with fear at this terrible event.

The darkness may well refer also to the judgement on Jesus, which is seen even more clearly in his cry which follows. The significance of Christ's having to die upon a cross is relevant here. The Jews applied to crucifixion the words of Deuteronomy 21:23: 'Anyone who is hung on a tree is under God's curse.' This is probably as near as we can come to an explanation of Christ's cry of desolation. **'About the ninth hour Jesus cried out in a loud voice,** *"Eloi, Eloi, lama sabachthani?"* **— which means, "My God, my God, why have you forsaken me?"** ' This cry, in Aramaic, used the words of Psalm 22:1. We know that God had not forsaken his Son in the sense of letting him down in his hour of need. That could not be. It was by the 'eternal Spirit' that he 'offered himself unblemished to God' (Heb. 9:14).

However, we can understand how God in his holy justice must turn away from one who is under his curse. The punishment that Christ endured in our place involved the wrath of God being poured out on him, manifested in this separation from him. All of us struggle to understand, still more to express, what is involved here. What it must have meant for the eternal Son to be deserted by the eternal Father is certainly beyond us. Nevertheless, the concept of the curse of God upon sin and sinners, here found in the person of Christ, is vital to our understanding of salvation. Failure to come up to God's standard results in the curse of the law. There is no excuse, no plea, that can counteract that. The only way that the curse, which began with Adam and Eve (Gen. 3:17) and is explained further in the law, could be removed from us, is if one without sin is made sin and a curse for us. So the apostle Paul explains, 'Christ redeemed us from the curse of the law by becoming a curse for us, for it is written: "Cursed is everyone who is hung on a tree"' (Gal. 3:13).

Our Lord's cry is misunderstood by **'those standing there'**. They think that he is 'calling Elijah' (Eloi/Eli = Elijah). The continuing mockery, **'Let's see if Elijah comes to save him,'** seems to indicate that the renewed offer of wine, in this instance put on a stick to raise it up to him, is not intended kindly. It again fulfils Psalm 69:21. We do not know whether the cry which Jesus uttered **'in a loud voice'** was simply a cry of anguish and agony, or refers to the triumphant words recorded in John 19:30: 'It is finished.' What is clear is that Jesus did not gradually weaken and die, for those on the point of death cannot cry with a loud voice. Rather, the words, **'He gave up his spirit,'** are to be taken literally. He dismissed his spirit, for he had 'authority to lay [his life] down and authority to take it up again' (John 10:18). The offering has been completed; the sacrifice has been made. Jesus, the one 'who had no sin', has been made 'to be sin for us, so that in him we might become the righteousness of God' (2 Cor. 5:21).

The effects (27:51-56)

It is important for Matthew that the consequences of Christ's death are made clear, as well as the response of those who were close by. First, he tells us that **'At that moment the curtain of the temple was torn in two from top to bottom.'** We are not told whether this was the inner or outer curtain. The outer curtain would be visible to more people; the inner one had the greater significance in relation to the offering of sacrifice. The explanation of the effect of the death of Christ, that 'We have confidence to enter the Most Holy Place by the blood of Jesus, by a new and living way opened for us through the curtain, that is, his body' (Heb. 10:19-20), suggests that this was the inner curtain or veil. The significance of this, as with so many events in the Bible, is both negative and positive. Negatively this would be seen as another mark of judgement upon the Jewish nation and their sacred place. One has only to remember the instinctive, if untheological, reaction to York Minster's being struck by lightning just after an unbelieving bishop had been consecrated there, to imagine the effect upon the Jewish people.

More positively we must conclude that the death of Jesus not only ended the whole Jewish sacrificial system of the law, but also opened the way into the Holiest of All for those who put their trust in him. Although the temple continued to exist for a generation it was now an anachronism. 'For what the law was powerless to do in that it was weakened by the sinful nature, God did by sending his own Son in the likeness of sinful man to be a sin offering' (Rom. 8:3). His one sacrifice achieved what generations and centuries of animal sacrifices could not do. Sinners are reconciled to God, justified through faith. They may now enter the very presence of God, whereas the high priest of the Old Testament could only enter even the typical presence of God once a year. Sin has been dealt with;

wrath has been removed. For the one who enters into the salvation of Christ by faith there is now no barrier between him and God. We may have unrestricted and uninhibited communion with God. There is no place now for priests or sacrifices, nor is there any place for a rebuilt and restored temple with sacrifices, even symbolic ones, as dispensationalists claim. The curtain was torn from the top, indicating that it was God who put an end to what had been intended to point to Christ, but which had been turned into an independent, but ineffective, way of salvation.

The consequences of Christ's death for the temple are followed by the consequences for the earth. First comes an earthquake: **'The earth shook and the rocks split.'** The timing of events after this is not clear. It is most likely that we should insert a full stop after **'the tombs broke open'**, so making a gap in the sequence.[1] When he was raised, **'The bodies of many holy people who had died were raised to life. They came out of the tombs, and after Jesus' resurrection they went into the holy city and appeared to many people'** (27:51-52). Exactly who these holy ones were and what happened to them later we cannot say. We do not know whether this was a resurrection like that of Jesus, or like that of Lazarus, although the former is more likely. Our ignorance of these matters does not really matter. It is the significance that counts.

First, the earthquake tells us that Christ's death has cosmic significance. It is a hint of the reconciliation and renewal of all things that will follow at Christ's return. It is a mark of the victory gained by the cross. Secondly, the raising of the saints assures us that Christ's death has defeated death. The title of John Owen's book sums this up: *The death of death in the death of Christ.*[2] Because sin has been dealt with, death, the consequence of sin, has also been dealt with. The sting of death has been drawn and the very fact of death will one day cease

(1 Cor. 15:54-56). It may be, thirdly, that the holy people are Old Testament saints, who rise as the first-fruits of Christ's death, pointing to the full harvest at his Second Coming. Once again, that final resurrection is certain because of Christ's death. It is significant that Matthew sets all these events in his account next to the death of Christ. He could justifiably have placed them next to his account of the resurrection, but he seems to want to stress the centrality and finality of the death of Christ.

There were various people around the cross at Golgotha. There were the soldiers under the command of a centurion and there were friends and followers of Jesus. Matthew tells us that **'When the centurion and those with him who were guarding Jesus saw the earthquake and all that had happened, they were terrified, and exclaimed, "Surely he was the Son of God!"'** Just what these Gentiles meant by this term is open to debate. However, it is clear that Matthew wants us to understand it in its fullest sense. It is true that there is no 'the' in the Greek, but this does not mean that we must translate as 'a son of God' in some semi-heathen sense. Titles customarily lacked the definite article and it is quite correctly translated as 'Son of God' or 'God's Son'. The idea seems to be that the centurion is recognizing the validity of Christ's claims. The onlookers had jeered at him as the Son of God. Now the earthquake and other events have convinced him that God is vindicating this man. The parallel is the Philippian jailer, for whom the earthquake demonstrated that Paul and Silas were indeed 'servants of the Most High God' (Acts 16:17,26-30). Jesus is what he claimed to be; God has confirmed it.

The disciples had deserted Jesus and fled, but **'Many women were there, watching from a distance. They had followed Jesus from Galilee to care for his needs. Among them were Mary Magdalene, Mary the mother of James**

and Joses, and the mother of Zebedee's sons.' These were women who loved him and knew that love means loyalty. They had served him sacrificially over the months and were not going to give up caring for him now. That is why Matthew reminds us that they had cared for the needs of Jesus. They had not remained out of mere curiosity or sentiment. They were still concerned with what they could do for him, as the following verses indicate. Real faith produces love, and love cares and gives, producing loyalty and even courage.

Burial (27:57-61)

Only one thing remained to be done. The body of Jesus must be cared for. So, **'As evening approached, there came a rich man from Arimathea, named Joseph, who had himself become a disciple of Jesus.'** John tells us that up to this point he had been a secret disciple 'because he feared the Jews' (John 19:38), but now he comes out into the open, taking his stand before the world. This could not have been an easy thing to do. Friends of criminals were liable to suffer with the guilty person. Joseph witnesses not in word only but in deed. In accordance with prophecy, Jesus 'was assigned a grave ... with the rich in his death' (Isa. 53:9). It may have been Joseph's social position that helped him to approach Pilate to ask for Jesus' body, for permission to bury a criminal, especially one accused of treason, was not always given by the Romans. His request was granted, perhaps because Pilate had never been convinced of Jesus' guilt.[3]

Joseph made careful preparations to bury Jesus in a suitable manner. He **'took the body, wrapped it in a clean linen cloth, and placed it in his own new tomb that he had cut out of the rock'** (27:59-60). The newness and cleanness are appropriate for one who was the holy Son of God. For Joseph to do this represented some sacrifice. The tomb had been prepared for his own use and would probably not be used again. **'He rolled a big stone in front of the entrance to the tomb and went away. Mary Magdalene and the other Mary were sitting there opposite the tomb.'** Thus one of Christ's oldest disciples and one of his newest join together in loving and practical service of their Saviour.

In considering these things we must preserve a balance. The essential matters here are the crucifixion, death and burial of the Lord Jesus. Christianity is good news about certain historical events, not a philosophical system. However, the mere historical events have to be interpreted and Matthew has provided that interpretation by the way he has presented them. He has highlighted the details which link Christ's death with significant Old Testament prophecies, like Psalm 22 and Isaiah 53, which stress the purpose of his dying — to pay for the sins of his people, to die that they might be justified. Together with this he has mentioned the details of the mockery, which by contrast show not only his kingship, but also his sonship and saviourhood. Matthew wants us to see that while Jesus could not take up the challenges that they made if he was to save us, nevertheless the terms they used were accurate. He did trust God. God did want him and delight in him. He did save others and will save others because of his death. He is truly God's Son.

This Gospel of Matthew preaches the gospel of Christ. It demands a response. We must make a choice, whether we stand with those who mocked and jeered, especially the religious leaders of the Jews, or with those who saw and responded in faith. We must ask whether our faith matches that of the centurion, who accepted that all Jesus' claims were vindicated. We must consider whether our love equals that of the women who, unlike the men, persevered in love and care for their Saviour. We must ask ourselves whether our devotion approaches that of the new disciple, Joseph, who served Jesus in a practical and costly way in a situation fraught with danger. Jesus has borne the curse and endured the judgement and wrath of the Father. We must make our response in faith, love and service.

46.
The King, risen and reigning

Please read Matthew 27:62 – 28:20

It is sad that Christians generally hear about the resurrection of Christ only at Easter-time. It is frankly surprising that many preachers choose this important topic only then. One consequence of this is that the resurrection is not seen in its proper context. True, it is usually related to the cross, but there is more to the context in Matthew's Gospel than that. Matthew encloses his account of the resurrection within the setting of the guard and their report afterwards. This *inclusio* gives us the context for the resurrection: Christ's triumph over his enemies. What we have here is the final stage of the opposition to Christ manifested by the Jewish leaders. At the very point of their apparent triumph they are defeated and have to acknowledge this, even if only privately, by their attempt to hide it from the people.

In addition to this there is an implied contrast between the guards, the servants of the Jewish leadership, and the women, the servants of Christ. Their reactions to the resurrection contrast radically. In this way Matthew sets the challenge of the resurrection before us. Are we with the guards or with the women? Are we on the side of the Jewish leaders or of Christ? When Matthew has dealt with this, he turns to consider the future of the kingdom. Several times Christ has referred to this reunion in Galilee, where he commissions the apostles for their kingdom task. This has to be seen as the outworking of the victory and triumph of the resurrection, based on the cross, which concludes the Gospel, and thus begins the story of the spread of the kingdom.

The guard at the tomb (27:62-66)

A guard is set on the tomb, not immediately after the burial of Christ but on the Sabbath. There were two Sabbaths during the feast, the feast-day itself plus the weekly one. So Matthew describes this day as **'the one after Preparation Day'**, that is Friday. The Jewish leaders approached Pilate and requested him to set a guard on the tomb until the third day. The reason they gave was that **'While he was still alive that deceiver said, "After three days I will rise again."'** They seem to have been taking Christ's prediction more seriously than the disciples did, but there is no suggestion that they believed it would actually happen. Rather they feared that **'His disciples may come and steal the body and tell the people that he has been raised from the dead. This last deception will be worse than the first.'** Pilate's response, **'Take a guard'**, should probably be translated as 'You have a guard of soldiers' (NRSV/ESV). This would explain why later the soldiers report, not to Pilate, but to the chief priests. **'So they went and made the tomb secure by putting a seal on the stone and posting the guard.'** Matthew's readers, of course, know that Jesus rose from the dead and it may be that Matthew's use of the word 'secure' is consciously ironical.

In the providence of God the guard will be able to confirm that the events Matthew is going to record really did happen. They cannot prove that the disciples did not steal the body, for they were not put there until the day following the burial, but the events of Easter morning, and especially the emptiness of the tomb, they can confirm.

The resurrection (28:1-15)

While the guards are in position as tools of the Jewish leaders to thwart the supporters of Jesus, some of those supporters come to the tomb. They know where to come because they have already been there while Joseph was rolling the stone across the entrance (27:61). Suggestions that they got lost and went to the wrong tomb are simply ridiculous. Matthew does not say anything about spices and anointing the body. He simply tells us that **'After the Sabbath, at dawn on the first day of the week, Mary Magdalene and the other Mary went to look at the tomb.'** In this way the women who had witnessed the crucifixion (27:56) and the burial (27:61) are present to observe the amazing and terrifying events associated with the resurrection.

In fact, there is no description of the resurrection itself, here or anywhere else. What we have are the accompanying circumstances: **'There was a violent earthquake, for an angel of the Lord came down from heaven and, going to the tomb, rolled back the stone and sat on it.'** There is no suggestion that the stone had to be removed before the Lord could rise, only that it had to be taken away so that people could see that the tomb was empty. As well as the earthquake, which again implies the terrible judgement of God, the very appearance of the angel was calculated to impress and, indeed, terrify the guards: **'His appearance was like lightning, and his clothes were white as snow.'** This vision of power and holiness, symbolized by the whiteness of the clothes, so terrified the guards **'that they shook and became like dead men'**. The striking appearance of the angel of the Lord testified to Christ's victory over them and over sin, Satan and death.

The women too, quite naturally, were afraid, but the angel reassured them: **'Do not be afraid, for I know that you are looking for Jesus, who was crucified.'** Their errand, looking for Jesus, puts them in a different category from the guards.

They clearly love the Saviour. The message to them is not one of judgement or terror, but consolation: **'He is not here; he has risen, just as he said. Come and see the place where he lay. Then go quickly and tell his disciples.'** We should note the obvious absence of Jesus' body, the stress on fulfilled prophecy, this time of our Lord's own prediction of his resurrection, and the urgency of the command to go and tell the disciples. The message for the disciples, **'He has risen from the dead and is going ahead of you into Galilee. There you will see him,'** also takes up the words of Jesus in 26:32.

The women hurried away from the tomb with mixed emotions: **'afraid yet filled with joy'**. The angel's comforting words were not sufficient to remove the fear, such was the effect of the earthquake and the angel's glorious appearance. Nevertheless they **'hurried'** to obey. On their way to **'tell his disciples'**, they were confronted by Jesus himself. He greeted them with a comforting, **'Do not be afraid'**, so they **'came to him, clasped his feet and worshipped him'**. He then repeated the instructions to tell his disciples to go to Galilee, where **'they will see me'**. The repeated words are, of course, important. It is not enough for them to know that Jesus has risen from the dead. They need to know that his attitude to them is one of love and concern, that although they deserted him and fled he still calls them his **'brothers'**. Although they have let him down, he will keep his promise to meet with them in Galilee. They may expect once more to take up their position as his disciples and apostles.

'While the women were on their way, some of the guards went into the city and reported to the chief priests everything that had happened.' Matthew contrasts the loving obedience of the women with the servile obedience of the guards. The obstinate unbelief of the Jewish leaders is shown here. Confronted by the evidence of their own soldiers that something quite remarkable has happened — an angel has appeared and the tomb is empty — they still do not reconsider their attitude to Jesus. It takes more than a miracle to change hearts (see Luke 16:31). Without the work of the Spirit they cannot and will not believe. Instead, they **'devised a plan'** to bribe the soldiers with **'a large amount of money'** to say that **'His disciples came during the night and stole him away while we were asleep.'** They promised to shield them from Pilate's anger and keep them out of trouble. This whole response is quite ludicrous. If the guards were asleep, how did they know that it was the disciples who came and stole the body? Thus the chief priests and elders tried to defend their interests. They had no concern for the truth of the matter, only to defend their position.

In fact, as we might expect, the facts became known, as is often the case, and so, comments Matthew, **'This story has been widely circulated among the Jews to this very day.'** Only Matthew records this incident of the guards and it may well be that his reason for including all this is that the false story was being spread in his own circles and he felt the need to squash it completely. In contrast to the false account, Matthew gives us the witness of the women, which is interesting, since women were not allowed to be witnesses in Jewish courts. This testifies to the genuineness of his account, since no one would invent a situation where the truth of the gospel depended on the witness of these allegedly unreliable female witnesses! In the providence of God, of course, the very enemies of Jesus were also witnesses — hostile but effective. When doubters deny the reality of the resurrection, we may appeal to the accounts of Matthew and the other Gospelwriters. However, most of these doubters simply reject the biblical evidence altogether. They regard not only the resurrection itself, but all the stories of the witnesses, guards, earthquakes and angels as fabrications. When this is the case — which is not always, of course — then it is only the amazing history of the church and the transformed lives of Christ's people that can make the doubters think again and consider the possibility that the resurrection really happened. This makes the last few verses of the Gospel both relevant and important.

The Great Commission (28:16-20)

Verses 16-20 record Christ's meeting with the Eleven, which he had set up by his own command and the message given to them through the women. Christ's ministry has now come full circle. It began in Galilee (4:12-16); now it concludes on a **'mountain'** in the same area. It is important to note to begin with that this is not a different version of the account of the ascension. That event occurred in the vicinity of Bethany, near Jerusalem (Luke 24:50-53). The ascension is related to the enthronement of Jesus as both Lord and Christ and this section is connected with his reign also. However, this is a different occasion with a different emphasis. Matthew tells us that **'When they saw him, they worshipped him; but some doubted'** (28:17). The meaning of this is not clear. If they doubted why did they worship? Probably it is only the Eleven who worship. They have already seen Jesus on at least two occasions and have no doubts. However, there may have been others with them and some of these may have doubted whether this was really Jesus — he was apparently at a distance from them to start with and then **'came to them'** — whether he had really risen, or, perhaps, whether they ought to worship him in this way. It is possible that these are the 'more than five hundred of the brothers' to whom Jesus appeared, according to Paul (1 Cor. 15:6), but this cannot be proved. The important point is that Jesus was worshipped.

Matthew's Gospel has been very much concerned with the Jewish people, but all the way through there has also been an

emphasis on the fact that the kingdom is to spread to the whole
world. In these final verses of the Gospel this universal aspect
is made explicit. Four times Jesus uses the word **'all'**: all authority, all nations, all things he has commanded and at all times.
The basis for his command concerning the spread of his kingdom is that **'All authority in heaven and on earth has been
given to me.'** He is returning to the right hand of the Father,
where he will reign and from where he will order the affairs of
his kingdom on earth. He will be seated at God's 'right hand
in the heavenly realms, far above all rule and authority, power
and dominion, and every title that can be given, not only in the
present age but also in the one to come. And God placed all
things under his feet and appointed him to be head over everything for the church' (Eph. 1:20-22). After all the weaknesses
and suffering associated in this Gospel with his title Son of
Man, the kingly and divine aspects of that title will be seen
clearly. Worship of this Lord, then, must bring obedience.

In the light of this, **'therefore'**, they must **'go and make
disciples of all nations, baptizing them in the name of the
Father and of the Son and of the Holy Spirit'**. The Great
Commission is to 'disciple' all nations, not just to 'teach' them
(AV). What has been foreshadowed in the Old Testament and
occasionally in our Lord's own ministry now comes to full
fruition in the preaching of the gospel in the whole world. In
this way the nation bringing forth the fruit of the kingdom will
come into being. Christ's worldwide kingdom is to be established in every nation. The means of making disciples is, of
course, the preaching of the gospel of salvation through repentance and faith. This is how the apostles became disciples
and this is how they will continue Christ's work.

Jesus appoints baptism as the initiatory sacrament of the
new covenant, replacing circumcision, which had had the same
function and similar meaning in the old covenant with Abraham.
That ordinance was not only restricted to the Jews. It was

limited to males and also involved blood. Thus it was unsuitable for the universalism of the new covenant after blood sacrifices were completed. The words 'in the name of the Father and of the Son and of the Holy Spirit' are often referred to as a baptismal formula, but this is unhelpful. The baptisms recorded in the book of Acts do not use this 'formula'. It may be convenient to use the words in the administering of baptism, but that is not the point. The word 'in' should be 'into', using baptizing in the same way as in 1 Corinthians 10:2. It means and signifies merging with, joining in union (cf. Rom. 6:3-4), and so coming under the leadership and lordship of the triune covenant God. It is significant that we find here three persons but only one name, pointing to the doctrine of the Trinity. This is parallel with the priestly blessing of the old covenant. Aaron and his sons pronounced a threefold blessing on the Israelites and this is described as putting God's name on them (Num. 6:22-27). In baptism the name of God, Father, Son and Holy Spirit, is put upon the disciples, signifying their discipleship.

The next part of the instructions involves **'teaching them to obey everything I have commanded you'** (28:20). Discipleship, although often linked with the teacher and pupil relationship, is more than mere learning. They are to obey or observe; they are disciples, not students. This avoids the false dichotomy between evangelism and edification which haunts the church. Is the church's main task to win souls or edify believers? Discipleship includes both. It is, of course, significant that the disciples are to be taught 'all things'. It has sometimes been argued that the Great Commission applied only to the apostles and that the missionary mandate ended with them. By any standard this is contrary to the whole ethos of the new covenant, but in any case 'all things' must include the Great Commission itself. The command to evangelize and make disciples of all nations is thus self-perpetuating. It is given not just to the apostles but to the church — the church of every era.

Jesus encourages his people with the promise of his continuing presence with them: **'And surely I am with you always, to the very end of the age.'** Where two or three are gathered together in his name, he is with them (18:20). Similarly, when his disciples obey his command to go and make disciples of all nations he will be with them. The wonderfully motivating promise of Joshua 1:5 and Haggai 1:13 is repeated here with the same implication of strength for service. The assurance at the very beginning, that 'God [is] with us' (Immanuel, 1:23) is repeated at the end. It has been far too common for Christians to plead this promise while simply sitting at home and ignoring the command to make disciples. The setting of the promise here is clearly related to Christ's commission and we have no right to claim it unless we are actively pursuing the spread of the gospel to all nations. The promise applies to 'all the days', even 'to the very end of the age'. (By the way we should note that such a promise is irrelevant if the commission was only for the apostles.) Jesus is looking to the consummation of all things, at the end of the age, when he will return and his final and glorious kingdom will be established with the new heavens and the new earth. He will be with his people to aid and strengthen until everything is accomplished.

Conclusion

It has often been noted that while each of the main five sections of the Gospel concludes with a lengthy discourse, this last section does not. However, the Great Commission instructs Christ's disciples to take the teaching of the first five sections — 'everything I have commanded you' — and spread it throughout the world. We have here an implicit reference to the work of the Holy Spirit, through the church, taking Christ's place as another Paraclete, convicting the world of sin, righteousness and judgement. For Matthew the message of the church is the same as Christ's message to his disciples, enshrined in these five great discourses. They could be used, therefore, to sum up what Jesus has taught according to Matthew, as a pattern for the work and ministry of the church .

The Gospel began with the assertion that God's King has come to reign, to establish the kingdom of heaven. The time has come for Old Testament prophecy to be fulfilled and God's purpose of salvation to be put into effect. So, at beginning of his ministry, Jesus began to preach, 'Repent, for the kingdom of heaven is near' (4.17). The first major discourse includes this call to repentance by entering through the narrow gate (7:13), and then describes the righteousness of the kingdom displayed in the fruits of repentance (7:20). Our message must call on men to believe in the King, to repent of sin and 'to seek first his kingdom and his righteousness' (6:33).

In this way men and women will share in the salvation that the King came to bring, leading them also to work for the coming of the kingdom through the preaching of the gospel. Disciples are not to be self-centred, but fulfil the words of Jesus: 'Freely you have received, freely give' (10:8). To this end we must both show compassion like Christ's and pray him 'to send out workers into his harvest field' (9:36-38). This coming of the kingdom is not immediate. The next section and the third discourse show that the kingdom will come through the preaching of the word, the sowing of the seed, but that there will be a long period of growth in the midst of problems and difficulties before the final judgement comes (13:37-43).

The fourth section is particularly concerned with the church, the community of the kingdom (16:18; 18:17). True discipleship is manifested not only by faith, but also by self-denial and taking up one's cross (16:24). Christ's church is not a formal, human organization, but a living, spiritual organism. It will grow and develop, showing a concern for the weak and demanding holiness and unity, especially manifested in love and forgiveness (18:10,35). Finally, Christ's teaching looks forward to the consummation of the kingdom. The Jewish nation will be judged and the kingdom handed over to a nation, including both Jews and Gentiles, which will bear the fruit that God wants (21:43). The benefits of this kingdom come only by grace (20:15), but there will be works of righteousness and obedience, which will prepare believers for the testing of that final day (22:12,14; 25:13,21,40).

However, all this teaching is of no use apart from the person and work of the Lord Jesus Christ himself. Throughout the Gospel, Matthew has chronicled how Jesus revealed himself to his disciples and even to the people in general. A high point came when Peter declared his faith in Jesus as the Christ, the Son of the living God (16:16). Christ's Messiahship and deity have been manifested throughout. Grace and truth have been shown in his words and deeds. Finally, however, the opposition to him grew, culminating in the arrest, trial and crucifixion of the Lord Jesus. This was not failure, but what God had purposed (20:28). The dying and rising again of the Son of Man, the Son of God, must be at the forefront of the message that the Great Commission envisages. Those who preach the gospel are disciples of the crucified and risen Lord, servants of the King who reigns, living and working for him, spreading his truth and the knowledge of his salvation until he returns at the very end of the age.

Notes

The following abbreviations are used in these notes:

Carson   D. A. Carson, *Matthew* in F. E. Gaebelein, ed. *The Expositor's Bible Commentary,* vol. 8, Zondervan, 1984

France   R. T. France, *The Gospel according to Matthew,* IVP, 1985

Hendriksen   W. Hendriksen, *The Gospel according to Matthew,* Baker, 1973, Banner of Truth, 1974

Morris   L. Morris, *The Gospel according to Matthew,* Eerdmans/IVP, 1992

Ridderbos   H. N. Ridderbos, *Matthew,* Zondervan, 1987

LXX   Septuagint

mg.   margin

Introduction
1. T. V. Moore, *The Last Days of Jesus,* Banner of Truth, p.xi.
2. The technical term for this modernist critical method is 'Redaction Criticism'.
3. For further information, see Carson, Moo and Morris, *An Introduction to the New Testament,* Apollos, pp.19-61.
4. Morris, p.17

Chapter 1 — Jesus the Christ
1. Stan Telchin, *Betrayed,* Marshalls.
2. Helen Shapiro, *Walking back to happiness,* HarperCollins, p.184f.
3. Carson, p.68.
4. *Ibid.,* p.70, note 17.
5. See G. Goldsworthy, *Preaching the whole Bible as Christian Scripture,* IVP, pp.89, 225.
6. Barry Webb, *The Message of Isaiah,* IVP, p.62f; David Peterson, *Christ and his people in the book of Isaiah,* IVP, p.57f.
7. J. A. Motyer, *The prophecy of Isaiah,* IVP, pp.84-6; also, 'Content and context in the interpretation of Isaiah 7:14, *Tyndale Bulletin,* 21 (1970), p.118f.

Chapter 2 — King Herod and King Jesus
1. C. H. Spurgeon, *The full harvest,* Banner of Truth, p.357f.
2. Matthew's insertion of 'by no means' formally contradicts Micah 5:2. However, the point being made in both places is that Bethlehem's only claim to greatness is as the birthplace of the Messiah (see Carson, p.87f.).
3. Carson, p.86.
4. Carson, p.97.

Chapter 3 — Jesus and John the Baptist

1. For an important exposition of the idea of kingdom as the controlling theme of Scripture, see Graeme Goldsworthy's *Gospel and Kingdom* (Paternoster Press, 1981).
2. The usual translations of Isaiah 40:3 imply that the way to be prepared, rather than the herald, is in the desert. Presumably both can be true, although it is also possible that the Hebrew accents are wrong and that Isaiah should be translated as in Matthew (see Carson, p.101).
3. France, p.90.
4. 'This baptism like the whole of John's preaching had a clearly eschatological character. It served to assure anyone who was baptized that in the way of conversion he would obtain the remission of his sins in the face of "the wrath to come" ' (Herman Ridderbos, *The Coming of the Kingdom,* P & R, p.382).
5. The Greek *en* might be translated 'in', 'with' or 'by (means of)'. Both the fact that 'in fire' is unlikely and that in Luke 3:16 'with water' is simply the dative case show that here we must translate it as 'with'.

Chapter 4 — A declaration of war

1. Cited by John Blanchard, *Sifted Silver,* Evangelical Press, p.303
2. The number forty in the Old Testament is usually linked with a time of testing, as with the fast of 'Moses at Sinai (Ex. 34:28; Dt. 9:9,18) and that of Elijah on the way there (1 Kg. 19:8); the mountain (v. 8) perhaps reinforces these allusions. But in view of the explicit reference to Israel's wilderness experiences throughout the narrative, the forty years of Israel's hunger (Dt. 8:2-3) are probably more directly in mind' (France, p.98).
3. In the days when the social gospel was particularly popular, it was common for evangelical preachers to counter it by saying that Jesus was being tempted to be 'an economic Messiah' by providing food for the multitudes or, in relation to the temptations, a sensational or worldly Messiah. While these were typical errors, which he did, and we must, avoid, this interpretation misses the main point.
4. Peter Craigie, *The Book of Deuteronomy* (The New International Commentary on the Old Testament), Hodder and Stoughton, p.185.
5. Carson, p.113.
6. Luke places the last two temptations in the reverse order. Neither account claims to be chronological, so there is no question of contradiction or error. However, most commentators believe that Matthew is the original, in the light of the Lord's dismissal of Satan after the third temptation. Luke has presented them differently for reasons which have not yet been satisfactorily explained.
7. Do not be put off by the technical term 'hermeneutics'. It is simply a useful shorthand for 'principles of interpretation'.
8. The idea of the Son of God worshipping God is strange to some, but must be understood in relation to his human nature, in which he also trusted and obeyed the Father.
9. The distinction between teaching and preaching is not between addressing believers and unbelievers, as it is sometimes thought. Still less does it distinguish

between a midweek teaching ministry and preaching 'in church' on Sundays! Teaching describes the nature and manner of the activity — instruction — while preaching tells us that it was proclamation of the gospel and of the King. The work of the ministry is preaching by teaching.

Chapter 5 — Kingdom characteristics

1. The relation of Christ's Sermon on the Mount to the Sermon on the Plain in Luke 6:17-49 is not clear. Even D. A. Carson confessed (in his *Exegetical Fallacies*, Baker, 1984, pp.42-3) to having changed his mind on this, so I may be allowed to ignore the matter here.
2. This was the title of a book on social responsibility by David Sheppard, Bishop of Liverpool.
3. Phillip D. Jensen & Tony Payne, *The Good Living Guide,* St Matthias Press (now The Good Book Company), p.13.
4. Herman Ridderbos, *The Coming of the Kingdom,* Presbyterian and Reformed Publishing Company, p.188
5. Carson, p.132 (italics mine). I have given an unusual number of quotations to support this interpretation as it is generally neglected or even rejected.
6. C. S. Lewis, *They Asked For a Paper,* Geoffrey Bles, p.198.
7. Carson, p.135.
8. See the hymn, 'Eternal Light! Eternal Light!' by Thomas Binney, *Christian Hymns,* No 5.

Chapter 6 — A surpassing righteousness

1. John Pollock, *Wilberforce,* Lion Publishing, 1978, p.97.
2. *Ibid.,* p.38 (my italics).
3. *Ibid.,* p.69.
4. Geoffrey Bles, 1962.
5. For further information and help on this readers in Britain are encouraged to consult The Christian Institute, P.O. Box 1, Newcastle upon Tyne, NE7 7EF. Internet: http://www.christian.org.uk
6. The NIV's 'God has come to help his people', though less literal, brings out the real meaning of the verb.
7. J. C. Ryle, *The Christian leaders of the Last Century,* Nelson, 1873, p.166.
8. From the hymn, 'Hark! the voice of love and mercy', by Jonathan Evans, *Christian Hymns,* No. 209, verse 3.
9. France, p.115.
10. *Westminster Shorter Catechism,* Question 14.

Chapter 7 — Christ and tradition

1. According to Carson, p.149, 'Raca' is the transliteration of the Aramaic word for 'imbecile'.
2. The AV's 'without a cause', qualifying 'angry' in verse 22, should probably not be read, on textual grounds, but it does fit with the fact that not all anger is sinful, as does the addition of the word 'easily' in 1 Corinthians 13:5. However, both additions detract from our Lord's strong insistence on not being angry.

3. In a gospel context it is often maintained that when we are exhorted to 'be reconciled to God' (2 Cor. 5:20), it means that we alone have to remove our enmity; there is no enmity or wrath on God's side to be removed. However, the usage in Matthew 5:24 shows that the offended one's attitude has to be changed, too. The verb is applied only to the offender, because it is his fault; the offended person has no sinful responsibility for the breach. Nevertheless his wrath has to be dealt with.
4. It is difficult to see the relevance of the hand to this particular sin. It may be that the right hand is here a euphemistic description of the male sexual organ (cf. Isa. 57:8, see Carson, p.151).
5. D. M. Lloyd-Jones, *The Sermon on the Mount*, vol. I, p.243.
6. The introduction to this verse is briefer than in the other links and also includes the connective particle δε.
7. See Morris, p.122, footnote 126, quoting Lenski.
8. W. Shakespeare, *Hamlet*, Act III, Scene 2, lines 234-5
9. See *The Mikado*, Act II.
10. The outer cloak could not legally be taken away (Exod. 22:26).
11. Leon Morris, *Luke*, IVP, p.130
12. See Carson, p.157.
13. Some deny that God loves even the non-elect, but this passage must mean that he does. The parallel is strict. Similarly, since they are sinners, it must be unmerited grace that gives them good gifts. This does not alter the fact that God has a special, saving love and grace for those whom he has chosen before the foundation of the world.

Chapter 8 — Giving and praying
1. Older versions have 'alms-giving' in verse 1. The best manuscripts have 'righteousness', which functions as an introduction to the threefold structure that follows.
2. Indeed, the word 'openly', found in the AV/NKJV, is probably an addition added later, perhaps to make explicit the contrast with 'in secret'.
3. Article, 'Hyper-Evangelism' in *The Banner of Truth* magazine, issue 6, May 1957. Those who would reject this as 'nit-picking' may also think that his reference to a church building as 'the house of God' is most unbiblical.
4. From the hymn, 'Jesus shall reign', *Christian Hymns*, No. 273, verse 2.

Chapter 9 — Praying and fasting
1. The word is translated 'downcast' in Luke 24:17, where it is used of the disciples on the way to Emmaus.

Chapter 10 — Treasure without anxiety
1. Carson, p.180.

Chapter 11 — Judging and being judged
1. See Carson, p.187.
2. See France, p.145.

3. Some interpreters regard the roads as leading up to the gates, comparing these verses with Luke 13:24-25. However, the natural order of the words suggests the reverse, as I have taken it.

4. Some manuscripts do omit 'gate' in verses 13 and 14, but 'the overwhelming weight' of the evidence supports its inclusion.

5. France, p.149.

Chapter 12 — Authority to heal

1. It is widely recognized that Matthew's order in this section is deliberately not chronological, but topical (according to subject). It must be emphasized that this is not an error; he does not claim to be writing in chronological order and 'Most of his "time" indicators are very loose' (Carson, p.196f.)

2. 'The Greek word was used for various diseases affecting the skin — not necessarily leprosy', i.e., the modern Hansen's disease (NIV footnote). This, however, does not alter the typical, spiritual interpretation of the biblical condition.

3. From the hymn by Joseph Hart, *Christian Hymns,* No. 474.

4. It may be that verse 7 should be read as a question with the 'I' stressed: 'Shall *I* come and heal him?' In other words, Jesus may be probing: What does the centurion actually want? Does he realize that he is a Gentile speaking to a Jew? Does he really believe Jesus can do this? (See Carson, p.201).

5. This error is referred to technically as 'an over-realized eschatology'.

Chapter 13 — The appointed time

1. See the extended note in Carson, p.209ff.

2. This was a technical term at that time for the afflictions which would come upon the Jews when Messiah came.

3. From the hymn, 'When we cannot see our way', *Christian Hymns,* No. 744.

4. Kenneth E. Bailey, *Through Peasant Eyes,* p.26. The whole section, pp.22-31, actually based on the parallel passage in Luke 9:57-62, is well worth consulting.

5. *Ibid.,* p.29. Bailey is actually referring to Luke's third man, but the point is the same.

6. *Christian Hymns,* No. 697.

7. The fact that Mark and Luke only mention one man need not trouble us. If there were two men, then of course there was one, and they are at liberty only to concentrate on him.

8. Carson, p.219

Chapter 14 — Authority and faith

1. France, p.166f.

2. See Peter Bloomfield, *Esther — The Guide,* Evangelical Press, Appendix A: 'Should Christians fast too?' p.157ff.

Chapter 15 — Workers in the harvest field

1. From John Milton's poem, *Lycidas.*

2. 'Cananaean', which Matthew actually uses here, is the Aramaic form of 'zealot'.

3. The discrepancy between Matthew and Mark here is probably because Mark speaks of the total equipment, while Matthew forbids 'extra' provision.

4. See the meaning of 'the end' in the context of chapter 24:6,13,14. Carson discusses the verse at some length and comes to the same conclusion, adding: 'The connection is not with v. 22 alone but with vv. 17-22, which picture the suffering witness of the church in the post-Pentecost period *during a time when many of Jesus' disciples are still bound up with the synagogue*' (his italics), pp.252-3.

5. See Carson's comments on this passage, p.253.

6. From the hymn 'Begone unbelief,' by John Newton (1725-1807), *Christian Hymns,* No. 697.

7. From the hymns 'Jesus to Thee our hearts we lift' and 'And are we yet alive?', both by Charles Wesley, *Christian Hymns,* Nos. 802, 345.

Chapter 18. Judgement or rest

1. Carson, p.272.

2. For a discussion of this see Paul Helm, *The Providence of God,* IVP, pp.55-68 and D. A. Carson, *How long, O Lord?,* IVP, p.145ff.

3. See *Christian Hymns,* Nos. 22 (John Fawcett), 100 (Joseph Addison) and 604 (Charles Wesley).

Chapter 19 — The Sabbath and the Servant

1. ' "The one greater" is neuter ... i.e. "something greater" (NIV mg.). The neuter, however, can refer to persons when some quality is being stressed rather than the individual per se (Turner, *Syntax,* p.21)' (Carson, p.281).

2. Luke 6:6 makes this explicit: 'On another Sabbath'. However, the fact that Jesus went **'on from that place'** means that this must be the case anyway.

Chapter 20 —Two kingdoms

1. An argument directed against a person rather than the position he is maintaining.

2. G. C. Berkouwer, *Studies in Dogmatics: Sin,* Eerdmans, p.340. The whole chapter, pp.323-53, is worthy of note.

3. *Ibid.,* p.340 (italics his).

4. *Ibid.,* p.341 (italics his).

5. *Ibid.,* p.340.

Chapter 21 — The parable of the sower

1. Much relevant and helpful material in this connection is to be found in Kenneth E. Bailey, *Poet & Peasant* and *Through Peasant Eyes* (combined edition, Eerdmans, 1983).

Chapter 22 — More encouraging parables

1. Much confusion arises because interpreters take the expression 'the kingdom is like' to mean that the first-mentioned element is to be identified with the kingdom. In fact, it is much more general: 'The way the kingdom works is like the following procedure...'

2. The title of his spiritual autobiography.

3. Commentary on Matthew 8:12, Hendriksen, p.398.

4. See 'The Martyrdom of Polycarp' in Henry Bettenson (ed.), *Documents of the Christian Church*, The World's Classics, Oxford University Press, p.12.

Chapter 23 — Jesus and the world
1. See Faith Cook, *Selina, Countess of Huntingdon,* Banner of Truth, p.69.
2. *Ibid.,* pp.127,105. We must remember that in her day the term 'Methodist' was used as an insulting description of any evangelical Christian, including Anglicans.

Chapter 24 — Walking on water
1. *Christian Hymns,* No. 698.
2. *Ibid.,* No. 697
3. See Carson, p.345.
4. Cf. 1 Sam. 7:12.

Chapter 25 — Clean and unclean
1. The term *qorban* is actually used in the account in Mark 7:11.
2. William Lane, *The Gospel of Mark*, The New London Commentary on the New Testament, London: Marshall, Morgan and Scott, p.251.
3. The word used for 'basket' here denotes a different kind of container, one more likely to be found in a Gentile area.
4. Carson, p.359.

Chapter 26 — Son of Man, Son of the living God
1. Albright and Mann, cited in Carson, p.369.
2. Carson, p.369.

Chapter 27 — Suffering and glory
1. Benny Hinn, on Trinity Broadcasting Network, November 1990, cited in G. Richard Fisher and M. Kurt Goedelman, *The confusing world of Benny Hinn*, Personal Freedom Outreach, Saint Louis, Missouri, p.99.
2. From his explanation of his Ninety-five Theses, published in 1517, quoted in James Atkinson, *Martin Luther and the birth of Protestantism*, Penguin Books, p.156.
3. *Ibid.,* p.152.
4. From a letter dated 10 July 1518, cited in *ibid.,* p.168.

Chapter 28 — The disciples' failure and privilege
1. From the hymn, 'Father of Jesus Christ, my Lord,' by Charles Wesley, *Christian Hymns,* No. 748.

Chapter 29 — Christ's little ones
1. See B. B. Warfield's most helpful essay, 'Christ's "little ones"', in *Selected Shorter Writings of Benjamin B. Warfield*, vol. 1, edited by John E. Meeter, Presbyterian and Reformed Publishing Company, pp.234-52.

2. See Warfield's following essay, 'The angels of Christ's "little ones"', *ibid.,* pp.253-66.

Chapter 30 — Discipline and forgiveness
1. 'The Greek could just barely be taken to mean 70 x 7 (490) instead of 70 +7 (77); but it follows the LXX of Gen. 4:24 exactly, which is a rendering of the Hebrew 77' (Carson, p. 406). It may be very significant that Genesis 4:24 refers to Lamech's revenge. Jesus is making the point that, far from avenging ourselves, we must forgive.

Chapter 31 — Marriage and the kingdom
1. Much of this debate is more technical than is appropriate for a Welwyn Commentary. For a reliable and helpful consideration of these issues see Carson, p.410ff, and also, Stephen Clark, *Putting Asunder,* Bryntirion Press, pp.74-100.
2. Carson, p.411.
3. See Clark, *Putting Asunder,* pp.92,107,108,142, on Jewish custom as well as the *lex Julia de adulteris* enacted by the Roman emperor, Augustus.
4. Clark, *Putting Asunder,* p.65.
5. See Jay Adams, *Marriage, Divorce and Remarriage,* Presbyterian and Reformed, pp.32-5
6. See my, 'Marriage: sanctity or indissolubility?' in *Evangelical Times,* January 1993, reprinted July 2000.
7. Carson and Clark, and possibly Morris, link Jesus' words to verse 10, while France and Hendriksen refer them to verse 9. The practical conclusion is more or less the same in each case.
8. Clark, *Putting Asunder,* p.98.

Chapter 32 — Grace, not status
1. Carson, p.410.
2. See David Kingdon, *Children of Abraham,* Carey Press, p.86, and John Murray, *Christian Baptism,* Presbyterian and Reformed, p.65.

Chapter 33 — The last will be first
1. Herman Ridderbos, *The Coming of the Kingdom,* Presbyterian and Reformed, p.209; see also p.199.
2. Iain Murray, *D. Martyn Lloyd-Jones,* vol. 2, *The fight of faith,* Banner of Truth, p.64
3. Craig L. Blomberg, *Interpreting the Parables,* Apollos, p.222.
4. From John Newton's hymn, 'Begone unbelief', *Christian Hymns,* No. 697.
5. Corrie ten Boom, *The Hiding Place,* Hodder and Stoughton/Christian Literature Crusade, p.220.

Chapter 34 — True greatness
1. See Peter O'Brien, *Colossians, Philemon* (Word Biblical Commentary), Word Publishing, p.79.
2. Carson, p.432.
3. Richard Hobson, *What hath God wrought,* Elliot Stock, pp.127-8.

Chapter 35 — The declaration of kingship

1. 'It is simply an arrogant put-down: sightless eyes and helpless legs are enough to repel any attack of yours' (Dale Ralph Davis, *Out of every adversity — Expositions of the Book of 2 Samuel,* Christian Focus, p.52).
2. From the hymn, 'Come, ye sinners, poor and wretched', by Joseph Hart, *Christian Hymns,* No. 474.
3. Carson, p.438.
4. Carson, p.444.

Chapter 37 — Kingdom controversies

1. See B. B. Warfield, 'The Old Testament and Immortality,' in *Selected Shorter Writings,* vol. I, Presbyterian and Reformed, pp. 339-47

Chapter 38 — Hypocrites!

1. The Pharisees were not all teachers, but many were. Matthew's description, therefore, seems to refer mainly to those Pharisees who were teachers — to those teachers who were Pharisees. We may simply refer to the Pharisees, as Jesus himself does in verse 26: 'Blind Pharisee.'
2. The best texts omit verse 14, which appears to have been inserted from the parallel passages in Mark 12:40 and Luke 20:47. It may be purely a coincidence that this reduces the number of woes to the perfect seven.
3. See France, p.329.
4. There is a problem over the identity of this Zechariah. The one who fits the context — martyred in the temple courtyard and whose death is recorded at the end of the Hebrew canon in 2 Chronicles 24:20-22 — is said to be the son of Jehoiada, not Barakiah. However, this may be a similar case to the other prophet Zechariah, who is said in Ezra 6:14 to be 'the son of Iddo', who was actually his grandfather (See Carson for a full discussion).
5. On the morning of his execution, he wrote, 'I have followed holiness, I have taught the truth, and I have been most in the main things.' See Maurice Grant, *No King but Christ,* Evangelical Press, p.197.
6. Tim Shenton, *Christmas Evans,* Evangelical Press, p.174.

Chapter 39 — The end of the age

1. The word for 'coming' here is *parousia,* see later note.
2. In the parallel passages in Mark 13:4 and Luke 21:7, the report of the disciples' question is limited to the subject of the temple's destruction. It is, therefore, probably correct to assume that Matthew's report is also concerned with the one event, which the disciples may have thought would occur at the end of the world.
3. 'The Roman army carried ensigns consisting of eagles and images of the emperor to which divine honours were often paid by the army. No greater abomination could meet the eye of the Jew than the ensigns to which idolatrous worship was rendered' (J. Marcellus Kik, *Matthew Twenty-Four,* Presbyterian and Reformed, p.44). Kik's whole exposition of Matthew 24 is worth careful consideration. It is now published as part of his volume, *An eschatology of victory.*

4. Carson, p.501
5. See the detailed description in Kik, *Matthew Twenty-Four,* pp.57-62.

Chapter 40 — That day
1. Carson, p.513.

Chapter 41 — Coming to judge
1. *Oxford Dictionary of Quotations,* p.251.
2. From the hymn, 'Lord, it belongs not to my care', *Christian Hymns,* No. 757.
3. The expression is France's, p.354.
4. John Bunyan, *The Pilgrim's Progress,* Oxford University Press (The World's Classics), p.159.
5. From the hymn by Philip Doddridge, *Christian Hymns,* No. 780.
6. See R. W. Dale, *History of Congregationalism,* Hodder and Stoughton, p.144.

Chapter 42 — The Passover Feast
1. See Carson, pp. 528-32, for a detailed and convincing study of this issue.
2. One reason for this is the AV translation of 1 Corinthians 11:24, based on inferior texts. Luke 22:19 says that his body is 'given for you', emphasizing the sacrificial character of Christ's death.

Chapter 43 — Testing times
1. From the hymn, 'O Christ, what burdens bowed thy head', by Anne Ross Cousin, *Hymns of Faith,* No. 294.
2. *Ibid.*
3. See Peter T. O'Brien, *The Epistle to the Philippians,* NIGNT, Eerdmans / Paternoster Press, pp. 211-16.

Chapter 44 — Crown of thorns
1. France, pp.376-7, See also Carson, pp. 549-52.
2. The words literally mean, 'You said', rather in the manner of the modern colloquialism, 'You said it,' or 'You're telling me'. The same expression is used in 26:25.
3. From the hymn, 'Man of sorrows', by Philipp Paul Bliss, *Christian Hymns,* No. 221.
4. Carson, p.571.

Chapter 45 — Crucified, dead and buried
1. See J. W. Wenham, 'When were the saints raised?', JTS 32 [1981]: 150-52, cited in Carson, pp.581-2.
2. *The Works of John Owen,* vol. 10, ed. W. H. Goold, reprinted by the Banner of Truth Trust, pp. 140-421.
3. See Carson, p.584.